'This book is one of the most powerful and well written sociological treaties on power and criminalisation of this decade. It demonstrates the inherent weaknesses of much of mainstream sociology, advocating with great force and empathy the need for critical analysis of the forces of marginalisation and exclusion and for seeing the criminal justice system "from below".'
Professor Thomas Mathiesen, Professor of the Sociology of Law, University of Oslo, Norway

'An important contribution to criminological theory, grounded in the author's deep knowledge of troubling public issues and long-time commitment to social justice.'
Professor Emeritus Tony Platt, California State University, Sacramento, USA

'This latest book by Phil Scraton represents the culmination of many years of activism and intellectual work across a range of contemporary political and social issues that inform critical criminology. This book is 'dangerous' scholarship in the best sense of the word: it takes us on a critical journey through policing, deaths in custody, and the rise of new forms of control over working class and marginalised young people. From working with Irish travellers in the 1970s to working with women in prison today, Scraton draws on his experience of the importance of critical research. The book challenges intellectuals to 'speak truth to power', to excavate the logic and language of control and at the same time to forge links with marginalised and oppressed groups. This book is critical research at its finest. It deserves not only to be widely read, but to be understood and acted upon.'
Professor Chris Cunneen, NewSouth Global Chair in Criminology, University of New South Wales, Australia

'Phil Scraton has worked at the cutting edge of critical criminology for more than a quarter-of-a-century. *Power, Conflict and Criminalisation* both synthesises his work and defines new directions. Passionate and scholarly, the book is a tour de force. It is an essential read for teachers, researchers and students alike. In fact, anyone with a concern for "big questions" of justice and injustice will want to read this book'.

Professor Barry Goldson, The University of Liverpool, UK

'Scraton's scholarship is responsible intellectualism at its best; this is critical social research that provides original insights about the consequences of authoritarian state polices on people's lives. His interviews powerfully account the pain and difficulties experienced by those labeled by such regimes as outsiders. These poignantly told stories of outsiders, in prisons and marginalized communities, reveal the unheard voices of the powerless and expose the secrets of the powerful. Scraton's work follows from the classic scholarship on the 'outsider' by Becker, Cohen, Fanon and others, and it goes beyond this scholarship in its capacity to simultaneously expose the often unrecognized truths about people subjected to state coercion and the strategies of the powerful to hide their responsibility for furthering their repression. Indeed, the aspirations of critical sociologists and criminologists of the 1970s for politically engaged and meaningful social science research is finally realized in Scraton's path breaking studies – each shows what it means for a scholar to be fully responsible to people who have become the subject of academic research and for the consequences of his intervention into the institutions that control them. In his efforts to enrich critical theory and practice, Scraton always remains deeply humane, courageous, and true to the interests of real people and their life situations.'

Professor Kristin Bumiller, Professor of Political Science and Women's and Gender Studies, Amherst College, USA

'This book is critical scholarship at its best. It is a provocative and persuasive account of how state sanctioned regimes of truth are corrupted and distorted in ways that deny justice to the most deserving. It provides an engaging and insightful understanding of oppressive government techniques by uncovering how state officials subvert 'truth' through institutional and discriminatory networks of abusive power. Phil Scraton remains one of the most influential and thought-provoking critical socio-legal thinkers of our time and this book's call for knowledges of resistance is both inspiring and timely.'

Professor Reece Walters, Professor of Criminology, The Open University, UK

'This text is not only an essential expose of structural inequalities and an incisive critique of authoritarianism in advanced democratic societies but also a telling reminder of how critical criminology can be mobilised as resistance.'
Professor John Muncie, Professor of Criminology, The Open University, UK

'Phil Scraton's latest book is written with verve and passion. It is a blast from the margins that makes a strong statement for the relevance of critical criminology to important social questions. The dramatis personae include Travellers, the suicidal, and troubled and troublesome young persons. By adopting the 'view from below' old problems are placed in new contexts and comfortable assumptions are challenged.'

Professor Ian O'Donnell, Professor of Criminology, University College, Dublin, Ireland

'Children are told by their parents to tell the truth. Yet, in contemporary society the 'truth' is frequently the first casualty of peace, much less war. Why and how this is the case is a key theme of this book. Writing with great passion and wisdom, Phil Scraton takes the reader on a journey that challenges orthodoxy, authority and the powerful. By placing people, events and situations into context, and by exposing the information that authorities try so hard to suppress, the book offers not only examples of critical social research, but a substantiated methodology for the doing of such research. It is an argument that speaking truth ought not to be the preserve of the very young - it is a core responsibility for all those who purport to seek democracy, justice and equality in our daily lives. To speak truth to power is to dissent from the superficial, the ideological and the official. It is to utter what needs to be said in the face of unfreedoms, mystifications, obfuscations and the tyrannies of terror. This requires social research that is thoughtful and thought-provoking; social analysis that is sensitive yet bold. This is the great achievement and contribution of this book.'

Professor Rob White, Professor of Sociology, University of Tasmania, Australia

'Scraton paints a powerful and moving portrait of the institutionalized abuse of power that resides at the heart of law and order politics. The book offers readers the rare privilege of hearing first hand the experiences of those, so often talked about but rarely heard, that reap the human costs of policies that transform social, political and economic problems into security problems.'

Associate Professor Jude McCulloch, Criminology and Criminal Justice Studies, Monash University, Melbourne, Australia

Power, Conflict and Criminalisation

Drawing on a body of empirical, qualitative work spanning three decades, this unique text traces the significance of critical social research and critical analyses in understanding some of the most significant and controversial issues in contemporary society. Focusing on central debates in the UK and Ireland – prison protests; inner-city uprisings; deaths in custody; women's imprisonment; transition in the north of Ireland; the 'crisis' in childhood; the Hillsborough and Dunblane tragedies; and the 'war on terror' – Phil Scraton argues that 'marginalisation' and 'criminalisation' are social forces central to the application of state power and authority regulating dissent and imposing compliance. Each case study demonstrates how structural relations of power, authority and legitimacy, particularly the inequalities of class, 'race', sectarianism, gender, sexuality and age, establish the determining contexts of everyday life, social interaction and individual opportunity.

Power, Conflict and Criminalisation explores the politics and ethics of critical social research, making a persuasive case for the application of critical theory to analysing the rule of law, its enforcement and the administration of criminal justice. This all-embracing book is indispensable for students in the fields of criminology, criminal justice and socio-legal studies, social policy and social work.

Phil Scraton is Professor of Criminology in the Institute of Criminology and Criminal Justice, Queen's University, Belfast. His primary research includes: the regulation and criminalisation of children and young people; violence and incarceration; the politics of truth and official inquiry; critical analysis. His most recent books are *Hillsborough: The Truth* (2000) and *Beyond September 11: An Anthology of Dissent* (2002).

Power, Conflict and Criminalisation

Phil Scraton

Routledge
Taylor & Francis Group

LONDON AND NEW YORK

First published 2007
by Routledge
2 Park Square, Milton Park, Abingdon, Oxon, OX14 4RN

Simultaneously published in the USA and Canada
by Routledge
270 Madison Avenue, New York, NY 10016

Transferred to Digital Printing 2008

Routledge is an imprint of Taylor & Francis, an informa business

© 2007 Phil Scraton

Typeset in Sabon by Taylor & Francis Books

British Library Cataloguing in Publication Data
A catalogue record for this book is available from the British Library

Library of Congress Cataloging in Publication Data
Scraton, Phil.
  Power, conflict and criminalisation / Phil Scraton.
    p. cm.
  Includes bibliographical references.
  1. Criminology–Research. 2. Criminal justice, Administration of. 3.
Social policy. I. Title.
  HV6024.5.S38 2007
  364–dc22
        2007019695

ISBN 978-0-415-42241-3 (pbk)
ISBN 978-0-415-42240-6 (hbk)
ISBN 978-0-203-93553-8 (ebk)

Contents

Acknowledgements

My first acknowledgement is to three women who died prematurely and who, each in their own way, contributed enormously to this book: my Mum, Hannah, who always had faith in my work; my close friends Hilary Arnott and Sita Picton – incisive, persistent, questioning minds. I miss them but I have fine memories.

Setting out, intimidated and unsure, I was taught by the late Joe Martindale, a fine tutor who stimulated students to discover for themselves the experiences of others living everyday lives. Owen Gill, then a researcher at Liverpool University's Sociology Department whose immersion in a Birkenhead community I knew well (Luke Street), provided a wonderful ethnography. Joe and Owen reinforced my commitment to challenging social and political injustice. In the 1970s working with Traveller families in Liverpool, with the Huyton and Toxteth communities, and prisoners in Walton, strengthened that commitment.

Writing and teaching at the Open University was a great experience and I learnt much from the Course Teams, particularly Mike Fitzgerald, Stuart Hall, Greg McLennan, John Muncie and Joe Sim. At Edge Hill University Kathryn Chadwick, my long-term 'partner-in-criminology' and close friend, and I established the Centre for Studies in Crime and Social Justice incorporating Masters/PhD programmes and eventually the first-ever degree in Critical Criminology. Over two decades we enjoyed working with many excellent undergraduates and postgraduates. I want to thank all involved in the Centre's work over the years, especially Alana Barton, Eileen Berrington, Helen Elderfield, Barbara Houghton, Ann Jemphrey, Helen Jones, Margaret Malloch and Lizzy Stanley.

In the mid–1980s Joe Sim, Paula Skidmore and I were commissioned by Sarah and Jimmy Boyle of the Gateway Exchange to research into prison protests in Scotland as part of an independent inquiry. Kathryn Chadwick and I researched deaths in custody and, following the 1989 Hillsborough Disaster, The Hillsborough Project was commissioned. I worked with Sheila Coleman, Ann Jemphrey and Paula Skidmore on the project and with Margaret McAdam on later research. Thanks to all.

Established in 1993, the Centre's Young People, Power and Justice Research Group was a fine initiative, meeting regularly on Sundays: thanks to Marc Bourhill, Vicki Coppock, Karen Corteen, Howard Davis, Barry Goldson, Deena Haydon and Ingrid Richter. Howard, Deena, Julie Read, Polly Wright and I worked together on subsequent early intervention research. Howard and I also developed the aftermath of disasters research, and the ESRC seminar series that followed was a truly remarkable experience. Thanks to all who participated and to Ann Jemphrey, who organised the programme.

More recently I have been supported by colleagues and postgraduates at Queen's University, especially in the Institute of Criminology and Criminal Justice and the Human Rights Centre. My thanks to Jean Allain, Graham Ellison, Lisa Glennon, Colin Harvey, John Jackson, Ruth Jamieson, Caroline Keenan, the late Stephen Livingstone, Shadd Maruna, Anne-Marie McAlinden, Kieran McEvoy and Katie Quinn. I was a member of the Queen's-based team commissioned in 2003 to carry out the children's rights research for the Northern Ireland Commissioner for Children and Young People – thanks to Ciara Davey, Clare Dwyer, Ursula Kilkelly, Rosemary Kilpatrick, Laura Lundy, Siobhàn McAlister and Linda Moore. This work also brought me into contact with many people working in the vibrant children's sector. Thanks to Sara Boyce, Tara Caul, Sheri Chamberlain, Siobhán Craig, Paula Keenan, Paddy Kelly, Natalie Strain, Pauline Leeson, Elaine McElduff, Edel Quinn, Koulla Yiasouma, the Derry Children's Commission and the staff and directors of Include Youth.

With Linda Moore of the Northern Ireland Human Rights Commission, whom I first worked with at Edge Hill, I researched conditions for women and girls in prison in the north of Ireland from 2004 to 2007. Linda is an excellent researcher and a good friend. Thanks also to colleagues at the Commission, the former Chief Commissioner, Brice Dickson, and his successor, Monica McWilliams.

Much appreciation to all my friends in the European Group for the Study of Deviance and Social Control – a great forum for critical debate and mutual support – especially Andrea Beckmann, Nils Christie, Francesco Faiella, Didi Gipser, Martti Grönfors, Päivi Honkatukia, Louk Houlsman, Karen Leander, Ida Koch, Maeve McMahon, Thomas Mathiesen, Beppe Mosconi, Dave Orr, Joan and Mick Ryan, Alvise Sbraccia, Dave Scott, Steve Tombs, Francesca Vianello, Reece Walters, Tony Ward, Steve Wright and Heiner Zillmer. I have benefited greatly from visiting scholarships to Sydney and Melbourne. Thanks to the research postgraduates with whom I worked and to Dave Brown, Moira Carmody, Kerry Carrington, Chris Cunneen, Michael Dudley, Fran Gale, Russell Hogg, Debbie Kilroy, Murray Lee, Craig Minogue, Sharon Pickering, Scott Poynting, Charandev Singh, David Tait and especially to my good friends and collaborators at Monash, Bree Carlton and Jude McCulloch.

So many people, directly and indirectly, have contributed to my work: A. Sivanandan, Siva, and all my good friends at the Institute of Race Relations; Tony Bunyan, Trevor Hemmings and all at Statewatch; Deb Coles,

Helen Shaw and the staff of INQUEST; all at the Pat Finucane Centre, Derry, at Relatives for Justice, Belfast and Coiste na n-Iarchimí, Belfast. The scholarship, commitment and support of Noam Chomsky, Stan Cohen and Stuart Hall has been – and remains – inspirational.

I am indebted to friends who, personally and intellectually, have been so supportive over the years: Lilly Artz, Sara Boyce, Kristin Bumiller, Flair Campbell, Pat Craddock, Anna Eggert, Julie, Leo and Maria Fallon, Barry Goldson, Paddy Hillyard, Barbara Hudson, Sue and Chris Hughes, Janet Johnstone, Karen Lee, Mark Lusby, Deirdre Mahon, Agnieszka Martynowicz, Laurence McKeown, Laura McMahon, Mark Minchinton, Alan Morris, John Muncie, Mick North, Denis O'Hearn, Mahesh Patel, Tony Platt, Denise and Paul Prescott, Edel Quinn, Don Richmond, Bill Rolston, Sheila Scraton, Colin Sefton, the late Teri Sefton, Ann Singleton, Tony Souza, Jan and Eddie Spearritt, Pete Strange, Marilyn and Tony Taylor, Phil Thomas, Mike Tomlinson, Margaret Ward, Frances Webber, Juliet Wells, Isabel Wilson (McBeath), Leah Wing, Margaret and Ian Wright.

To my family: Deena Haydon whose research, insights and love have contributed so much; Paul Scraton, Katrin Schoenig and grand-daughter Lotte; Sean Scraton and Sandra Prepens. Wonderful sons and partners.

Finally, and most significantly, my profound respect and deepest gratitude to the women, men and children whose stories fill these pages. Their strength, courage and resistance against all odds constantly remind us why critical analysis as resistance is so important.

Phil Scraton
Belfast
April 2007

Preface

It was a beautiful late summer's day. We struggled with heavy bags across the crowded Ponte degli Scalzi. Still more stone steps took us to Santa Lucia's booking hall and a one-way ticket to Verona. Our time on San Giorgio with friends from the European Group had been memorable. Discussion, comradeship and stunning views across the busy Canale della Giudecca to San Marco.

Venice is a remarkable city: the Jewish ghetto, the historic working-class Giudecca, Castello's back streets and bars, the islands and the rock and roll of the *vaporetti*. Relaxing into the brief train journey to Verona we had no notion that within 24 hours our lives – personal and political – would be turned upside down. That warm, sun-lit evening we ate in the Piazza dei Signori, wandering back to the hotel through narrow, marble-paved streets. It was 10 September 2001.

Waking to a hot day we walked the city, from the castle walls along the river, eventually arriving at Juliet's balcony. Needing shade, we set off for the hotel. Visiting the Roman Arena was an afterthought. We strolled along high-walled passages, their worn, stone floor a legacy of two thousand years and millions of feet.

A fraction of a second – that's all it took. Laughing and joking – I slipped, my leg trapped under my body. The deep, nauseous pain of serious damage. Lying motionless, brought down by a makeshift disability ramp. Hardly able to walk, the pain unbearable, I made it to the hotel and then by taxi to hospital.

The consultant examined my injured leg. Indifferent, aloof, he was distracted. 'You have no ligament trouble. But the plane it crashes into two towers at the World Trade Center. And at the Pentagon. Possibly 10,000 dead. The towers, they collapse. The Pentagon is on fire.' Then, matter-of-fact, he told me to rest. Most probably it was a ruptured muscle.

The following morning the taxi collected us from our Verona hotel and delivered us to the cheap flight home. Little did I know that I had severed the quadriceps tendon, the blood from ruptured muscles swelling my thigh. In the weeks after surgery I suffered pulmonary emboli to both lungs. Rushed to the Intensive Care Unit, I faced my own mortality. Bush and

Blair, meanwhile, faced the mortality of others as they prepared to bomb Afghanistan.

That moment, so close to dying, dramatically contrasted with the sure fatalities, mutilation and displacement inflicted on a country already in ruins. Blood clots, no more than a simple twist of fate, set against the purposeful, planned and ruthless execution of death and destruction, reported by allied spin-masters as 'collateral damage' or 'casualties of war'. Some irony, that the very state providing the means to save my life simultaneously mobilised the means to destroy others. And it did so in our names.

Between initial surgery and my time in intensive care I was so overwhelmed by the appalling racism unleashed against anyone assumed to be Muslim and so immobilised by my injuries that I emailed friends and contacts with a request for 3,000 words voicing disapproval against the imminent offensive against Afghanistan as the obvious precursor to Iraq. Responses arrived as I lay in the ICU, scared to close my eyes in case I never awakened. My crisis passed and I was relocated to the general ward among hateful, racist outbursts often directed towards our doctors and carers in their absence. Weeks later I was home, the 'project' under way. First, however, I was behind schedule for an article to be published in a book on Critical Criminology. I completed it in a couple of weeks. It caused me to reflect on the writings that had influenced my research. Having nearly died, and still incapacitated, 'thinking time' virtually extinct in modern academic life was now freely available to me. *Beyond September 11: An Anthology of Dissent* was written and edited during early convalescence and my contributions therein form the basis of a chapter in this book.

Revisiting these events locates this text in its moment of conception. Following my recovery one of the first public lectures I gave was at Liverpool, in the Department of Sociology where I had studied over 30 years earlier. It was an emotional moment, not least because many friends turned up, but also it was a retrospective on my research. Later in the year I went to Helsinki for the European Group's annual conference. The recently formed European Criminology Society was also in Helsinki and it was suggested that our Group should present a symposium on critical analysis. I was volunteered as one of four contributors and condensed my Liverpool retrospective into twenty minutes. Gerhard Boomgaarden was in the room and he introduced himself as Commissioning Editor at Routledge. In a ten-minute conversation *Power, Conflict and Criminalisation* was conceived.

We kept in touch. I had moved to Belfast and was working on two commissioned research projects: on children's rights and on women and girls in prison. They were completed and published a year later. Finally, the proposal for *Power, Conflict and Criminalisation* was submitted and accepted. I guess what follows is my story. It is not written as a definitive text on critical criminology nor is it presented as a complete overview of the significant contemporary contributions made by critical researchers into 'crime' and harm, criminal justice and social justice. It is a personal reflection on three decades of empirical research, teaching and writing, acknowledging key influences on a shared perspective as it evolved and took shape. If we acknowledge faithfully our sources, those who made us pause for thought, the 'mix' is sure to be eclectic. A paragraph in a book, a phrase in a lecture, a comment in a research interview, a hard choice in a campaign meeting, a discussion in a tutorial are part of that mix. Like any interaction these are interpretive moments that cohere in the mind of the observer, the participant.

I was always drawn to empirical research and I feel at home, whatever the circumstances, in conversation. As a child in a working-class family, people's experiences fascinated me and reminiscences, though elaborated, well rehearsed and often hilarious, were memorable times when everyone came together. I was also aware from an early age that not all stories had happy endings. In fact, I realised that many of the 'significant others' in my life were profoundly unhappy, regularly ill and relatively poor. They smoked heavily, drank regularly and died young. Yet we were supposed to be living in the 'golden age' when all were, or could aspire to being, middle class. One of a handful of children from my primary school to go to grammar school, I was immediately confronted with the dynamics of what would now be described as 'social exclusion'. I left within two years.

Studying Sociology at Liverpool University was a decision taken after further education college, with the blessing of my Mum alone. Most people hadn't a clue what it was I was doing and those who listened responded with comments about 'common sense' or 'doing something worthwhile'. After a term sitting through 101 Research Methods I thought they had a point. As I look back, the question that crossed my mind at the time seems to have even greater relevance now: How could anyone make social research boring? The answer at the time, of course, was the detachment of much sociological analysis from the real world, at least the real world I inhabited.

The more I became familiar with the 'founding fathers', as they were known, the more I visualised the chasm between structural functionalism and its 'domain assumptions' within the discipline and the structural relations of class, gender, sexuality, 'race' and age that dominated my life and Toxteth, the community in which I was living. Then I read C. Wright Mills' *The Sociological Imagination* (Wright Mills, 1959). All the way from America it connected me to so many authors whose work is referenced throughout the following pages. Involved in the occupation of the University Senate House, the red flag flying from its roof, in anti-Vietnam War and anti-Apartheid protests, and experiencing first hand the racist policing of Toxteth, my studies suffered. But I had also been introduced to the work of Frantz Fanon.

Reading critical work, particularly neo-Marxist and feminist writings, I realised that researching, writing and teaching the 'view from below' was what really excited my sociological imagination. I was also gripped by the injustices I saw all around me, on the streets, in factories, schools and prisons. The raw edge of racism was blatant, sexual exploitation was unmissable and poverty was everywhere despite the relocation of inner-city workers and families to 'promised lands' on the urban periphery. In Toxteth, for example, the politics of subjugation was interwoven with a distorted politics of morality so poignantly caught by James Baldwin (1964: 28):

> In any case, white people, who had robbed black people of their liberty and who had profited by this theft every hour that they lived, had no moral ground on which to stand. They had the judges, the juries, the shotguns, the law – in a word, power. But it was a criminal power, to be feared but not respected, and to be outwitted in any way whatever. And those virtues preached but not practised by the white world were merely another means of holding Negroes in subjection.

Relations of power are implicit, occasionally explicit, throughout this book. Research over three decades maps social and political conflict in the context of increasing state authoritarianism and its popular appeal. It also shows how the political and ideological processes underpinning criminalisation are dynamic in the implementation of and justification for punitive state responses. While several chapters draw on research already published, occasionally using modified earlier passages, the objective throughout is to retain the accuracy and integrity of the original research interviews.

The first chapter presents the case for critical social research while acknowledging its starting points. It also discusses the responsibilities and struggles associated with research into sensitive issues and the problems of conducting ethnographic research into state institutions. Nine chapters are each related to research projects set in their time but revisited in 2007. They blend qualitative methods with documentary, case and content analyses. The final chapter returns to my theoretical starting point, tracing the development of critical criminological theory and its relevance to the projects, their inception and their analysis.

* * * * * * * * * * * * * * * * * * *

The sun streamed in through the high, elevated windows of the assembly hall. It was 1960, a Roman Catholic primary school on Merseyside. Despite the bright morning, the sense of foreboding was as tangible as it was unusual. The head teacher, accompanied by his male deputy and the parish priest, a blessed trinity high on the stage, were uncharacteristically stern, so detached.

The girls were asked to leave with their teachers, the boys instructed to sit cross-legged on the polished wooden floor. The Head's voice echoed around the school hall. The girls and the women teachers left. A pro-

longed, silent pause was broken by the opening and closing of the heavy doors at the rear of the hall. Each boy simultaneously heard and felt the vibration of more than one person walking. Two male teachers, one in front of the other, walked down the 'aisle' made by the two groups of cross-legged boys. Between them was a tiny figure. Ten years old, one of seven brothers and sisters; poor and undernourished.

Led on to the stage, he was delivered from teacher to Head. The boys had no idea what was happening but shared a collective terror, desperately trying not to wet themselves. The Head spoke gravely and deliberately: 'Boys. You know there has been someone stealing from the shop near the school. Never, not for one minute, did we think that a child from this school was responsible. But last night we were informed that one of our boys had been caught.'

He stood motionless and condemned before his accusers, his judges, his punishers. The words that follow will never fade: 'You have let yourself down, you have let your family down, you have let this school down. But most of all . . . ' he paused, 'you have let God down.' He was to be taught a lesson, a punishment to fit a crime, a punishment to serve as a deterrent to the rest.

Taking a bamboo cane from behind a table the Head took the boy's left hand and caned it, then his right hand and then, bending him over the table, he caned his backside. Multiple blows delivered by a grown man. He was walked from the stage and through the hall. Trembling, the boys glanced from the corners of their eyes. His gaunt face was expressionless but tears ran freely down both cheeks from dark, sunken eyes.

That morning adult authority, derived and sanctioned by the school, the state and the church, had been administered. Adult power to define, discipline and punish stood uncontested, legitimated by the institutions of which it was a cruel, harmful and subjugating manifestation. Yes, a lesson was learnt, but it was not the one intended.

1 Challenging academic orthodoxy, recognising and proclaiming 'values' in critical social research

On 'knowing'

> Your clever academics befriend us for a few months, they come down to our site, eats our food and drinks our tea. Some of them even lives amongst us. Then they disappear to their nice homes and university libraries. Next thing we know they're giving lectures on us, writing books about us ... what do they know about our struggles? How can they know our pain? We live it all the time. Our persecution lasts a life-time, not just a few months. Give us the tools to say it right and we'll tell you like it is. You know what we call them on our site? Plastic Gypsies.

Roy Wells, then President of the National Gypsy Council, spoke these words in 1975 at the launch of an academic report into the deterioration in relations between house-dwellers and Travellers. Flanked by academics and policy makers he reminded the audience of local authority councillors and officials what it felt like to be in the goldfish bowl of academic research, of the distance between researchers and the researched and of the experience of alienation when the control of a people's destiny lay elsewhere. He refused to be the 'token Gypsy' on someone else's stage and, with good grace and great oration, he instructed investigators and interventionists that the diverse cultures comprising the Traveller population were neither a curiosity for the voyeuristic gaze nor an alien within. He was under no illusion about the purpose of government-funded research. It would, as it always had, inform new strategies of surveillance, regulation and control. It would result in laws and policies to 'discipline' Travellers in a move towards the longer-term objective of enforced assimilation.

At the time I worked with Irish Traveller families in Liverpool. As a researcher I knew the realities and difficulties of being an insider–outsider. On the site daily, I spent more time there than most Traveller men. Involved with the on-site Travellers' school, in contesting imminent evictions and in reading and writing letters for families, I was an 'insider' in terms of trust. Yet I was an outsider in every other way, struggling with the seemingly implicit contradictions of my research. While I experienced the apparent vagaries of an ever-changing 'community' and came to some understanding of its historical and contemporary realities, I witnessed the direct impact on families of unremitting interpersonal and institutionalised racism.

I visited the West Midlands where, during a technically unlawful eviction, three children had died in a fire as a trailer (caravan) had been ripped from its jacks. Writing from jail, Johnny 'Pops' Connors (1973: 167) describes the experience of being an Irish Traveller in mid–1970s West Midlands: 'my wife kicked black and blue by the police in her own trailer three days before the baby was born; my little son very badly injured and my trailer smashed to pieces; the hospital refused to treat us; the councillors said kick them out at all costs'. My first research experience of extreme race hate raised questions well beyond the scope of any academic methodology course I had studied. What kind of men would recklessly evict Travellers, killing their children in the process? What kind of state, supposedly an advanced, inclusive, democratic state, would sanction such acts of brutality? What kind of an investigative and inquisitorial system would deliver verdicts of accidental death? Why did academic research and the care professions seem unconcerned?

Back in Liverpool on the windswept site of urban dereliction that was Everton Brow, the undesignated home to over 50 Irish Traveller families, the local community demanded evictions and threatened violence. A leaflet dropped through letter boxes in neighbouring streets:

> TINKERS OUT
> THE RESIDENTS OF EVERTON ARE SICK OF THE FILTH AND SQUALOR BROUGHT TO THEIR COMMUNITY BY IRISH TINKERS. LOCAL COUNCILLORS PROMISES HAVE COME TO NOTHING. IF THESE DIRTY PARASITES ARE NOT REMOVED WE WILL DO THE JOB OURSELVES. THEY ARE A DANGER TO THE HEALTH OF GOOD AND DECENT FAMILIES. THIS IS AN ULTIMATUM: GET THE TINKERS OUT, OR ELSE.

Soon after, a leading Warrington councillor called for a 'final solution' to the 'Gypsy problem'. Given the genocide directed against Roma throughout the Holocaust, his comment was calculated to instil fear within the local Traveller population. Gypsies, classified as genetic asocials by the Nazis, remained the ultimate, collective illustration of 'otherness'. Even their mass deaths were erased, their suffering 'largely absent from discussions of the Holocaust, as they are absent from the monuments which memorialise it' (Clendinnen 1998: 10–11).

In this climate of hate Howard Becker's portrayal of 'outsider' was literal. Community leaders and their elected representatives denied legitimacy to Traveller communities, their cultures or ways of life, refusing to negotiate any terms of acceptance. The daily reality of life on Everton Brow was local authority harassment, local community attacks and police brutality. Evictions happened at first light and self-styled, private-hire bailiffs were undiscriminating and unremitting in using force. While men and women defended their homes and families, their children screamed in fear. There were no case studies, ethical guidelines or briefing papers to advise the fledgling researcher on her/his place and role in such circumstances. Academic conferences were as distant in their analyses of such events as were most contributors from the action.

Writing on the hidden history of Aboriginal oppression in Australia, Henry Reynolds recalls meeting two young Aboriginal girls sitting on a dirty mattress on a prison cell floor, surrounded by shards of glass. A bucket for defecation, the air was stale with the stench of urine. Both girls, one bleeding, stood before Reynolds, ashamed. He wondered what dreadful crime had they committed. There was no crime. They had sworn at their teacher and been imprisoned for a day. He was shocked by the arbitrary and 'grossly disproportionate' punishment. Yet it was rationalised 'within the parameters of what was thought normal on the island'. Reynolds concludes, 'it seemed so utterly out of place in the modern Australia I knew about ... if such manifest injustice could flourish in 1968, whatever had been done in the past? If this could be done to children, whatever punishments were meted out to adults? Why didn't I know? Why hadn't I been told?' (Reynolds 1999: 7–8).

Three decades on from the Everton Brow evictions, on a cold March day in 2004, I and my co-researcher, Linda Moore, visited the punishment block of the high security Mourne House women's unit within Maghaberry jail in the north of Ireland. A 17-year-old young woman, by international standards a child, was held in a strip cell for no reason other than that the adult regime could not manage her self-harming behaviour. She was cut from her feet to her hips, from her hands to her shoulders. The skin between cuts had been scoured raw. She had used Velcro tabs on her anti-suicide gown. The tabs removed, the gown was held in place by sellotape. She was deprived of underwear, even during menstruation. The cell was bare, no mattress, no pillow, nothing except an 'anti-suicide' blanket and a small cardboard potty for defecation. She slept on a raised concrete plinth. Locked in isolation 23 hours each day her situation was desperate. She felt compelled to self-harm:

> I was in a hospital out there [in the community] and I still harmed myself then. I'm not getting the right treatment. They don't understand why I cut myself and I tell them I have to do it. It's my only way of coping. I seen Dr [the psychiatrist] and he gave me medication which helped ... I shouldn't be down here. There's nothing to do. It's worse in the night. I hear voices and see things. But no-one helps me. I should be in the hospital wing. This place needs a women's hospital or a special wing for nurses to control and deal with women with problems. They could have got people in to talk to me. To help me deal with my drink and drugs problems. I've had no counselling since I've been in here.
> (Interview, March 2004)

Considered a 'suicide risk', she had been accused of inciting other women prisoners to self-harm or take their own lives. Part of her 'care plan' was 'optimal contact' with staff and prisoners. Isolated from other prisoners, she had minimal interaction with staff. Women held 'down the Block' were checked 'two or three times an hour' through the day and 'roughly once an hour at night' (Interview, Prison Officer, March 2004). 'Checks' amounted to 'looking into the cell' through a spy-hole. Staff–prisoner contact was left to individual officers' discretion.

In her home town the young woman's doctor had removed her from his register, 'so I had no doctor to set up my medication'. She 'took other stuff to calm me down' and 'tried to stick a glass bottle in my neck'. Charged with possessing an offensive weapon, she was imprisoned. For nine days she was held in the male prison hospital, then transferred to the punishment block: 'That night I tried to hang myself and they wouldn't take me back over.' The 'voices' told her to self-harm and it 'released the pain'. Sleeping without a mattress was 'terrible ... you keep changing positions', the potty was 'a disgrace' and she had no personal contact with officers. During menstruation, 'They just give you a wee sanitary towel' but it was 'hard' to keep in place without pants (Interview, March 2004).

As we walked from the cell, her words on tape, the emotional mix of sadness, anger and incredulity was overwhelming. Her circumstances typified the 'duty of care' provided to women and girls imprisoned within an advanced democratic state constantly proclaiming values of 'moral renewal' at home and abroad. I reflected on Henry Reynolds' questions: if such 'manifest injustice' prevailed in 2004, what had been done in the past? If 'this could be done to children' what was the fate of women prisoners? How had a process involving doctors, nurses, probation officers, clergy, prison visitors as well as prison officers and their managers become so institutionalised, so accepted, so routine, yet hidden from the world outside? Academics had researched recently in the prisons, why were they unconcerned?

Answers, at least in part, are found in the negative reputation ascribed to female 'offenders' and self-harming children classified as 'behaviour' or 'personality disordered'. As with the social and societal reaction to Gypsies and Travellers, cultural and political representation is not happenstance but reflects a 'system of presuppositions and principles that constitute an elite consensus, a system so powerful as to be internalised largely without awareness' (Herman and Chomsky 1988: 302). Alternative discourses are rooted in challenging the purposeful, propagandist constructions of what is published as 'official history' and embedded in 'official discourse'. Through personal exploration and revealing context, a process of reinterpretation and understanding, 'knowing' offers the antidote to the official suppression of truth and the denial of responsibility, underpinned by witnessing and recording.

Having observed a 'stark and compelling' abuse of power by a prison doctor and two health-care officers during his extensive, in-depth research into health care in male prisons, Joe Sim (2003: 239–40) raises three questions:

> Do they accurately reflect the reality of the interactions that took place? What did I feel about these events both as a critical academic and as a human being? How should I bear witness to them?

Responding, Sim borrows a phrase from Lucy Maher's research: 'being there'. He had witnessed a distressed, sick prisoner threatened, cajoled and dismissed by captors wielding immediate discretionary power. The prisoner's 'subjugation was intensified and his acute distress remained untreated'. It was one of numerous encounters with those

> in the hospital wings because they were physically ill, psychologically distressed, had attempted suicide, or simply needed psychological and sometimes physical protection from the everyday ravages of prison culture. They were thus near the bottom of the prison hierarchy. Conducting the research – 'being there' – was often a gruelling experience which was saturated by a sense of outrage, not only at the abject and corrosive conditions in which the prisoners were detained and examined, but also at the often callous, off-hand and brutally capricious medical treatment they received ...
>
> (Ibid.: 241)

Sim captures the dilemmas of critical research in process. His observation of the power dynamic was neither amorphous nor tangential. It was specific, blatant and painful. 'Being there' at that moment bore witness to an act of unacceptable yet institutionally normalised degradation. It raised issues of intervention, interpretation, responsibility, complicity and identification. It lies at the heart of critical research, setting out to challenge official discourse and the protected boundaries of academic disciplines through seeking alternative interpretations of social and political reality.

Establishing a critical research agenda

In the 1960s sociology emerged as a seemingly significant site of critical analysis, challenging the very ethos and questioning the independence of the academic institutions in which it was based. Yet in the USA the early development and eventual consolidation of social science disciplines serviced the needs of giant corporations through cradle-to-grave management of workers and their families. Beyond the factories, they operated to politically manage the poor, the unemployed, the 'problem populations' and the neighbourhoods in which they lived. This included working as architects of the apartheid policies and practices that condemned Native Americans to increasingly restrictive reservations, while regulating 'non-white' immigration and migration. Despite some notable exceptions, academic social scientists produced 'knowledge' useful to a political economic form predicated on, and reproductive of, structural inequalities. Not only were social sciences complicit in capitalist expansionism, they were on hand to contain social and political conflict through mapping social, economic and criminal justice interventions. State welfare programmes appeared to identify and administer to the needs of the marginalised and the destitute, but in reality they managed the consequences of communities fractured by economic exploitation, endemic unemployment, inadequate housing and chronic ill-health.

In 1959 C. Wright Mills published *The Sociological Imagination*, in which he mounted a blistering attack on the 'inhibitions, obscurities and trivialities' of mainstream social science research (Wright Mills 1959: 20). His analysis exposed academia's servile and servicing association with state institutions and giant corporations. He was 'opposed to social science as a set of bureaucratic techniques which inhibit social enquiry by "methodological pretensions", which congest such work by obscurantist conceptions, or which trivialise it by concern with minor problems unconnected with publicly relevant issues' (ibid.). The lives, experiences and opportunities of ordinary people, their neighbourhoods, their communities and their associated tensions had been decontextualised. In the shadow of McCarthyism and the chill of Cold War politics sociology's critical edge had diminished. Its 'tendencies' were 'towards fragmentary problems and scattered causation', its direction 'conservatively turned to the use of the corporation, army and the state'.

Within social sciences, the city, the neighbourhood and the street had been reduced to social laboratories: a disconnected and ahistorical context. People's experiences, values and opportunities were neglected as state departments and corporate interests commissioned research that denied social inquiry its critical potential. The independence and integrity of academics had become compromised by close association with the military–industrial complex. State welfare programmes, employing 'social scientists' with professional training in social work, health, welfare and other related areas prioritised policy and practice interventions based on classification and regulation over care and advocacy. State-sponsored academic research could not be considered independent, rigorous or value-free. Wright Mills (ibid.: 193) argued that social scientists were hired for their utility; as 'technicians' who accepted 'problems and aims' defined by the powerful, who were ideologically compromised by the promotion of 'their prestige and authority'.

A contrasting, radical framework was required, dedicated to understanding and explaining day-to-day realities. This was to be found in the 'sociological imagination', critically self-reflective of personal context and understanding of 'the intersections of biography and history' operating between the 'personal troubles of milieu' and 'the public issues of social structure' (ibid.: 7–8). Personal troubles were found in the unique experiences of 'self', the direct associations of interpersonal relations. Yet public issues 'transcend these local environments of the individual' being derived in the 'larger structure of social and historical life' (ibid.: 8). He identified structure as shaped, regulated and reproduced through relations of power, legitimacy and authority. For Wright Mills, to understand social structure, the intricacies of institutions and to be 'capable of tracing ... linkages among a great variety of milieux', was 'to possess the sociological imagination' (ibid.: 11).

Wright Mills' critique challenged the dominant functionalist orthodoxy within post-war sociology. In academic institutions it dispelled the assumption, not shared on streets or in neighbourhoods, that 'society' was stable, integrated and smoothly functioning. It rejected the depiction of state institutions and large-scale corporations as consensual, meritocratic organisations benevolently accommodating a plurality of respectful, competing interest groups. In 1960s USA the struggle for civil rights in the Deep South, the emergence of revolutionary groups such as the Black Panthers, the rise of civil protest, the antagonism of large-scale corporation bosses towards unions, the anti-Vietnam War movement and the consolidation of second-wave feminism reminded academics and politicians that they lived in anything but an evenly balanced, consensual society. Not only were deep social and material divisions transparent, but the foundations had been laid for the growth of the prison-industrial complex.

As Elliott Currie (1998: 185) has since observed, the US stood 'at a crossroads' in structuring a 'response to urban violence'. The President's 1967 Crime Commission and the Kerner Commission on urban disorders 'reflected a remarkable degree of consensus about urban violence and its remedies', and sought a 'balanced approach to crime'. While accepting the need for a well-resourced and effective criminal justice system, the commissions 'insisted that we could never imprison our way out of America's violent crime problem'. A sustained offensive on 'social exclusion' was required: 'reducing poverty, creating opportunities for sustaining work, supporting besieged families and the marginalized young'.

The alternative 'road', however, emphasised incarceration. Currie notes how right-wing opportunist politicians and media commentators characterised the USA as being 'insufficiently punitive', portraying 'rehabilitative efforts' as 'useless', while 'social conditions', identified as 'breeding grounds for violence', were presented as irrelevant in explaining the rise in violent crime (ibid.: 186). Welfare interventions 'against poverty, joblessness, and racial discrimination were part of the problem, not part of the solution'. Criminals were 'coddled' and excused, the poor's 'resolve' was 'weakened' by handouts and a 'climate of permissiveness' had been 'spawned' (ibid.).

It was in this politically charged climate that Howard Becker delivered his presidential address to the Annual Meeting of the Society for the Study of Social Problems. Whether military expansionism abroad or penal expansionism at home, Becker argued that contemporary sociologists studying 'problems that have relevance to the world we live in' found themselves 'caught in the crossfire ... to have values or not to have values' (Becker 1967: 240). His attack on the relationships between academic sociology, US state institutions and cradle-to-grave giant corporations was unrelenting in challenging value freedom as a core assumption within social science research. In this context social theorists and active research-ers were given little room for manoeuvre. Yet Becker called for them to 'get into the situation enough to have a perspective on it'. Famously, he demanded that his academic colleagues reveal their 'personal and political sympathies', thus disclosing 'whose side' they were on.

In *The Coming Crisis in Western Sociology* Alvin Gouldner (1971) also rejected value freedom as deception. Consistent with Wright Mills, he explored in some depth how issues of structure, power and legitimacy had been deliberately evaded by academics operating as social engineers or welfare technicians financially and intellectually indebted to the established order rather than as social investigators researching the contexts and con-sequences of structural inequalities. Expressing a deepening concern about social voyeurism, however, Gouldner (1973: x) warned that academics were drawn to 'dangerous' neighbourhoods to observe 'wayward' life-styles, functioning as 'zoo-keepers of deviance'. His concern was the avoidance of 'patronising the concrete and smaller worlds' of everyday life. Defending 'field research' that accessed communities, groups and indivi-duals on their terms, Ned Polsky (1971: 137) argued that sociology 'isn't worth much if it is not about real live people in their ordinary life-situations'. He rejected the fetish within criminological research of 'pre-cise, controlled techniques of observation' that lifted people out of context. Gouldner's objective, however, was the development of a reflexive sociol-ogy that contextualised social and cultural relations in their material his-tory and their political-economic present. Only then could issues of power, legitimacy and authority be understood and analysed.

These issues were at the heart of the sociological imagination, the 'suc-cess' of which

> is intimately related to the struggles of oppressed people for equality, self-determination and social justice, because these are the groups that are actively seeking liberation, intellectually and politically. To stand for the sociological imagination is not a fashion or an aesthetic choice: ultimately, it commits one to social change.
>
> (Krisberg 1975: 19)

In acknowledging powerlessness, particularly the extent to which the ideological construction of outsider status was internalised and accepted rather than rejected or resisted, this debate was pivotal in consolidating the development of critical analysis. It emphasised that social research, whatever its specific focus, had to engage with the material world, its history, its ideologies, its political economy, its institutional arrangements and its structural relations. The road for critical researchers was uphill, given the exponential rise in the relative surplus population, the 'astronomic growth of the police and criminal justice budgets, subsidized in the main by the working class' and the withdrawal of 'desperately needed social services' (Platt and Takagi 1981: 39). The state drew its support from 'law and order ideologues' committed to 'depict[ing] the horrors of "street crime" and devis[ing] new methods of punishment'. On its payroll were the 'brightest and best criminologists ... eager to perform this function and prove their loyalty' (ibid.).

Breaking the silence

Thus, to fully grasp and interpret social action, interaction and reaction, critical analysis requires the interweaving of the 'personal', the 'social' and the 'structural'. Knowledge, and its processes of definition, acquisition and transmission, cannot be separated from the determinants of 'existing sets of social relations' (Harvey 1990: 2). The challenge for 'critical methodology' is 'to provide knowledge that engages the prevailing social structures ... oppressive structures [such as] those based on class, gender and race' (ibid.).

> Critical social research does not take the apparent social structure, social processes, or accepted history for granted. It tries to dig deep beneath the surface of appearances. It asks how social systems really work, how ideology or history conceals the processes which oppress and control people ... [it] directs attention to the processes and institutions which legitimate knowledge ... [it] involves a critique of 'scientific' knowledge which sustains [oppressive structures].
>
> (Ibid.: 6)

Lee Harvey's critique of the positivist and phenomenological perspectives within sociological research proposes a critical perspective 'delving beneath ostensive and dominant conceptual frames, in order to reveal the underlying practices, their historical specificity and structural manifestations' (ibid.: 4).

The underlying 'premise' of critical analysis is 'that "knowledge", including the formalized "domain assumptions" and boundaries of academic disciplines is neither value-free nor value-neutral' but 'is derived and reproduced, historically and contemporaneously, in the structural relations of inequality and oppression that characterise established social orders' (Scraton and Chadwick 2001: 72). Yet the critiques of mainstream social science theories are only part of the story. Within the political management processes of advanced democratic societies, official discourse confers legitimacy on power, thus underpinning the exercise of authority. For Foucault (1980: 131) each society operates a deeply institutionalised 'regime of truth' comprising 'the types of disclosure which it accepts and makes function as true; the mechanisms and instances which enable one to distinguish true and false statements, the means by which each is sanctioned; the techniques and procedures accorded value in the acquisition of truth; the status of those who are charged with saying what counts as true'.

Just as information is manufactured through professional conventions and industrial processes within the mass media, so truth is produced through the political processes of government. While not totally determining, the 'production of truth and the exercise of power are inextricably interwoven' (Scraton 2002a: 28). As Foucault (1980: 94) concludes, power 'never ceases its interrogation, its inquisition, its registration of truth'. It 'institutionalises, professionalises and rewards its pursuit'. Discourses of academic and state institutions, employing constructs such as 'state security' and 'public interest', combine and produce formally sanctioned knowledge. For Cohen (1985: 196) the 'logic and language of control' provides state institutions and their professional agents with an unrivalled, and often uncontestable, 'power to classify'. It is in their 'methodologies, techniques and functioning' that 'established bodies of knowledge' consolidate. Yet it is a process of legitimacy derived in, and supportive of, 'the determining contexts of material power relations' (Scraton 2002a: 29).

Critical social research sets an oppositional agenda. It seeks out, records and champions the 'view from below', ensuring the voices and experiences of those marginalised by institutionalised state practices are heard and represented. Through in-depth, contextual analysis it unlocks the potential of turning 'cases' into issues (Sivanandan 1990). This is the transcendence of 'local environments' to include the 'larger structure of social and historical life' envisaged by C. Wright Mills in his discussion of personal troubles and public issues. It is the application of the sociological imagination 'to change the world, not only to study it' (Stanley 1990: 15).

In disclosing and analysing the 'underlying mechanisms that account for social relations', a significant dimension of critical social research is its stimulation of 'dramatic social change from grassroots level' (Neuman 1994: 67). It challenges the portrayal of the marginalised, the excluded and the oppressed as helpless or hopeless victims of circumstance. It recognises the collective strength and formidable articulation of people galvanised to resistance by the insensitivity, recklessness and neglect of state institutions and corporate bodies. In his in-depth study of state killings in the north of Ireland, Bill Rolston (2000: xv) notes how British state institutions 'degraded the ideal of human rights over three decades'. Yet campaigners, many of whom had suffered loss, 'struggled to uphold the ideal in the most hostile of environments'. As a consequence 'private ills were transformed into public issues' and 'individual experience became a spur to political action' (ibid.: 319).

In circumstances where individuals or communities experience the brunt of poverty, racism, sexism, homophobia or ageism it is difficult for the social investigator not to be partisan, not to 'take sides'. Yet, with a few notable exceptions, academics remain silent when oppression within liberal democratic states is institutionalised. Research that focuses on serious civil disorder, the differential policing and regulation of communities and the use of state-legitimated force, and negligence by those in authority, is conceived, formulated and realised in volatile circumstances. Its agenda, *a priori*, is political. Interviewing people in the immediate aftermath of arrest, bereavement, court cases and so on brings the researcher face-to-face with raw emotion. It is not feasible, in the heat of such moments, to be free of moral judgement or political conviction. But the researcher's experiences, values and commitment are not necessarily inhibitions to fact finding, bearing witness or truth telling. If anything, critical research offers analyses of great integrity and honesty. For, rather than claiming some mythical 'value-neutrality', or sanitised, controlled environment, critical social researchers position their work, identify themselves and define 'relevance'.

As academic departments depend on local and central government to commission 'independent' research and evaluation there is often concern, usually indirectly expressed, that critical research could jeopardise lucrative and regular contracts and consultancies. An inherent problem in researching the powerful from the standpoints or experiences of the powerless is the discretionary use of institutional power to inhibit, or prohibit, access. Associated with such inhibition is the selective commissioning or appropriation of knowledge through which particular academic perspectives are ascribed credible status by the powerful in the context of a prevailing 'politics of truth'.

In denying funding to critical work, in challenging its methodological rigour, pressure is exerted on departments, universities, learned societies and independent research bodies to reconfigure their work. Jupp (1989: 158) concludes that the most 'serious threats' to the publication of research findings come from sponsors and influential gatekeepers 'who have the power to protect their interests'. Yet 'mainstream' social research adopts a 'most dangerous relationship to power: the categories and classifications, the labels and diagnoses ... being both stigmatizing and pejorative' (Hudson 2000: 177).

Researching controversial deaths

Nowhere is that 'dangerous relationship' more apparent than in the silence within mainstream social research regarding deaths in controversial circumstances. In 1979, within months of each other, two deaths involving the police received massive publicity but despite their significance were, and remain, conspicuous by their omission from most texts on policing. In April 1979 Blair Peach, a New Zealand teacher, was brutally killed by members of the Metropolitan Police Special Patrol Group as he walked home with friends from an anti-fascist demonstration. Two months later, Jimmy Kelly, a 54-year-old unemployed man in ill health, died on the charge-room floor of a Liverpool police station following arrest by several Merseyside Police Officers. The cases galvanised friends and relatives of people who had died in custody to form INQUEST: United Campaigns for Justice. What soon emerged from a systematic analysis of these cases (see: Scraton and Chadwick 1987a; 1987b) was the 'yawning gap between official discourse, inquiries or [inquest] verdicts and alternative accounts provided by bereaved families, [prison] regime survivors, rights lawyers, community workers and critical researchers' (Scraton 2002b:112).

Having researched these cases and as a founding member of INQUEST, my work on deaths in custody expanded into researching deaths in other controversial circumstances, including the Hillsborough and *Marchioness* disasters, the Dunblane Primary School shootings and the treatment of children and women in prison. It also involved work on violence in prisons and the arbitrary use of force by the police against targeted individuals and groups. Such research requires 'being there' or 'bearing witness' and occasionally takes the researcher to a different place. As the photographer Don McCullin (2002: 120) asks, when do you put down the camera and 'do something'? When do you pause as a researcher and directly intervene, give evidence or expose what is happening before it is too late? Researching deaths in controversial circumstances, institutional negligence and interpersonal violence, particularly involving the police, prisons, young offenders' institutions, special hospitals and so on, presents political as well as methodological and ethical challenges.

In my research, wherever possible I used taped, semi-structured interviews enabling personal stories to be told and relived. Storytelling, however, should not be restricted by the 'structure' of interviews. When people do 'memory work' they reflect as well as remember, occasionally making connections for the first time. Often the unexpected, the profoundly personal, is revealed. So vast was the scope of primary research, in the numbers of participants and the length of interviews, that the process of extracting and abridging the core elements of each testimony was onerous. In these circumstances it was vital that data selection did not result in distortion or inappropriate weighting. Extracts, their use and publication, were discussed with participants to ensure nothing was taken out of context nor meanings changed. This consultation included exploration of the potential implications of publication. At each stage of the process they retained the right of withdrawal.

Despite the different contexts and circumstances of the various research projects, the Hillsborough and Dunblane research, alongside in-depth interviews with families bereaved by the Lockerbie and *Marchioness* disasters (see Davis and Scraton 1997; 1999), revealed marked similarities and consistencies. In each case powerful political and economic interests, with much to lose, were implicated. In the immediate aftermath procedures were dominated by interagency conflict, particularly concerning the operational role and priorities of the police. As in the deaths in custody research, the bereaved complained of insensitive and unacceptable treatment by the authorities. This involved poor communications, absence of reliable information, misinformation, lack of humanity in handling the process of body identification, inadequate provision for receiving and interviewing the bereaved, and inappropriate procedures of inquiry. The concern voiced across all projects and cases was that families were, at best, marginalised and ignored and, at worst, excluded and abused.

Marginalisation and exclusion extended beyond the immediate aftermath to the processes of inquiry, investigation and inquests or fatal accident inquiries (Scotland). Lack of disclosure and/or selective presentation of evidence combined with inaccessible medico-legal processes and discourses inhibiting understanding and restricting participation. Yet, as major 'public interest' cases, the families found themselves projected into the international media spotlight. With deflection of blame and denial of liability foremost in the legal and media strategies of those in authority, grieving close relatives were impelled into initiating and defending campaigns for greater transparency while protecting the reputations of loved ones. It was in this volatile and occasionally vituperative climate that the research operated, regularly providing procedural explanations and personal support to distressed families and survivors.

With the consent and participation of bereaved families, an application was made to the Economic and Social Sciences Research Council to fund a series of eight international research seminars. The series examined all aspects of the aftermath of disasters and other controversial deaths, including deaths of civilians in the north of Ireland. It brought together family group representatives, campaigners, lawyers, journalists, academics, emergency service workers, counsellors and social workers. The core group, comprising the initial researchers and family participants, set the agenda, established the focus of each seminar and invited outside participants. They shared lead roles in seminar presentations. Two bereaved participants had previously published significant personal accounts (Partington 1995; North 2000). The seminars provided a unique forum for discussion of this work, incorporating and promoting its content and analysis. In evaluating the seminars the bereaved and survivors unanimously agreed the personal benefits of being involved. One bereaved mother stated that 'research into disaster cannot claim academic integrity if it fails to place at its centre the experiences of the immediate victims and their families. This, for me, is the only credible starting place.'

A bereaved father noted that the bereaved and survivors 'are rarely consulted about how they were treated. Not only does this diminish, even nullify, the value of such [research] reports, but also means that valuable lessons are lost.' The seminars enabled shared 'common experiences', revealing 'universal themes of insensitivity, collective indifference and distortion' by those in authority. They provided 'a forum ... not simply for emotional outpourings' but one in which the experiences of 'victims' were discussed 'in a broader context provided by those whose expertise ensured that the conclusions reached were always made objectively'. A bereaved mother commented that people 'who have lived through extreme experiences represent awkward questions'. She considered the seminars addressed these questions 'head on, with courage and imagination'. She continued: 'Sometimes I would feel almost euphoric on the long drive home. I suggest that was because I got my say – and a hearing. You could see it in the faces of others – they were being believed.'

The significance of the seminars was well illustrated by the following statement from a bereaved sister: 'This innovative research has been an invaluable, two-way, mutual process which has enabled a rare blend of healing and scrutiny in its underlying quest for a more compassionate, more just and more honest way forward for those affected by disasters'. The long-term success of the research projects into controversial deaths, including the subsequent range of publications and the seminars that followed, was a consequence of the close, mutual relationship between researchers and participants. It established a foundation of shared trust and skills on which further applied research, and the dissemination of its findings, was constructed and developed.

'Speaking truth to power'

> Whether the 'truth' sets you free is neither here nor there. The choice is between 'troubling recognitions' that are escapable (we can live with them) and those that are inescapable. This is not the 'positive freedom' of liberation, but the negative freedom of being given this choice. This means making more troubling information available to more people. Informed choice requires more raw material: statistics, reports, atlases, dictionaries, documentaries, chronicles, censuses, research, lists ... regular and accessible (Cohen 2001: 296).

Critical research is concerned with disclosure at two distinct but related levels. As argued earlier, it is about the revelation of context; locating moments, events and responses within their structural determinants. Returning to Wright Mills, 'personal troubles', at this level, can be fully understood and explained only in the structural relations of social and historical conditions. The second level concerns discovery of 'troubling recognitions' that have been denied, neutralised or reconstructed. The disclosure and dissemination of 'troubling information' is the responsibility of the critical researcher, whether academic or investigative journalist. Herein lies alternative discourse, building on case studies to transform personal troubles into public issues, making troubling recognitions accessible and contesting regimes of truth.

Returning to my early days working with Irish Travellers, I recall standing with Jimmy Loveridge amid the rubble, mud and squalor of the Everton Brow Travellers' site. The City Council was determined to evict, to use whatever force necessary to escape its statutory obligations to provide for its Traveller population. Jimmy was talking about the pub on the hill. That day he'd gone in and ordered a pint of beer. No one responded; 'the fella just looked straight through me'. Naively I asked, 'Did he have a "No Gypsies" sign on the door?' Jimmy smiled wryly and responded, 'No ... it wouldn't be lawful'. There was a long pause before he added, 'He's got the sign in his head'. When politicians talk of tackling 'social exclusion' and academics promote 'social capital' they seem oblivious to the experiences of 'outsiders', of what it takes to deal daily with the dimensions of 'otherness'. One moment 'otherness' means invisibility, the next it is the full-on, physical force of state intervention: harassment, eviction, injury and even death. One moment – the attitudinal racism of interpersonal conflict; the next – the institutionalised racism of state policies and practices.

For mainstream policies and practices to be formulated and enacted they not only require institutional authority but also claim the legitimacy of academic 'knowledge' and professional discourses. In vocational training, applied research and much-vaunted 'evidence-based' evaluations, the objective is to establish regimes of truth represented as objective, scientific and value free. Take the disciplines/professions most influential in processing the cases discussed above: medicine and the law. Each claims dedication to the 'common good': medicine for care and cure; law for rights and justice. Yet they are connected implicitly to maintaining and reproducing the *status quo*. The 'due processes' of legal or medical inquiry rarely confront powerful political-economic interests. These are core elements within Foucault's regimes of truth. Yet, despite considerable obstacles, not all doctors, lawyers and academics accept the set professional agendas; they form alliances with campaign and support groups to encourage and validate the 'view from below'.

Critical research is often questioned about objectivity and validity. The assumption being that because it sets out to expose 'troubling recognitions', with the intention of 'righting wrongs' or promoting socio-legal reforms, its objectivity is essentially skewed. Certainly there are ethical dilemmas. Discipline-based ethical codes provide guidelines detailing researchers' responsibilities towards research participants. They prioritise safeguards to protect the physical, social and psychological 'best interests' of the researched, who should not be adversely affected by their participation. The impact of the research process, however, cannot always be predicted. While guaranteeing privacy or anonymity, neither of which is afforded legal privilege, revisiting deeply sensitive issues is always an emotional, and often painful, experience. In encouraging people to recall and reflect, researchers have to be prepared for unexpected disclosures and, occasionally, personal discoveries brought on through participation. Disclosure and discovery are not necessarily empowering and regularly emphasise vulnerability. This is particularly significant when powerlessness is institutionalised (for example, research into imprisonment, mental health, bereavement, childhood). Critical researchers should be accountable for handling a process that requests traumatised participants to relive their suffering. As the research seminars show, personal support cannot be restricted to conducting a sensitive interview. The more substantive and enduring needs of participants must be identified and prioritised.

All qualitative research is predicated on establishing personal, moral and political relationships of trust between the researcher and the researched. In-depth research sets out to achieve maximum openness in these relationships. In addressing vulnerability, however, there are ethical imperatives. Consent should be given without expectation or pressure and should be based on full and accessible information regarding the purpose, funding, objectives, presentation and publication of the research. Anonymity and confidentiality should be guaranteed unless participants agree otherwise. The right to withdrawal and the right to deny permission to publish should, be established at all stages of the research. Findings should be discussed fully with participants and any further use of data, by other researchers or through submission to archives, should receive consent. The decision to disseminate and publish findings carries with it a responsibility regarding the 'facts' as found and the risks faced by participants whose accounts enter the public domain. The personal, social and institutional implications of publication, particularly regarding media and official responses, require informed discussion between researchers and participants.

As the following chapters demonstrate, however, guarantees and safeguards cannot be applied equally to all participants. The powerless are afforded greater protection, including confidentiality, than the powerful. Institutions and their officers are called to account, while the bereaved and survivors give their testimonies. Ethical codes are adjusted in the face of power and its institutional relations. Each project discussed in this text reveals the difficulties associated with addressing conflicting interests between powerful state institutions, their officials, and the relatively powerless. Interviews with senior officials and established professionals, particularly in circumstances where institutions are under scrutiny, usually are prepared and rehearsed by participants. Their purpose is to deflect criticism, negotiate or even reconstruct events. While the 'conditions' of the interview should always be honoured – anonymity, confidentiality, 'off the record' comments and so on – officials undertake interviews to represent and protect the interests of corporate bodies or state institutions. Revelatory research uncovering abuses of power requires a 'public interest' defence, more often attributed to investigative journalism.

In this context, informing official representatives of the purpose of the research, and the possible institutional consequences of participation, is not always achievable or desirable. Beyond this lies the difficult and often dangerous terrain of covert research. The methodological defence of full participant observation is that those being researched are unaware of being the subjects of study, thus enabling the researcher to more accurately 'tell it like it is'. In critical work, covert research provides a means of accessing powerful and inherently secretive institutions and their operations. If disclosure is formally denied or partially granted, uninhibited access is prevented. Put another way, the 'public interest' ends justify means which, in ethical terms, could be criticised for negotiating principles that underpin informed consent.

Clearly, critical research can, and does, subject the researcher to levels of personal and professional commitment which carry serious consequences. Working on controversial cases brings suspicion, marginalisation and hostility, as powerful interests defend their corner. It also leaves researchers open to accusations of 'over-identification' with their 'research subjects', of 'idealising' the 'view from below', of distorting the analysis in pursuit of political agendas and of exploiting the 'vulnerable' to build academic reputation. In the publication of critical accounts and making them accessible to a wide audience, the libel laws are weighted heavily in favour of powerful interests and individuals who have the resources at their disposal to initiate proceedings at the drop of a name. Within the academy, anonymised peer review polices and regulates the funding and publication of critical social research. I have experienced directly and personally the impact of each of these inhibitions, including informal approaches to my employers, the censoring of primary research reports and anonymous threats to me and my family. The most profound personal impact, however, is derived in bearing witness to the depths of people's pain and suffering and the consequences on their lives of the uphill struggle for truth, justice and acknowledgement. Yet this is where the foundation of critical research is laid. Hearing, recording and contextualising these testimonies, ensuring that they are afforded the credibility they are due, are the prerequisites to answering the questions with which this chapter opened.

In confronting 'inescapable', 'troubling recognitions', in delving beneath the spin, manipulation and deceit of official discourse and in pursuing alternative accounts, critical social research is concerned with speaking truth to power. As cases collectively transform into issues, platforms for significant societal change are established. Protagonists and defenders, however, are unlikely to recruit support for this mission in the corridors of power or the cloisters of the academy. Yet critical social research has a broader agenda. Providing the 'raw material' that is the stock-in-trade of alternative accounts, and stimulating informed debate and active participation, recasts research as a form of resistance. In this sense it is a necessary prerequisite and healthy manifestation of democratic societies.

2 'Unreasonable force': policing marginalised communities in the 1980s

Throughout Britain during the late 1970s heavy-handed policing in working-class communities, on picket lines and in black and Irish neighbourhoods drew criticism from campaign and civil liberties groups, politicians and the media. In 1979 a sequence of events occurred in Knowsley, Merseyside that led to serious allegations of excessive use of force by police officers from Merseyside Police's K Division. I had lived in Huyton a few years earlier and knew the area well. Following the death in custody of Jimmy Kelly, I began researching the case in the context of other events in the area. It was soon apparent that virtually no research existed on deaths in custody and none on the coronial system. I attended the inquest and was eventually involved in the submission of the case to the European Court.

In April 1979 Blair Peach, a New Zealand teacher, was clubbed down and killed by a member of the Metropolitan Police Special Patrol Group as he walked away from an anti-fascist demonstration in Southall, London. Later the police entered an African-Caribbean community centre, lined the stairs and batoned everyone as they tried to leave the building. Not only were the police heavily criticised for protecting a racist demonstration through the heart of an Asian community, they were held responsible by an independent committee of inquiry for killing Blair Peach and for brutalising black people. With families bereaved by deaths in custody we formed INQUEST: United Campaigns for Justice.

Two years later there was a full-on community uprising in Toxteth. Drawing on the work of Stokely Carmichael I argued that inner-city uprisings were a consequence of institutionalised racism within the custom and practice of local government and state agencies, a charge dismissed by the 1981 Scarman Report into the disturbances. In October 1985, following a minor confrontation in Toxteth, the Merseyside Police sealed off the community and deployed its Operational Support Division (OSD). The OSD literally took no prisoners, dealing out summary justice on the streets. Chanting monkey noises, drumming their riot shields and shouting sexist abuse they made it clear that their revenge was long overdue. Yet chief constables, government ministers and mainstream criminologists continued to deny or simply ignore the existence of institutionalised racism in policing Britain's black, Asian and Irish communities. It took the death of Stephen Lawrence in 1993, the appalling treatment of his family by the Metropolitan Police and the Macpherson Report to confirm from above what communities for generations had known from below.

The summer of 1979

The late 1970s police view of Liverpool and its people is well illustrated by James McLure's 'portrait of a police division'. According to the then Chief Constable, Kenneth Oxford, McLure's account 'faithfully portrays the frequently hectic, often dangerous task' facing the police in a place where 'crime and disorder are ever-present and have always been so throughout the turbulent history of the city' (in McLure 1980: 10). McLure concurs, cementing the negative reputation of the community. Liverpudlians were characteristically flawed by an 'evil streak' manifested in 'an astonishing propensity for gratuitous violence'. He interviewed a 'softly spoken' veteran officer who described the induction of a recruit into the division:

> To his left, the North Sub (sub-division), and it's a bit of a desert island on that side. All those cliff-dwellers in high rise flats; the bucks running wild and a few buckesses too ... then straight in front of him the market-place: all that glitters, merchants and moneylenders, beggars and meths-drinkers lying about legless! Then to his right, the South Sub: the jungle noises and even more the jungle behaviour of clubland; then yellow country, Chinatown; then, up in the right-hand top corner, black people country, Upper Parliament Street ... if he's coming on nights, he'll probably see five sort of stockades with campfires burning; places he can get in out of the cold and safe from a hiding ...
>
> (Ibid.)

To the Merseyside Police Liverpool had 'the country's worst law and order problem', fuelled by a genetic and/or culturally learned propensity to violence. It was a form and level of violence associated with territory, the occupancy of sinister neighbourhoods – 'jungle land', 'black people country', the 'yellow peril'. No one escaped this inner-city patchwork of lawlessness posing an ever-present threat to the law-abiding middle classes. Hard-line policing was the established antidote to hard communities. The 'war zone' imagery was not restricted to the custom and practice of differential policing on the street but underpinned operational policies and priorities. There were 'stand-offs' throughout the 1970s between the black community and the police. Streets were barricaded to keep out police patrols. What had not been foreseen was the flashpoint in McLure's 'cliff-dwelling', predominantly white, neighbourhoods of Knowsley, a metropolitan district of Merseyside containing the postwar developments of Huyton and Kirkby New Town.

People used to know where they stood, how far they could go ... I don't just mean knockin' off [stealing] but in havin' a joke with the Bobbies an' that ... but after the bust-up at the Huyton Park you daren't say a word to them. Just put your head down an' keep walking.

(Interview, August 1979)

On 15 June 1979 at the Huyton Park Hotel, K Division police officers mounted a raid, 'an organised police operation', to investigate breaches of licensing laws. The community was convinced it was a reprisal for damage inflicted on a police vehicle the previous week. Another confrontation occurred the following night at the Eagle and Child public house. There were five arrests and two officers were injured. Arrests at the Huyton Park were limited to 'drunk and disorderly' and 'assaulting the police'. Three of those arrested claimed they had been assaulted by the police and subsequently officers had perjured themselves in court. Two were acquitted and 14 people lodged formal complaints against the police for assault and perjury. Following the Eagle and Child incident one man, Peter Jeonney, was sentenced to three years' imprisonment for affray and assault. His convictions were quashed on appeal, the court ruling the police evidence inconsistent and unreliable.

Meanwhile on 21 June, in Huyton Police Station, a drunken 56-year-old man suffering with a heart condition died in custody, having been arrested in controversial circumstances. He had been drinking in the Bluebell public house and was making his way home across derelict land. People noticed him because he was singing loudly. A police car drew up and two officers confronted him. They attempted to push him into the back seat of the two-door car. They admitted squeezing his testicles. He lurched out of the car and on to the ground. Other police arrived and eyewitnesses stated the man was assaulted on the ground before being carried to the floor of a police minibus. He was semi-conscious. Unloading him at the police station, officers dropped him on to his head. Now unconscious he was carried into the charge-room, laid on his back on the floor where he urinated and died. Jimmy Kelly's injuries were extensive, including a fractured jaw. According to one pathologist, they were consistent with a severe beating.

Concern over heavy-handed policing led to the founding of the Jimmy Kelly Action Committee and community–police tensions consolidated. On 2 August the police attempted to quell a disturbance between neighbours in Prescot. Entering a family's house they arrested a couple and their son. The mother was hospitalised and all three were charged with causing actual bodily harm, criminal damage and obstructing the police. Eventually and without explanation all charges were dropped. Three weeks later the police dispersed one of the many street dice games. 18-year-old Michael Cavanagh fled the scene. He alleged that when the police caught him he was kicked in the side and taken to the police station without medical attention. Later he was rushed to hospital. His ribs were fractured and he lost a kidney and his spleen. None of the complaints made in these cases was upheld, thus compounding the breakdown in public confidence in the police.

Huyton's post-war housing was developed under industrial estates legislation and investment that preceded the implementation on Merseyside of the 1946 New Towns Act. These out-of-town developments brought young families from the inner city to mainly medium- and high-rise housing where financial enticements drew light industry to a ready supply of labour. Within one generation they were blighted by job losses as light industry withdrew in search of cheaper labour and new grants. With 80,000 jobs lost and registered unemployment at 13 per cent throughout the Merseyside Special Development Area, the Huyton and Kirkby estates, previously heralded the 'New Jerusalem', bore the brunt of structural unemployment and intergenerational poverty. The cynical concept of 'natural wastage' coined by employers with shrinking workforces left disillusioned school-leavers to bear the brunt of unemployment. At the time all that was offered in place of traditional apprenticeships and secure factory work were short-term, government-funded training schemes with no prospects guaranteed. The schemes were cosmetic and deeply resented. Families whose elders remembered well the union struggle against casualisation on Liverpool's docks were witnessing the return of cheap, easily disposable and unprotected labour.

Structured unemployment and endemic poverty inevitably induce an underground, 'hidden' economy sailing close to the wind of illegality. It is an economy of survival, of scamming welfare benefits, moonlighting, handling stolen goods and street gambling. These activities, alongside a growing drugs trade, were well known to the police, as were the pubs that accommodated informal trading. Police acceptance and toleration of the street economy was conditional on it remaining low key and modest. Other than a change in the divisional command structure there was no explanation for the sudden arrival of hardline policing in Knowsley. It had the hallmarks of a clampdown on low-level crime and what later would be characterised as 'antisocial behaviour'. The impact was instantaneous, drawing an organised response from the communities as trade unions, local councillors and Harold Wilson, Huyton's MP, demanded explanations from the Chief Constable and the Police Committee for the shift to aggressive policing. Lady Margaret Simey, leader of the Labour group on the Police Committee stated:

We are simply rubber stamps. We have the right to ask for information, the Chief Constable has the right to refuse. We should be having a discussion with the Chief Constable about the reasons the public are agin the police ... The answer is a political one. It is not a police one. And the Chief Constable is in a right political pickle over Knowsley.

Within weeks the policing crisis in Knowsley became a national issue. Harold Wilson called for a public inquiry into Jimmy Kelly's death in custody, the Knowsley District Council passed a no-confidence motion on policing within the area and BBC's *Panorama* broadcast a special investigation. On the programme, Margaret Simey stated the police had 'taken over the whole field of political decision' with local authority police committees 'opt[ing] out of their responsibility' (*Newsline*, 3 October 1979). She described the new generation of chief constables as 'very intelligent, very efficient' but 'unwilling to share their powers with elected representatives'. The Chief Constable responded sharply to criticisms levelled against his policies and his force. He considered the BBC's investigations 'impertinent and presumptuous' (ibid.). Councillors and Police Committee members were 'vituperative and misinformed', his officers subjected to a 'one-sided trial' by 'some sections of the media' and 'others of dubious political intent' (*Liverpool Daily Post*, 31 October 1979). James Jardine, the Chair of the Police Federation dismissed critics as 'the usual ragbag of people who spend their time sniping at the police service' (*New Statesman*, 30 November 1979).

At the subsequent Police Committee meeting the Chief Constable refused to elaborate on a press statement he had released previously. Margaret Simey was dismayed by his failure 'to co-operate' with the committee, concluding that members were 'reduced to "okaying" administrative items' (*Liverpool Daily Post*, 31 October 1979). The West Midlands Police investigation of the complaints against K Division continued into 1980. The Conservative Chair of the Metropolitan District Council, Sir Kenneth Thompson, accused the Chief Constable as 'arrogant ... he talks of his police force. It isn't, it's our police force'. The episode reflected the 'distant authoritarianism of certain ego-inflated chief police officers ... a small group of intriguers who shape public opinion' (*Liverpool Echo*, 19 May 1980). John Hamilton, Leader of the Labour group, concurred, noting that the conflict between the committee and the Chief Constable was 'symptomatic of a number of chief constables who are talking in this vein'. He concluded that the committee's powers were 'nearly nonexistent' (*Municipal Review*, July 1980).

On 24 March 1980, nine months after his death in police custody, Jimmy Kelly's inquest resumed in the cramped, heavily policed Whiston Coroner's Court. Ten seats were allocated to the family and ten for the general public. Family, friends and campaigners were well aware that many journalists would attend. They queued through the night on the snow-laden pavement in the freezing cold to secure extra seats. Rain-soaked and cold, they took their places as the Coroner warned the all-male jury to exclude from the mind the 'rumours, speculation and fantasy' and the possibility of a 'distorted and biased picture' previously constructed through selective media reporting of the case (Inquest Transcript, Day 1). The uniformed police presence was extraordinary. Officers from the division in which Jimmy Kelly had died staffed the car park, allocated passes, lined the stairs to the court and escorted family to and from the toilets. The layout of the court, its poor acoustics and inadequate consultation rooms distressed the family: 'There's no privacy ... if you want to discuss how it's going [with the barrister] there's always someone listening in' (Interview, March 1980).

While coroners warn juries that inquests are not trials, that any clear indication of liability would lead to postponement, in controversial cases they are often the only site of public inquiry, providing the only opportunity for the bereaved to hear the circumstances in which their loved one died. Given the high profile of the case and the allegations made by civilian witnesses in the media, the inquest was instantly adversarial, with leading Queen's Counsel pushing the boundaries of permissible cross-examination. Witnesses were identified as 'pro-police' or 'anti-police' and were treated accordingly. Those critical of the arrest of Jimmy Kelly were questioned severely by the QCs for the Police Federation and the Chief Constable. It was clear that each witness had been thoroughly investigated by the police. Personal details of their past, non-payment of bills, sexual innuendo, conflict with the law, school suspensions and any behaviour that could be used to discredit their reliability were presented in condemnation. They were portrayed collectively as irresponsible, antisocial and criminal individuals inhabiting a community infected with a pathological hatred of the police. It was also suggested in court that there had been intimidation of 'pro-police' witnesses within the community. A young man was dramatically escorted from the court, having been identified as a suspect. It was a theatrical moment, yet he was not charged with any offence and no explanation was given. Allegations of witness intimidation remained unsubstantiated. Jimmy Kelly's niece was unforgiving: 'It was stage-managed, a set up. Who was the bloke? None of us knew him. It was done to impress the jury and the cops were in on it' (Interview, March 1980).

During the inquest the Action Committee, family and friends wrote to Harold Wilson. They considered the police investigation and the coroner's inquest were so closely related that undue 'police influence' dominated proceedings:

> As far as we are concerned the use of the unusual discretionary powers vested in the office of coroner has produced a situation in which the proceedings have been conducted more like a trial than an inquest. The victims of that trial so far have been Jimmy Kelly and the witnesses. The hostile, emotive climate gets us no nearer to providing a context in which the truth might be established.
>
> (Letter, undated, March 1980)

Many civilian witnesses found it difficult to recall sequentially the precise details of the events recorded in their initial statements but all remained adamant that the police had used unacceptable levels of force during the arrest. They also considered that Kelly had been treated harshly after he had been subdued. Three young boys denied there had been any assault by the police. The four arresting officers stated that Jimmy Kelly had been drunk and aggressive. The first officers at the scene admitted using force. One officer had sat on him on the rubble-strewn ground and punched him 'three or four times' in the stomach. Under cross-examination his fellow officer agreed that the punches must have been to the face, because the officer was astride Jimmy Kelly's chest. It was admitted that in attempting to put him into the car they had grabbed him by the testicles and somehow he had somersaulted out of the car on the driver's side, on to his head. The police having requested back-up, Jimmy Kelly was restrained by one officer standing on his feet while another knelt on his chest. Handcuffed, he was carried to a minibus and transported on the floor of the vehicle.

The police case was that, in the circumstances, the force used had been reasonable. Kelly's treatment after arrest was not contested other than inconsequential points. The Coroner summed up the evidence, instructing the jury that for a verdict of unlawful killing they 'would have to be satisfied beyond all reasonable doubt that, first, unreasonable force had been used ... secondly that the deceased had sustained injuries which were the consequence of that unreasonable force and thirdly such injuries effectively caused the death' (Inquest transcript, Final Day). The jury returned a unanimous verdict of 'death by misadventure' caused by heart failure, with the contributory factors of acute alcoholic intoxication and exertion. The family interpreted the verdict as being self-inflicted death: that by drinking heavily in the full knowledge of his heart complaint and resisting arrest, Jimmy Kelly had brought death on himself. The Chief Constable welcomed the verdict, stating that it 'cleared the individual officers involved and the Merseyside Police from the many allegations and criticisms which were made after this incident occurred which have now been found to be without substance' (*The Guardian*, 18 April 1980).

In his 1979 Annual Report the Chief Constable commented:

> The tragic Kelly case was further cited to illustrate my reluctance to inform my police authority [committee] of matters pertinent to their responsibility: again completely unfounded and untrue, but unfortunately seized upon by those who question the accountability of chief police officers.

Given the context of other events in Knowsley, Margaret Simey demanded a public inquiry into the case. It was rejected by the newly elected Thatcher government. In September 1980 the Chief Constable presented a progress report on the internal investigation into K Division. It found 'no grounds' for the prosecution of officers or for disciplinary action. Further, there was 'little doubt that the more obdurate critics will continue to denigrate the police, as is their wont, and will attempt to transform individual transgressions by police officers into a universal condemnation of the police system' (para 18). Outcomes and conclusions drawn from the internal investigation remained exclusively the property of the Chief Constable. The Merseyside Police report and the West Midlands report were not submitted to the Coroner or the Police Committee. Despite eyewitness accounts across a range of cases, critical media coverage, political concern and a strong community-based campaign regarding police abuses of power and lack of accountability, the Chief Constable had the last word. Meanwhile, a major confrontation was brewing in another part of the city.

The summer of 1981

In 1980 street protests by the black community in St Paul's, Bristol brought into sharp relief the city's long history of racism. Bristol, like Liverpool, had grown wealthy on the back of the slave trade. Its black communities were well established, as was endemic racism trapping young people in ghettoes. The following year, in Toxteth, barricades were on the streets and initial confrontation escalated into a full-on community uprising. On Upper Parliament Street the symbols of Empire were burnt to the ground. That summer police from throughout Britain were deployed on Liverpool's streets. To those unfamiliar with the city and its history, the conflict came as a surprise. Its depiction as 'riot' fulfilled an image of random, chaotic spontaneity. It also deflected attention from the recent history of endemic racism. It failed to explain that in 'taking on the police' many in the black community were embarking on a reasoned response to free themselves of unacceptable differential policing.

In 1970s Liverpool racism was prevalent: on the street, in the schools, throughout public institutions and private enterprise. Few Liverpool-born black people served in the city's shops. They were conspicuous by their absence in the corridors and offices of the City Council. Most lived in Toxteth, close to the University but a world apart. It was walking distance from the city centre, but on Saturdays the police patrolled the junction of Bold Street and Renshaw Street, turning back black youth and lighting a slow-burning fuse of resentment. Police–community relations were confrontational, not least in the military-style, long-wheelbase, reinforced Land Rovers – known as 'meat wagons' – deployed exclusively on Toxteth's labyrinthine streets. The Merseyside Police made night and day forays into the heart of the community, stopping and searching, randomly raiding houses. In 1971 Margaret Simey, who lived in Toxteth, stated the 'black community' was 'fed up of being hounded'. She continued:

No-one is safe [from the police] on the streets after 10pm. One gang we know has given the police an ultimatum to lay-off within two weeks or they fight back. It could lead to civil war in the city.

(in Scraton 1981: 24)

Throughout the 1970s disproportionate levels of unemployment; discrimination in schools, work and housing; few social amenities; and hard-line policing blighted the lives of those living in Toxteth. Reports and inquiries presented a mass of evidence demonstrating the racism inherent in the marginalisation and subjugation of the black community. In 1978 the community experienced national, public humiliation as a consequence of a BBC *Nationwide* programme presented as a reassurance to black people that the police were not racist. A commentary by Martin Young, later published, noted that the police 'are the first to define the problem of half-castes in Liverpool':

Many are the products of liaisons between black seamen and white prostitutes in Liverpool 8, the red-light district. Naturally, they do not grow up with any kind of recognisable home life. Worse still, after they have done the rounds of homes and institutions, they gradually realise they are nothing. The Negroes will not accept them as blacks, and the whites assume they are coloureds ... the half-caste community on Merseyside, more particularly Liverpool, is well outside recognised society.

(*The Listener*, 2 November 1978)

Young's statement, reflecting the attitudes of police officers he interviewed, gave credibility to the implicit racism behind the crude, reductionist stereotypes broadcast. He challenged the 'pinko, liberal attitudes' evident in the anti-racist debate: 'when you are suddenly faced ... with the stark reality of villainy, when you see the total contempt that the hardened criminal feels for society and the law, you have to think again about the efficiency of the powers we allow the police'. Young had visited Liverpool, met the police and looked criminality in the eye. Rather than questioning the strength and depth of racism and its implications, he presented an argument for the extension of police powers.

Following the prime time television broadcast, the local community held a public meeting but neither the BBC nor the Merseyside Police offered an apology. As police–community relations deteriorated further, the Merseyside Area Profile Group submitted evidence to the 1980 Home Affairs Committee on Racial Disadvantage, warning that police harassment and aggression towards black youth had escalated. The Chief Constable was in denial, oblivious to the depth of concern voiced repeatedly by community leaders, local politicians and academic researchers. In his 1980 annual report he wrote that police–community relations were 'in a very healthy position and I do not foresee any difficulties in the future'. It was a miscalculation of some magnitude.

Within weeks, between 6 July and 15 August 1981, 690 police support units from 40 British police forces were deployed on Toxteth's streets; 781 officers were injured, 214 police vehicles were damaged and over a million pounds was spent on associated police costs. In Toxteth 320 people were arrested, over 300 in other Merseyside areas; and one young man was killed by a police Land Rover driven at speed on the pavement. Not involved in the disturbances, simply venturing outdoors made him a target, following the Chief Constable's statement that 'law-abiding people should get off the streets'. Another young man suffered severe back injuries when a Land Rover was driven into the crowd. As part of what the Chief Constable labelled 'positive police policy' the Land Rovers were 'deployed into the crowd to break it up'. For the first time in Britain, CS gas was fired 'to regain the control of the streets from the rioters'. As a consequence of the use of 'barrier-penetrating' projectiles against people four civilians were seriously injured. The Chief Constable subsequently accepted that the cartridges fired 'were of a type not designed for use in public order situations' (*Evidence to the Scarman Inquiry*, 1981: 6).

In late July, still reflecting on the Knowsley episode, the Police Committee established a working party into police–community relations. It took evidence from community groups, professional bodies and the police, presenting its first report in late October. The Committee also requested a full report from the Chief Constable on the police handling of the disturbances. In the heat of the conflict he had denied that it was in any way 'racial' but 'exclusively a crowd of black hooligans intent on making life unbearable and indulging in criminal activities' (*The Guardian*, 6 July 1981). Yet his subsequent report was not written in that context and had the benefit of considered reflection. 'Public Disorder on Merseyside: July–August 1981' was only five pages in length, focusing on the use of CS gas, police tactics, complaints and prevention of disorder. It proposed the introduction of foot patrols in Toxteth, a crash officer-training programme 'aimed at influencing the attitudes of officers' that would prevent 'a police over-reaction to incidents occurring within the force and particularly within Toxteth'. Local communities would be involved in consultations about police policies. The Chief Constable's schematic report contrasted significantly in tone and content with his report to Lord Scarman, who was conducting a Home Office inquiry into disturbances in Brixton, which he had extended to include other cities.

To Scarman, Chief Constable Oxford portrayed Toxteth as a community of pathological criminality within a city 'beset by problems of violence and public disorder throughout the centuries' (Oxford 1981: 4). The 'true Liverpudlian' had an 'aggressive nature' and 'belligerent attitude'. Historically the 'Liverpool populace' had developed a 'turbulent character': 'problems which multiplied and were aggravated by large-scale immigration of

Irish ... enough remained to aggravate the problems of poverty, unemployment and overcrowding, which then, *as now*, were the *breeding grounds for violence*' (ibid.: emphasis added). Then arrived 'appreciable numbers of Welsh rural labourers who were attracted to a flourishing city'. Other 'foreign nationalities' and 'foreign exiles' arrived until after the Great War, which brought a 'remarkable increase in the number of coloured immigrants ... initially seamen who stayed and married local white girls'. Oxford's potted history was consistent with the account given to Martin Young for the *Nationwide* programme that had caused so much tension within the community. Oxford's conclusion connected immigration and settlement to violence and disorder:

> The black community, like the Chinese, has been a feature of Liverpool life for generations. Each of these communities *brought with them* associated problems, disputes and tensions, which on occasion spilled over into outbreaks of violence.
>
> (Ibid., emphasis added)

Persistent street confrontations in Liverpool's history had 'for many years fulfilled her reputation as a tough, violent city to the present day'. Its people had a reputation as 'proportionately tougher, more violent and more pugnacious'. Their collective attitude was 'belligerent' finding 'expression in violent disturbances similar to ... the most recent outbreaks in Toxteth'. He represented Toxteth as the 'natural homing ground for immigrants', the location for 'so-called mugging' where 'street prostitution is customary and there is a flourishing drug traffic' (ibid.: 28).

Absent from this account was the history of the Merseyside working-class experience of casual labour, structural unemployment, poor housing, discriminatory public services and hard-line policing. In fact Oxford justified discriminatory, differential policing on the grounds that certain identifiable communities posed a disproportionate threat, thus requiring greater regulation. His account was also consistent with the veteran officer's instructions to the new recruit in McLure's study. Liverpool people had a negative reputation, their natural and cultural inheritance being aggression and belligerence, but within the broad categorisation lay subcategories of greater lawlessness and violence. From Oxford's evidence Scarman noted the 'particularly high incidence of crimes of violence' within Liverpool. Toxteth was the 'scene for a high proportion of that crime' (Scarman 1981: 64). Community-based allegations of racist policing, harassment and violence were lost in the rhetoric of 'breeding ground', 'natural homing ground', 'cultural deficiency' and moral degeneracy. As Scarman took evidence, I was drawing a quite different conclusion:

> Racism is a long-endured inhumanity in Liverpool's black and Irish communities. The picture painted by the city's well-known politicians

is of a harmonious, integrated, cosmopolitan city. This ignores the brutal reality of the inter-war period when the first generation black community was continually the butt of white racism ... it also veils the institutionalisation of that racism within the practice of local government and state agencies.

(Scraton 1981: 24–5)

Not only did the British state do little to provide reasonable living standards for the working class in inner cities and towns, it also failed to provide effective protection for black or other ethnic communities against racism at either personal or institutional levels. Instead, the law was enforced differentially and rigorously in and against these communities. Saturation policing, using special taskforce units, encouraged an aggressive, siege-like mindset within the police. Offensive methods emerged and consolidated as force policy elevated racism from a personal to an institutional level. However visible in policing, institutionalised racism permeated all state agencies, corporate bodies and private enterprises.

To those familiar with communities in turmoil it was clear that the 1981 disturbances were a direct consequence of generations of institutionalised racism in the city, the police and the courts. Years of reports, independent research and parliamentary evidence revealed that the depth and scope of racism within policing had been disregarded persistently by chief police officers. It was barely disguised. In Liverpool's Admiral Street police station, on the fringe of Toxteth, Merseyside Police officers operated what they called 'coon races'. Each officer on duty put money in a 'kitty' and the first back to the station with an arrest of a black person won the money. Uncompromising policing of black youth throughout Britain's black communities, including routine stops and searches on the dubious grounds of 'suspicion', demonstrated the prevalence of institutionalised racism.

Yet, in what was to become a most influential government report on policing, Scarman (1981) interpreted institutionalised racism as 'discrimination against black people ... knowingly, as a matter of policy'. He stated, 'If the suggestion is being made that practices may be adopted by public bodies as well as private individuals which are unwittingly discriminatory against black people, then this is an allegation which deserves serious consideration.' But he found neither the 'direction' nor 'policies' of the police to be racist. Scarman concluded: 'I totally and unequivocally reject the attack made upon the integrity and impartiality of the senior direction of the force' (ibid.: 64). He found no evidence of 'deliberate bias or prejudice'. Extending beyond Brixton and the Metropolitan Police, he denied 'institutional racism' existed in Britain, while accepting that 'racial disadvantage and its nasty associate racial discrimination, have not yet been eliminated' (ibid.: 135).

Among Metropolitan Police officers, he found evidence of 'ill-considered, immature and racially prejudiced actions ... in their dealings on the streets with young people' amounting to 'an unthinking assumption that all black people are criminals' (ibid.: 64). Yet 'such a bias is not to be found among senior officers'. 'The criticism', he said, 'lies elsewhere – in errors of judgement, in lack of imagination and flexibility, but not in deliberate bias or prejudice' (ibid.). Racism, when found, was 'occasional' and confined to 'the behaviour of a few officers on the street'.

For Scarman the existence of racism within an institution, however prevalent, was an aggregation of racist attitudes rather than being deep-rooted and institutionalised. In contrast, two years later a Metropolitan Police-commissioned Policy Studies Institute report on police–community relations exposed the extent to which Scarman's view of racism was blinkered. The report provided evidence that linking black people to crime was an all-pervasive assumption within the Metropolitan Police. It concluded that racial harassment and racial violence was not taken seriously at a senior command level, that racism led to routinely aggressive and intimidatory policing. Police racism was identified as inherent within a culture of values derived in white, male respectability and manifested via a 'cult of masculinity'.

The autumn of 1985

In 1985, following a series of incidents in Toxteth, a number of allegations were made to the Police Committee and to its chairperson, Councillor Margaret Simey, concerning insensitive policing and police harassment of black people in the community. Community meetings were held at which a range of problems was raised by community representatives: the deployment of the Operational Support Division (OSD) in Toxteth using unmarked vehicles; aggressive and racist policing against black people in the city centre; the use of unreasonable force in evicting black demonstrators from a City Council meeting; selective searches of 'black only' properties following a bank raid; a raid on Toxteth Sports Centre; the stereotyping of black people as criminals, despite Scarman initiatives in training; the inadequacy of the police complaints system and the 'reality' of police reprisals against complainants (Report of the County Solicitor and Secretary, 26 June 1985, Merseyside County Council). These allegations were repeated in September 1985 at a meeting of the Police/Community Liaison Forum, attended by the Deputy Chief Constable. The picture portrayed by many black people was one of containment within Toxteth through hostile and racist policing in the city centre and by the 'heavy presence of police on the perimeter of the Toxteth section with vehicles operating sirens and containing numbers of police officers ... causing disturbance and concern to some residents' (Notes of the meeting, 24 September 1985, Merseyside County Council).

Margaret Simey recorded her concern about the number and consistency of allegations. There had been a measure of success between the police and the Toxteth community through a community policing initiative, but this appeared to be collapsing. On 1 October 1985 matters came to a head. Following a well-publicised court case at the City Magistrates' Court, involving four men prosecuted over the death of a London man in Toxteth two months earlier, a crowd returned to the community. A police station window was broken and several vehicles and people were attacked. Cars were torched and traffic halted. It was early evening and the police dispersed groups of youths. Operational command was under the local superintendent. Without warning and without his knowledge or approval, a Police Support Unit (PSU) and other mobile units from the OSD were deployed into the area (Interview, Margaret Simey, October 1985). Interviewed in the wake of the event, the superintendent stated that the OSD's deployment in full riot gear contributed to the unrest on the streets (*The Observer*, 7 October 1985).

Witnessing the OSD's arrival on the streets was the Archbishop of Liverpool, the Most Revd Derek Warlock. He recalled:

At first there was an explosion of frustration after events at the Magistrates' Court. By 7.30pm it was evident that it was under control. At 9.00 I found a lot of anger – black and white – about the intensity of the police reaction. Then the police suddenly appeared in riot helmets and shields. They were told that if they would go, we would clear up and get everybody off to bed. I do not want to make judgements, but I did see things that were regrettable. Police communications had broken down – vehicles were moving around very fast and on pavements. That is dangerous.

(*The Observer*, 7 October 1985)

In a joint letter to Margaret Simey, Archbishop Warlock and the Bishop of Liverpool, David Sheppard, stated the police 'cordoned off the area and sent in a large number of riot police and armoured vehicles ... and there seems to have been mounting anger at this show of force ... the price seems to have been high in damage to good relations built up through community policing in recent years' (Letter, 11 November 1985). From the moment the OSD arrived it was impossible for people to move in or out of the area. At the height of its intervention transit vans and Land Rovers were driven at fast speed on pavements, stopping to deploy riot officers, truncheons drawn, on to the streets. People were 'targets' by being on the streets and the Archbishop of Liverpool was pinned to a wall. A letter from a priest to Margaret Simey stated:

I saw half a dozen officers leap on a man while I was shouting 'He's drunk'. One after another they leapt at him with truncheons, almost fighting with each other to find a part of the man to hit.

An off-duty fireman witnessed the assault. He went to help the priest rescue the drunken man. He was convinced 'the only reason that they did not attack us at that stage was because the priest was with us' (Statement, Liverpool Law Centre). The drunken man jumped on to a police van and the police 'came swarming around ... and began to beat him hard'. He continued:

> Suddenly a group of police officers turned on me. I could estimate that about thirty of them paid special attention to me and there was absolutely nothing I could do to defend myself. I cowered against the wall and ducked my head down in the hope of protecting myself. I offered no resistance at all but in spite of that blows were rained on my head, back, shoulders and kicks to my body. I was badly gashed on the back of my head and had to receive medical treatment. I had four or five stitches in my head.
>
> (Ibid.)

Numerous statements from civilian eye witnesses testified to extreme racism, hostility and brutality throughout the police operation. At a later residents' meeting the common view was that vehicles had been deployed in a haphazard and dangerous manner, at speed and with screeching brakes, along pavements and directly at onlookers. The community considered the police offensive to be deliberately provocative. It had 'frightened and angered people and was thought to have precipitated the much worse civil disorder which followed' (Notes of meeting, 4 November 1985). A black community worker stated:

> They were driving at greater speeds this time than they had been earlier. The engines were revved up and a great deal of noise was made. Vehicles would turn off into side streets and do U-turns and go round and back again. Vehicles were going up and down the streets scattering people ... they were intent on clearing us and others like us who were simply watching quietly to see what would happen next.
>
> (Ibid.)

Apart from the unlawfulness of the dispersal tactics, the main complaint concerned the level of violence directed purposefully towards black people. The Toxteth meetings heard numerous complaints and accounts of police racism. As the police officers exited their vehicles they moved into side streets in large numbers, 'banging their shields and shouting "Come on you black bastards"'. The local residents were 'called "nigger", "coon", "whore", "slag", and various other derogatory names by these officers' (Notes of meeting, 28 October 1985). One community worker stated:

> There must have been several dozen police all in riot gear and they were walking along the street in rows that filled the whole street. They

were banging their truncheons on their shields ... and seemed to be trying to work themselves up into a frenzy ... the shout that went out was 'Come on you black bastards'. They were shouting and screaming as they broke into a run ... I was disgusted and distressed by their organised, frenzied shrieking.

(Ibid.)

A black woman stated:

They were all in full riot gear and they approached us. In particular one of them grabbed me by the arms. He said 'Get home!' and then 'Fuck off, you slag'. I replied in anger 'Don't tell me to fuck off. And I am not a slag. Look, I live here.' Quite a few of the policemen then took up the cry of 'Slag'. They began shouting it at me and I began to walk away. One of them in particular shouted after me 'We got it right the first time, you are a slag'.

(Ibid.)

What shocked so many witnesses was the police use of indiscriminate violence against anyone who happened to be on the streets:

There was another young lad about 16/17 standing by a shop. A police officer jumped out of the back of the van and went towards him. He grabbed the lad and started to beat him with his baton. Another officer joined the officer who had hold of the lad and started punching him and hitting him with their batons ... they sandwiched him between two vehicles. They started hitting him with their batons, booting him and punching him and one of the officers shouted 'Gary, lay off him'. The police put the lad into one of the vehicles and drove off ... The other vehicle with the officer 'Gary' in it went towards Princes Road and Princes Avenue and stopped at the lights there. An officer jumped out and threw a baton at the first car that went past. His fellow officers shouted 'Gary, what have we told you, get back in the van' ... At about 10.30pm we were standing on the estate of Granby Street where a Land Rover was parked ... An officer jumped out of the back, got hold of a young woman, hit her in the face with a baton, pushed her to the floor. Someone shouted 'Unit 3 get back in the van'. He didn't get back in the van he just kept hitting the woman. The CO shouted again, 'Gary I have told you to get back in the van and control your temper'.

(Ibid.)

The range and consistency of statements from residents, clergy and community workers provided a body of evidence confirming the escalation of police aggression that arose from a single incident. Given the post-Scarman commitment to community policing initiatives and the formal complaint made by the local superintendent to his senior officers over the handling of the October events (*The Observer*, 7 October 1985), the main issue turned on the operational policy and organisational control of the OSD. Without internal consultation an operational decision had been taken to transfer command from the local superintendent. In reporting to the Police Committee the Chief Constable stated:

> At 6.05pm the control of the incident, which until this stage had been exercised by the Divisional Chief Superintendent from his Divisional Command Post, was transferred to the Incident Control Room at Force Headquarters under the direct command of the Assistant Chief Constable (Operations) in order that the deployment of manpower and resources could be fully co-ordinated.
>
> (Chief Constable's Report to the Police Committee,
> 15 October 1985, para 3)

The Toxteth community meetings presented the Deputy Chief Constable with eye-witness accounts alleging that the OSD had been 'out of control'. He replied that each unit was under the direct control of an inspector. What was not clarified was whether the problems of communication between the local commander, the OSD and other Police Support Units were due to 'different divisions operating on different radio channels or whether it reflected a more fundamental question of "who's in charge"' (Report of the County Solicitor and Secretary, 20 November 1985, para 24). The evidence confirmed that, once deployed, the OSD operated on its own unit-based discretion. Certainly, that was how it was perceived and experienced on the street. Racist abuse and beating riot shields were raised as examples of unacceptable policing with the Deputy Chief Constable. He 'did not condone the use of such language', but pointed out 'the stress under which officers in such situations operated' (ibid.: para 21). The Police Committee was invited to consider whether 'shields are beaten in such situations in order to raise morale of officers or to frighten onlookers'.

Finally, throughout the confrontation officers could not be identified by rank or number. This caused problems in accessing those in command and identifying officers against whom people wanted to make complaints. Some witnesses claimed that officers had removed their numbers from their clothing. The Deputy Chief Constable stated this practice would not be repeated. The Report of the County Solicitor and Secretary to the Police Committee listed serious issues arising from the Toxteth incidents: the use of the OSD and the nature of the police operation as being possibly 'unnecessary and provocative; the use of vehicles and the accepted requirement for the use of minimum force; the allegations of racist abuse and random violence by the police; the level and quality of operational control'.

Some time later ...

Reflecting on the influence of the Scarman Report, Lee Bridges (1999: 306) notes how it moved beyond the contemporary policing of black communities to 'a whole school of race criminology in Britain, which adopts a pathological approach and seeks to downplay the impact, both of police racism and racial discrimination in general on Afro-Caribbeans'. Evident from subsequent events in Liverpool and in many other British towns and cities was that differential policing, incorporating racism, continued virtually unchallenged within most UK police forces. Undoubtedly it was bolstered by Scarman's denial of institutionalised racism. This denial, coupled with complacency, was exposed tragically in the police response to and investigation of the racist murder of Stephen Lawrence in April 1993.

The Metropolitan Police reaction to the killing, in the immediate aftermath and throughout the investigation, was heavily criticised by the Lawrence family and its lawyers. The failure to accept the attack and murder as racist and to question known, named suspects, allowed the attackers to dispose of incriminating evidence and establish alibis. Four years after the attack the coroner's inquest returned a verdict of unlawful killing, with an added rider that Stephen Lawrence was the victim of a 'completely unprovoked racist attack by five white youths'. The family demanded a public inquiry. In July 1997 the Home Secretary, Jack Straw, appointed Sir William Macpherson 'To inquire into the matters arising from the death of Stephen Lawrence ... in order particularly to identify the lessons to be learned for the investigation and prosecution of racially motivated crimes' (Macpherson 1999: 6).

The Macpherson Report was thorough in detailing the murder of Stephen Lawrence and its aftermath. Its conclusion appeared uncompromising. There had been 'fundamental errors' in an investigation 'marred by a combination of professional incompetence, institutional racism and a failure of leadership by senior officers' (ibid.: 317). The internal Metropolitan Police review of the case was 'flawed' and had 'failed to expose these inadequacies'. Despite the Police Commissioner persistently denying institutionalised racism within the Metropolitan Police, Macpherson disagreed. He defined 'institutional racism' as a 'collective failure of an organisation to provide an appropriate and professional service to people because of their colour, culture or ethnic origin'. Its presence 'can be seen or detected in processes, attitudes and behaviour which amount to discrimination through unwitting prejudice, ignorance, thoughtlessness, and racist stereotyping which disadvantage minority ethnic people' (ibid.: 321).

Macpherson made 70 recommendations, including: openness, accountability and the restoration of confidence; definition of racist incident; reporting and recording of racist incidents and crimes; police practice and investigation of racist crime; family liaison (by police); the handling of victims and witnesses; prosecution of racist crimes; police training (first aid, race awareness); employment, discipline and complaints; stop and search; recruitment and retention; prevention and the role of education. The impact was instant and far reaching. Although rooted in the police handling of a single racist murder, the recommendations had implications for all organisations.

As Jenny Bourne (2001: 13) observes, Macpherson raised the profile of 'the extent of racist violence in Britain, the way miscarriages of justice could take place and the incompetence and racism of the police force'. Given that chief constables, government ministers and the media had continued to deny the existence of institutionalised racism in policing Britain's black, Asian and Irish communities Macpherson's report was significant. Regrettably, it had taken the death of Stephen Lawrence, the appalling treatment of his family by the Metropolitan Police, and the Macpherson Report to confirm officially that which had been endured by communities for generations.

While Macpherson was acclaimed as far sighted and radical he defended police policies and placed all responsibility on institutionally accepted racist practices and individual, personally held racist attitudes. He confirmed the existence of *institutional* racism within and across institutions. *Institutionalised* racism, however, is more profound. This is racism as a prevalent ideology underpinning policies, priorities and practices within institutions, rather than solely an expression of an institution's policies, priorities and practices.

3 'Lost lives, hidden voices': deaths and violence in custody

From 1983, with Kathryn Chadwick, I continued my earlier research on deaths in custody. We attended inquests, acquired transcripts and interviewed bereaved families. It soon became apparent that the inquest system was an inadequate and inappropriate forum for settling controversial cases, not least because the coroner's court is one of inquiry rather than liability. Yet for many families it was a court of 'last resort'. While the research focused in part on deaths resulting from the application of restraint during arrest or in custody, of particular concern were instances of people taking their own lives in circumstances that might have contributed to their deaths.

In 1985 we were contacted by Jimmy Boyle and Sarah Boyle, co-directors of the Gateway Exchange in Edinburgh. The Gateway Project worked with young people, particularly those with drug and alcohol dependencies, and on prison reform issues. Over a four-year period seven young men, several of whom were children, had taken their own lives at Glenochil Detention complex. Initially we could not gain access to the complex, but we interviewed children and young people who had been inside, gathered depositions from the Fatal Accident Inquiries (the Scottish equivalent of the inquest) and monitored the Scottish Office Inquiry. Soon after the Inquiry report was published we visited the complex and observed the regimes in operation. The research contributed to the book In the Arms of the Law, *published in 1987.*

In November 1986, following a rooftop protest at Peterhead Prison in north-east Scotland, the Gateway Exchange held a series of public meetings under the Scottish Prison Service motto 'Dare to Care'. The meetings heard detailed allegations of brutality from prisoners' letters, former prisoners and prisoners' families. Prison protests soon extended to other Scottish prisons, escalating to hostage taking and a further rooftop protest at Peterhead. Along with Joe Sim and Paula Skidmore, I was commissioned by Gateway to conduct research into the protests as part of an independent inquiry. Research access to the prison was denied but we took written evidence from 45 prisoners in addition to prisoners' letters sent to Gateway between 1984 and 1986. Prison managers and officers used threats and intimidation to prevent prisoners participating in the research and working with the researchers. Despite these inhibitions, many prisoners wrote detailed, verifiable accounts of their experiences.

In November 1987 the Gateway Independent Inquiry published its report, The Roof Comes Off. *It made 17 recommendations including the closure of Peterhead. In 1991 we published the book* Prisons Under Protest. *Despite refuting the research at the time, a senior member of the Scottish Prison Service later stated that the research had been taken seriously, contributing significantly to long-term, fundamental reform within the Scottish Prison Service. He endorsed the research findings but stated he would deny our conversation should we 'go public'. From 1988 until 2003 I organised annual research field trips for my students to Scottish prisons and young offenders' institutions.*

Behind locked doors

The legacy of twentieth-century incarceration in Britain and Ireland is characterised by the application of habitual, institutionalised violence against men, women and children. At the sharp end of the continuum of locking people away lives were lost, from childhood through to old age in mental institutions whose regimes were harsh, inhuman and degrading. Survivors of punitive regimes operated by the state and, in Ireland, the Church, recount lives lost to psychiatric and surgical experimentation and to arbitrary and indiscriminate applications of force. They reveal great courage and determination, their private resistance to public degradation eventually securing release. Classified 'feeble-minded', 'dangerous', 'immoral' and/or 'imbeciles', their imprisonment not only appropriated their freedom but for decades eroded their human potential, their social capacity. Then came the closure of institutions and liberation of sorts. No explanations, no apologies and no acknowledgement of the institutionalised brutalisation of locked-in wards.

In considering the dynamics of incarceration it is important to visit the 'extreme' where enforced mutilation, electrically induced convulsions, drugging and ritual humiliation were endured. Bodies and minds constituted unrestricted test sites in medicine's obsession with the identification and eradication of individual pathology. The incarcerated feared the perpetrators. White-coated professionals formalised and, in casual demonstrations of powerful discretion, legitimated physical abuse. In tandem were routine, informal assaults by untrained and vindictive 'care' staff. The long-term incarcerated also feared for absent friends – the disappeared. It was a rational fear of death by unlawful killing: failed experiments, fatal side-effects of 'new' drugs, restraints that killed and suicides of despair. These were the consequences of licensed assault. The wheels of the night trolley heralded the departure of another premature death.

Informed and endorsed by the pseudo–scientific principles of eugenicism, these punishing regimes were not confined to Nazi barbarism or other forms of totalitarian rule. They were central to routine treatment administered to those classified and researched as mentally disordered throughout social democracies; forming an invisible and virtually autonomous archipelago of incarceration in mental institutions and special hospitals. For such regimes to exist, to remain hidden from independent scrutiny, professionals within and beyond the network were commissioned. They were implicated through an unquestioning acceptance of classifications made by powerful definers and their failure to inquire into the dubious circumstances of unexplained deaths. Doctors, nurses, care workers, psychologists, psychiatrists, coroners, pathologists, police officers, lawyers, administrators, clergy remained silent, ambivalent, accepting; and someone pushed the trolley.

How is all this known? Through personal accounts of those who survived. They provide an alternative to official discourse, to the diagnoses and to the scant hospital records of nether worlds. As the mental hospitals closed, the stories of those dispossessed of much of their lives were told and received as contemporary testimonies of a bygone era. Revisiting that oral history with a view to establishing individual responsibility and institutional accountability was never contemplated. Yet democratic states that proclaim the checks and balances of interrelated, formalised processes of legal, political and professional accountability persisted in reassurances of transparency for their public institutions. Behind the high walls of special hospitals, the bolted doors of psychiatric units and prison wings, those imprisoned continue to be subdued by a lethal mix of tranquillising and antipsychotic drugs, supervisory neglect, staff brutality and defensive managements. Like the abandoned mental institutions, high-security special hospitals and most prisons remain closed worlds.

Writing on prisons as 'closed systems', David Leigh (1980: 91) interviewed a senior prison officer about the death of a long-term prisoner in the prison's hospital wing. The prisoner 'had been making a considerable row, shouting and banging the door of his cell'. Leigh continues:

> It had been decided to quieten him down. 'About ten officers tore into his cell and set about him.' The prisoner was a big man, the cell was tiny. The prisoner died. The medical staff on the hospital wing were all aware of the circumstances, the prison administrators were in a suppressed roar of anxiety, and no inquest had been held.

The Home Office reported the man had been 'found dead' and 'asphyxiation' was recorded as the cause of death. According to Leigh, the authorities admitted there had been a struggle but death was accidental following the use of restraint. Leigh concludes:

The only evidence that could contradict the prison officers' official version came from my source [the senior officer] who was unable to testify [at the inquest] ... The dead man had no relatives to make a fuss on his behalf. If a newspaper printed an unsubstantiated accusation, it would run the risk of heavy libel damages ... There was to be no police investigation. And so, the man died violently, in 1979, in a British prison, and the circumstances of his death were successfully covered up.

(Ibid.: 92)

In August 1980 Barry Prosser was found dead in a locked prison cell at Winson Green Prison, Birmingham. His injuries were consistent with a heavy beating – his body bruised from head to toe, his stomach and oesophagus ruptured. A man with a history of mental depression, he was in prison on remand, awaiting reports following arrest for criminal damage to his home. He caused a disturbance in the main prison and was removed to a 'quiet cell' in the prison hospital. Two pathologists told the inquest that they concluded he had been the victim of a vicious attack. The officer in charge of the hospital stated to the police that he had visited the cell once to administer a sedative. Twelve officers were called to the cell and Barry Prosser was held down and injected. Officers stated that he did not resist and force was not used. No record was made in the incident logs.

Prisoners gave evidence that three officers, including the officer in charge, had gone earlier to the cell and that was when the assault had taken place. The Coroner was 'horrified' by the evidence and by the regime and procedures in the prison hospital. The jury took just 15 minutes to reach its verdict that Barry Prosser had been unlawfully killed. The Coroner submitted the inquest transcript to the Director of Public Prosecutions. He also made a submission to the Home Office, drawing attention to the deficient regime and the lack of health care. Three officers were tried for murder and were acquitted due to lack of evidence. Consistent with the case reported by Leigh, a prisoner had been unlawfully killed in the closed environment of a prison hospital and no individual was held responsible. Twenty-one years later the Director General of the Prison Service, Martin Narey, commented that Winson Green was one of six 'hellhole' prisons, a place where 'Barry Prosser was kicked to death by staff, none of whom was convicted for his unlawful killing' (*The Guardian*, 6 February 2001).

Official investigations and inquests into such cases and more general allegations of inhuman and degrading treatment have been hindered by powerful staff and management interests. Prisoners consistently report that threats and intimidation by staff are means through which the 'view from below' is silenced. Within closed institutions staff are given permissive discretionary powers, yet there are minimum mechanisms for guaranteeing transparency. 'Control and restraint' methods are used with impunity to inflict arbitrary punishment on 'difficult' prisoners. Harsh measures (body-belts, strip searches, force-feeding, punishment-block isolation), endorsed by medical professionals, form part of the 'management' of the most vulnerable and distressed prisoners. These conditions are also inflicted on children and women who arrive in prison with serious, identifiable mental conditions. Other prisoners develop psychiatric problems as a consequence of prison conditions and regimes, leading to transfer from mainstream jails to special hospitals. And a growing number of men, women and children are isolated on suicide observation while inside.

'Short, sharp, shock'

On 10 October 1979, Home Secretary William Whitelaw announced to Conference the first Thatcher government's response to the 'law and order crisis'. In promising a 'short, sharp, shock' regime for young offenders in custody, he gained a euphoric reception. 'These will be no holiday camps,' he trumpeted, 'life will be conducted at a swift tempo ... there will be drill.' The applause was sustained, the delegates rapturous. Undoubtedly Whitelaw's words echoed down the spotless, scrubbed corridors of every detention centre and young offenders' institution in Britain. They gave sustenance to authoritarian staff whose contact with young prisoners was predicated on the use of physical force, verbal humiliation and social isolation as the primary instruments of instilling discipline into wayward children and young people. His message was loud and clear; its consequences were devastating.

In Scotland the principal detention centre was located at Glenochil, opened in 1966. For 17 years it received first-time offenders sentenced to a fixed term of three months. This changed in 1983, when the 1980 Criminal Justice (Scotland) Act was implemented. Under Section 45 of the Act, the Prison Department allocated male young offenders, aged between 19 and 21 and sentenced to between four weeks and four months, occasionally up to five months, to a detention centre. The 1975 Criminal Procedure (Scotland) Act required that, in imposing a custodial sentence, account should be taken of 'any information ... concerning the offender's character and physical or mental condition'. Those 'physically or mentally unfit to be detained in a detention centre' should be transferred to a Young Offenders' Institution.

At Glenochil, Whitelaw's 'holiday camp' jibe could not have been further from the truth. It had established a fearful reputation as a hard regime before the introduction of 'short, sharp, shock'. The Detention Centre comprised three wings, with an overall capacity of 182 prisoners, referred to ironically as 'trainees', in single-cell rooms. Clothing, bedding and equipment were presented 'military style' and each cell was basically equipped, including a plastic chamber-pot. Toilets and ablutions facilities were located at the end of the landing and could be used only during unlock.

In 1984, 1,037 prisoners passed through the Detention Centre at a daily average of 156. They experienced a physically demanding regime comprising physical training, running, drill and domestic cleaning, rather than education and constructive activities. In the early weeks, prisoners were castigated and cajoled into putting effort into physical tasks and a colour-coded system of tokens, related to earnings, was used by the staff to assess 'achievement'. Failure to achieve brought a charge of 'offending against discipline for lack of effort' and automatic loss of remission. 'Achievers' eventually graduated from scrubbing floors to working in the laundry, the garden or the kitchen. The only education programme available was 'remedial', also taking second place to physical training and drill. The token system dominated the Detention Centre's routine. Even the length of visits was dictated by where prisoners were located on the ladder of achievement. Two visits were permitted each month and new arrivals were entitled to a mere 30 minutes, increasing to 45 minutes and then to an hour, according to the 'grade' achieved. These brief moments of 'informal' contact with relatives and friends were in stark contrast to the daily routine beginning at 5.45am with slopping-out the contents of the plastic chamber-pot.

From this point, prisoners were under a rule of silence, with commands shouted at them by prison officers. Movement was also military style, with prisoners marched to breakfast, marched back to their cells, change of clothes, inspected for work, marched to work, marched to tea-break, marched to their cells, change of clothes, inspected on parade and marched back to work. By 1pm the prisoners had changed their clothes three times, been inspected twice, marched everywhere and had remained in total silence. The routine continued throughout the day. At 8pm, following a lengthy period spent in isolation in their cells, prisoners were allowed 30 minutes' recreation. For five days each week prisoners were able to talk to each other for only 30 minutes daily. At weekends only those prisoners who had achieved the highest grade were allowed evening recreation. The others were confined to their cells. Those receiving the maximum two visits each month – and not all did – were regularly deprived of recreation at weekends. The rule of silence created an atmosphere of mental isolation. At weekends that mental isolation was consolidated by long periods of physical isolation. Under the 1980 Act, this form of regime was imposed on all young offenders given custodial sentences of less than four months.

Observing the regime gave a clear appreciation of the discipline imposed on the children. At lunch they were brought from their work and other activities and lined up, silent, in rows, along a wide corridor. Uniformed prison officers stood at the front and back of the lines and patrolled the corridors. The boys stood expressionless, arms to their sides. Orders were shouted by officers, many of whom had the peaks of their caps pulled down over their eyes, military style. They referred to each other as 'Mr'. Each line in turn was instructed to move and the boys immediately went into a parade-ground jog along the corridor at right angles into the canteen corridor and in through the door of the canteen. They continued the jog around the outside of the canteen, peeling off to their tables, where they jogged on the spot until all were in the room. On an order shouted above the tramp of the feet, they stopped. On a further order they sat down. The canteen remained silent except for the consumption of food and the movement of patrolling officers. Many officers had shirt sleeves rolled to their elbows, revealing military and loyalist tattoos.

The boys were returned to their landings in similar style. Cell inspections were thorough, with boys standing to attention alongside their beds. Despite the poor condition of the building, the landings and cells were scrubbed clean, beds turned down military style and clothes folded neatly. On inspection, any deviation from the expected layout drew the wrath of the officer, shouting his displeasure into the face of the child. A feather on a bed resulted in the officer throwing the mattress to the floor and ordering the child to remake it 'properly'. Lining the corridors, awaiting barked instructions, the sullen, pale-faced boys fixed their eyes on their jailers. It was a collective stare of silenced resentment.

The Glenochil Young Offenders' Institution, opened in 1976 and receiving prisoners whose sentences were over nine months, was located on the same ex-National Coal Board site as the Detention Centre. It was a purpose-built, high-security institution separated from the Detention Centre by double fencing. At the time, it was the largest Young Offenders' Institution in Scotland, accommodating short-sentence prisoners considered security risks or classified 'management problems' in other young offenders' institutions. Its reputation was the 'end of the line' for the young 'hardmen' of custody. Consequently, it had a tough punishment block, formally the 'segregation block', and a harsh regime.

The Young Offenders' Institution consisted of four halls, A to D, of 124 cells, each hall divided again into three landings accommodating 40 or 42 prisoners each. Landings were on either four or five levels with 13 or 14 cells per level. Levels were closed off at night, all gates and cell doors controlled electronically from a central operations room. The Institution's capacity was 496, an allocation rarely approached. The average daily population early in 1985 was 270 and during 1984, 473 young offenders were admitted. Because the average length of sentence was much higher the turnover of prisoners in the Young Offenders' Institution was significantly less than the Detention Centre.

D Hall was dedicated to assessment and induction, holding prisoners for their first month. Psychological screening tests were used alongside work-related aptitude tests. Prisoners were also assessed by teachers and social workers, with a collective 'team' assessment at the end of each month to decide on allocation to Glenochil or to an 'open' allocation. These early assessments in the Young Offenders' Institution initiated a grading and progression system within which 'promotion' resulted in a different shirt colour, longer visits, privileges and higher wages. Promotion was granted through discretionary staff judgements and included assessment of cleanliness and attitude. Progression through the halls brought increased access to recreation, the 'privilege' of making hot drinks during recreation (B Hall) and the wearing of T-shirts and watches (C Hall).

Unlike the Detention Centre, the Young Offenders' Institution provided education programmes other than remedial, and the daily routine, starting at 6am with the electronic unlocking of the cells, appeared more relaxed. Prisoners were allowed to talk at meal times and were 'moved' rather than marched around the prison. Work was more constructive and programmed, and there was a brief period of recreation after lunch, before afternoon work. Prisoners were locked in their cells while the officers had meal breaks. Evening recreation was two hours, including an opportunity to go to evening classes. At 8.45pm the young men were locked in their cells for the night. In the induction hall and the post-assessment hall, recreation was restricted to four nights, with none available on Saturdays or Sundays. Visiting was limited to weekends and, depending on the grade achieved, the length of visits varied between 30 minutes and an hour.

Within the Institution, as in most male prisons, a strong internal hierarchy existed among prisoners. It was based primarily on violence, intimidation and facing-down. Formally labelled the 'inmate culture', this internal structure of intimidation and bullying was presented by managers and staff as little more than the occasional acts of a few individuals – the 'aggressive behaviour of a minority'. Glenochil Young Offenders' Institution, however, with its size and its reputation for a tough regime, exemplified the institutionalisation of male violence. On the landings, those with physical disabilities or learning difficulties, the unassertive, the weak, the sex offenders and the loners were subjected to a relentless barrage of physical torment and mental torture. They were extorted, verbally harassed, physically beaten and constantly threatened. On exercise, or alone at night in their cells, they underwent a constant hail of abuse, including direct incitement to 'top themselves'. Attempts to garner support from prison staff constituted the worst offence against another prisoner – 'grassing'. Inevitably it led to a beating. Yet the bullying and torment were visible and audible to staff. The permanence of this internal regime of male violence and its routine acceptance demonstrated its institutionalisation. Not only was the 'inmate culture' and its hierarchy of violence recognised, it was actively mobilised in the staff management of the landings as a form of control and containment.

If the rule of silence, heavy discipline and limited recreation created conditions of mental and physical isolation in the Detention Centre, the endemic verbal harassment and physical violence in the Young Offenders' Institution created a climate of fear and aggression. 'Doing time' in either regime was about negotiating and handling punitive conditions created formally (institutional) and informally (cultural). To cope without 'bottling out' was to demonstrate publicly, with maximum visibility, that the regimes, the staff, other prisoners presented no fear. This applied to how prisoners perceived each other and extended to how officers responded to prisoners. To the management, the prison officers, the medical staff and other associated professionals, the regimes were rational, consistent and appropriate. Consequently, 'failure to cope' was identified as a problem within the individual, rather than a symptom of harsh conditions within a punitive structure. Those children and young men who expressed their rationality and sensitivity by occasionally breaking down and crying soon learnt to cry alone.

On 16 October 1981, Edward Herron, almost half way through a 15-month sentence for theft and fire-raising, was found dead in his cell in the Young Offenders' Institution. The Fatal Accident Inquiry (FAI) determined the cause of death as cardiac arrest brought on by inhaling solvents. These were paint thinners he had taken from a work shed. Exactly one year later, Richard MacPhie was found dead in his cell in the Young Offenders' Institution, three days into a three-month sentence for road traffic offences. The Inquiry determined the cause of death as asphyxia due to the inhalation of vomit and hanging. With these two cases began a sequence of deaths at Glenochil unparalleled in the custody of young people.

By 13 April 1985 a further five young men had died in the complex. Of the seven deaths, all young men aged between 16 and 19, five occurred in the Young Offenders' Institution and two in the Detention Centre. The *Scottish Mail* (2 June 1985) claimed there had been a further 25 suicide attempts at the complex during the previous four years. Based on FAI transcripts and Sheriff's determinations, the five deaths can be outlined as follows:

Allen Malley, died 1 November 1982, ten days into a three month sentence for road traffic offences. The FAI determined that he died from asphyxia caused by hanging.

Robert King, died 14 August 1983, ten months into a three year sentence for road traffic offences, culpable and reckless driving and assault. The FAI determined that he had not intended to commit suicide but had an 'unhealthy interest' to 'see what hanging felt like'. In short, it was an experiment that went wrong.

William MacDonald, died 16 February 1984, five days before his release following a three month sentence for stealing a tin of glue and assault. At the time he was 'on report' for fighting and he expected loss of remission. The FAI determined that while he died of asphyxiation due to hanging, his death probably was not deliberate suicide. Sheriff Principal Taylor, who had conducted the FAI on Robert King, considered William MacDonald's death was an attempt to 'draw attention to himself, get sympathy or special treatment'. He had 'misjudged the extent to which he could go, or had bad luck with the loose end of the knot in the sheet getting caught'. Put another way it was a pretence that went wrong.

Angus Boyd, died 18 February 1985, was found dead in the segregation unit of the Detention Centre. He was two months into a three month sentence and his failure 'to comply with the routine of the Centre' had ensured the whole of his sentence had been spent in the segregation unit. He had been on 'strict suicide observation' until ten days before his death. The FAI, again conducted by Sheriff Taylor, determined he had committed suicide while suffering mental illness.

Derek Harris, died 13 April 1985, was found dead in his cell. He had been threatened by another prisoner and faced further charges the probable outcome being a further term at Glenochil. Initially sentenced to detention centre training he had been transferred to the Young Offenders' Institution. The FAI, again conducted by Sheriff Taylor, determined he had committed suicide by hanging. His death was 'an outburst of despair at the situations which confronted him, with which he could not cope'.

In November 1984 the Secretary of State for Scotland accepted Sheriff Taylor's recommendation to review precautionary suicide and parasuicide procedures at Glenochil. From the outset, the broader political and structural contexts within which children and young people were held at the complex were outside the Review Group's remit. The eight person Review Group, chaired by Derek Chiswick – a university forensic psychiatrist – included three members who worked full time at Glenochil. Its medical orientation was evident in the direction and weighting of the eventual report and its recommendations (Chiswick Report 1985). The Review Group noted and accepted 'patterns' of suicidal behaviour in prisons and risk 'indicators' associated with them. As presented, these behavioural 'patterns' were the consequence of a hidden logic that placed particular individuals 'at risk' through inherent vulnerability. A further assumption accepted without question by the Group was that many prisoners were manipulative and threatened suicide so that they could be relocated and placed on strict suicide observation. Chiswick portrayed staff as fair and considerate, doing a difficult job in a highly pressured environment under a media spotlight that exacerbated their defensiveness and anxiety.

The classification 'strict suicide observation' (SSO) was initiated on landings by referral to prison hospital staff. A Hall accommodated 13 prisoners on SSO. There was also provision in the Detention Centre in its punishment block and in nine modified cells on the landings. During 1984, 75 prisoners (7 per cent) in the Detention Centre and 89 (10 per cent) in the Young Offenders' Institution were on SSO for periods from two days to one year. In considering the SSO regime, however, the fundamental contradictions between custody and care were brought into sharp relief. The Review Group was aware of the privations of SSO but attributed responsibility for its 'highly punitive element' to prisoners choosing relocation from the mainstream and to troublemakers who had 'contaminated' the SSO regime (Chiswick Report 1985: para 6.3.2). It was a remarkable conclusion, given Chiswick's negative appraisal of the regime.

SSO cells were not conducive to restoring sound mental well-being. They were places of deprivation rather than positive engagement. Apart from their spartan design, their windows were fixed with ventilation through a permanently open grille. In winter months cells were 'extremely cold' (ibid.: para 5.5.1). Electric lights were never switched off, compelling prisoners to cover their heads so as to sleep. Non-destructible blankets were a coarse canvas weave, as was the canvas gown: a 'short-sleeved, knee-length garment shaped in a similar style to a pinafore dress' (ibid.: para 5.6.1). No clothing, including underwear, was allowed except for slippers. Association forbidden, the young prisoners were held in solitary confinement: 'the regime consists essentially of the inmate sitting in his room [cell]' (ibid.: 5.6.2). Exercise was confined to 30 minutes walking up and down the landing, work was occasional basic cleaning and two sessions of physical training were offered each week.

The daily SSO routine was punitive, including the removal of mattresses. Prisoners were 'observed' through the cell-door spy-holes every 15 minutes day and night to ensure that they 'to all intents and purposes appear[ed] normal' (ibid.: para 5.6.11). There was no conversation between staff and prisoners. It was a regime of isolation matched by silence. The 'appearance' of normality was the priority. On the other side of the locked door the child or youth sat on a hard chair in a rough canvas gown alone with one paperback book and a Bible. Seventy-two times a day, as regular as a church clock, an eye appeared at the spy-hole, reminding the young prisoner that there was life beyond the door. This was the 'treatment' afforded to those considered to have such a serious 'mental condition' that they required 'strict suicide observation'. The SSO regime adopted a medical model in defining risk of self-harm and suicide while constructing a punitive model as an appropriate response. It was a disturbing example of the classic contradiction of administering 'treatment' in the context of punishment. As the 'appearance of normality' was logged, children and young men were condemned to further anguish.

The regimes in the Glenochil complex were dominated, as Chiswick recognised, by a 'macho culture'. Rather than identifying and challenging the culture of masculinity, Chiswick recommended the introduction of women staff to generate a perception of safety, encourage good behaviour and reduce tension. The culture of masculinity, however, was not restricted to prisoner-on-prisoner bullying. Hostility and violence was institutionalised, ever present in staff relationships with prisoners. It was how the system worked. Staff also used the routine aggression between prisoners and the hierarchies it generated as a mechanism to manage and control the landings. What 'short, sharp, shock' had delivered was official recognition, or legitimacy, for the institutionalised violence already prevalent in children's and young people's institutions. Drill, physical exercise, menial tasks, isolation and silence, alongside the excessive aggression displayed by bullying male staff, brought Whitelaw's conference platform commitment of 'no compromise' to fruition. As any semblance of rehabilitation and reform was lost to embitterment and resentment, seven children and young people died, 25 came close to death and hundreds were held in draconian conditions.

The roof comes off

Peterhead prison, 34 miles north of Aberdeen on Scotland's far north-east coast, was built using convict labour and opened in 1888. With a chequered history of diverse use, by the 1980s it accommodated male prisoners serving sentences over 18 months for whom allocation to a training prison was deemed inappropriate. No remand prisoners were held at Peterhead. In late 1985 there were 281 operational cells and a daily population averaging 188. The majority of prisoners were higher security long termers. The prison had an established reputation for tough regimes and severe punishment, the latter regularly administered informally by male officers who closely identified with Peterhead and its distinctive culture. In 1971 a Home Office researcher noted the 'wide gulf between staff and prisoners' (McMillan 1971: 2). Violence was 'endemic' and a 'wall of silence' prevailed as prisoners accepted punishment 'without argument'. Peterhead had evolved as a brutalising and alienating prison:

> At one end of the continuum of institutionalised violence was the daily routine of bullying and intimidation; at the other was the inhumane, torturous punishment of the cages. Standing naked before prison officers in a 'cage' 9 feet by 6 feet, the prisoner underwent a full body search three times a day. The solitary confinement and personal humiliation of the cages represented the ultimate loss of dignity for any individual receiving punishment. The prisoner remained entirely at the mercy of the prison officers and accounts of prisoners who went through the cages describe how officers regularly exploited their absolute discretionary powers.
>
> (Scraton, Sim and Skidmore 1991: 15)

The violence of Peterhead, the sense of isolation not only in the prison but in the prison system as a whole, led to prisoner protests and roof-top demonstrations in 1972. A full day's round trip from the Edinburgh–Glasgow urban belt that is home to the majority of Scotland's population, Peterhead was literally 'out of sight, out of mind'. While the media responded to the protests as confirmation of the violence of the men held in the prison, the reality was different. When the prisoners ended their protest they were beaten by staff and their sentences were extended.

Throughout the 1970s there were hunger strikes, cell fires, overuse of segregation in strip cells, and calls within government for Peterhead's closure. Following a roof-top protest in 1979, three officers were tried for assaults on prisoners administered as retribution. Hearing graphic evidence from prisoners of the beatings they had endured, the Sheriff returned not guilty verdicts, although he considered the prisoners' evidence had carried a 'certain ring of truth'. While the Scottish Prison Officers' Association continually portrayed media and politicians' concerns as mischief, accounts from prisoners alleged severe and arbitrary beatings by staff. The official line was that a small number of violent prisoners were determined to disrupt the prison and assault staff. They were portrayed as beyond management. The confrontations within the prison continued throughout the early 1980s, with 12 prisoners convicted of 'mobbing and rioting'. By 1985 the prison appeared out of control as allegations and counter-allegations provided clear evidence of violence and retaliation. Despite all evidence to the contrary, Scottish Office Minister Ian Lang reassured the public he was 'impressed with the atmosphere' and that conditions in Peterhead were 'extremely good'. Within a month, in October 1986, prisoners took a prison officer hostage and occupied the roof of the prison.

Protests spread throughout Scotland's prisons and in June 1987 prisoners took two officers hostage inside Peterhead, holding one for five days. It was ended when officers stormed the cells. Despite long sentences handed down for the 1986 hostage taking, in September 1987 a siege in D Hall resulted in three prisoners holding an officer hostage, occasionally parading him on the roof and threatening to kill him. After 105 hours the siege was ended by the SAS. As protests continued at other prisons the violent humiliation of a veteran prison officer on Peterhead's roof overshadowed the underlying malaise within the prison. Prisoners' demands for an inquiry into the running of the prison, its harsh regime and Victorian conditions, were lost in their public display of aggression. The Scottish Prison Officers' Association and the Prison Governors' Committee united in condemning the actions of a small, violent group of intransigent prisoners. The injustices of the regime, insanitary conditions, violence, victimisation and bullying, mistrust and poor management in the context of a decrepit estate, remained unresolved issues.

Prisoners' accounts, provided to the researchers, revealed Peterhead as a prison in which fear prevailed. Most felt unsafe and for two-thirds fear was a 'predominant factor' in their daily lives. Prisoner-on-prisoner violence was significant:

At any time a prisoner can snap and go crazy. The screws don't give a damn as long as it isn't their heads on the chopping block.

I have been threatened on numerous occasions, and my life is in danger ... So when no-one seems interested I have to resort to demonstrations and protests to bring attention to my plight in prison.

You can cross someone at any time not even realising you've done it, an incident could flare up and you could find yourself in the wrong place at the wrong time and end up involved unwittingly.

I feel safe most times but paranoia creeps upon you, so you know others can be paranoid also.

I have been assaulted four times by other prisoners two of which left me with large, visible scars for life. All of which made it necessary for me to be housed in the annexe at Peterhead.

For many prisoners, tensions in Peterhead were all-pervasive and were responsible for hostility between prisoners, encouraging and sustaining predatory and bullying behaviour:

Due to the tense atmosphere that is almost constant, one feels on the edge of what could end up an explosive situation.

Peterhead is a dangerous place to be in for a great many reasons. It is not easy to avoid trouble when there is constant unrest on either side.

It is almost impossible to live at peace with each other due to our situation and tempers can flare up quite easily over the least little thing.

No one feels safe in prison. I for one don't. That's why I end up in so much trouble ... I fear dying, loneliness, going insane, solitary confinement.

The use of solitary confinement, particularly the silent cell, was corrosive. On average, prisoners were held in solitary for three months but several had been held in isolation over 12 months. Its impact was debilitating and lasting:

My head aches from morning until night. To put another human being into that silent cell you would have to be barbarous. The effects are severe! The thought of returning to Peterhead is very frightening. I've been locked up in the silent cell for 8 days ... When you step into the cell you see a box. That's the silent cell. Around this is all their strip lights and big heaters. The inside is about 3 square yards. There are two spy holes and two small air vents. It's a human furnace. I've had headaches all week. Sitting there in this cell is like having a band clasped around your throat.

The violence of prison officers, however, was the most threatening issue for prisoners in Peterhead. While some prisoners stated their reluctance to respond fully and specifically in writing to questions concerning staff violence, 71 per cent reported suffering assaults by staff and 62 per cent had witnessed assaults by staff on other prisoners. Many prisoners noted that assaults usually took place 'behind closed doors', in the absence of other prisoners:

> You hear it going on, the fighting and kicking, you hear your mates screaming but you're powerless. Either you protest and shout, knowing you're next or you put your pillow over your head and block it out.

In responding to questions about staff violence, prisoners stated their fear of victimisation. While some refused to comment, others reported assaults or witnessing assaults, but refused details. The reasons given included: 'the questionnaire is subject to censorship'; 'my lib. [liberation] date is imminent, and I want it to stay that way'; 'I'm allowed to fill in this questionnaire as long as I stick to standing order (M).' This was a reference to a potential charge for making false allegations. There was universal disdain for the official complaints procedure. Many prisoners formalised complaints, pursuing them outside the prison, but they considered the process ineffective. Drawing attention, being ascribed a reputation as a troublemaker, intimidation and victimisation were significant deterrents, particularly the threat of being 'put on report for making false allegations' and the fear of taking a beating: 'if they get away with it once, they'll do you'. Prisoners were resigned to what they considered the futility of the complaints system. Typical responses were: 'What's the point?'; 'It's a waste of time.'

There was a collective lack of faith and trust in what prisoners identified as a system that 'fabricates' and 'rewrites' evidence, denied legal representation and 'takes their word over ours'. The lack of trust in staff and management undermined the procedures for operational accountability regarding staff violence. It also contributed significantly to a climate of paranoia and fear:

> Such is the atmosphere in Peterhead that you learn not to trust anyone. In my opinion, a situation created by staff. My motto: 'On guard'.

> I have experienced staff telling other prisoners that I have been grassing other prisoners for no apparent reason other than to put con

against con and not con against screw ... When things are tense in here you can't help being afraid.

According to prisoners' accounts, the tension provided an ever-present backdrop to specific moments or flashpoints, usually occurring over petty issues leading to direct confrontation:

There's a total breakdown in communication between prisoners and staff. At any time trouble can flare. If you're singled out you are beaten or simply restrained even though you haven't struggled. Restraining technique is virtual strangulation.

During any incident or argument staff are liable to lash out first, due to fear, and this is frightening as it usually involves anything up to 6 of them. Six lashing out with sticks can cause some damage to a person.

You have to tread softly with staff as they can, and do, what they like with no comebacks. An assault here, or a report there. When there is the first sign of trouble they run out of the hall, lock you in and refuse to let you out. I was stabbed in the prison. Even after warning the authorities, they just don't care and they won't get involved. [Is this fear a predominant factor in your daily life?] Yes, very much so.

Assaults by staff and witnessing brutality against other prisoners constituted the most serious indictment of the Peterhead regime. Those prisoners willing to share their experiences provided graphic accounts:

One evening, while going to my cell at lock up time, an officer started shouting at me for no apparent reason. Then he pushed me into a cell and started punching me about the head. As I wasn't in any fit state to defend myself, I put my hands through the windows to make him stop because it would attract attention. It resulted in another officer pulling the screw off me. I was then dragged down to the cells. The next day I was put in front of the Governor and charged with assault. The officer said I had assaulted him ... The Governor didn't believe my side of the story. He said his staff don't go around beating up prisoners. I was sent to see the psychiatrist.

I have been quite lucky, one assault only. Punched, kicked, wrists bent, neck bent, ankles twisted, this was me being 'restrained' after an incident protesting the way another inmate had been treated.

They forced an internal search on me without a doctor and an officer jumped on my arm in the cell-block in Peterhead.

Christmas Day '86 they set about me with riot sticks for throwing a cup of tea out my door. They charged me with assaulting them with a knife and gun. I was found not guilty of these charges.

I have been very badly assaulted in the past by some staff. I have had my leg broken, my head bust open, and my face very badly marked.

I've had too many assaults to mention in various penal establishments. In PH only once – assault involved batons, feet, hands.

Several times, the most serious being in the yard leading to the silent cell. 4 staff beat me up which led to me being taken to an outside hospital for X-rays on my head plus bruising on my body and legs and face.

Informal 'punishments' were often followed by serious charges against prisoners, resulting in loss of remission, solitary confinement or further prosecution. Often this resulted in further beatings as prison officers 'taught cons a lesson':

They accused me of escaping down a tunnel and I was put in front of the VC [Visiting Committee]. They took 60 days remission and locked me up for 28 days in the punishment block. They kicked me unconscious for protesting and when they came back it was the same brutality all over again, beaten, stripped, handcuffed and thrown into an empty cell.

The initial incident was not always as dramatic as attempted escape. One prisoner catalogued other 'typical instances':

I refused to go to a 'separate cell-block' so I got punched, kicked, and dragged; Lit a fire in a cell in solitary confinement to keep warm so I got a black eye off the staff; Fingers fractured while being escorted to cell block after attempted escape; Nose broken after taking hot water for tea after being refused permission.

In the aftermath of more organised disturbances or protests, prisoners were charged in the courts. Yet the use of calculated violence by MUFTI (Minimum Use of Force Tactical Intervention) teams or 'riot squads' was a clear demonstration of reasserting control of the landing or hall:

After the riot in '79 I was beaten unconscious for my assaults on staff, when my brother threatened the staff's families with revenge. I had my head split open with a baton in the silent cells.

The last time officers, clad in semi riot-gear, riot sticks like baseball bats, further officers outside my door: [date provided]. Struck by baton, used like bayonet, kidney, left leg gave way, jumped all over me, mainly booted, handcuffed arms up my back, squeezed testicles, etc (usual) internal life endangering injury, 10 inch scar, med. reports max. 24 hour life expectancy without emergency op. 16 hours left on floor, no doctor unless a deal that I fell.

How safe I feel depends on the situation at a given time, especially when the MUFTI squad are operating; then no one is safe.

1984; A Hall was destroyed; I was put into a windowless cell, with nothing apart from a mattress, 18 solid weeks. A 'pneumatic con-solidated drill' with a jack hammer attachment pounded the floor of the above cell. One night I lit a fire in the hope that I would be taken from A Hall. The officers came in force dragged me from the cell, hit me with fists, sticks and kicked me all over the place, tried to break my arms and choke me.

Prisoners also reported 'routine' assaults by officers on other prisoners:

I saw my friend, T.P., being beat up in the exercise yard; my friend J.B. beat up on the corridor, another man in the hall.

Saw a member of the staff punch a guy then they grabbed him and forced an internal examination on him.

I saw an inmate assaulted on exercise at PH by 3 members of the staff. Witnessed this from my cell window.

I saw a prisoner punched in the face for refusing to drop his under-pants without an M.O. present. I have heard prisoners getting beaten up but everyone is locked up before this takes place.

I have seen prisoners being put on report in the past for next to noth-ing and dragged to the cells and hit with sticks ... I have seen it all.

Over many years, in many prisons, the instances I have personally witnessed of prisoners being assaulted by prison staff are too numer-ous to enumerate.

Prisoners routinely experienced minor 'instances' of assault. Prisoners who did not accept that the prison regime was based on fear, intimidation and staff bullying were dismissed as naive or colluding. The more serious cases raised the most profound concern:

The most recent was a man being kicked near to death and being left in a cell for 5 & half hours before the Authorities would call a doctor. The man was badly injured and had to undergo an emergency operation to save his life. I was a witness.

Of all the liberties I witnessed among them was an assault on a young cripple. This particular day his sticks were at surgery being adjusted. He intervened in a slanging match on behalf of another prisoner, the officer seized him by the throat and punched him 3 times or so in the face, officer later said that he had hit him with a stick. [The prisoner] got 14 days for assault.

I saw him [a prison officer] whack a man over the head with several sets of steel handcuffs, bursting his head open which was later stitched up. I was only 4 yards away, as were 5 other prisoners ... At the time the warder hit the man on the head, five warders were holding on to the man; they all denied the warder hit the man with the cuffs.

Once I saw a man almost beaten to death by about 15 screws ... Only extensive surgery saved this man's life. The screws used 'riot-sticks' as well as the 'black aspirin' [their boots].

I heard an inmate being assaulted on Xmas night, battered with sticks. Heard the screams, he was taken to hospital. I saw him the next day with his arm all bandaged up and in a sling plus a bruise on cheek.

[My] bruises were witnessed by a few prisoners one of which was placed on report and lost 14 days remission because he vented his anger at the state I was in. Only verbally I might add. The assault had taken place in the separate cells area.

These accounts are a selection of many accounts of extreme brutality in the prison. Prisoners described violence at both ends of the spectrum, from violence directed outwards to self-harm. Their poignant experiences of suffering showed how 'hard men' identified with the anguish of others while remaining frustrated and angry at the callous indifference of the institution and its officers:

The guy has slashed his own face twice in the past couple of weeks. What state of mind is the poor guy in? Not one person has lifted a finger to help him.

At the other end of the spectrum was the statement of intent, the response suggesting that, regardless of the consequences, violence would always be resisted through violence:

My views on violence are simple enough: if they have a license to inflict brutal beatings – then you must do likewise at the earliest opportunity as a defensive act to show them you're prepared to stand none of it. I don't believe in abusing or assaulting warders because they are locking me up. I treat them as they do me.

The only way I can communicate with these people is in a cell block. By tension, abuse, violence, hatred and excrement. They won't allow for a man to change, so fuck them. No way will they be able to talk to me because when I talked they didn't listen. Fuck them.

Allegations of brutality at Peterhead were not new. For many years prison officers were accused of routine assault, taking a 'pound of flesh' before prisoners were formally charged. A masculine culture had evolved in which officers asserted authority through demonstrations of superior physical strength. The institutionalisation of male violence was not unique to Peterhead. Staff brutality, denied by the Scottish Prison Service, the Scottish Office, the Scottish Prison Officers' Association and prison officers, requires consideration in the broader context of the prison regime. The entrenched dynamics of prisoners and officers within the prison created a context in which physical assaults, by prisoners on prisoners, prisoners on staff and staff on prisoners, were institutionalised as custom and practice. Most prisoners in the study were distrustful of the criminal justice process of which the prison was an integral yet invisible part. In the daily operation of the prison, officers were the ultimate authority of control, discipline and restraint.

The violence of men

The Glenochil research showed clearly how, through the authority and discretionary powers vested in its custodial institutions, the state initiated punitive and unconstructive regimes of containment for children and young people in conflict with the law. Most had experienced childhoods in marginalised working-class communities, housed in schemes where structured unemployment prevailed, amenities were minimal, futures bleak and small-scale 'crime' part of learnt survival. The determining ideology within the detention complex was correction through punishment, discipline through compulsion. It reinforced the physicality and aggression at the core of hegemonic masculinity. In a predatory environment where emotion, compassion and fear were signs of weakness, inviting bullying from staff and other prisoners, self-harm and suicide were not difficult to explain. Yet the inquiry into the deaths in Glenochil sought explanation in the 'inadequacies' of the boys and the asocial relationships between them.

This was consistent with existing primary research into deaths in police and prison custody. It demonstrated how negative imagery and established ideologies, 'deeply institutionalised in the British State', were mobilised to justify 'the marginalisation of identifiable groups', successfully deflecting responsibility away from state institutions (Scraton and Chadwick 1987b: 220). The political management of identity constituted 'a process of categorisation which suggests that the "violent", the "dangerous", the "political extremist", the "alien", the "inadequate", the "mentally ill", contribute to their own deaths either by their pathological condition or their personal choice' (ibid.: 233).

At Peterhead the use of violence by prison officers was explained and justified through pathologising the 'hardmen' in their custody. Mobilising this imagery in popular discourse reached an unprecedented level in 1991 when prisoners took possession of part of Strangeways jail in Manchester. The prisoners occupied a section of the overcrowded, insanitary Victorian prison, accessed medical supplies and broke out through the roof. Dramatic, sensational and highly visible, the roof-top protest lasted 25 days. While negotiating teams attempted to end the protest by day, hovering helicopters blasted music by night. Within 24 hours of the siege starting, all national newspapers and television bulletins led with the story that drug-fuelled prisoners had systematically murdered other prisoners in the course of the 'riot'. Initially put at 20, the roll-call of the dead eventually reached 30. There was no doubting the story's veracity: 'Sex perverts butchered in their cells'; 'Drug crazed lynch mob torture and murder ... '; 'My son saw six killings'; 'Bodies cut up and dumped in sewer'.

As headlines became more salacious the press and broadcast media reported that victims had been processed through 'kangaroo courts'. Following merciless beatings, sex offenders were castrated, strung up from accommodation landings, cut down and butchered. Day after day, newspapers elaborated the story under mastheads including 'Massacre at Strangeways' and 'Slaughter at Strangeways'. Yet these events did not happen. No prisoners were hung, no summary executions took place, none had been butchered and there were no castrations. The media silence, following realisation that the gory details of the Strangeways disaster had been fabricated, that reporters and editors had been duped by uninformed 'official' reports and off-the-record briefings by prison officers and their Association, was in marked contrast to the frenzy of the initial reporting. Yet the most significant story in English penal history, the 'Strangeways massacre', ran for weeks. Unattributed allegations, supported by inducements to those willing to offer false 'eye-witness' accounts, remained uncontested by officials who had access to the prison throughout. Reluctance to deny was taken as verification.

The most troubling aspect of the media coverage was journalists' willingness to accept that prisoners would commit such atrocities. Alongside this was the unquestioning acceptance among the general public and in political debate that they had. It demonstrated how deeply rooted was the pathology of dangerousness in popular discourse. The challenge for critical research, as shown in the Glenochil and Peterhead cases studies, is to literally 'get inside' places of detention and expose that which otherwise would remain hidden or disbelieved. Reflecting on the Peterhead research, Jimmy Boyle (1991: vii) commented that it revealed 'the unheard voice of the underdog' providing a 'powerful indictment of our so-called democracy ... vividly reminding us that there is another story which, until now, has remained untold – that of the prisoner'. The research into custody deaths and prison protests heard and projected the voices of those silenced and vilified within total institutions. It challenged the pathologisation of prisoners, so much the stock-in-trade of media sensationalism and politicians' sound-bites. And it contributed significantly to long-term, fundamental reform within the Scottish Prison Service.

4 'Negligence without liability': the scale of injustice after Hillsborough

The 1989 Football Association (FA) Cup semi-final between Liverpool and Nottingham Forest was held at Hillsborough Stadium, Sheffield. I was at home, about to listen to the game on the radio when my young son, Paul, shouted that there were crowd problems at the match. BBC Television had interrupted coverage of world championship snooker to go live to Hillsborough, where what was to become one of the most serious UK disasters of recent times was happening before the world's media. It was clear from the coverage that people were dying. In the days that followed, Liverpool's stadium, Anfield, became a shrine to those who died and a 'mile of scarves' was created across Stanley Park to Everton's ground, bringing thousands together in silent tribute. The grief of bereavement, especially for those whose loved ones and friends had died, was soon exacerbated as those in authority used every means available to place responsibility for the disaster on Liverpool fans.

Given my previous research on controversial deaths and my knowledge of public inquiries and coroners' inquests, it was suggested that I should research the aftermath of Hillsborough. I was familiar with football and its policing, having been a regular at Anfield since I was a child. Liverpool City Council commissioned the research and Sheila Coleman, Ann Jemphrey, Paula Skidmore and I established The Hillsborough Project. In 1990 it published Hillsborough and After: The Liverpool Experience, *covering the Home Office inquiry under Lord Justice Taylor, the media coverage of the disaster and the appalling treatment endured by bereaved families and survivors in the immediate aftermath. In 1995 we published* No Last Rights: The Promotion of Myth and the Denial of Justice in the Aftermath of the Hillsborough Disaster, *focusing on the longest inquests in English legal history, other legal proceedings and the persistent negative media coverage. Following the screening of Jimmy McGovern's award-winning drama documentary in 1996, Lord Justice Stuart-Smith's judicial scrutiny of new evidence in 1998 and access to all police statements, I published* Hillsborough: The Truth *in 1999. The text was later revised to include the 2000 private prosecutions of two senior police officers.*

Fatal negligence

> They didn't know what I'd been through. I'd lost someone dear to me,
> fought to survive and others died around me. People died before my
> eyes and no-one helped. It was chaos and I know some could have
> been saved. They didn't want to know at the inquest. No questions
> about the first aid on the pitch, about carrying people on hoardings,
> about the police in the gymnasium. None of that. But I was there and I
> saw it with my own eyes. But they didn't want to know. It [the
> Inquest] was all a sham.
>
> (Hillsborough Survivor, interview, March 1991)

On 15 April 1989 at the Hillsborough Stadium in Sheffield a fatal crush
occurred on the terraces at one of the UK's most important soccer matches.
As a result 96 men, women and children were killed, hundreds physically
injured and thousands traumatised. Many involved directly or indirectly
never worked again and others died prematurely, the longer-term consequences of post-traumatic stress. What happened is uncomplicated and,
mostly, uncontested. For the second time in successive years, Liverpool
played Nottingham Forest in the FA Cup semi-finals. Hillsborough stadium, the home of Sheffield Wednesday Football Club, was hired by the
Football Association as a neutral venue. Coincidentally, the match was a
carbon copy of the previous year's semi-final and the pre-match arrangements were virtually identical (South Yorkshire Police Operational Orders,
1988 and 1989).

A sell-out, ticket-only match, Liverpool fans were allocated one end of
the stadium, including the West Stand (seated), the Leppings Lane terrace
(standing) and the North Stand (seated). Stadia such as Hillsborough were
nearly a century old. Modifications had been made, some areas upgraded,
but the essential fabric of the terracing, concrete steps on packed earth,
remained much the same as it had always been. Prisoners of their history,
such stadia squatted uneasily amid the compact terraced housing of long-
established working-class communities. Formerly vast and uncovered, they
were constructed when few travelled by car. Standing spectators, their
movement up and down the terraces restricted only by crush barriers
anchored intermittently, were packed on to crumbling, unsafe steps.

Entry to the stadium for all 24,256 Liverpool spectators was through 23
outmoded, malfunctioning turnstiles, set back off a bend in Leppings Lane
within a small, confined area. Access was via six low, double gates, boun-
ded by a corner shop and a fence above the River Don. In June 1986
Inspector Calvert of the South Yorkshire Police wrote an internal memorandum warning of the dangerous bottleneck. The turnstiles did 'not give
anything like the access to the ground ... needed by ... fans' (Memorandum, 11 June 1986). Supporters had become 'justifiably irate because of
the inefficiency of the system, which was turned on the police and could

have resulted in public disorder'. His assessment concerned ordinary club matches; an FA Cup semi-final guaranteed a full stadium. Yet the memorandum went unheeded.

The 15 April 1989 was a beautiful, early spring day. For Liverpool fans travelling by train, coaches, transit vans and cars the last thing on their minds was danger. Coaches and transits were stopped *en route* and searched by police. Once in Sheffield, all were directed to designated car parks, searched and briefed by South Yorkshire Police officers. Those travelling by train were escorted to the stadium. An instruction on the match tickets requested spectators to be inside the stadium 15 minutes before kick-off. Delays on the road and rail journeys, including police stops and searches, brought thousands of Liverpool fans into the city throughout the hour before the 3pm kick-off. Many converged on the stadium after 2.30pm.

Within minutes the congestion at the turnstiles overwhelmed the police. Lack of stewarding and no filtering of the swelling crowd, together with malfunctioning turnstiles, made a serious crush inevitable. Police on horseback were trapped, fans struggled to breathe. The senior officer outside radioed the Match Commander in the police control box inside the stadium. After some hesitation, viewing the crush on CCTV monitors, Chief Superintendent Duckenfield acceded to the request to allow entry through an exit gate, bypassing the turnstiles.

Fans, four or five abreast, walked unstewarded and without police direction through the exit gate, down the 1 in 6 gradient tunnel beneath the West Stand and on to the Leppings Lane terrace. The tunnel was directly opposite the gate. In an unfamiliar stadium the fans did not know that the tunnel led into two divided central pens, 3 and 4, behind the goal. Pens like cattle pens. Fences to the side, at the front – and no way back. The side pens remained sparsely populated as fans sat on the terrace steps, reading newspapers and match programmes.

Over 2,000 fans entered the already packed central pens. With twice the designated number of people on the steps, compression was immediate. Faces were jammed against the perimeter fence, people went down underfoot and at the front of Pen 3, a barrier collapsed under the weight of a tangled mass of bodies. As the match kicked off the thunderous roar of the crowd drowned out the screams of the dying. Initially, the police did not respond. In the control box above the south end of the terrace, a short distance from the central pens, Duckenfield failed to identify the severity of the situation. Officers on the perimeter track were under explicit orders not to unlock the tiny perimeter fence gates, one per pen, without the authorisation of a senior officer.

Eddie Spearritt's evidence captures the hopelessness and desperation of the pens:

> The crush came ... it wasn't a surge. It was like a vice getting tighter and tighter and tighter. I turned Adam 'round to me. He was obviously

in distress. There was a police officer, about five or six feet away and I started begging him to open the gate. I was screaming. Adam had fainted and my words were 'My lovely son is dying' and begging him to help me and he didn't do anything. I grabbed hold of Adam's lapels and tried to lift him over the fence. It was ten feet or thereabouts with spikes coming in. I couldn't lift him. So I started punching the fence in the hope I could punch it down. Right at the beginning when I was begging the officer to open the gate, if he'd opened it I know I could've got Adam out. I know that because I was there.

(Scraton 2000: 60–1)

The police failure to close the access gates into the tunnel and redirect fans to the side pens before allowing so many so quickly into the stadium was compounded by the failure to respond immediately and effectively to the desperate crush on the terraces. Eventually the two perimeter gates were opened, revealing the full horror on the terrace below. It was impossible to evacuate the dead and dying quickly, given the restricted access. Bodies were dragged from the pens and laid on the pitch. The match was abandoned at 3.06pm as fans and some police officers tried to resuscitate those who had lost consciousness. Fans tore down advertising hoardings for use as makeshift stretchers. They ran the length of the pitch, carrying bodies to the stadium gymnasium. Only 14 of the 96 who died made it to hospital. The agreed major incident plan was not operationalised.

As these deeply distressing scenes unfolded directly in front of the police control box, Duckenfield was 'unable to give an accurate account of what the situation was other than a possible pitch invasion' to the Assistant Chief Constable (Statement: 12). Soon after 3.15pm Duckenfield informed two Football Association senior officials that Liverpool fans had forced open an exit gate, causing an 'inrush' into the packed central pens. Subsequently he stated: 'The blunt truth [was] that we had been asked to open a gate. I was not being deceitful ... we were all in a state of shock ... I just thought at that stage I should not communicate fully the situation ... I may have misled Mr Kelly' (Taylor Inquiry Transcripts, Day 8: 112–13). He did. Duckenfield's lie was reiterated to the waiting media. The BBC's initial bulletins reported that gates had been 'broken down' by 'large numbers of ticketless fans' determined to force entry (Scraton 2000: 113). Within minutes, this untruthful account was broadcast worldwide. Jacques Georges, then President of FIFA, publicly railed against 'people's frenzy to enter the stadium come what may, whatever the risk to the lives of others'. They 'were beasts waiting to charge into the arena' (*Liverpool Echo*, 17 April 1989). Liverpool fans were presumed responsible for the deaths of 'their own'. Within the hour, the lens of hooliganism was firmly in place.

Soon after Duckenfield 'misled' the FA officials, Chief Superintendent Addis, Head of South Yorkshire CID, was given responsibility for managing the incident. He took control of the stadium gymnasium, now redesignated a temporary mortuary. Rather than transport bodies to Sheffield's purpose-built Medico-Legal Centre, the decision was taken to lay them out in body bags on the gymnasium floor, photograph their faces and give each body a number corresponding to the relevant photograph. The gymnasium, stated Addis, was 'an ideal situation, if you don't mind me saying so, to put all the eggs in one basket' (Interview, March 1990).

The Coroner, Dr Stefan Popper, arrived at approximately 6.45pm and, following discussions with the police, took the unprecedented decision of recording the blood alcohol levels of all who died, including children. He 'realised that the vast majority were in fact extremely young' but 'we were doing them for all' as age was 'no guarantee that alcohol is not ingested'. He considered it entirely justifiable 'given where it [the disaster] happened and all the circumstances surrounding it' (Inquest Transcripts, Day 1, am: 1–2). It was a decision that immediately and publicly implied that those who died might have contributed to the disaster.

> It was a received agenda already set by Duckenfield's lie and senior officers' initial assessments. It guaranteed that allegations of drunkenness would remain centre stage. It deeply hurt the bereaved as they realised that the naming of their dead would imply the shaming of their lives.
>
> (Scraton 2000: 89)

What followed was an inhumane and damaging process of identification. People seeking information were directed to a disused boys' club. There, in appalling conditions, they were held without information, until being bussed to the gymnasium. They queued throughout the night, awaiting their turn to enter the gymnasium foyer. Over 80 poor-quality, numbered photographs of faces in body bags were displayed on screens.

Inside, the gymnasium was divided into three sections. Furthest from the entrance, bodies were laid out in body bags; each body allocated a police officer, each police officer given a bucket of water and sponge or cloth to wipe clean the faces of the dead. The central area housed police officers on 'breaks', 'around the walls ... sitting down eating chicken legs' (Senior Ambulance Officer, Interview, March 1990). Close to the entrance, an area was laid out with tables and chairs. It was here the police took formal statements of identification from the bereaved.

Following the distress of viewing the photographs, relatives stood at the gymnasium door while bodies were brought on trollies. Body bags were unzipped, the police 'just showed you the head. I bent down to cuddle [him], they hawked me up and told [us] that they [the bodies] were the property of the Coroner and we couldn't touch him. They quickly zipped the bag up, ushered us away and they were gone' (Bereaved Mother, Interview, June 1998). A bereaved father stated, 'They virtually manhandled us, sort of grabbed our shoulders, grabbed our arms ... they didn't want me to stay for a second longer than was necessary' (Interview, January, 1990). According to another mother, 'they didn't give the poor people who were killed any dignity ... I bent down to kiss and talk to [my son] and as we stood up there was a policeman who came from behind me ... trying to usher myself and my husband out ... I had to scream at the police officer to allow us privacy ... the total attitude was, you've identified number 33 so go!' (*After Dark*, Channel 4, 20 May 1989).

Told that the procedure was for identification only, forbidden to touch, caress or kiss loved ones, the bereaved were led to the tables where they were subjected to a barrage of questions about those they had just identified. Did they have criminal records? Had they ever been ejected from football grounds, expelled from school? Did they drink? The procedure, more akin to an interrogation than identification, went on through the night. It demonstrated a callous disregard for the trauma of sudden bereavement and reflected a fast-consolidating police perspective: the full responsibility for the tragedy lay with fans' drunken, violent behaviour.

The following day Prime Minister Margaret Thatcher visited Sheffield accompanied by Home Secretary Douglas Hurd. She was briefed that there 'would have been *no* Hillsborough if a mob, who were clearly tanked up, had not tried to force their way into the ground (Sir Bernard Ingham, press secretary to the Prime Minister, personal correspondence, 13 July 1994).

Inquests and inquiries

The Home Secretary appointed Lord Justice Taylor to conduct an inquiry 'into the events at Sheffield Wednesday Football Ground on 15 April 1989 and to make recommendations about the needs of crowd control and safety at sports events' (Taylor 1989: 1). He also appointed the West Midlands Police to assist the inquiry, while simultaneously conducting the criminal investigation and servicing the inquests as 'coroner's officers'. The inquiry team processed 2,666 telephone calls, 3,776 statements and 1,550 letters. Taylor's *Interim Report*, published within four months, established 'overcrowding' as the 'main cause' of the disaster and 'failure of police control' as the 'main reason'. Taylor criticised Sheffield Wednesday Football Club, their safety engineers and the local authority for failing to issue an up-to-date licence for the stadium. His most damning conclusions were directed against South Yorkshire Police.

Senior officers had been 'defensive and evasive ... neither their handling of problems on the day nor their account of it in evidence showed the qualities of leadership to be expected of their rank'. It was 'a matter of regret that at the hearing, and in their submissions, South Yorkshire Police were not prepared to concede that they were in any respect at fault for what had occurred' (Taylor 1989: 50). Duckenfield's 'capacity to take decisions and give orders seemed to collapse'. No 'necessary consequential orders' had been issued after he had sanctioned the opening of the gates and he failed 'to exert any control' once the disaster unfolded. His 'lack of candour' triggered 'a widely reported allegation' against fans (ibid.).

Taylor's indictment of the police, alongside his exoneration of the fans' behaviour, took many commentators by surprise. In December 1989 the South Yorkshire Police accepted civil liability in negligence and paid damages to the bereaved. Subsequently, in a House of Lords judgment, Lord Keith concluded that the Chief Constable had 'admitted liability in negligence in respect of the deaths and physical injuries' (House of Lords Judgment, 28 November 1991). In a later Divisional Court judgment Lord Justice McCowan stated that the force 'had admitted fault and paid compensation' (Divisional Court Judgment, 5 November 1993). These words were repeated in the House of Commons by the Attorney-General (*Hansard*, 26 October 1994: col 981).

In March 1990, following consultation with the Director of Public Prosecutions (DPP), the Coroner resumed the adjourned inquests on a 'limited basis' ahead of decisions regarding criminal prosecution or disciplinary action. His 'preliminary hearings', or 'mini-inquests', for each of the deceased were unprecedented. They were limited to medical evidence, recording blood alcohol levels, establishing the location of bodies prior to death, and identification. Consideration of the specific circumstances in which people died was not permitted. Sparse and often inaccurate evidence concerning each case was summarised and presented in court by a designated West Midlands Police officer. Witness statements on which summaries were based were neither disclosed nor cross-examined. The jury heard a confusing mix of interpretation, selection and conjecture presented, unchallenged, as fact. Unable to access primary statements and cross-examine the evidence, bereaved families were left with many deeply personal questions unaddressed.

Four months later the DPP concluded there was 'no evidence to justify any criminal proceedings' against any organisation involved and 'insufficient evidence to justify proceedings against any officer of the South Yorkshire Police or any other person for any offence' (Letter from the Head of the Police Complaints Division to the Chief Constable, 30 August 1990). The inquests resumed in generic form, running from 19 November 1990 to 28 March 1991. Altogether, 230 witnesses were called and 12 interested parties (six of whom were police interests) were represented. A single barrister represented 43 families. Disclosure of evidence was limited and police witnesses reasserted the issues discounted by Taylor: fans' drunkenness, hooliganism, violence and conspiracy to enter the ground without tickets. Survivors, called to give evidence, felt they were 'on trial'. The following comments (Interviews, March 1991) were typical.

> I felt I had done something wrong. I was a witness but I wasn't treated like one with the line of questioning.

> I remember thinking at the time, 'It's supposed to be an inquest but it's more like as if you're a bank robber' ... you were being grilled.

> Their tone was hostile towards me. Every time I didn't give them the answer they wanted they would look down at their papers and find something else to try to trap me with. It was as though I was a defendant ... as if I had to defend myself. That's the way I felt. That shouldn't have been the case.

> I felt disappointed because I wasn't given the chance to say the things that I thought were important.

> Afterwards, I felt 'What's the use?' I came away thinking no-one believes me anyway.

Summing up, the Coroner steered the jury towards 'accidental death' as a verdict that could 'straddle the whole spectrum of events' including 'carelessness, negligence' where 'someone would have to make compensation payments in civil litigation' (Inquest transcripts, Day 75, 21 March 1991: 63). Accidental death would not necessarily mean exoneration 'from all and every measure of blame'. There could have been 'very serious errors', but being 'incompetent is not the same as saying that a person is being reckless' (Inquest transcripts, Day 78, 26 March 1991: 31). The jury deliberated for two days, returning a majority verdict of accidental death.

The Police Complaints Authority intended to bring disciplinary proceedings against the Match Commander and his assistant, Bernard Murray, for 'neglect of duty'. Duckenfield, however, resigned on ill-health grounds and the case against Murray was withdrawn. Six families took test cases to the Divisional Court, aiming to quash the verdicts on the grounds of irregularity of proceedings, insufficiency of inquiry and discovery of new evidence. Supporting the Coroner, the judges considered that the inquests had been properly conducted, evidence had not been suppressed and the jury's direction had been 'impeccable'. In June 1997, following publication of *No Last Rights* (Scraton, Jemphrey and Coleman 1995) and the screening of Jimmy McGovern's award-winning drama documentary *Hillsborough* (ITV, December 1996), Jack Straw, the new Labour government's Home Secretary, announced an independent judicial scrutiny 'to get to the bottom of this once and for all' (*The Guardian*, 1 July 1997).

The unprecedented scrutiny, by former MI6 Commissioner Lord Justice Stuart-Smith, reviewed evidence not available to previous inquiries or investigations. It had to be of such significance that in his opinion it would have resulted in prosecutions or changed the outcomes of the Taylor Inquiry or the inquests. Stuart-Smith visited the South Yorkshire Police and met 18 bereaved families in closed sessions. In February 1998 he presented his report to the Home Secretary, who greeted it as 'thorough', 'comprehensive', 'dispassionate', 'objective' and 'impartial'. Stuart-Smith concluded that neither the Taylor Inquiry nor the inquest was flawed and the so-called 'new' evidence did not add 'anything significant' to that already known (*Hansard*, 18 February 1998: cols 1085–97).

Submissions made to Stuart-Smith by the author and a former South Yorkshire Police officer revealed that on the evening of the disaster police officers were told not to write in pocket books but to handwrite 'recollections' of the day. These could contain emotions, comment and opinion as they were solely for the 'information of legal advisers', were 'privileged' and not subject to disclosure (Former South Yorkshire Police Officer, Interview, November, 1997). They were gathered by senior officers, submitted to the force solicitors and returned to Detective Superintendent Denton, Head of South Yorkshire Police Management Services, as part of a consultation process of 'review and alteration' (Correspondence between Hammond Suddards Solicitors and South Yorkshire Police, 15 May 1989). A review team of senior officers transformed the recollections into formal statements. Following the alterations, the officers concerned were invited to sign their statements. It amounted to a systematic, institutionalised process of review and alteration intended to remove all criticisms of the police.

Over 400 officers' 'recollections' were passed to the solicitors, with 90 recommended for alteration. Analysis of the documents shows that the alterations protected the interests of the force, and Stuart-Smith had made this point strongly in interviews with Denton and the former South Yorkshire Chief Constable. Denton informed Stuart-Smith that the police 'had their backs to the wall' and it was 'absolutely natural for them to concern themselves with defending themselves' (Transcript, Meeting between Stuart-Smith and Denton, 1 December 1997). The former officer recalled that after the disaster a 'certain chief superintendent' took him and his colleagues for a drink. He had said, 'unless we all get our heads together and straighten it out, there are heads going to roll' (Interview and Transcript, Meeting between Stuart-Smith and former officer, 24 October, 1997).

Stuart-Smith was unimpressed and simply concluded that in a few cases 'it would have been better' not to have made alterations. At worst it revealed an 'error of judgement' but did not amount to 'unprofessional conduct' (Stuart-Smith 1998: 80). There would have been serious implications in finding otherwise. It transpired that the West Midlands Police investigators, the Treasury solicitor, the Coroner and Lord Justice Taylor were aware that statements had been written as personal recollections under guarantee of non-disclosure, and then transformed into final statements through an orchestrated process of review and alteration.

While Lord Justice Taylor had condemned senior police officers, their actions on the day and their evidence to his inquiry, he had condoned their privileged access to the investigations and inquiries and the reconstitution and registration of the 'truth' to best advantage the police interests. His silence on the process of review and alteration compromised his inquiry.

Bereaved families and their lawyers were severely hindered and disadvantaged by non-disclosure of evidence and the clandestine reconstruction of police statements. The DPP's decision not to prosecute on the grounds of insufficiency of evidence provided no indication of the quality of evidence in his possession. At the inquests the selective presentation of evidence by West Midlands officers prevented disclosure of the original statements and their cross-examination. The South Yorkshire Police held all the evidence and used it to establish and sustain their defence.

Private prosecution, public scrutiny

Two years on from Stuart-Smith's report, on a hot July day at Leeds Crown Court, Duckenfield and Murray faced a ground-breaking private prosecution brought by bereaved families. It followed years of campaigning to establish criminal liability and to force disclosure of key documents, witness statements and personal files on the deceased. The prosecution case was straightforward. People died in the pens because they were trapped, crushed and asphyxiated. According to the prosecution, the crush occurred because both defendants were 'grossly negligent, wilfully neglecting to ensure the safety of supporters'. While accepting that 'these men's inertia, their abject failure to take action' was not the 'only cause of this catastrophe', that Hillsborough was 'old, shabby, badly arranged' and that a 'police culture' prevailed which 'influenced the way in which matches were policed', the prosecution argued that 'primary and immediate cause of death' lay with the defendants' failures; negligence of 'such gravity that it amounted to a crime' (Alun Jones QC, Opening Speech, 11 June 2000).

As the case progressed, both former officers, their legal costs underwritten by the South Yorkshire Police Authority, sat impassively alongside their legal teams. Day after day families filled the court. What they all knew, but could not disclose, was that the Judge had already decreed that if found guilty neither man would go to prison. In presenting his committal ruling four months earlier, he took a 'highly unusual course' to 'reduce to a significant extent the anguish being suffered', commenting that 'the thought of being convicted for a serious offence must be a strain on anybody'. The 'greatest worry' for a police officer was the anticipation of imprisonment (Ruling, Leeds Crown Court, 16 February 2000). The judge considered that the former officers would risk serious injury, even death, in prison. Custody, therefore, would not be an option.

The prosecution called 24 witnesses, each of whom stated that the overcrowding in the central pens was evident even from a distance. Duckenfield declined to give evidence. Murray, 'haunted by the memory of Hillsborough', was remorseful but denied negligence. Defence witnesses comprised a few local residents and character referees. After weeks of legal wrangling, CCTV footage and cross-examination, Mr Justice Hooper placed the four-part manslaughter test before the jury. First, foreseeability:

that 'a reasonable match commander … allowing a large number of spectators to enter the stadium through exit gate C without closing the tunnel would create an obvious and serious risk of death to the spectators' in the central pens. Second, could he have taken 'effective steps … to close off the tunnel' thus 'preventing the deaths?' Third, was the jury 'sure that the failure to take such steps was neglect?' Fourth, was the failure 'so bad in all the circumstances as to amount to a serious criminal offence?' (Research Notes, 11 July 2000).

In his closing speech for the prosecution Alun Jones QC (Research Notes, 12 July 2000) argued the police 'mind-set' was hooliganism at the expense of crowd safety, amounting to a serious failure best illustrated as 'neglect'. There had been no 'split-second decision' but 'slow-motion negligence'. The 'clear, cogent and overwhelming' view from 'all four corners of the ground' was that the pens had been dangerously full when the exit gate was opened. Given that all prosecution witnesses had recognised overcrowding, it would have been obvious from the police control box.

Duckenfield's counsel denied that he had 'unlawfully killed those 96 victims' (Research Notes, 13 July 2000). The events had been 'unforeseeable and unique', creating a 'physical phenomenon' without precedent in the stadium's history. It had occurred in the tunnel and projected people forward with such ferocity that those in the pens were crushed to death. His explanation was that a small minority of over-eager fans, possibly those who had caused crushing at the turnstiles, were responsible for the explosion of unanticipated force in the tunnel. It was a far-fetched yet convenient explanation; a 'hidden' cause that could not be verified.

Murray's counsel contested the prosecution's notion of 'slow-motion negligence' (Research Notes, 13 July 2000). The disaster 'struck out of the blue'; deaths were unforeseeable. No reasonably competent senior officer could have anticipated the sequence of events that unfolded. While there were deficiencies in policing Hillsborough, the defendants alone should not 'carry the can'. The prosecution, he proposed, was an exercise in scapegoating.

Mr Justice Hooper reminded the jury to judge the case 'by the standards of 1989' when 'caged pens were accepted' (Summing-up, Research Notes, 12–18 July 2000). Penning had been an acceptable 'response to hooliganism'. The defendants had to be judged as 'reasonable professionals', meaning 'an ordinary, competent person – not a Paragon or a prophet'. The jury also had to carefully evaluate the circumstances. When the exit gate was opened 'death was not in the reckoning of those officers'. They responded to a 'life and death situation' at the turnstiles and the jury had to accept it 'was a crisis'. The judge warned, 'be slow to find fault with those who act in an emergency'.

In an insensitive comment that offended the bereaved, the judge instructed, 'the *mere* fact that there has been a disaster does not make these two defendants negligent'. A guilty verdict would reflect negligence 'so bad to amount to a very serious offence in a crisis situation'. He put two questions: 'Would a criminal conviction send out a wrong message to those who have to react in an emergency and take decisions? Would it be right to punish someone for taking a decision and not considering the consequences in a crisis situation?' Yet these questions, repeated later when the jury sought clarification of the relationship between negligence and serious criminal act, were concerned with policy rather than evidence.

After 26 hours' deliberation the judge agreed to accept a majority verdict. Bernard Murray was acquitted and the jury was discharged without reaching a verdict on Duckenfield. The judge refused an application for retrial. A bereaved father reflected the families' feelings: 'I never expected a conviction, especially after the judge's direction. But people on that jury held out and the case went all the way' (Interview, July 2000). Yet the families felt vindicated in taking the prosecution. While the DPP had ruled against a prosecution on the grounds of insufficiency of evidence, seven weeks in Leeds and a deadlocked jury suggested otherwise. Families stressed the private prosecution was 'not about revenge', nor was it an attempt to attribute *all* blame and *all* responsibility to two men.

The case over, the Crown Court's automatic doors opened and, one by one, families emerged on to the pedestrian walkway. Television cameras, press photographers and journalists stood back as the bereaved and survivors, their tears now dried, walked from the court for the last time. One camera continued to record the calm and dignified exit. It was operated by a West Yorkshire Police video surveillance team. In their lens were relatives and friends of many of the 96 men, women and children killed at Hillsborough Stadium. It was, at best, an insensitive and unnecessary intrusion at a time of profound grief. Justifying it as 'evidence gathering', the police claimed to have had 'intelligence about some threat to Mr Duckenfield and a potential threat for some disorder'. To the families this was the final, enduring act of the seven-week trial of two senior police officers. It was an act which once again sullied their reputation and that of their loved ones. 'All through the years we've been made to feel like criminals', said a bereaved mother, 'but this is the last straw. What did they think we were going to do?'

Media representation and the sociology of reputation

In the immediate aftermath of Hillsborough the press published explicit photographs and graphic descriptions of the dead and injured. While recognising the difficulties faced by those broadcasting, filming, photographing and reporting the disaster as it happened, production and editorial decisions encouraged and condoned intrusive journalism. This included: attempting to photograph the dead as bodies were transferred from the temporary mortuary; entering hospital wards uninvited; door-stepping the bereaved; posing as social workers; monitoring funerals. While it was to be expected that public concern and interest in Hillsborough would be considerable – at that time 94 people had died, many were in hospital, the media was present in numbers and it involved a major annual event in the soccer calendar – the level of media attention was, and remained, considerable.

As the full impact of the disaster consolidated, attention inevitably focused on causation and responsibility. In any controversial situation these are difficult and complex issues to report accurately, analytically and respectfully. More than ever before, editors and journalists compete in a shrinking market-place. Consequently, quality is often sacrificed to quick-fire sensationalism, hype and voyeurism. It is a climate in which accurate, ethical and balanced reporting is regularly compromised; a semi-fictional world in which readers are invited to believe the worst. Distortion prevails, with baying headlines competing to attract the attention of potential customers.

Three days after the disaster the *Sheffield Star* (18 April 1989), under the headline 'Drunken Attacks on Police: Ticketless Thugs Staged Crush to Gain Entry', published police allegations that Liverpool fans not only caused the deaths but attacked rescue workers and stole from the dead. The report included an allegation that 'yobs' had 'urinated on policemen as they gave the kiss of life to stricken victims'. Local politicians and Police Federation representatives, without any substantiating evidence, reiterated the allegations. The following day *The Sun* cleared its front page to pronounce: 'THE TRUTH: Some Fans Picked Pockets of Victims; Some Fans Urinated on the Brave Cops; Some Fans Beat Up PC Giving Kiss of Life' (19 April 1989). A further eight newspapers carried the allegations, including 'sex jibes over a girl's corpse' (*Sheffield Star*, 19 April 1989). It later transpired that *Sun* editor, Kelvin Mackenzie, had considered running the headline 'You Scum' (Chippendale and Horrie 1992: 283). From the outset, Duckenfield's instant reaction to blame the fans and exonerate the police had established a seemingly legitimate constituency. Unsurprisingly, the allegations originated in off-the-record briefings given by senior police officers. That grain of reliability, invented and manipulated, was sufficient to publicly condemn those suffering the trauma of the disaster. It determined the course of events in the immediate aftermath and set a wider, longer-term media and political agenda.

The Sun episode led to a mass boycott on Merseyside, but it was the most extreme case of many unfounded allegations which, had they been made against named individuals, would have resulted in libel actions. What followed was a rush to judgement in which the media employed the 'informed' opinions of experts and gave considerable coverage to statements attributed to official sources, particularly the police. Over time Hillsborough became synonymous with soccer-related violence and the hooliganism debate that had exercised politicians, journalists and academics throughout the 1980s. It dominated news reports of Lord Justice

Taylor's inquiry (May/June 1989) and the Coroner's inquests (April/May 1990; November 1990/March 1991). In particular, and despite Taylor's emphatic rejection, police allegations of fans' mass drunkenness and threatening behaviour continued unabated.

A particularly serious example was a *Sunday Telegraph* article (4 February 1990) by Simon Heffer, titled: 'BLAME THE HOOLIGANS, NOT THE STADIUMS'. Assessing Taylor's findings, Heffer stated:

> The problem at Hillsborough, though Taylor was reluctant to say it, was one of hooliganism. However much it may outrage Liverpool, 95 Liverpool fans were killed by the thuggishness and ignorance of other Liverpool fans crushing into the ground behind them. It serves no purpose to prevent the fans who caused the crush from facing that responsibility.

The *Observer*'s John Naughton stated it was misconceived to not apportion blame 'to the football multitudes who consistently behave so swinishly' (11 February 1990). Although those who died 'deserve our sympathy', Naughton asked, 'what about the other fans – the ones who milled round the gates and stampeded down the tunnel into the pens simply because they couldn't bear the thought of missing the kickoff?'

In a written response to complaints about his comments Naughton stood by his assessment of the cause of the disaster (Personal correspondence, 13 February 1990). Others in authority, and with immediate media access, reiterated similar sentiments. In a television interview the ex Chair of Sheffield Wednesday Football Club, Bert McGhee deflected attention from the condition of the stadium, its stewarding and policing: 'Many, many hundreds of people came to Hillsborough without tickets in the knowledge that if they created enough mayhem the police would open the gates. And that is exactly what happened' (*Liverpool Echo*, 16 March 1990).

South Yorkshire's Chief Constable, Peter Wright, heavily criticised the Taylor Inquiry for its rejection of 'mass drunkenness' as a determining factor in the disaster. Under the headline 'HILLSBOROUGH POLICE CHIEF ATTACKS JUDGE', the *Daily Mail* (6 February 1990) quoted Wright: 'What I found difficult to understand was the finding that there was drinking among a percentage of the fans, and that they were under the influence of drink, but that it had no effect on the events.'

Anticipating the inquests, Wright also suggested, 'there were other factors in the disaster which he hoped would emerge at the coroner's inquest and give people a different view of what happened' (*The Guardian*, 6 February 1990). Bereaved families lodged formal complaints to the South Yorkshire Police Authority against the Chief Constable. These drew the following response from Bernard Dineen (*Yorkshire Post*, 30 April 1990):

Everyone with a scrap of sense knows that drink was a contributory factor at Hillsborough: why crucify the police for saying so? What do Liverpudlians want? A declaration that no Liverpool fans have ever been known to indulge in alcohol; that they spend their entire leisure time sipping bitter lemon and debating the finer points of philosophy? Why are they so unwilling to face the truth?

This casual, persistent victim blaming was well illustrated by an 'idle' comment made by Terry Wogan on a chat show with Bobby Charlton, when he suggested that *unlike* soccer's other disasters, Hillsborough was 'self-inflicted'. Broadcast at peak-viewing time, this revealed just how penetrative were the consolidating myths of Hillsborough. The constant pressure felt by the bereaved was to justify or defend their loved ones.

In the longer term, the media coverage developed two distinct but closely related themes: consolidation of the myths surrounding the disaster and Merseyside's ascribed negative reputation. Analysis of the press coverage of the Taylor Inquiry, the inquests and other legal procedures demonstrates the persistence of an agenda set in the immediate aftermath (Scraton, Jemphrey and Coleman 1995). Whenever acts of crowd violence occurred at other venues, even in other countries or at international matches, Hillsborough was mentioned. Invariably, in such reporting Hillsborough was associated directly with the 1985 Heysel disaster and its associated crowd violence. Alongside violence were constant references to drunkenness.

The decision by the Coroner to record the blood alcohol levels of the men, women and children who died added to the speculation that drunkenness played a significant part in the Hillsborough disaster. Taking samples from the dead inferred that, through their irresponsibility, those who had consumed alcohol had contributed to their own deaths and to the deaths of others. Blood alcohol levels were revealed at the opening of the personal inquests. While many fans had no trace of alcohol in their blood, *The Sun* (19 April 1990) relentlessly compounded its initial offensive coverage, proclaiming: '15 HILLSBOROUGH DEAD TOO DRUNK FOR DRIVING'. The report described:

Fifteen of the Hillsborough soccer tragedy dead had DRUNK so much they would have been unfit to drive, an inquest heard yesterday. At least two had TWICE the legal drink-drive alcohol limit in their blood. And tests showed that 51 of the dead – more than half the total – had been drinking.

In addition to widely reported claims of forced entry, hooliganism and drunkenness, was the allegation that many hundreds of Liverpool fans, intent on entering by any means possible, conspired to arrive at the stadium without tickets. With allegations of violence, robbery and degradation of the dead fresh in the public's collective mind, the intensity of criticism directed towards Liverpool supporters' behaviour was an enduring feature of the entire inquest period (April 1990–March 1991). Duckenfield's initial lie became part of a much wider and deeper deceit. The recording of blood alcohol levels by the Coroner, the orchestration of fabricated allegations by police officers and the reaffirmation by senior officers of charges of 'hooliganism' left a durable impression, reinforced and seemingly legitimated by journalists, politicians and academics.

Following a serious confrontation between English fans and the Rotterdam police, David Evans MP, remarked that the Hillsborough disaster, as 'everyone in football knows although they won't say it, was caused by thousands of fans turning up without tickets, late and drunk' (*Today*, BBC Radio 4, 14 October 1993). Brian Clough, Nottingham Forest's manager at Hillsborough, wrote that he would 'always remain convinced that those Liverpool fans who died were killed by Liverpool people' and 'had all the Liverpool supporters turned up at the stadium in good time, in orderly manner and each with a ticket, there would have been no Hillsborough disaster' (Clough 1995: 258). His widely reported comments reignited the public debate about Hillsborough and hooliganism. Faced with widespread criticism from a range of sources, Clough remained unrepentant. On national television he repeated his allegation that 'Liverpool people killed Liverpool people' (*Sunday Mirror*, 6 November 1994). Reflecting on Liverpool City Council's call for a boycott on his autobiography, he retorted, 'half of them can't read and the other half are pinching hubcaps ... There must be a hangar somewhere where they keep all those hubcaps – as well as about 54,000 stolen car radios' (*Mirror*, 8 November 1994). There was astonishment, hurt and anger among the bereaved and survivors and many wrote to Clough (see: Scraton, Jemphrey and Coleman 1995: 276–85).

Academic researchers also accepted the police-media accounts of the connection between the disaster and violence at Hillsborough. Writing on soccer hooliganism, Kerr (1994: 18) reflected on the 'chaotic horror at Hillsborough' initiated by a 'late inrush of spectators' who 'had run into an already full enclosure of Liverpool fans, causing a desperate crush'. Young (1991: 540) listed Hillsborough as one of 13 international 'noteworthy incidents of sports-related collective violence' between 1955 and 1989: '94 fans' [*sic*] had been 'crushed to death as fans arriving late attempted to force their way into the game'. Cohen (1991: 143) wrongly attributed allegations about Hillsborough to Heysel: 'some fans ... urinated on the dead, on police and on ambulance men'. Using McPhail's 'behavioural categories' to analyse 'crowd behaviours' Lewis and Scarisbrick-Hauser (1994: 170) reviewed evidence in contemporary football crowd safety reports. They introduced four 'new' categories: 'climbing, falling, kicking, and public urinating'. Regardless of evidence, location or circumstances, they attributed 'surging', 'jogging', 'climbing', 'falling' and 'public urinating' to fans at Hillsborough. For Cohen (1991: 146), Hillsborough revealed the city of Liverpool's 'darker side: a massive drugs problem, endemic unemployment and a resultant capacity for mass disorder'. Liverpool fans had developed a 'ferocious reputation' bearing 'the hallmarks ... of Neanderthal man'.

Condemnation of the fans was not restricted to media accounts or academic publications. For example, a curious yet revealing reference appeared in Minette Walters' (2001: 142) novel *Acid Row*:

> Gaynor, who had seen footage of the Hillsborough Stadium disaster, when football fans had been mercilessly crushed by a stampede of people behind them, was terrified that a catastrophic surge would cause the people against the wall to be suffocated.

Here the myth of stampeding fans, merciless in their determination to watch the game, whatever the fatal cost to others, was casually reinforced to a mass readership 12 years after Duckenfield's lie had been exposed.

These extracts illustrate the wide-ranging media, political and academic commentaries on Hillsborough. They represent the longer-term 'drip, drip' effect always associated with the consolidation of negative reputation, whether derived from fact or fiction. Occasionally its consequences were tangible. Awaiting the delayed arrival of bereaved families due to give evidence to his scrutiny in Liverpool, Lord Justice Stuart-Smith pointedly asked, 'Have you got a few of your people or are they like the Liverpool fans, turn up at the last minute?' (Research Notes; Scraton 2000: 169). In 2000 at the opening of the private prosecution at Leeds Crown Court, the judge warned bereaved families that 'any display of campaigning, written or verbal, would constitute intimidation and considered contempt of court' (Research Notes, 6 June 2000).

The negative reputation ascribed to Liverpool fans was further developed and exploited by a broader attack on Merseyside as a region beset by violence, militancy and arrogance. When thousands turned out to show compassion for the dead and solidarity with the bereaved, it was reported as a public display of self-indulgence, self-pity and mawkishness. The specific untruths of the events at Hillsborough became compounded by more generalised untruths about Liverpool and its people. In 1993, following the tragic killing of James Bulger by two 10-year-old boys, the dominant image, so strong in the coverage of Hillsborough, was that of a place beset by violence, fear and a disdain for authority. Auberon Waugh (*Daily Telegraph*, 3 March 1993) was unrelenting:

> It is said that Liverpool's problems are all due to unemployment. I wonder what Liverpool's unemployment is due to. I fear it may be due to the stupidity as much as the unpleasant habits of the people who live there. All the clever people left it long ago.

The connection to Hillsborough was exemplified by *The Guardian*'s head-line 'HEYSEL, HILLSBOROUGH AND NOW THIS' (20 February 1993). According to Ian Jack, in his article 'A CITY ACTS UP', only Liverpool 'has the capacity to turn a deep but very particular and personal tragedy into a wake' (*The Independent on Sunday*, 28 February 1993). Liverpool people, he claimed, played to script 'as if they expect it now, mugged by one disaster after another until a peculiar kind of martyrdom has become part of the municipal character'. Writing in *The Sunday Times* (28 February 1993) under the headline 'SELF-PITY CITY', Jonathan Margolis set out to reveal the 'dark and ugly side' to that character 'which has belied the cheeky Scouse image it loves to promote'. For Margolis, the 'most liberal of people can turn out to hate, or at least be irritated by Liverpudlians ... however much you like the city Liverpool culture seems nevertheless to combine defeatism and hollowcheeked depression with a cloying mawkishness'. Focusing insensitively on Liverpool football supporters, he asked: 'Does anyone dare wonder how many of the Anfield faithful solemnly observing a minute's silence at last week's home match were, to put it crudely, getting off on the "city in mourning" theme?' Like Jack, Margolis inferred that ordinary Liverpool people wallowed in, even enjoyed, loss of life in their communities. Inevitably, constant commentaries on 'self-pity', 'martyrdom' and 'cultural mawkishness' preceded references to Heysel and Hillsborough. Margolis wrote:

> In what one liberal commentator described post Hillsborough as the 'world capital of self-pity', everyone tells you that the atmosphere after the Bulger murder was just like Hillsborough. Indeed, Hillsborough is mentioned in every conversation. Yet in two weeks, the name of Heysel, where bad behaviour by Liverpool fans helped lead to the deaths of 39 Juventus supporters, was never brought up. The inevitable taxi driver, oddly enough a coloured South African, explains without apparent irony: 'That's because no Liverpool lives were lost at Heysel'.

Again, using another unattributed source, Margolis quoted a sportswriter: 'Looking back, the way the Heysel boys were treated was monstrous. All those Italian fans were dead and the Liverpool boys were heroes'. Ian Jack pursued a similar theme, also running Heysel and Hillsborough together:

> Football remained to give the city its chief identity and its only cause of celebration. But then the football began to go wrong. In the summer of 1985, supporters of Liverpool FC crashed through the barriers at the Heysel stadium in Brussels and 39 people, most from Turin ... were crushed to death. Four years later at the Hillsborough stadium in Sheffield, 95 Liverpool supporters died in another crush ... The first incident produced collective guilt, the second – for which Liverpool

people were not to blame, collective anger and self-pity. The victims were said to have 'died for football' or at least 'not died in vain' ... Thus Liverpool learned to dramatise itself, to show its stigmata.

Margolis was equally unsympathetic in penning a spiteful conclusion:

> The tragedy is ... that Liverpool is stuck in a groove, refusing to listen to criticism, clinging to past charms and triumphs, desperate not to be seen as provincial but managing to appear just that by cutting itself off from the world. When the world is against you, how gratifying it must feel to know that you really do walk alone.

The cynical response of the media was to denigrate the compassion felt by many people, typified by the *Sunday Times* headline. During the coverage of the James Bulger case, the seal was set on the negative reputation of Liverpool, transmitted on television and reported in newspapers and journals worldwide. Plays, television drama, autobiographies, disaster texts, articles, features, comment pieces, editorials, chat shows, news items, political interviews and reviews each provided vehicles for the persistence of the myths of Hillsborough and the systematic, almost obsessive, denigration of the city of Liverpool and those inhabiting the Merseyside region. None of the authors or commentators could be made accountable for their errors of judgement. There is no collectivised right to privacy, no right to accuracy and no right to redress. It is an indictment of the effectiveness of the formal complaints procedures, established under the auspices of self-regulation, that untruthful and damaging reporting lived on. It caused immeasurable pain and suffering to the bereaved and the survivors, compounding the institutional injustices while clearly influencing legal and policy outcomes associated with the disaster.

The politics of denial

Writing on the abuse of power within states that systemically violate human rights, Stan Cohen (1993) argues that the 'unwillingness to confront anomalous or disturbing information' extends to 'democratic-type societies'. This can involve 'a complex discourse of denial'. It is a discourse bolstered by the 'language of legalism'. States, 'proud of their democratic credentials' and 'sensitive to their international image, cannot easily issue crude literal denials' (Cohen 1996: 528). Consequently, official discourse implicates the rule of law, harnessing its processes and procedures to conduct a sophisticated 'legal defence'. Discussing the production and publication of human rights reports on oppressive regimes, Cohen notes three forms of reaction: 'the "classic" discourse of official denial'; 'the strategy of turning a defensive position into an attack on the critic'; 'the disarming type of response, characteristic of more democratic societies, which partially acknowledges the criticism' (ibid.: 521). Within the 'classic' discourse are: 'literal denial (nothing happened); interpretive denial (what happened is really something else); implicatory denial (what happened is justified)' (ibid.: 522).

At Hillsborough, operationally the South Yorkshire Police had a '*de facto* responsibility for organising the crowd' (Popplewell 1985: 12). This was implicit in the pre-match briefings and explicit in the police Operational Order for the day. In planning, virtually no attention was paid by the police to crowd safety or assessment of risk. The unambiguous priority was crowd control. As the scale of the disaster emerged, senior police officers immediately were aware that their planning, organisation, decision making and performance would be scrutinised. Consequently, at the highest level the police reconstructed events to realign blame to the victims. First, to paraphrase Stan Cohen, they participated in 'interpretive denial', claiming that Liverpool fans conspired to force entry into the stadium, thereby causing death and injury. In other words, 'what happened' was really 'something else'. Through this reconstruction the police embarked on 'literal denial' of their collective and individual culpability (they did nothing wrong). Duckenfield's lie, however, was revealed and the Coroner's decision to record the blood alcohol levels of all who died was contested. Thus the police moved to 'implicatory denial'. The decision to open the gate without closing access to the tunnel and preventing fatal overcrowding was recast as justifiable to deal with a 'drunken', 'violent', 'ticketless' mob at the turnstiles.

Deeply painful processes of marginalisation and exclusion cannot be analysed or understood without consideration of political, economic, cultural and ideological contexts. States that use the rhetoric of tolerance, of rights and liberties within a declared politics of pluralism are not averse to conferring 'outsider' status on identifiable individuals, families, communities and 'lifestyles'. Often occurring through open condemnation of 'others', this amounts to dissociation and questions their morality, their very humanity. As Cohen demonstrates, the withdrawal of 'shared humanity' is nothing less than dehumanisation. Closely associated, at least in popular discourse, with dehumanisation is the related process of demonisation, through which established, ascribed negative reputations are consolidated. Once any claim on humanity has been denied, openly rejected, anything goes. Subsequently, any dreadful act, however base, can be attributed without question. This process unfolds within a purposefully orchestrated vacuum of decontextualisation; the marginalised, the excluded, the 'enemy' within or without, removed from their structural, material circumstances. How convenient it then becomes for state institutions to promote denial and rationalisation. In denying what 'really' happened, in abdicating responsibility for those killed or injured, state institutions purposefully, sometimes cynically, neutralise their actions, their omissions, while condemning their condemners.

Despite a grudging acceptance of their 'liability in negligence', the police steadfastly refused to acknowledge their central role in the disaster. From the Chief Constable down, the South Yorkshire Police strategy, in off-the-record briefings with politicians and journalists and in reviewing and altering the initial statements of their officers, was to condemn the condemners. This was made possible through privileged access to, and management of, evidence given to the police within the processes of inquiry and investigation. Beyond this, they exploited the negative climate surrounding 'football hooliganism', particularly regarding Liverpool fans' assumed culpability at Heysel. These were essential ingredients in the process of condemnation. Duckenfield's lie, blood alcohol levels, the 'ticketless' conspiracy theory, the indefensible treatment of the bereaved, the purposefully constructed allegations in *The Sun*, each contributed to the demonisation of the survivors and the dead. Marginalised as 'other', the dead, the traumatised and the survivors together experienced dissociation from 'genuine', 'law-abiding' football supporters. Jacques Georges' comments about 'beasts', together with senior officers' references to 'animals', completed their marginalisation, using an explicit vocabulary of dehumanisation. Each element of denial and neutralisation was intrinsic to the police reconstitution and formal registration of the 'truth'. Reconstructed as the inevitable outcome of drunkenness, disorder and violence, actively promoted and propagandised as indicative of the 'enemy within' a tolerant social democracy, Hillsborough was decontextualised. The central issues of environmental safety, crowd management and duty of care were deflected and neutralised by a discourse and defence constructed around self-infliction: the fans brought it on themselves.

Despite Lord Justice Taylor's condemnation of senior police officers, Hillsborough demonstrates how state institutions within social democracies can employ discourses of deceit, denial and neutralisation to protect, even exonerate, the interests of the 'powerful'. In this case 'truth' was constructed as a reflection of an established 'hierarchy of credibility', yet reinforced by propaganda subordinating and disqualifying the accounts of the marginalised. The 'mechanisms', 'means', 'techniques' and 'procedures' specified by Foucault as underpinning society's 'régime of truth', lay barely disguised beneath the surface of Hillsborough's official discourse and legal defence. They informed the degradation of the bereaved throughout the identification process, denying them even minimal access to their loved ones.

It took eight years for the Hillsborough families to access 'body files' on their loved ones. Each file contained the pathological evidence, a 'continuity chart' of locations, photographs and witness statements. This was the first disclosure of evidence held by the South Yorkshire Police and many of the body files were littered with factual inaccuracies, contradictory statements, contestable assumptions and ambiguous identifications, their reliability untested in court. Much of the documentation significant to the case was missing or mislaid. It is not possible to verify the 'deals' struck verbally in the corridors of influence or in unrecorded meetings.

No part of the legal process or procedure after Hillsborough was untainted by the reconstitution of the 'truth'. As a long-term, complex case study into policing, inquiry and accountability it demonstrates the necessity for change in professional cultures and attitudes, discretionary powers, public inquiries, inquests and police disciplinary codes. It remains an extraordinary feature of Hillsborough that it received virtually no attention in the academic literature and 'standard' texts on police powers and accountability. As this chapter has shown, deep political and ideological assumptions, coupled with professional self-interest and survival, combined to demonise the victims, to deny their 'truth', to disqualify their experiences and to undermine justice. The state's failure to address its deep-rooted and endemic practices of demonisation, denial and disqualification, amounts to disturbing complacency.

The structure, procedures and appropriateness of official inquiries, controversial inquests, criminal prosecutions and their inter-relationships have to be evaluated in terms of their individual and collective deficit in revealing truth and delivering justice. For the bereaved and survivors of Hillsborough, the due processes of investigation, inquiry and criminal justice failed. Compounding their suffering has been, and remains, the torment of injustice: paltry compensation payments, flawed coronial procedures, inappropriate inquest verdicts, unacceptable police practices, and the failure to prosecute or discipline those responsible. In that context acknowledgement of the 'truth', recording and registering the 'view from below', however painful, has been essential in memorialising the dead.

5 'Licensed to kill': the Dunblane shootings and their aftermath

My research with Dunblane families overlapped the Hillsborough Project. Most people remember precisely where they were when they heard the news that there had been fatal shootings at a primary school in Scotland. I received a telephone call from a journalist friend on his way by car to Dunblane from Edinburgh. He told me that children and teachers had been shot by a gunman who had walked into the school and opened fire. Some had died. He wanted information on what might have happened and what leads might be followed. I couldn't help him other than to tell him to treat families with respect and not to rush to judgement. As the media covered the tragedy it was apparent that most journalists took the route of extreme pathology. The perpetrator was a 'loner' who had an 'unhealthy interest' in young boys. Within hours the explanation for the deaths of 16 young children and their teacher was summarised in one word: 'pervert'.

A year later I interviewed bereaved families. The research interviews throughout this chapter were conducted in Dunblane in June 1997. By this time the Cullen Inquiry into the shootings had reported, but what emerged from the interviews was an issue touched on only briefly by the official inquiry. It concerned the treatment of the bereaved by the Central Scotland Police throughout the day of the shootings. As a consequence of this research two parents, Isabel McBeath and Mick North, became good friends and key contributors to an ESRC research seminar series on the aftermath of deaths in controversial circumstances. They were joined by the bereaved and survivors of Hillsborough and other disasters. The series, over two years, contributed significantly to developments in the care and treatment of the bereaved in the aftermath of tragedies and their participation in inquiries and inquests. Mick North wrote Dunblane: Never Forget, *published in 2000.*

Death in a Primary School

Not far from Stirling, Dunblane is a beautiful, idyllic cathedral city, no bigger than a large village. It is often described as a gateway to the Scottish Highlands. Its name is now the persistent reminder of the terror of an appalling tragedy. Early in the school day on 13 March 1996 a lone gunman walked calmly into the gymnasium of Dunblane Primary School and, using semi-automatic weapons for which he had licences issued by Central Scotland Police, shot dead 16 five- and six-year-olds and their teacher, Gwen Mayor. A further 10 children and three teachers were injured. Having fired 105 rounds in under four minutes, Thomas Hamilton took his own life. Police officers arrived at the school at 9.50am, the emergency services seven minutes later. A 'major incident plan' was put into operation and the Chief Constable was soon at the school. Within minutes, a Stirling Royal Infirmary medical team arrived and evacuation of the injured began. By 10.35am backup theatre teams were on duty at the hospital and within the hour the injured had been admitted in order of medical priority. Only one of the children who died was admitted to hospital alive (Cullen 1996: 11–15).

The school was cordoned off and by 10.30am between 200 and 300 people waited outside for news. The only telephone in the school and all available mobile phones were blocked and the police radio system lacked security. As the crowd swelled, parents of Primary 1 children were escorted to a nearby hotel, where those of children in Primary 1/13, Mrs Mayor's class, were separated and transported in minibuses back to the school staff room. Other parents were not reunited with their children for 2–3 hours. It took four hours to identify the injured children. Police withheld information from families until all the children who had been killed were identified, mainly by teachers. The class register had not been taken and, with Mrs Mayor dead, help was sought from nursery teachers who previously had taught some of the children. They visited the gymnasium on several occasions to try and identify those children who had died.

The police also decided that teams, each comprising two officers and a social worker, would be assembled, briefed and allocated to each family. It was their role to provide information, counselling and support. These teams did not begin work until 1.45pm, with the last family informed at 3.30pm, six hours after the shootings. Until that moment families were held in the staff room without any information concerning the incident, the injuries or the deaths. They were not even told that the incident had ended. One mother recalls feeling 'terrified' that her daughter might have been taken hostage.

Eight days after the tragedy a public inquiry, chaired by Lord Cullen, was established by the Secretary of State for Scotland. The inquiry's terms of reference were: 'To inquire into the circumstances leading up to and surrounding the events at Dunblane Primary School on Wednesday 13 March 1996, which resulted in the deaths of 18 people; to consider the issues arising therefrom; to make recommendations as may seem appropriate; and to report as soon as practicable' (Cullen 1996: iii). Cullen received over 1,600 letters, petitions supported by 33,379 signatures, 123 written submissions, numerous published documents and academic papers.

He took oral evidence over 26 days between 29 May and 10 July 1996 and presented his final report on 30 September 1996.

The police knew from the outset they were dealing with Thomas Hamilton. One of the first officers into the gymnasium described him as the 'nutter from Stirling'. Over the years Hamilton had been the focus of rumour, innuendo and accusation concerning his self-appointed boys' club activities. Cullen established that from 1981 to March 1996 Hamilton ran 15 clubs, using secondary schools as venues. While there had been two allegations of indecency, much of the concern was speculative. In 1981 Hamilton had been 'discreetly removed from the Scout movement' because of 'his homosexual tendencies' (Unattributed memorandum to the Director of Education, cited in Cullen 1996: 26).

As controversy dogged his boys' clubs, opinion polarised about Hamilton's approach and the activities he offered. George Robertson MP, whose son attended the Dunblane club in 1983, had been concerned by the pervasive climate of militarism he had witnessed on a visit. He considered middle-aged men ordering around young boys who were stripped to the waist to be reminiscent of the Hitler youth. In contrast, Hamilton continually produced references and petitions from parents portraying him as an inspirational leader who cared deeply for the boys in his care. Complaints continued, however, and the local authority, the Commissioner for Local Administration in Scotland and Members of Parliament became embroiled in the controversy. It was decided that Hamilton had suffered injustice through subjection to malicious and unfounded allegations. His activities continued.

In 1988, following the early return of a young boy to his family, Central Scotland Police officers, alerted by the Strathclyde Police, visited Hamilton's summer camp. The camp was considered poorly run and most boys alleged physical assaults by Hamilton. Discrepancies in the boys' evidence and inconsistencies in parents' opinions of Hamilton inhibited prosecution. He responded by making an official complaint against the police. The officers were exonerated. A protracted exchange followed concerning Hamilton's persistent allegations that he was being intimidated and harassed by people determined to end his activities. Concerns re-emerged in 1991 and a second police investigation into his summer camp activities was initiated.

At the time of the investigaton a Central Scotland Police detective sergeant attached to the Child Protection Unit realised Hamilton had a firearms certificate. First granted in February 1977, by 1991 it had been amended or renewed on eight separate occasions. In a memorandum to headquarters the investigating officer recommended its withdrawal, but the Deputy Chief Constable wrote 'no action'. Consequently the recommendation was not recorded in the firearms file nor in criminal intelligence records. On the day he walked into the school gymnasium, Hamilton was licensed to hold four handguns, two rifles and 3,000 rounds of ammunition.

From 1991 onwards, Thomas Hamilton's activities, both residential and in his boys' clubs, were the focus of complaints, investigations and monitoring. This included reports to the regional children's panels, police inquiries and regional staff. The case against Hamilton was considered at a senior level within the local authority and by the Procurator Fiscal's office. The regional council repeatedly decided against withdrawing his access to school venues because no charges had been brought and the ombudsman would again find in his favour. Hamilton's bitterness, however, escalated and he claimed systematic victimisation by the authorities.

By 1995 Hamilton's clubs were in decline and, in open letters to parents, he alleged he was the victim of a smear campaign. In January 1996 he sent a letter to primary school head teachers, including the head of Dunblane. The letter stated:

> At Dunblane Primary School where teachers have contaminated all of the older boys with this poison even former cleaners and dinner ladies have been told by the teachers at the school that I am a pervert. There have been reports at many schools of our boys being rounded up by the staff and even warnings given to entire schools by Head Teachers during assembly ... I have no criminal record nor have I ever been accused of sexual child abuse by any child and I am not a pervert.
>
> (Cited in Cullen 1996: 53)

Hamilton continued to write letters and make telephone calls to prominent politicians and he wrote to the Queen as Patron of the Scout Association. Hamilton was now known throughout the local authority, to members of parliament, head teachers and the police. His boys' clubs remained publicly controversial and it was accepted that he held a gun collection and considerable stocks of ammunition. Against this backdrop, Hamilton methodically planned his violent attack on children and staff at Dunblane Primary School. As the horror of the killings confronted senior officers on entering the gymnasium on the morning of 13 March 1996, so the full realisation of questionable certification and unheeded warnings must have dawned.

'Monstering' Thomas Hamilton

The sheer scale and brutality of Hamilton's attack was as unpredictable as it was inconceivable. Whatever the warning signs, however inappropriate the issuing of permissive licences, it was impossible to foresee such a terrible outcome. Being 'weird', or any of the other labels attached to Hamilton, gave no indication of his potential as a purposeful mass killer. Within hours of the killings the national and international media were in full cry. The 'innocence' of childhood was immediately juxtaposed with the 'evil' of the man. An evil not reducible solely to his appalling acts, but also to his well-established, pathological reputation. Typical newspaper mastheads were: 'Massacre at Dunblane' (*Express*, 14 March 1996); 'Massacre of the Little Ones' (*The Sun*, 14 March 1996); 'Massacre of the Infants' (*The Guardian*, 14 March 1996); 'Slaughter of the Innocents' (*Daily Record, Daily Star, Mirror, Herald*, 14 March 1996). Hamilton was a 'madman' (*Daily Record; Mirror*) 'monster' (*Daily Star; Daily Mail*), 'devil' (*The Sun*) and 'misfit' (*Express*). Journalists quickly established that he was well known to the authorities, from local councillors to council officials and MPs. It was his 'interest in young boys' that caught the collective imagination of the press: 'pervert scout master' (*Daily Record*); 'Kiddie perv' (*Daily Star*); 'sordid misfit' (*Express*); 'shabby weirdo' (*Daily Mail*); 'Mr Creepy' (*Independent*); He had 'doted on boys' (*The Guardian*), was a loner with 'fantasies' (*The Independent*), who had taken 'sleazy snaps' (*Mirror*).

In the immediate aftermath, with a few notable exceptions, the media missed key issues. Rather than investigating the complexities surrounding the licensing of Hamilton's armoury, and his apparent obsession with instilling discipline into young boys through quasi-militaristic activities, most coverage dwelt on his unsubstantiated reputation as a sick, perverted, paedophiliac loner who held a grudge against the 'community', authority and the police. Yet the more considered evidence indicated an articulate, participative, yet discipline-obsessed man – consistent with the traditions of strict, character-building regimes of physical training and outward bound.

A more contextual, analysis was provided by an in-depth investigative article in *Scotland on Sunday*:

> In short, Hamilton did not live in a void. He lived among us all. To write him off as an exception misses the point: exceptions are not born. They are made, by circumstance and experience, by the slow drip of alienation, isolation and paranoia. We do not understand the men who ran Nazi death camps, but we do know that for the most part they were men made exceptional by their circumstances ... we must see beyond the convenient labels that describe Hamilton as a sick pervert and an evil psychopath. The danger now is that history is rewritten in an effort to demonise Hamilton's past as an alternative to confronting the more frightening reality that nothing he ever did could have indicated the depths to which he was capable of sinking. That is by far the hardest truth to bare.
>
> (Ahmed *et al.* 1996: IV)

While unremitting stereotyping of Hamilton as a sexual predator dominated media coverage, journalists were fulsome in praising the professionalism and efficiency of the police and crisis support in the immediate aftermath. News stories reported how parents had been divided into groups, taken to a local house where, accompanied by the police and social workers, they were kept informed. According to one report, 'Everything was done to keep things as normal as possible, to shield the children from the magnitude of what had happened' (*Scotland on Sunday*, 17 March 1996). Senior reporters and news managers praised the police for a 'fantastic job' in providing 'regular briefings' and 'more than enough information' (Reuters reporter, in Preston 1996: 9). It amounted to an 'impressive ... media operation' which recognised and responded to the 'needs of journalists ... the need to feed the press with information' (BBC Home Assignments Editor, in Preston 1996: 22–3).

Consequently, the press received 'as much of the pertinent information as necessary so that they would not interfere with the investigation or bother grieving families' (Van Heil and Hoo 1998: 3). The police senior press officer, drafted in to Central Scotland to capitalise on his experiences at Lockerbie, described the media as a 'hungry beast'. He continued, 'If you feed the beast, the beast will be happy, otherwise the beast will go looking for food' (ibid.).

The families' perspective

The most obvious and consistent aspect of sudden disaster or tragedy is how the most extraordinary circumstances occur in the most ordinary of contexts. In Dunblane it was just another day as children were dropped off at school, parents left for work, others cleaned their houses and the small, peaceful community went about its out-of-season business. A primary school is the hub of a community's provision for its young children, epitomising care, safety and trust. It is where children go to share their lives, their growth and their development with peers, friends and neighbours. As parents, teachers and children began their day, the last thing on their mind was a lone gunman determined to kill children and teachers at random.

News of the shooting and possible fatalities broke into every UK radio and television broadcast. Parents, extended families and close friends of those with young children in Dunblane rushed to the school. Isabel Mac-Beath, at home close by, was with her young baby, Catherine. She 'put the baby in the push chair' and went up to the main road where 'it was absolute mayhem ... the school is just around the corner' (Interview, June 1997). She arrived at the school in minutes. Other parents were at work or travelling, only receiving the news some time later.

Rod Mayor, whose wife Gwen was the Primary 1/13 class teacher, left the house first. He had a 50-minute drive to a client in Forfar, followed by a longer trip to Aberdeen. They kissed goodbye and he set off. After his first meeting he picked up two messages on his in-car phone. The first, from one of his two daughters, Esther, told him there was an emergency. The second was from a friend who suggested he should tune into local radio. Almost immediately he received a third call, from his other daughter,

Deborah, studying in London. She was panic-stricken, telling him that she had seen a newsflash about a shooting at Dunblane Primary School. She said there were fatalities.

He contacted Esther and she confirmed the seriousness of the incident. Heading for Dunblane, he telephoned the school and spoke to a man whose voice was unfamiliar. Rod gave his name, explaining that his wife was the Primary 1/13 class teacher. He was informed that no details would be divulged and he should try the helpline number. Driving frantically, he realised that Gwen might be dead or injured. The helpline was permanently engaged but he heard the 12.30pm news broadcast. It reported two adults dead: 'I knew then that Gwen was involved. Call it intuition, whatever, I had a feeling ... I just knew it was her' (Interview, June 1997). Esther phoned again and he told her to 'expect the worst'.

At about 8.30am that morning Mick North, whose wife Barbara had died two years earlier, drove his daughter, Sophie, to the pre-school Kids' Club. They hugged and he set off for Stirling University, where he worked as a senior academic. Soon after 11am, a colleague told him there had been a shooting at the school. With two other colleagues, each with children at the school, Mick tried to phone Dunblane Police Station. The line was engaged and they left immediately for the school.

Kareen Turner's daughter, Megan, took the school bus with her friends and Kareen set off for Stirling, where she was on a school placement with Primary 1 children as a trainee nursery nurse. At 11am she was told there had been a shooting at Dunblane involving a Primary 1 class. She could not get through on the phone. Her 'head spinning', she drove to a nearby high school where her mother was a teacher. She had already left for Dunblane and Kareen followed. When she arrived another parent told her that Megan would be safe because the shooting involved Mrs Mayor's class. 'But she's in Mrs Mayor's class', replied Kareen.

Initially, the situation at the school was chaotic as the enormity of the tragedy impacted on teachers, the police and medical staff arriving from the nearby health centre. The gymnasium was the scene of unimaginable carnage, pain and suffering. Hamilton had also fired rounds from the gymnasium into other areas of the school. Apart from the dead and dying, there were 13 injured, some critically. At the outset, however, it was clear that the focus was Mrs Mayor's class.

Decisions were taken quickly to restrict access, cordon off the school and isolate Primary 1 parents. As Isabel MacBeath approached the school she was 'pretty calm because Mhairi's classroom was on the second floor and any siege situation, I thought, would be on the ground floor'. Intercepting Isabel at the end of the road, the police established that Mhairi was in Primary 1. Isabel was instructed to go to a nearby hotel. On arrival she was upset by a 'fairly senior officer' who told parents: 'Don't worry, it's only Mrs Mayor's class'. Isabel went 'weak at the knees' and thought 'Christ, it's *just* Mrs Mayor's class'. She had already heard a rumour, via the media, of 16 fatalities. It eventually turned out to be accurate, but at the time it was unsubstantiated and no one knew how 'the media had got hold of this information'. While accurate information had been leaked to the press early on, families had no way of knowing whether or not it was conjecture.

Mick North arrived approximately three-quarters of an hour later. He recalled confronting a barrier at the end of the road up to the school. Allowed through, he was stopped at a second barrier and directed to the hotel.

> When we reached the hotel I was given a cloakroom ticket and told to wait for my number to be called. I think mine was in the 40s or 50s and the only number I remember being called was 9 ... [a friend] assured me that it wasn't Gwen Mayor's class, though I don't know how she got this incorrect information. I guess there were a lot of rumours flying around. After 5 to 10 minutes a police officer came in and said that it was only Mrs Mayor's class.
>
> (Interview, June 1997)

The Primary 1/13 parents were separated from others and told to walk to a private house close to the school. It took a couple of minutes. As they left the hotel, personal details were not recorded. At the private house the police took names and addresses; they appeared to be 'completely out of their depth ... they were shouting at us, you know, panicking' (Bereaved mother, Interview, June 1997). Mick North confirmed her account, witnessing the officer in charge 'at one point shouting at an arriving parent'. A mother commented:

> There was one police officer, he sticks out in my mind and he was shouting and one of the parents whose child is still alive asked, 'Are the children hurt, are there any injuries?' And he said, 'Yes. Yes'. And then someone said 'Are there any children dead?' This stupid policeman replied, 'Yes. It could be worse. It could be worse.' What he probably meant was, 'Yes your child could be injured or, it could be worse, they could be dead.'
>
> (Interview, June 1997)

This created 'pandemonium' as parents were 'crammed in' to the small room. Social workers and educational psychologists had arrived and were 'moving around the room trying to say soothing things to us ... it was just ridiculous'. About an hour passed, then families were told by the police that they were to be moved again, this time to the school. Mick North recalled the unfortunate sequence of events:

> We were taken in Ambulance Service patient transport vehicles. They couldn't drive directly from the house to the school without

reversing ... I had already been surprised to see that a crowd of press photographers and TV cameramen had been allowed to assemble opposite the school entrance ... [and] no attempt was made to stop them taking photographs of distressed parents entering the school grounds or the house. The reversing manoeuvre was performed in front of the massed ranks of press photographers. Nothing was done at this time to stop them taking photographs. I would have preferred to have walked to the school.

(Interview, June 1997)

Isabel MacBeath remembered being 'desperately cold' and her baby Catherine crying. The police could not accommodate all parents in the transport vehicles 'so they crammed some into one and I had to wait for the next ... and they still told us nothing ... it still hadn't occurred to them to tell us the incident was over'. She continued:

There was this ridiculous manoeuvre when they put us on these three buses and reversed us out slowly in front of the press so they could take as many photographs as they wanted. Why didn't they simply get us to walk to the school? It's just around the corner.

(Interview, June 1997)

Entering the school through a side door parents were ushered to the staffroom. It was packed. They were given no information concerning the incident or the police-led organisation unfolding around them. Mick North stated:

Shortly after we got to the staffroom some families were called out. We weren't told why. Even after they had left the staffroom was still crowded. There were rumours that twelve children had been killed and that seemed like the number of families who had been called out. Some of us consoled ourselves with the fact that there were too many families left to match this.

(Interview, June 1997)

Later it emerged that those called at this stage were parents of children who survived. Taken from the staffroom without explanation, some were reluctant to leave friends behind. A friend of Isabel MacBeath was driven to the hospital, where she was reunited with her son. He was injured but fully conscious. He said 'Mummy, I've been waiting for you for so long, where have you been?' According to Isabel the delay was 'certainly part of his trauma ... he desperately wanted his mummy yet she [had been] stuck in a room without any information'.

Those remaining in the staffroom continued to speculate, desperately trying to glean information or reassurance from the police officers at the door of the staffroom. On his occasional visits the inspector was 'brusque'.

While parents remained 'calm', the 'atmosphere in the room was tense'. Isabel MacBeath felt that senior officers with whom they had contact were unable to handle the situation. One 'got really ratty with me':

> He kept saying 'Two minutes! Two minutes!' It was like, 'I've got a job to do here'. I thought, 'Yes, but you're not directing traffic, this is about dead children.' And they lied to us ... I said to him, 'We would like you to take our concerns to your superior officer, we need to see someone senior.' He said 'Yes, I'll go and do that.' And my doctor, who had arrived at the staffroom, told me that at that moment he saw the officer leave the room and just hang around outside. He never went near a senior officer. His job was to shut us up. There were two women police officers put on the door, on the inside, and by then we were really angry and one of them was in tears.
>
> (Interview, June 1997)

Mick North confirmed that families were repeatedly told they would be given information within minutes but 'this went on for about an hour and a half'.

> After a while we realised there were members of school staff, clergy and local doctors in the room. I found the presence of the clergy particularly unnerving; one female cleric dressed in black wandering around silently touching people on the shoulder. It was like the angel of death visiting. None of these people could tell us anything though we subsequently found out that they knew our children were dead.
>
> (Interview, June 1997)

According to a bereaved mother, the police 'were running around like headless chickens ... they panicked'. Her friend arrived and was 'milling around' for a while before being told where she was.

> He said he was wandering around ... in and out of rooms. Some people, without authorisation, were also wandering around while others, desperately needing to get into the school, and who had official permission, couldn't get in ... My social worker was sent to the school and the police wouldn't let her in ... she had to stand outside with a mobile phone saying 'I've been sent here but the police won't let me in'.
>
> (Interview, June 1997)

By 1pm families had been offered coffee, tea and cheese sandwiches but no information. For Isabel MacBeath the situation was desperate.

> My daughter, Catherine, the baby, was in a Terry nappy ... since 7 in the morning ... she was soaking wet, she was shivering, she was

crying, she was distressed. I kept saying to a midwife, who happened to be there, 'Can't you just get me a nappy?' At one point I said, 'I'm leaving, I have to go home to get nappies for this baby.' And the police prevented me from leaving. It's my big regret, my big regret, I wish I'd insisted on leaving because either they would have arrested me, which I don't think they would have done, or – and this is more likely – they would have told us something … Yet I am quite an assertive woman but remember feeling cowed by them. I remember thinking, 'We have to do what the police want us to do because they're in charge here.' It wasn't just that they botched it. They consciously made decisions that were stupid, in which the parents were just an administrative inconvenience.

(Interview, June 1997)

Isabel remained 'haunted' by what she identified as her 'failure' to leave the staffroom and challenge the police: 'If you could have sneaked out of a window and switched on the first radio or television you came to, you would have known more.' The parents continually reminded the Inspector how long they had waited without information. They felt treated 'unsympathetically'. It was clear to them that 'his orders were to hold us in the staffroom and that's what he was doing'. Another father recalled:

We had an idea of what had happened. I can't believe that there were some teachers actually in the staffroom with us who had [earlier] been involved in the identification who were then sent in to comfort us and told not to say anything. To put these people in that position was outrageous. Not one senior police officer, no-one above inspector came in – and he only did for seconds at a time.

(Interview, June 1997)

A bereaved mother 'hadn't twigged that people coming in and out of the room knew'. She was being comforted by her doctor and 'didn't know that my doctor knew'. She said to him that she wanted to leave and he replied, 'I don't think you should'. The police had instructed them 'not to say anything' to the parents about the identity of the dead children.

As time went on the 'trauma' for Isabel MacBeath was 'not knowing, being stuck in that room with my other baby in distress, not knowing'.

I felt awful, absolutely awful. I didn't know if she [Mhairi] had been desperately frightened, if she was stone dead, if she was brain-damaged. It was absolutely horrendous. Mhairi lived for a little while [she died at the hospital]. I would have liked to have known, to have gone and seen her in her hospital bed. They kept us hanging on, like cattle, and told us nothing … they were so rude.

(Interview, June 1997)

Convinced that Gwen had been shot, Rod Mayor arrived at the school at 1pm. After a brief discussion between senior officers he was allowed through the cordon, accompanied by an officer.

> Another uniformed man and, I assumed, a detective, came down to see me. He asked me to go with him ... and they put me in this room which I know now was the library. As soon as we arrived I said, 'I need to know whether my wife is injured, dead or what.'
>
> (Interview, June 1997)

The police officer stated that he 'didn't have the information available but would come back to me in a few minutes'. Rod was left, alone, in the school library. It was soon after 1pm and he decided to give the police until 1.30pm. Minutes after Rod arrived at the school, Esther introduced herself to an officer at the gates and asked if her father was there. The officer confirmed that he was in the school, 'but we don't know where'. Esther was taken to the staffroom and asked officers to find Rod: 'They told me again he was there, but they didn't know where.' She 'knew it was mum's class because I'd been at the hospital ... the fact that dad was there, in the school, yet they couldn't or wouldn't tell me where, meant there was something wrong'.

At 1.30pm, still in the library, Rod went to the police officer outside the door. He said, 'Look, I'm Mr Mayor and I've been in here since just after one o'clock. I need to know what's going on. If no-one comes in the next few minutes I shall leave and find out what's happening.' About ten minutes later the detective who had shown Rod to the library returned. Rod confronted him:

> I said, 'I need to know. Time's going on and I need to know. Is it the worst scenario?' He said, 'I can't tell you. We don't have information available.' So, I said 'In that case I'm going. And I'm going across, outside. I'll find out from somebody what the hell's going on.' And he said to me, 'Well, in that case, Mr Mayor, it is the worst scenario.' It sounds strange, but it was quite logical, I simply said, 'Right, I need a phone, I need to tell my daughters.' He said, 'We don't have a phone'. 'That's not a problem ... I've a fixed in-car phone.' He said, 'Well, in that case, Mr Mayor, we do have a phone.' It was right there, in the library.
>
> (Interview, June 1997)

Rod Mayor was devastated. His worst fear was realised. Gwen was dead. The police had left him, alone, in a state of ignorance; their insensitivity compounded with deceit. He stated:

> On reflection, two blatant lies were told, absolutely out-of-this-world blatant lies. One, he said he didn't know, and he did ... And then there was no phone, and there was.
>
> (Ibid.)

One hour and ten minutes after arriving at the school, Rod Mayor telephoned Deborah in London and told her of Gwen's death. He tried to contact Esther but her mobile phone was not responding. In fact, she was only yards away in the staffroom. They were reunited half an hour later at 2.45pm, an hour and three-quarters after Esther had arrived at the school. Rod commented:

> I can't understand how or why they kept us apart for so long. There'd obviously been some sort of decision made that if and when I arrived I was to be taken somewhere separately. I don't know on what basis they came to that decision ... If they were putting all the suspected bereaved families together, why wasn't I put in that category? Obviously my daughter was.
>
> (Ibid.)

Being told

In his inquiry report Cullen states the 'process of breaking the news to the parents of deceased children did not begin until 1.45pm' because communicating appropriate information to parents was to be carried out by a 'family liaison team' of 'two police officers and a social worker' (Cullen 1996: 15–16). The teams had to be 'assembled and briefed ... instructed to provide them [the bereaved] with continuing counsel and support'. Further, the police 'decided that they should be entirely certain as to the identity of the deceased children ... lest any parents be misinformed'.

The delay, precise time and procedure adopted in confirming the identities of the children who died remained contested. A parent, among the first to be taken from the staffroom, stated it was 'precisely 2.32pm'. Yet in evidence to the Cullen Inquiry police officers were adamant that all families were informed by 2.30pm. Cullen accepted that the last parents were not taken from the staffroom until 3.30pm. He concluded: 'delays were entirely unacceptable, especially when they were combined with the distressing effect of lack of any information' (Cullen 1996: 17).

Still surrounded by clergy, educational psychologists, doctors and others, each of whom knew details of the shootings, parents were called by name from the staffroom. It was, recalled a mother, 'impossible to describe what it was like waiting for your name to be called out, not knowing what you were going to be told ... hoping for the best but fearing the worst'. Another stated, 'It seemed to take ages, rather than taking us all together they did it family by family over what was nearly a two hour period'. Called from the staffroom, the Turners met their liaison team:

> The policewoman asked me to sit down. She held my hand and told me Megan had been killed. Strangely, I felt anger. I was angry that I

had been kept waiting for so long ... furious that it had taken them hours to tell me that my daughter had been murdered ... I wanted to be with her. If she was still in the gym, I wanted to be there. I just needed to be beside her.

(Kareen Turner quoted in Samson and Crow 1997: 27)

Not knowing her unconscious daughter had been rushed to hospital, Isabel MacBeath was escorted from the staffroom at 2.40pm, although when she later accessed her file the police claimed she was informed at 2.10pm.

They took us out of the room, and I'm still nursing this fractious baby. He [the police officer] said 'My name is Detective Constable [name] and I'm a police officer serving with ... ' I interrupted saying, 'I don't care who you are, I want you to tell me what's happened'. He said, 'There's been an incident at the school.' I mean, I knew that, and thought, 'Cut the crap'. I just shouted, 'You will have to tell me what has happened to my daughter.' And he said, 'Well, I'm sorry, she has been one of the victims.' He couldn't bring himself to say 'dead'.

(Interview, June 1997)

Mick North was sitting with a friend in the staffroom. He remarked it was about the time that Sophie would normally have finished class and gone to the school-based Kids' Club: 'That's why I never had any doubts about the time I was told of Sophie's death.'

At about 2.40pm I was called out of the room. Olwen [his friend] came with me and we were taken to one of the school huts. The support team was a social worker, a plain-clothes police constable and a uniformed police constable.

(Interview, June 1997)

Mick and Olwen were addressed as 'Mr and Mrs North'. He explained that his wife had died and Olwen was a friend: 'a school record card should have been available which indicated that Sophie only had one parent. They had ample time to find out information about personal circumstances.' They were told there had been a 'shooting incident and sixteen children had been killed'. Mick 'guessed that Sophie was dead and he [the police officer] confirmed it'. They were informed that Gwen Mayor had been killed and the gunman had taken his own life. Asked to wait, Mick 'stormed out of the room'.

[The police officer] came after me and touched me on the sleeve at which point I threw his hand off me. I shouted at them that I had been left waiting for hours to be told that Sophie was dead so why should I wait any longer. It was suggested that they arrange a car to take me home and I agreed to wait. I apologised for shouting.

(Ibid.)

Despite the time it had taken to brief the liaison teams and establish a procedure for giving information to the families, the confusion continued. Martyn Dunn remembered sitting in the staffroom 'and they came in and said, "Oh, there's still people waiting". They thought they'd told everyone.' Pam and Kenny Ross could not understand the delay:

We were the second last to be called. We realised things were bleak. People coming in and out of the room must have known we were about to be told. A doctor sat, holding my hand and I kept saying that it didn't look good ... 'Joanna's gone, she has to be', but 'why are we left?'

(Interview, June 1997)

Still unsure whether 'the parents guessed who I was', Esther Mayor 'didn't know what was happening or what to think ... your mind just goes'. Knowing a teacher had died, but not knowing who, knowing her father was in the school, but not knowing where, she was in turmoil:

It was very, very stressful ... you hear people being called out ... you don't know why and you don't know anything. Some of the parents had been there since just after 10 in the morning. It was worse for them.

(Interview, June 1997)

After demanding to know what had happened to Gwen, Rod was introduced to his family liaison team, one police officer and one social worker: 'Even the liaison team didn't know that Esther was in the building ... they had the briefing but didn't know.' Esther stated that 'whatever they did' with her details 'it wasn't good enough'. She continued, 'They didn't pass on crucial information to the social workers and then I was left in that room ... whatever happened to that information?' In fact it was Rod who confirmed Gwen's death to Esther at 2.45pm. Neither could understand why they were not informed of her death on arriving at the school. Gwen's identity had been known from the outset: 'They knew exactly who she was. They knew she was dead when I arrived at the school. Once they had my name, Esther Mayor, they knew.'

Eileen Harrild, the PE teacher working with Gwen Mayor's class in the gymnasium, was one of the first to be shot. She was hit twice in the arms, in the hand and in the chest before Hamilton gunned down Gwen, the supervisory assistant Mary Blake, and the children. Rushed to hospital, Eileen was told immediately her injuries were not life-threatening. She underwent emergency surgery. At 11am her husband, Tony, was called to the hospital and put in a room. He was anxious to know the class involved because his two youngest children were at the school. Repeated requests for information from the police were frustrated and he was instructed to telephone the school. Unable to get through on the phone, three hours after arriving at the hospital he overheard a conversation suggesting it had been a Primary 1 class.

The Harrilds' two older children were at the local high school. While Tony went to pick up the younger children, a family friend went to the high school, where the two boys feared the worst for their mother. Eileen recalled:

> [They] had only heard radio newsflashes, having been told that there were two adults and, at that time, they assumed, eleven dead children. Knowing that there were normally only two adults in the gym, myself and the class teacher, they assumed ... I was dead. They assumed this for almost five hours.
>
> (Emergency Planning Society, 1999: 37)

Eileen considered the dissemination of 'accurate information' to those families 'directly affected' should have been an immediate priority. The effective 'co-ordination of information between the two schools would have helped the many families affected that morning'. Clearly, the delay in providing her husband and children with accurate information caused considerable distress: 'unnecessary silence can be very destructive, accelerating the fear, anxiety and anger'.

At the time of the shootings Anne Beaton was a district nursing sister and midwife at the Dunblane Health Centre. She was one of the first people to enter the gymnasium. After the injured had been triaged and evacuated, the Health Centre staff 'were taken by police to the Library where we were told the families would be brought to us while the news of the children was broken to them ... they would have somebody they knew with them when receiving the devastating news' (ibid.: 38). What followed, however, was quite different:

> ... once the social workers arrived they teamed up with the police personnel and the families were given the news by complete strangers. They did not know that one mother had recently lost her husband, that another father was widowed and other families' problems, we the Health Centre staff did know and would have been extremely sensitive. As it was, misery and grief were compounded by asking questions about relationships.
>
> (Ibid.)

What concerned Anne Beaton was that families would have been better supported had the skills, experience and close proximity of the Health Centre staff been used more effectively. Staff 'had known the children since birth' and had 'attended the injured and dead'. Yet when it came to confirming fatality the Health Centre staff 'were left totally isolated because it is practise that the police and social workers work together' (ibid.).

As children left school early, they walked a gauntlet of journalists and television cameras. They were released without information and were unprepared for the mêlée at the gates. Apparently, no checks were made on whether parents or family were at home. According to Dennis Currie, the assistance team co-ordinator, 'In the first few hours we were getting calls from children who had just returned to an empty house, had seen and heard the news, and needed somebody to talk to.' These calls were followed by others from families and friends wanting information that the team, 'stuck in a basement room' did not have: 'They often knew more than we did by checking the media' (quoted in *Community Care*, 28 March 1996).

Rod and Esther Mayor eventually left the school, accompanied by a social worker and a police officer. Rod recalls walking into the house where, only a few hours earlier he had kissed Gwen goodbye:

> You think to yourself, 'What the hell's going on here? I've got two people here who I've never met before half an hour ago'. It was a bizarre situation ... When we met they didn't know I had two daughters, there were two sets of grandparents. Gwen had a sister ... these were the people 'in' the equation ... a huge responsibility.
>
> (Interview, June 1997)

The social worker was 'very straight' with Rod and Esther, telling them 'she was in no position to give advice because it was a scenario they had no experience of'. Their liaison team 'was thrown in at the deep end'. Back at the house, immediate priorities were to arrange for Deborah to fly from London and to inform relatives; 'you don't want the family to hear about it on the radio'. And then there were journalists:

> When we arrived back on the day there were two cameramen taking photographs in the garden and we had to close the curtains. It was reported the next day that we were so grief-stricken we'd had to close the curtains. But that wasn't the reason, it was to prevent intrusion.
>
> (Interview, June 1997)

These matters were handled by the social worker and the police officer. Rod and Esther met Deborah off the flight. It was mid-evening and the impact of what had happened was beginning to sink in: 'at that stage I still didn't believe it had happened and you still have that hope, you *know* it can't be, that there's been a mistake ... until you actually see for yourself'.

When Isabel and Catherine arrived home a uniformed officer stood outside the house:

It was quite helpful. It meant that people knew, like having an 'angel of death' at your door ... people knew you had a dead child ... neighbours immediately knew and wouldn't come running across to ask if Mhairi was alright.

(Interview, June 1997)

A Flawed Inquiry?

A problem for public inquiries into tragic events is that while they should be held soon after the event, gathering evidence fresh in witnesses' minds, those directly involved are experiencing grief, trauma and suffering. Cullen's public hearing began just over two months after the shootings. Before it opened he met with the bereaved 'to discuss any concern or anxiety which they had with regard to the taking of evidence'. According to Cullen, they requested that 'details of the injuries suffered by individual victims' should not be explored and he agreed (Cullen 1996: 7). The Lord Advocate stated that while witnesses would give evidence under oath or affirmation, it was in the public interest that 'anything which a witness said in evidence ... would not be used in evidence against him or her in any criminal proceedings ... ' (Cullen 1996: 7–8). In other words, according to a bereaved father, 'we were assured that the objective would be to explore the truth and learn lessons ... no-one would hold anything back for fear of recrimination' (Interview, June 1997).

While other assurances were given concerning the provision of witness statements and the order of witnesses' appearance, 'the arrangement broke down ... and on some occasions we had no idea who would be appearing'. In a remarkable example of institutional insensitivity, the police officer who had overall responsibility for the parents in the staffroom on the day was allocated a similar responsibility for the duration of the inquiry. A bereaved mother considered this 'totally out of order ... he was arrogant, rude, unkind and the police were going to sit him in the inquiry with us'. According to a bereaved father, he 'was replaced at our request':

In spite of the promise of honesty the Inquiry was soured almost immediately ... To eliminate the need to call a number of witnesses [the officer in charge of the police inquiry] presented a summary of much of the evidence. It was delivered in such an arrogant manner. When asked if he knew of the parents' concerns about how they were dealt with on the day he said he had only become aware of them the week before.

(Interview, June 1997)

What followed shocked the families. Successive police witnesses reported significantly earlier times when families had been told of their children's deaths. According to a bereaved father, it was 'a concerted attempt to make out we had not been left waiting as long as we had'. In order to establish consistency between the police version and families' experiences, 'parents were approached by their support team police officers suggesting that they [parents] had got the time wrong'. Another relative was shocked at how 'the police just stood there and lied on oath – sticking to bizarre time-scales':

> These guys were giving evidence which was incensing us ... Rather than just admitting they were human and were not looking at their watch ... they were totally insistent that their timing and their version of everything was right ... It didn't seem particularly sinister at the time but it was distressing.
>
> (Interview, June 1997)

The pressure on other witnesses intensified. One social worker 'was subjected to tougher cross-examination than most police officers in order to verify times'. Given little notice of being called, according to a bereaved father, 'Not surprisingly, she confirmed our version of events'. Yet 'no police officer was called to explain the discrepancy between hers and their evidence'. A bereaved relative concluded 'it was us who were made to feel that we were the ones who were lying'.

The commonly held view of the bereaved was that on the day of the shootings senior police officers realised that the force would be closely scrutinised and severely criticised for allowing Thomas Hamilton, with all that was known about him, to amass an armoury of semi-automatic weapons and ammunition. Thus, while part of the delay in providing information to parents was due to inefficiency, incompetence and equivocation, behind the scenes the police were concerned with damage limitation.

At the inquiry, when challenged, the police regularly opted for denial. A bereaved mother commented:

> Senior officers ... simply said, 'I don't know. I don't have this information'. One guy didn't seem to know anything ... he'd come to a government inquiry to answer questions and he didn't have that information with him.
>
> (Interview, June 1997)

She continued:

> What happened on the day at Dunblane they [the police] had no control over. It was a straightforward, open and shut case. All the police had to do [at the school and immediately after] was to make everything easy and bearable for the victims but instead it was a catalogue of disasters. They had the opportunity to put it right at Cullen but they stood by their stories and lied.
>
> (Ibid.)

Whatever the shortcomings of the Cullen Inquiry, and bereaved families raised serious concerns over the failure to call a range of significant witnesses, it criticised the Central Scotland Police for its renewal of Hamilton's licence and not acting effectively on profound issues drawn to its attention concerning his unsuitability to hold a licence. It was this failure to act which led to the resignation of Deputy Chief Constable Douglas McMurdo. The shared opinion of many families, however, was best illustrated in the words of one bereaved father: 'As the Inquiry progressed it was difficult to consider it as anything more than a piece of public theatre so that the establishment could justify their position in public' (Interview, June 1997).

For the families, 'the big issue was handgun control ... we were focused on the handgun issue, this firearms issue'. The bereaved father continued:

> We were pessimistic about what Cullen would come out with ... We had never made a decision that we would become a campaign group but, almost subconsciously, we decided that if it was going to happen, it would have to come from us. Cullen didn't feel right ... we decided that it didn't matter what Cullen came out with we would campaign for a ban ... and that became all-consuming.
>
> (Interview, June 1997)

Doubting politicians, yet feeling the general public was sympathetic, the families 'educated ourselves' on the 'morality, the ethics, the civil liberties, the type of people who have guns' and the wider political debates. Another bereaved father agreed that campaigning for a ban meant neglecting other significant issues:

> It's consumed me right up until last week [June 1997]. I've now started to go back and I feel aggrieved about how we were treated at the time. For almost a year I've been concerned with guns, but I am now aggrieved by the way the police handled us. They gave the guy [Thomas Hamilton] a licence, that's one issue. The second is they treated us shabbily; they lied in court and got away with it ... the whole thing stinks, it's all been swept under the carpet.
>
> (Interview, June 1997)

Another father wrote to Cullen 'about the way we were treated, in the school, at the identification' but 'those questions I wrote to Cullen remain unanswered'. A mother who felt Cullen 'failed us' felt that the 'story' of the police behaviour on the day and at the inquiry 'has not been told properly'. At the time, however, focused on gun control and overwhelmed with personal grief, families found it 'impossible to sort out precisely just what's going on ... they [the police] are organised, concerned about their reputation and professional standing – we were a group of families torn apart by the loss of our children' (Interview, June 1997).

Mick North (2000: 137) notes that, after hearing three weeks' evidence to the Cullen Inquiry, there 'no longer appeared to be an obvious structure to the proceedings'. 'Naively,' he continues, 'I'd expected that a Public Inquiry would be conducted in a way that would help the public to understand.' Much of the inquiry dialogue 'was almost impossible to follow, the arguments couched in legal language with examples drawn from cases no lay person would know'. As the inquiry neared its end it became clear that the prosecuting agency in Scotland, the Procurator Fiscal, would not be questioned about why they had never taken a case against Hamilton. For the families, 'who wanted to believe that all relevant evidence would be heard', this issue was 'crucial'. North concludes: 'Examining the prosecution service in depth was not possible; this was one boundary that the Scottish judicial system would not or could not cross' (ibid.: 138).

Seeking 'truth' and acknowledgement

Some time after the inquiry, and following success at lobbying for gun control, families came to the conclusion that the full story had not emerged. Serious questions of police accountability remained unresolved, and parents exchanged letters with the Joint Police Board, but to no avail. Both the Joint Board and the Her Majesty's Inspector of Police Report recorded their satisfaction that Central Scotland Police responded appropriately and fully to the criticisms levelled against them. The bereaved, however, were not convinced, as the following three comments (Interviews, June 1997) demonstrate:

> Most of us are law-abiding citizens and you have this belief in the police that they are doing a good job. Now I wouldn't trust them as far as I could throw them. There has been much skulduggery over this, all they're bothered about is looking after themselves. I don't think there is anything now we can do. The door is shut, they covered up rapidly.

> This is not just a matter of justice and fairness, but of honour and integrity. I don't care if it takes every penny I've got, I'm going to keep on. What will that achieve? That I know there is nothing more I could have done. And also, something might happen, there may well be disclosure. We are convinced that there are things being buried around this case.

> I would like the truth to come out, the real story to be told, the gaps in the Cullen Inquiry to be filled in and the police to fully accept their responsibilities. I can't reconstitute my child but what I would like is that these very controlling, macho senior officers are seen as the old guard and are on the way out.

The shootings at Dunblane Primary School, as the bereaved relative quoted above stated, was an 'open and shut case'. An unprecedented tragedy with enormous consequences and implications, it was over in minutes. The direct cause was immediately known and the emergency response, evacuation of the injured, was obvious. Once the evacuation was complete, three priorities remained: the care and welfare of the children, teachers and rescuers at the school; the assessment and realisation of the psychosocial and material needs of the bereaved and survivors; the organisation of a sensitive and fully informed process of identification.

The inter-agency response failed the bereaved, yet the Central Scotland Police continued to defend the appropriateness of its handling of events on the day. As a bereaved father stated, at the inquiry police officers 'were asked, in hindsight, whether they would do anything different and they said no'. Further, the Director of Social Work considered the liaison between the senior police officers and social work managers had 'built up over years ... which meant that there was no friction ... and no negotiations were necessary' (quoted in *Community Care*, 28 March 1996). As Mick North (1999: 17) states:

> In the past, the Dunblane victims' families have criticised Central Scotland Police for their attitude towards us on the day of the shootings and for distorting events in evidence to the public inquiry. Adequate explanations have never been provided by Chief Constable Wilson, who appears unprepared to take responsibility for the actions or lack of actions of his force ... On March 13 we could have done with a little more human feeling from ... senior police officers. The victims' parents have never felt satisfied with the responses provided by Central Scotland Police or the Joint Police Board to questions they have raised. Evidence in the case should shed some interesting light on the culture inside the force.

According to the Director of Social Work, inter-agency management of the immediate aftermath was sensitive and efficient. Alongside the police account, it stands in stark contrast to the reality endured, suffered and recounted by bereaved families. What is striking and consistent about the bereaved parents' accounts is that the police clearly assumed control and, given the immediate questions over Thomas Hamilton's suitability to hold gun licences, their professional competence was compromised. Far from rendezvous points and quiet organisation, the arrangements for holding families, transporting them and identifying their needs were seriously deficient. More than one family was 'shouted at' and no information regarding the incident or its consequences was given.

Despite assurances that the major incident plan had been successfully operationalised, it emerged that the police-led decisions taken in the immediate aftermath were *ad hoc*. A bereaved mother was told by her assigned police officer that 'at one point a senior officer seriously put forward the idea of getting the parents to identify the bodies on the floor of the gym' only to be 'talked out of that' by healthcare staff (Interview, June 1997). A decision was then taken to inform the parents in the library, using the skills and local knowledge of the Dunblane Health Centre staff. This was abandoned and remains contentious, given the delays and the procedure eventually adopted.

The decision to put those teachers who had identified bodies into the staffroom, with bereaved parents who knew nothing of the incident or the deaths, was indefensible. Discussing one teacher, Rod Mayor stated, 'So she knew who was dead and who wasn't and she wasn't allowed to tell parents and it must have been absolutely horrendous for her ... she was told not to tell them anything ... giving anybody that burden was just unacceptable' (Interview, June 1997).

On the day of the shootings senior officers maintained a distance from the families. At the inquiry, according to a bereaved father, one officer stated that he 'had the role of liaison and communication with the parents'. But the majority of parents 'had never seen this guy until he set foot in the Inquiry'. During cross-examination it was suggested to him that his primary role was liaison with families, yet he had not entered the staffroom: 'I could not believe that they [the police] got away with something as basic as that ... a senior guy had a primary role on the day and he just didn't carry it out' (Interview, June 1997).

Claims that the management of the immediate aftermath were rehearsed and collaborative, involving multi-agency decision making, were not sustainable. For the bereaved, and the families of those who survived, the official response they endured was insensitive, unstructured and profoundly deficient. Possibly because of the realisation of their culpability in legitimating Thomas Hamilton's gun ownership, the police placed their priorities before those of the bereaved.

While Cullen committed his inquiry to openness and thoroughness, the bereaved were profoundly disappointed by its conduct and outcome. They were given no detailed information or explanation concerning the status of the inquiry or their entitlement to legal representation, Cullen's preliminary meeting with families promising an 'expectation of openness that wasn't fulfilled' (North 2000: 194). In selecting evidence, there was 'no clear overview of the strategy being adopted' and the legal procedures language of the inquiry represented 'an alien world to many of the families', denying their 'full participation in a supposedly public process' (ibid.). For grief-stricken families there was no time to prepare, to gain advice and information or to grasp fully the realities or potential of the process.

As the families subsequently argued, an official inquiry could not deliver a detailed and thorough examination of all relevant evidence if time and opportunity had not been given for all available information to emerge. North specifies several significant 'omissions' by Cullen in setting his inquiry's parameters: the 'link' between Hamilton and Dunblane concerning his 'problems' with the town; the failure to call witnesses to explore that link; the decision not to call successive Central Scotland Police Chief Constables; the lack of open discussion of Hamilton's suggested relationship with the Freemasons; the partial examination of discrepancies and deficiencies in the gun-licensing process; the lack of accountability of the Procurator Fiscal; the stark discrepancies in evidence between the police and parents over their treatment. North (ibid.: 197) reflects strongly felt and shared feelings about these discrepancies: 'Had there been a ruthless determination to establish the truth and to demonstrate that only the whole truth was acceptable, then those police officers who'd distorted the times ought to have been recalled ... to explain the discrepancy.'

At the close of his inquiry, Cullen placed the crucial internal police report on Thomas Hamilton under a 100 years' secrecy order. Following a campaign by the bereaved families, the ban appeared to be lifted early in 2003 by the Lord Advocate (under pressure from the Scottish Parliament). In fact, it became evident that 106 files had been subject to the secrecy order. The four Central Scotland Police reports released were 'edited' versions of the originals. Many of the other documents, not released and held in Scotland's National Archives, are police summaries or edited witness statements. Mick North stated that 'this raises questions about what was made available at the time of the Inquiry ... Everything was supposed to come out ... it seems the Crown Office was less than open' (*The Mail on Sunday*, 6 April 2003). The issue of non-disclosure and police editing supported North's (2000: 199) conclusion that Cullen's inquiry 'appeared unwilling to challenge the *status quo*', begging the question: 'Which public do they [official inquiries] serve?'

Finally, in 2005, the 106 files were opened to public scrutiny. Mick North examined thousands of documents contained in the files. He stated that reading the files 'confirmed what I already believed I knew about the role of the police and the involvement of the procurator fiscal service'. Each of the complaints against Thomas Hamilton had been 'viewed in isolation'. The documents also 'proved' that the police 'misled' the Cullen Inquiry concerning the times that families were informed. He concluded:

> Too often the inquiry appeared as a process run by the Establishment largely for the benefit of the Establishment in an attempt to minimise damage and to reassure the public that there was not too much to worry about. Yet the arrogant decision to hide these documents away has left a festering sore that has never healed. I hope lessons have been learned, about how society should deal with someone in a community who behaves persistently in an alarming manner, and about how a public inquiry should treat those directly involved in a tragedy.
>
> (Mick North, Public Statement, October 2005)

6 Children on trial: prosecution, disclosure and anonymity

When James Bulger was abducted and killed it was immediately apparent that those responsible were children. I was recently a child myself when Mary Bell was convicted of child killing and the memory of the publicity surrounding her trial remained vivid. In February 1993 the responses within the community, as neighbours turned against neighbours, were shocking. Between the tragedy and the arrest of two 10-year-old boys, false leads and police raids on houses brought, in their wake, vigilante attacks against those wrongly accused. Once arrests were made, angry mobs reacted with ferocity at the courts. A policewoman involved in escorting the boys told me that she feared for their lives. Following their murder convictions, the trial judge gave permission for both boys to be named, their photographs published. In most states none of these events, from the prosecution through to the publicity, would have occurred. The media-hyped, in some cases sponsored, demand for vengeance was exploited by opportunist commentators and politicians.

The Centre for Studies in Crime and Social Justice was nine miles away from the Bootle shopping precinct from where James Bulger was taken. Collectively, we were deeply concerned at the public reaction and media coverage surrounding the case, not least how such an exceptional case was portrayed as emblematic of growing lawlessness among children and young people. We formed the Young People, Power and Justice Research Group and in 1997 published 'Childhood' in 'Crisis'? It mapped the regulation and criminalisation of children and young people that followed, including the backlash against children's rights, the moral panic regarding 'feral' children, persistent young offenders and antisocial behaviour. With Deena Haydon, I visited a small town in Sweden were a child had been killed by two boys. We interviewed the police, social workers and others in the community. Unlike a similar case in Norway, the Swedish case was never made public and the boys stayed with family and were given full-time welfare support. When we showed the police and social workers the media coverage of the James Bulger case they were aghast that children, whatever they had done, could be treated in such a way. A year later I was interviewed on New Zealand radio prior to presenting a public lecture in

*Wellington on the implications of the case. The radio station switchboard
was jammed for several hours as people rang to voice outrage at my seemingly 'liberal' views on children, discipline and punishment.*

A child killed by children

The scenes outside South Sefton Magistrates' Court, Bootle, Merseyside in
1993 were unprecedented in recent history. A crowd of men, women and
children had to be restrained by police officers as they attempted to charge
a prison van. It was a frightening and disturbing experience, more so because
the targets of their wrath were two 10-year-old boys – indistinguishable in
appearance from those on the pavement hurling abuse. The 10-year-olds,
Jon Venables and Robert Thompson, were in the 'protective' custody of the
state, about to be committed for trial for the horrific killing of two-year-
old James Bulger. They were charged with murder and remanded to secure
units to await trial. The killing took place in February 1993, the trial in
Preston, at the Crown Court, in November. For nine months both boys
were imprisoned without counselling or psychological support, knowing
that eventually they would be tried as adults in an adult court. They had
relived the killing of James Bulger during hours of interrogation.

Undoubtedly, public outrage was heightened as the nation became a collective, armchair voyeur to the abduction. The event had been caught on camera,
albeit out of focus, hazy and flickering. It showed two primary-school boys,
one ahead of the other, the second leading the toddler by the hand. It remains
a haunting image, replayed and published a million times. From the miles
of routine CCTV tapes these were defining moments. The pair of confused,
sometimes difficult 10-year-olds, came to be projected internationally as
two of the most notorious killers in contemporary history. Yet no one should
feel at ease with the presumption of premeditation in the case of James Bulger's tragic death. Experience, understanding and knowledge of the world
of young children should instil doubts in any certainty that at the time of
the abduction, throughout the long walk which led eventually to the rail-
way line where the final assault took place, the boys had set out to kill.

Yet the decision to prosecute the children for murder, together with the
Court's decision that at the time each knew their actions were seriously
wrong, implied premeditation. The prosecution flew in the face of the 1969
Children Act intention that there should be no punishment of children
without proven moral responsibility. It also raised the children's rights
issue concerning whether young children are able to 'comprehend the
complexity of the investigation and trial process', whether they can
'meaningfully participate in their own defence' (Ashford 1996: 16). On this
basis it is questionable whether a fair trial could have been achieved.
Finally, and importantly in terms of Europe, only in Ireland other than
Britain would the children have been above the legally defined age of
criminal responsibility.

Allan Levy QC, a leading authority on children and the law, was 'unequivocal' in his response to the 'sad message' of the trial. Prosecution 'revealed the unacceptable face' of the criminal justice system providing 'an unpalatable insight into outmoded thought, reform denied and the appearance of political calculations' (*The Guardian*, 20 November 1994). The Penal Affairs Consortium (1995: 6) doubted whether 'such young children were able to comprehend the complexities of a lengthy prosecution and trial' and whether they should be subjected to the 'full glare of media coverage of a Crown Court trial'. Although tried as adults, such young children could not understand the language, procedures and conduct of the court, nor could they instruct their lawyers appropriately. The children were neither named nor identified until after the verdict, the court was open to the public and they were positioned on a raised platform. Ostensibly provided to enhance their participation in the proceedings, it ensured their every move and expression was scrutinised by journalists seeking to construct the personalities of the boys through observing their courtroom behaviour.

Twenty-five years earlier, however, similar issues occupied the minds of those who witnessed the prosecution of 11-year-old Mary Bell and her friend, Norma Bell, at Newcastle Assizes. Mary was convicted of the murder of two younger children and Norma was acquitted. Gitta Sereny attended the trial throughout, noting 'a jury trial for murder is a fearful matter, deliberately grave in its procedures and awesome in its effect'. Neither girl was prepared for the 'solemnity of the courts', for the two 'mutually incomprehensible languages' (of childhood and the law) nor for the crowds, the media and the public interest surrounding the case. She concluded there had been 'no sense that children are, in fact, any different from adults in their understanding of the proceedings and function of the court, and in their understanding of right and wrong ... they are tried as small adults' (Sereny 1997: 70–1). Effectively such 'deconstruction confers meaning without understanding' amounting to 'an institutional process of definition, ascription and categorization bereft of personal histories, familial complexities, and social significance' (Haydon and Scraton 2000: 421).

Despite these informed reservations, popular opinion, political opportunism and reactionary professional ideology united in conferring legitimacy on the public prosecution of young children for murder. In November 1993, at Preston Crown Court, the judge, as far distanced from the children in age as he was in social class, passed sentence framed by the words, 'an act of unparalleled evil and barbarity'. Complex issues about the boys, their lives, experiences and communities, about the roots of the killing and the intricacy of social and structural influences were submerged by an outpouring of adult condemnation. The press lost no time in presenting full page photographs of the now-named folk devils as 'Freaks of Nature' (*Daily Mirror*, 25 November 1993) who were 'Born to Murder' (*Today*, 25 November 1993). Another headline read 'How do You Feel Now, You

Little Bastards' (*Daily Star*, 25 November 1993). It encapsulated and reflected an adult nation's clamour for revenge.

A decade on, the foreman of the jury, Vincent Moss, criticised the judge's comments, stating that his 'pronouncement that they [the boys] were "evil" was just wrong – they didn't have the moral and intellectual capacity for this to be an accurate description' (*The Guardian*, 6 February 2003). Further, he questioned the boys' ability to participate in the trial: 'For them, the trial was traumatic and largely incomprehensible.' They 'could not understand why they were in court', faced with 'adults who were using language and concepts which had no reality for them'. The 'most cynical and irresponsible aspect of the whole affair', however, was the 'way in which so much of the press has worked to inflame and continue the parents' and the public hatred' towards Jon Venables and Robert Thompson.

A 'crisis' in childhood?

The killing of children by children is a rare event. In the decade prior to James Bulger's death just one child under five had been killed per year by a stranger and none by another child. Yet over 70 under-fives each year had been murdered by parents or adults known to them. Despite these unambiguous statistics, one of the UK's leading academics on child development, Professor Elizabeth Newsom, without any supporting evidence, claimed: 'The figures are very small now but what frightens me is that we *maybe* on the verge of something bigger' (*The Observer*, 28 November 1993, emphasis added). The 'figures' to which she referred did not exist. The only case was that of James Bulger. Yet Newsom's comments were widely reported, giving credence to the unsubstantiated outpourings in the press.

Writing in the *Sunday Times* (3 July 1994), Gerald Warner proclaimed, 'Civilisation menaced by adolescents from hell':

> What I did on my holidays the 1994 version. Put concrete block on railway line, am; abducted toddler from supermarket and beat him to death, pm. Who said that today's youngsters do not know how to make their own entertainment?

Quite apart from representing a rare crime as typical, almost casual, Warner trivialised the killing of James Bulger while using it to vilify a generation of children. The 'school population' released into 'general circulation' was 'life-endangering'. It was a population of 'sullen, introverted, ignorant and loutish young people' threatening the 'future of our country' and 'civilisation itself'. A 'nation of vipers' had been bred whose 'prevailing ethos is anti-social'. He attributed dysfunctional 'breeding' to 'two decades of political correctness' dominated and sustained by the 'Leftist thought police'.

At any other time Warner's article might have been dismissed as a reactionary rant against progressive trends but, in the context of the public condemnation that followed the trial, it represented the sharp end of a continuum of child rejection; a sharp end most accurately described as child hate, consistent with race hate, misogyny or homophobia. An atypical event was reconstructed as typifying a generation deficient in basic morality, discipline and responsibility. Hatred, usually reserved for cases marked by exceptional cruelty and brutality (as the killing had been portrayed), was extended to include a spectrum of 'antisocial', 'abusive' or 'offensive' behaviours. Thus, the atypical transformed into the stereotypical.

As the media-hyped debate raged, this 'continuum' was clearly evident. The killing of James Bulger was 'simply the worst possible example of amoral childish viciousness; horrible precisely to the degree that it was childlike – random, aimless, and without conscience' (Janet Daley, *The Times*, 25 November 1993). Throughout the UK, announced a *Sunday Times* editorial (28 November 1993), parents were 'viewing their sons in a new and disturbing light', wondering 'if the Mark of the Beast might not also be imprinted on their offspring'. Walter Ellis observed children at play 'with a frisson of apprehension and fear that was not there before ... we can never know which of them has the Satan bug inside him' (*Sunday Times*, 28 November 1993).

Novelist Beryl Bainbridge returned to her native Liverpool, where she was instantly confronted by children whose 'countenance was so devoid of innocence that I was frightened ... old beyond their years and undeniably corrupt. Women passing by said there's more of them than there used to be, they should have been drowned at birth' (*Daily Mail*, 20 February 1993). For the well-established columnist Lynda Lee Potter a 'nightmarish world' beckoned 'where children go rarely to school, roam the streets 'til midnight, know how to roll a joint, gloat over sick videos and think fun is tying a firework to the tail of a cat and setting it alight ... a world where children are growing up virtually as savages' (*Daily Mail*, 26 November 1995).

Thus, a rare and exceptional event gave rise to a prolonged and generalised condemnation of children, families and communities. The killing of James Bulger was portrayed as the extreme end of a developing continuum of children's aberrant and criminal behaviour. Franklin and Petley (1996: 138) demonstrate that 'brutal and hysterical press vilification' of the 10-year-old killers 'spilled over into more general assertions about childhood', characterising 'children as evil' and 'metamorphosing the traditional social construct of childhood "innocence" into its opposite'. Yet the debate was not confined, in content or scope, to the media. The police, particularly the Association of Chief Police Officers, continually lobbied politicians about 'persistent young offenders' encouraged into career crime through soft interventions such as cautioning. In this increasingly hostile representation, 'no-go areas' were depicted as neighbourhoods overrun by gangs of marauding, feral children. Gullible journalists became the conduit for the most lurid and exaggerated stories. Masked children, assumed to be armed, stared through the eye-holes of balaclavas from the pages of hyped feature articles, while television documentaries used night-sights on cameras to record the 'nastiest' behaviour from the 'worst' estates. A 'rat-boy', supposedly living rough among the ventilation shafts and cellars of flats and houses, 'prowled' a council estate in north-east England. The search for 'the worst child in Britain', for the youngest child to assault a teacher, for the 'bail bandits' and for the child 'most excluded from school' established a media pattern. It produced a diet based on over-generalisation and misrepresentation in which Home Office estimates of 'persistent young offenders' were marginally above one hundred. In the aftermath of the Bulger case, 'child crime' was ripe for political opportunism.

At the precise moment when the renewed moral panic over lawlessness required considered political judgement and sound leadership Prime Minister John Major called for a 'crusade against crime', a 'change from being forgiving of crime to being considerate to the victim' (*Mail on Sunday*, 21 February 1993). The Home Secretary, Kenneth Clarke, attacked 'persistent, nasty, little juvenile offenders' bereft of 'values' or 'purpose' while railing against social workers who mouthed 'political rhetoric ... about why children in their care are so delinquent' (*The World This Weekend*, BBC Radio 4, 21 February 1993). The Shadow Health Minister, David Blunkett, also criticised the 'paternalistic and well-meaning indulgence' that tolerated 'the sub-culture of thuggery, noise, nuisance and anti-social behaviour often linked to drug abuse' (*Daily Mail* 25 February 1993). Tony Blair, then Shadow Home Secretary, emphasised teaching the 'value of what is right and what is wrong', to resist the fast descent into 'moral chaos'. Challenging the prevailing 'moral vacuum' demanded policies 'tough on crime and tough on the causes of crime' (*The Guardian*, 20 February 1993). Nick Cohen identified a more cynical intent. Blair had 'employed a dead toddler to shift Labour to a hard line on law and order', leading directly to an inter-party 'arms race to see which could invent the sterner penalties' (Cohen 1999: 84). Within days, imprisonment for children and young people was high on popular and political agendas.

By October 1993, prior to the trial verdict, the new Home Secretary, Michael Howard, proclaimed the sound-bite principle, 'Prison Works', while unveiling '27 steps to crack crime' to a rapturous Conservative Party Conference. Grandstanding in an atmosphere akin to William Whitelaw's 1979 'short, sharp, shock' conference speech, Howard rekindled an earlier, previously censored statement made by a junior Home Office minister, David McLean: 'we are sick and tired of these young hooligans ... we must take the thugs off the streets' (*The Sun*, 7 October 1993). The atmosphere, within and outside the conference hall, was astonishing. Conference delegates rose to their feet to support one speaker's demand for execution, castration and flogging. This hit the headlines as 'Hang 'Em High, Hang 'Em Often' (*Today*, 7 October 1993). Receiving the punishment baton from his predecessor, Kenneth Clarke, Howard announced secure accommodation for 12- to 14-year-olds with the introduction of USA military-style 'boot camps'.

> Within months, James Bulger's death had become a catalyst for the consolidation of an authoritarian shift in youth justice ... replicated throughout all institutional responses to children and young people. It carried media approval and popular (adult) consent, reflecting the well-established Thatcher agenda of the 1980s.
>
> (Scraton 1997: 170)

Sentencing children

Convicted of murder and under 18, Jon Venables and Robert Thompson were sentenced to detention during Her Majesty's pleasure (HMp), a sentence 'in lieu' of a life sentence. The length of time they would serve would be determined by the Home Secretary, taking into account the trial judge's recommendation and the Lord Chief Justice's advice. Fixing the 'tariff' was an ambiguous mix of law, interpretation and Home Office policy developed over the previous decade to meet the requirements of retribution and deterrence. Prior to their release, the Home Secretary would be guided by the Parole Board's assessment of risk. The first review of a life sentence would take place normally three years before the expiry of the tariff to enable informed risk assessment and preparation for release. Ultimately, responsibility for release remained the Home Secretary's discretion.

In sentencing the boys, the trial judge, Mr Justice Morland, stated they would be 'securely detained for very, very many years until the Home Secretary is satisfied that you have matured and are fully rehabilitated and are no longer a danger to others' (cited in *T v UK Judgment*, Strasbourg, 16 December 1999). On 29 November 1993 he assessed the length of detention 'necessary to meet the needs of retribution and general deterrence for the offence'. He considered 'very great care' was necessary before release as the boys' backgrounds reflected 'great social and emotional deprivation', including regular exposure to 'abuse, drunkenness and violence'. To respond to such 'appalling circumstances' significant 'psychotherapeutic, psychological and educational investigation and assistance' was necessary. While an 18-year tariff would have been appropriate for adults, he settled on eight, entitling review at five. Eight years, he stated, were 'very, very many years for a ten or eleven year old. They are now children. In eight years' time they will be young men' (ibid.).

The Lord Chief Justice agreed that 'a much lesser tariff should apply than in the case of an adult' (*R v Secretary of State for the Home Department ex parte T and V*, House of Lords, 12 June 1997). Yet he extended the tariff to 10 years, with review after seven. A significant factor in both assessments was that, should the boys be released within 10 years, they would not be transferred to an adult prison. It reflected a well-founded concern that children and young people who experience a welfare-based and treatment-oriented regime in children's secure units are not well served by the harsher and more punitive regimes of young offenders' institutions or adult prisons. This tension is particularly marked when cases have been given widespread notoriety, an issue noted by the trial judge in advising that the boys should be protected from 'the very real risk of revenge attacks' (*T v UK Judgment*).

The intense public pressure surrounding the trial and its immediate aftermath refocused on the sentence. A petition, urging Michael Howard 'to take account of our belief that they should not be released in any circumstances and should be detained for life', was signed by 278,300 people. Another petition signed by 5,900 demanded a 25-year minimum sentence. The Bulger family received 4,400 letters of support for its campaign. Most controversial were 21,281 coupons published by *The Sun* newspaper and sent by readers to the Home Office. The coupon read: 'Dear Home Secretary, I agree with Ralph and Denise Bulger that the boys who killed their son James should stay in jail for LIFE.'

Howard disagreed with the judges, setting the tariff at 15 years with review at 12 years. The boys would be in adult prisons for their first assessment. Howard stated that he had weighed the judges' advice against the circumstances of the offence, legal representations, precedent and 'public concern'. The petitions and correspondence had been influential in arriving at his decision, particularly regarding the 'need to maintain public confidence in the system of criminal justice' (Goff in *R v Secretary of State*). A defining issue for the Home Secretary was the 'exceptionally cruel and sadistic' nature of the crime, perpetrated against 'a very young and defenceless victim' and 'committed over a period of several hours' (*T v UK Judgment*). Howard stated that had the boys been adults they would have received a minimum sentence of 25 years.

Howard was criticised by campaigners for being lenient. Others realised the implications of an executive decision that, in essence, was judicial. Troubled by the lack of separation of powers, a *Guardian* editorial (8 February 1995) stated: 'The last person who should be involved in sentencing is a highly political politician ... of all that breed Michael Howard, on his record, is the last to be called.' Allan Levy, QC, argued that Howard had persistently, 'exploit[ed] his hard-line views about the police, prisons and punishment in a bid to bolster his party politically' (*The Guardian*, 29 November 1994). Sentencing was a 'judicial process and not a political exercise'. Gitta Sereny was outraged, stating that, for an 11-year-old child, 15 years was the 'other side of the moon', a tariff without 'hope' potentially resulting in 'a situation in which they cannot but be corrupted' (*The Guardian*, 8 February 1994).

On 7 November 1994 leave was granted to Jon Venables and Robert Thompson for a judicial review of the Home Secretary's decision. It was argued that the tariff was disproportionately long, ignoring the needs of rehabilitation prioritised by the trial judge. In the Divisional Court, Lord Justice Pill and Justice Newman concluded that an HMp sentence obliged the Home Secretary to regularly review the period of detention imposed on children and young people. To establish 'an identified penal element' within an HMp sentence was unlawful. Neither punishment nor deterrence should influence the setting of an appropriate release date. It was unacceptable to set a tariff for children, who 'change beyond recognition during the running of the tariff period' (Goff in *R v Secretary of State*).

The Home Secretary appealed, and in July 1996 his appeal was dismissed. A majority ruling centred on the contradiction inherent in setting a tariff while continually reviewing the progress of children. The Home Secretary appealed to the House of Lords. By the time the appeal was heard, in June 1997, there was a new government and a new Home Secretary. In a majority ruling, the Lords dismissed the appeal, allowing a cross-appeal by Jon Venables and Robert Thompson on the grounds of procedural unfairness. As in the Court of Appeal, the Lords' judgments centred on duty of care, the welfare of children in custody, the judicial function of setting a tariff and the undue influence of public opinion on the Home Secretary's tariff.

According to Lord Goff, in implementing a 'penal element' the Home Secretary had adopted what amounted to 'a sentencing function'. Lord Hope noted a 'serious conflict between the process of tariff-fixing' by the Home Secretary and 'his duty to keep the period of detention under review'. The 'risk' was in 'replacing the duty of review with the blanket of rigidity'. It was an unacceptable risk given that it involved the rehabilitation and development of two young children. Lord Browne-Wilkinson considered that Howard's policy denied consideration regarding 'how the child has progressed and matured during ... detention until the tariff originally fixed has expired'. Throughout the tariff period, appropriate 'weight to the circumstances directly relevant to an assessment of the child's welfare' could not be established, thus denying the essential prerequisite of flexibility for the 'welfare of the child'. Fixing a tariff, without review, for a person's childhood infringed international treaty obligations. Failing to keep track of developing capacity and maturity while under sentence, not reviewing progress for the purpose of reintegration into society, would violate the UN Convention on the Rights of the Child and other international standards. Lord Hope was clear that a sentencing 'policy which ignores at any stage the child's development and progress while in custody as a factor relevant to his eventual release date is an unlawful policy'.

While the Lords' judgments focused on the legitimacy of tariff setting, Lord Hope was concerned that the long tariff precluded parole review until the children had 'ceased to be young persons and [had] been moved into prison conditions with adults'. As the Home Secretary had not provided evidence recognising his duty 'to keep the progress and development of the children under review', his tariff decision was procedurally unfair. It was informed by an improper application of discretionary powers and had failed to demonstrate an appropriate 'measure of detachment from the pressure of public opinion'. Lord Steyn accepted that public confidence in the criminal justice system was important but contested that there was no place for the excesses of public clamour and protest. As fixing the tariff was a 'classic judicial function', the Home Secretary should have responded 'with the same dispassionate sense of fairness as a sentencing judge'.

According to Lord Goff, there had been a palpable 'desire for revenge', including the 'infliction of the severest punishment upon the perpetrators of the crime'. While 'perhaps natural' it had been 'whipped up and exploited by the media ... degenerat[ing] into something less acceptable'. Responding to 'public clamour' had been an 'irrelevant consideration ... render[ing] the exercise of his [the Home Secretary's] discretion unlawful'. Referring to the *Sun* coupons, Lord Steyn considered the Home Secretary should have ignored the 'high voltage atmosphere of a newspaper campaign'. He had 'misdirected himself in giving weight to irrelevant considerations', which, having their intended impact, had 'influenced his decisions ... to the detriment of Venables and Thompson'.

Lord Hope argued that as an 'orthodox judicial exercise' the tariff fixing should have been confined to 'the circumstances of the offence and those of the offender and to what, having regard to the requirements of retribution and deterrence, is the appropriate minimum period to be spent in custody'. He concluded:

> Expressions of opinion [via petitions or a media-led campaign] however sincere and well-presented, are rarely based on a full appreciation of the facts of the case ... they cannot be tested by cross-examination or by other forms of inquiry in which the prisoner for his interest can participate. Natural justice requires that they be dismissed as irrelevant to the judicial exercise.

The newly elected government's Home Secretary, Jack Straw, announced his intention to revise the policy for fixing and implementing the tariff for young offenders imprisoned during HMp. He reaffirmed the practice of seeking advice from the trial judge and from the Lord Chief Justice in establishing appropriate 'punishment'. Combining that advice with representations 'on the prisoner's behalf', an 'initial tariff' would be set, with reasons for the decision provided. Cases would be monitored annually, using 'progress and development' criteria. At the mid-point a comprehensive report, informed by relevant legal representations, would be compiled for the consideration of the minister (*Hansard*, 10 November 1997).

A violation of rights

Applications presented in May 1994 by Jon Venables and Robert Thompson to the European Commission alleged six violations of the European Convention on Human Rights (ECHR). In March 1998 their applications were declared admissible to the European Court of Human Rights (ECtHR). Subsequently the UK government was held responsible for three ECHR violations in the trial and sentencing of the two boys. The public trial of children in an adult court was considered seriously 'intimidatory'. They were prevented from playing an effective part in the proceedings and the establishment of the facts and appropriate allocation of responsibility had been impaired. Together this amounted to a violation of Article 6. Further, the Home Secretary was neither independent nor impartial in setting the tariff, a further breach of Article 6. Finally, Article 5.4 was also breached because the tariff-fixing policy denied the right to a periodic review of detention by a judicial body. Other alleged breaches were not accepted by the Commission, but it concluded: 'the case raises complex issues of fact and law under the Convention, the determination of which should depend on the merits of the application as a whole' (*T and V v the UK*, 6 March 1996).

A *Guardian* editorial (16 March 1999) stated, 'No-one should be surprised by the Commission's ruling that the Home Secretary was wrong to intervene in the sentences'. Sentencing was a 'judicial process, not a political exercise'. It considered it anomalous that a trial of 11-year-old children could be judged unconstitutional because they had been unable to participate effectively, while not being considered inhuman or degrading. The editorial concluded:

> The trial did have a cathartic effect on a traumatised nation but few other nations would have allowed it. Should the interests of a nation outweigh the interests of offenders? That is a dangerous precept. Both children were severely traumatised. Strasbourg is ideally placed to balance the conflicting interests.

It would have been more appropriate to state the dilemma as the 'interests of the nation' set against the '*rights* of offenders'. If the denial of participation amounted to inhuman or degrading treatment it constituted a violation of rights, not interests.

In December 1999 the ECtHR delivered parallel judgments on the cases. Regarding the boys' submission that their cumulative experiences of the trial and its procedure amounted to inhuman or degrading treatment the Court held, on a majority of 12 to 5, that there had been no breach of Article 3. The boys proposed that, taken together, the age of criminal responsibility, the length and accusatorial nature of the trial, adult proceedings in a public court, overwhelming media and public presence, a jury of 12 adults, attacks on the prison van and the disclosure of identity amounted to violation. While the Court noted that Article 3 'enshrines the most fundamental values of democratic society', the alleged ill-treatment 'must attain a minimal level of severity'. The absence of an agreed age of criminal responsibility throughout Europe obstructed grounds for a breach of Article 3. While the Court considered that juvenile defendants' privacy should be protected, and the European Convention affirmed the desirability of media and public exclusion, it was not possible to determine ill-treatment had occurred at the minimal necessary level of severity for an Article 3 breach. Further, the state had not intended to humiliate or cause suffering.

The boys also alleged a breach of Article 6.1, the right to a fair trial. In Robert Thompson's case, a diagnosis of post-traumatic stress disorder, together with enforced absence of therapeutic work between the offence and the trial, were claimed to have restricted his ability to instruct lawyers. The psychiatric opinion concerning Jon Venables stated that at the time of the trial he had the emotional maturity of an eight or nine-year-old, did not understand the proceedings and was too traumatised and intimidated to effectively participate. The Commission had recognised the issues of mass publicity, severe intimidation and the denial of effective participation, and the Court agreed. Special measures adopted at the trial had not eradicated its 'formality and ritual', which would have appeared 'incomprehensible and intimidatory' to children. In being situated in a raised the dock the boys had been placed on public view. Whatever the skills of their lawyers, the inhibitions placed on the boys restricted appropriate consultation throughout the trial. Given their 'insecurity' and 'disturbed emotional state', the boys were considered incapable of cooperating in preparing their defence. Their inability to 'participate effectively' had denied them a fair hearing, and on a majority of 16 to 1 the Court held that Article 6.1 had been violated.

The boys argued that detention at Her Majesty's pleasure was severely disproportionate and its retributive element breached Article 3. While the House of Lords had ruled against the 15-year tariff, no replacement tariff had been set. Effectively, the tariff fixing remained a political or executive decision. There was continuing uncertainty concerning the boys' future and a real risk that the sentences would be completed in adult prison. The Court referred to international standards, noting that imprisonment for children should be limited to a minimum period and used as a measure of last resort. On a close majority of 10 votes to 7, however, it did not consider the punitive element in the tariff amounted to inhuman or degrading treatment.

The lawfulness of the boys' detention was challenged on the grounds that 'Her majesty's pleasure' was an arbitrary imposition on young offenders and disregarded personal circumstances or needs. It failed to consider minimum periods of detention and the well-being of the child. The Court unanimously upheld the UK government's submission that imprisonment comprised punishment, rehabilitation, and protection of the community. The boys submitted that in setting the tariff the Home Secretary, rather than an appropriate tribunal, performed a 'sentencing exercise', thus breaching Article 6. The Court agreed that tariff fixing was a sentencing exercise and, as a politician, the Home Secretary was neither a court nor tribunal independent of the executive. As a 'fair hearing by an independent and impartial tribunal' had not occurred, the Court held unanimously that Article 6.1 had been breached. Further, since conviction, the children had been denied the opportunity to have the continued lawfulness of their detention reviewed by a judicial body. The Court held unanimously there was also a breach of Article 5.4.

Following the domestic judgments, the ECtHR's rulings had been anticipated. While alleged inhuman or degrading treatment was not upheld, five judges specified significant issues that together amounted to substantial mental and physical suffering: treating 10-year-olds as criminally responsible; prosecuting 11-year-olds in an adult court; handing down indeterminate sentences. Their opinion was severe. The 'whole weight' of adult processes had been directed against children. It was a 'relic' from the past when children's physical and psychological well-being and best interests were neglected. The prosecution was retributive and vengeful, did not constitute justice and 'should be excluded'.

The dissenting opinion considered it paradoxical that while the children were held responsible as adults for their actions they were provided with a play area during adjournments. The adult court, length of proceedings and formality amounted to an 'experience' for 'children of this age in an already disturbed emotional state' that 'must have been unbearable'. Medical evidence demonstrated that the trial, followed by the lifting of restrictions on publishing their identities, had resulted in 'lasting' harm and significant suffering. The dissenting judges noted that Jon Venables cried throughout a trial that 'caused suffering and humiliation' beyond an inquiry that required the circumstances of the acts committed. Consequently, 'the minimum level of inhuman and degrading treatment' had been exceeded, and exacerbated by an indefinite sentence. Uncertain and anxious, the boys had been denied their status as children.

Home Secretary Jack Straw noted serious breaches of the European Convention 'relating to the trial process, to the way in which the tariff linked to their sentence was set, and the failure to subsequently review the tariff' (*Hansard*, 6 December 1999). In contrast, Michael Howard was appalled that the Convention could be 'applied to cases like this ... ' (ibid.). Bristling with indignation over the 'interference' of the ECtHR in domestic matters, editorial writers warmed to Howard's theme. The *Liverpool Echo* claimed the Court's intervention would be 'bitterly resented by those who feel we need no lessons from Europe on how to operate a just legal system in a democracy ... this European Court has no obvious claim to lecture us on how to behave' (17 December 1999). *The Sun* was as typically outraged as it was ill informed: 'Who gave a bunch of European lawyers, from countries with much less satisfactory and mature legal systems than ours, the right to dictate how British courts and elected British politicians should deal with child murderers?' (17 December 1999). According to the *Daily Mail*, the ruling originated from 'an outside court interfering in long-standing judicial and political procedures which have been democratically established and accepted by the British people' (17 December 1999). Minnet Marrin's jingoism was palpable: 'There is something rather monstrous … about a bunch of foreigners telling us what is right. And what a gallimaufry of foreigners they are too' (*Daily Telegraph*, 17 December 1999).

Undeterred by the logic and detail of the rulings, the press continued to defend the part played by public opinion in influencing the legal process. 'Surely', argued the *Daily Mail*, 'it is the job of democratic politicians to take account of public feeling.' While acknowledging that 'Public outrage may be unattractive', the *Daily Telegraph* claimed that 'revulsion from extraordinarily wicked crimes is still entitled to expression in sentencing. Jack Straw is better placed to judge that entirely proper outrage than a gaggle of lawyers in Strasbourg.' That the European judgments were consistent with those in the British courts seemed an insignificant detail to editorial writers. As with much of the parliamentary response, xenophobia was an easier option than handling the complexities of the injustices exposed by the judgments and dissenting opinions.

Press freedom v the right to life

The long-term consequence of Mr Justice Morland's decision to disclose the identities of Jon Venables and Robert Thompson was the inevitable pressure to disclose their details, particularly their whereabouts, at the time of their release from custody. Throughout their time in separate secure units in north-west England stories, many of which were fabricated, were published. As with Mary Bell, stories about the two boys captured the public's imagination. Allegations of violent behaviour fitted the popular image, fanned by the tabloids, that both boys were inherently, pathologically evil and beyond reform. Condemnatory stories were published, regardless of their origins or veracity. Those reporting positive progression towards release and resettlement brought resentment that the boys were having an 'easy', privileged experience at significant cost to taxpayers. As they approached 18 it became clear they would be released into the community from the secure units where they had experienced welfare-oriented regimes under social services. This would avoid transfer to more punitive regimes in young offenders' institutions run by the Prison Service. The decision was informed by a desire not to have positive 'rehabilitative' work undone and to ensure protection from attack and, possibly, death.

Anticipating release during 2001, Jon Venables and Robert Thompson applied to the High Court, seeking four injunctions protecting their new identities on release and withholding information concerning changes in physical appearance, location and their time inside the secure units. In January 2001 Dame Elizabeth Butler Sloss delivered her judgment. The defendants comprised three influential news groups that argued freedom of expression as a primary right. They considered anonymity to be against the public interest, in that people had a 'right to know' who was living in their neighbourhood. They also considered that any threats directed against the boys should be processed through the criminal justice system and not by injunctions. The case, the media interests argued, set a precedent in which 'the more detestable the crime, the greater the claim to anonymity'. They did not consider it desirable that former prisoners convicted of serious offences should be encouraged to 'live a lie'. Finally, they proposed that the media should be trusted to report the case accurately and responsibly.

Butler Sloss weighed 'a public interest that confidences should be preserved' against 'a countervailing interest favouring disclosure'. The core of the case was the balance to be struck between Article 10 of the ECHR, the right to freedom of expression, and Article 2, the right to life protected by law. Butler Sloss noted that freedom of speech constituted the 'lifeblood of democracy', providing a 'brake on the abuse of power by officials'. In guaranteeing the 'right to say things that "right thinking people" regard as dangerous or irresponsible' the 'press needs to be free of governmental and judicial control'. Any impediment on Article 10 had to be supported by 'cogent grounds recognised by law'. Under Article 2, however, the state had a duty to 'take appropriate steps to safeguard the lives of those within its jurisdiction' and its institutions 'must act if there is a real and immediate threat to life'. Two further articles also were relevant: Article 3, protection against inhuman or degrading treatment, and Article 8, respect for private or family life.

Butler Sloss stated: 'The most important issue by far is the assessment of the risk to each claimant if his identity and whereabouts were to be discovered when he leaves the secure unit and lives in the community.' In making an assessment of risk she relied on evidence from the secure units, including potential damage to their full rehabilitation and the 'relentless pressure' that had been exerted by the media on the units, that showed 'no signs of abating'. She also noted the boys' families had been forced to move home on several occasions. She listed 18 significant threats, including the following from James Bulger's family: 'The streets won't be safe' (Uncle); 'I have sworn to go looking for them ... after their blood' (Mother); 'We can't stop now and let these two animals be released. I will hunt them down' (Father). Butler Sloss quoted the *Mirror*'s claim that they 'would be lynched and no-one would shed a tear' for they 'took a baby's life, why should they have a life of their own?'

In drawing her conclusions, Butler Sloss accepted that the killing of James Bulger was 'truly horrific' and 'exceptionally cruel' and the subsequent climate surrounding the case had made sentencing difficult. Jon Venables and Robert Thompson were 'uniquely notorious'. Given the context and their reputations she considered that the media was 'uniquely placed to provide the information that would lead to the risk that others would take the law into their own hands', as there was a 'real possibility of revenge attacks'. The 'detection of the future identity in the community' of the young men on release constituted the 'single most important element of the case'. Thus, any information received in confidence should be preserved under Article 10 but connected to the 'safeguard of physical safety' in a case where there was a demonstrable possibility of 'fatal consequences'. She did not believe that the case set a precedent, as it extended the law in an exceptional case and future cases would have to demonstrate their uniqueness. She maintained that the media had not only shown an interest in the case but had demonstrated continued hostility. Reporting had not been restricted to facts but had extended into the initiation of events, particularly *The Sun*'s coupon campaign and the *News of the World*'s 'naming and shaming' campaign directed against alleged paedophiles. On this basis promises of 'editorial constraint' could not be trusted and the proposition of adequate remedies in law would be too late after any event. Butler Sloss concluded:

> From all the evidence provided to me, I have come to a clear conclusion that if the new identity of these claimants became public knowledge it would have disastrous consequences for the claimants, not only from intrusion and harassment but, far more important, the real possibility of serious physical harm and possible death from vengeful members of the public or from the Bulger family. If their new identities were discovered, I am satisfied that neither of them would have any chance of a normal life and that there is a real and strong possibility that their lives would be at risk.

Inevitably, the Butler Sloss ruling was reported prominently in the press. The *Independent* considered it the 'right decision' taken in the context of a tabloid press 'whose cant, hypocrisy, and vengefulness have few equals anywhere' (9 January 2001). Writing in the same edition under the headline 'A brutal crime in a brutal society', Deborah Orr argued that in 'whipping up' public hostility an 'irresponsible media' had 'made this injunction so very necessary'. Sections of the media 'do not flinch from promoting hate campaigns ... inciting people to take the law into their own hands'. What had been generated was a 'lynch-mob mentality'. She also criticised the parlous state of young offenders' institutions, so 'brutal' that the boys could not be transferred. In response to a 'balanced and humane' ruling, former *Mirror* editor Roy Greenslade noted the 'utterly disgraceful ... scream of rage' from newspapers who 'sought to gloss their bloodthirsty cries of vengeance by casting themselves as champions of the public interest' (*Guardian*, 9 January 2001). The concerted attempt to gain disclosure 'showed a streak of venality, even barbarism, which besmirches Britain's press'. Noting that both boys had shown 'deep remorse' the *Daily Express* (9 January 2001) concluded:

> Only a misguided and dangerous desire for vigilante vengeance would be served by revealing the details of the boys' new lives. If the court had pandered to the sickening baying for blood that has surrounded this case, we would have returned, in effect, to the savage days of the lynch mob.

Predictably, given its singling out by Butler Sloss, the *Sun* broke a front page 'exclusive': 'LUXURY LIFE OF BULGER KILLERS'. The 'boy killers' had 'led an amazing life of luxury since being caged', resulting in a 'whopping £1.6 million' being 'lavished'. The story continued: 'Tax payers have footed the bill for plush rooms with VIDEOS and TRIPS to the seaside as well as for the finest EDUCATION money can buy ... they have had the kind of privileged upbringing – including one-to-one tuition – their poverty stricken families could only dream of. Former truant Thompson has passed five GCSEs and is studying for his A levels'. Computers were 'state of the art', family visits were 'unlimited', rooms were 'comfortable, well-furnished' and diets were 'healthy, well-balanced tailored to their individual needs'. The cost was estimated as 'ten times' the fees at Eton. In a similar vein, the *Daily Mail* (9 January 2001) considered that Butler Sloss's judgment 'mocks justice' in that 'the more heinous the crime the greater the courts' indulgence towards the perpetrators'.

This coverage drew an intended response from those whose loved ones had been killed by violent acts. The spokesperson for Mothers against Murder and Aggression stated:

> It is an utter scandal that these two wicked and twisted thugs have been treated as if they are a pair of victims themselves. They have enjoyed lifestyles far more beneficial and comfortable than if they had never been involved in James Bulger's murder. What kind of society takes two boys responsible for such an appalling and cruel act and showers them with care and attention? The way that these two have been treated, you would have thought that they were a pair of angels ... this sends out a message to youngsters that crime DOES pay – and that it pays very well.
>
> (*The Sun*, 9 January 2001)

Denise Fergus, James Bulger's mother, was 'disgusted by the special treatment these two now get at every turn'. It made her 'blood run cold to think they are being patted on the back and rewarded after the cruel, pre-meditated murder they carried out'. It remained a 'comfort' knowing 'they will always be haunted and hunted and will never be able to live in peace' (*Liverpool Daily Post*, 9 January 2001). At the time of their release in June 2001 the *Daily Star* denounced their eight years in prison as a 'sick joke', arguing that it 'sticks in the throat that Thompson and Venables will get new lives, paid for at a huge price from the public purse' (23 June 2001). The *Star* quoted Denise Fergus as saying that the 'murderers have walked away with a life of luxury'. The Government and the Parole Board had been 'sucked in by two devious murderers ... '

Interpreting the 'backlash'

What was so disturbing about the unfolding aftermath of James Bulger's killing was the strength of the backlash against progressive and successful developments in education, youth work, youth justice and child welfare. It assumed a 'loss of decency', 'corrupted innocence', 'ill-discipline', 'law-lessness', 'nastiness', 'barbarism' and 'moral malaise' generated by 'dis-membered families' and educational decline. A review of the reactionary media and political debate, highlights that the aligned processes of marginalisation and demonisation were tangible. As the venom was released in newspaper articles and through broadcast features, the underlying ideology was palpable, quickly translated into academic discourse and criminal justice policy.

Three pre-eminent trends were discernible within this dominant, adult ideology. First was the reaffirmation of idealised childhood combining 'innocence', 'protection' and 'inexperience'. Not innocence, protection and inexperience as positive constructions in the negotiation of personal and social development, but as negative conditions better described as ignorance (innocence), dependency (protection) and silence (inexperience). The language of risk and danger, seemingly 'protecting' children by taking them off the street, fearful of 'strangers', under the presumption that 'home and family' is a place of safety and security, ignores or denies the reality of risk and danger for many children. Defining children as inexperienced or limited in their understanding of the worlds they occupy effectively silences them. Lack of consultation dominates the private and public domains that contextualise children's lives, reminding them that active participation in the decisions that define their destiny, including establishing the parameters of 'best interest', is for adults only. Meanwhile there has been virtually no progress in tackling poverty, structural unemployment and homelessness, the material conditions that also constitute experiential dynamics of harm for children and young people.

The second trend was the reconstitution of adult authority underpinned by the powerful adult construction that, left to their own devices, children would be barbarous and wild. Much of what was written around the

Bulger case referred to William Golding's *Lord of the Flies*, as if it could be relied on as an empirical cautionary tale. It was a remarkable irony, given the apparently insatiable appetite that much of the adult, patriarchal world has for violence, brutality, war and destruction. In its operation, adult authority assumes legitimacy for 'prevention', 'discipline' and 'correction'. These are presented as negative constructs. Prevention is manifested as surveillance: the child monitored, assessed and classified from the earliest age. Discipline becomes subservience: an unquestioning, passive, silent child – a child under threat, under curfew. Correction rarely means anything but punishment – the realisation of the threat. Within schools, for example, statementing, suspension and exclusion are each elements of a continuum of correction. At the same time, there is a continuing call for a return to corporal punishment administered on the basis of 'just deserts'. But the real harm of correction is endured in the secure units, young offenders' institutions and US-style boot camps where the fine line separating 'hard discipline' from physical force is routinely crossed.

The third trend, and probably most contentious as a 'category' in itself, was the ideological whiff of child hate. As stated earlier, unlike racism, misogyny and homophobia, there is no recognisable parallel depicting the systemic and interpersonal prevalence of harm, abuse, degradation, exploitation, fear, rejection and exclusion suffered by children in their daily encounters with adult worlds. Children's pain makes news only when cases are so extreme, the brutality so callous, that they shock. The climate of fear, the rituals of degradation and the calculus of violence are most accurately interpreted and understood as a continuum. In the chastisement of children, the administration of physical punishment, it is adults who decide on degree, necessity and appropriateness. This is the prerogative of adult authority. Adults alone, particularly in the private domain, draw the line of legitimacy within the continuum. So prevalent is the assumption of the 'right' to define that the state intervenes at its peril.

Child hate not only has a presence in the physicality inherent in the punishment and sexual abuse of children, it emerges as a powerful expression, unwitting maybe, of adult hegemony. The images constructed by the vocabulary of demonisation and condemnation are rooted in a disdain for children as active participants in their own destinies; by a fear of children's rights as challenging adult authority and, ultimately, adult power. While that power is usually interpreted as legitimated in the two interrelated but distinct domains of the 'public' and the 'private', the reassertion of adult power also operates at both structural and social levels and through the pre-eminent institutions of the state and the family. Adult power is imposed without negotiation or consultation. It amounts to a dominant and dominating ideology supporting a politics of adultism. Legitimated, reinforced and reproduced through professional discourses, adultism is expressed via a language of exclusion and denial, confirming children and young people as outsiders; the 'other' to adult essentialism.

Obviously, not all shifts in the law, in policy or in professional guidelines are to be interpreted as manifestations of child hate or can be reduced to being no more than the outcome of some universal adult conspiracy. The relationship between structure and agency is more complex than that. Yet, as this chapter has shown, political and interventionist agendas set by the perceived 'crisis' in childhood are reactive, authoritarian and persistent. Together they reduce to and regress into a political backlash, disregarding the advances in children's rights. It is ironic that the renewal of open authoritarianism occurred during the same period that the ritualised, rather than ritual, abuse of children in local authority homes, church schools and young offenders' institutions was revealed. At a time when the British government found itself before the European Court in a concerted attempt to reinstate corporal punishment in private schools. At a time when bullying, 'taxing', self-harm and suicide of young men and women in custody reached unprecedented levels. And at a time when the age of criminal responsibility was lowered, thus feeding the rising spiral of incarceration, already exceptional in the western European context.

In this climate, how easily tabloid journalism became conflated with sound-bite academia. Following publication of the Gulbenkian Foundation's 1995 report of the independent Commission on Children and Violence, 'leading psychologist' Professor Richard Lynn, long-time proponent of physical punishment, stated: 'The objective of the commission is to abolish the last sanction on badly behaved children – the right of parents to administer physical punishment ... the result will be a further breakdown of law and order and yet more crime' (*Daily Express*, 10 November 1995). On the same day, *The Sun* editorial unsurprisingly gave its unreserved support for familial violence in terms close to Lynn's position: 'A gentle smack teaches a child there are punishments for those who break the rules ... listen to the do-gooders and children will just run wild'. As Muncie (1999a: 44–5) concludes:

> If adolescence is viewed as a period in which young people are deprived and deficient of standards of morality and discipline, then it is appropriate to treat their condition through systems of supervision, guidance, training and support ... if adolescence is viewed as a period in which youth is essentially depraved and dangerous then interventions requiring a formal criminal justice response are legitimized ... Given the limited discourses of danger, depravity and deficiency that routinely surround the 'youth problem' non-intervention is rendered unthinkable.

In the case of Robert Thompson and Jon Venables an exceptional and deeply troubling case was mobilised politically as a moral panic over 'threatening children' to divert the direction of progressive reform. It was not simply a 'threat' in the physical sense, although that remained a persistent theme in much of the media and political coverage. More significantly, it was perceived as a threat to adult authority and hegemony. Meanwhile, the structural and social relations through which adult power is maintained and reproduced remain intact. While not all manifestations of this power relation, either unwittingly or in intent, are negative, it is a power routinely and systematically abused.

7   'Asbo-mania': the regulation and criminalisation of children and young people

In 1997 I was invited to a public meeting called to discuss crime, particularly involving young people, in Skelmersdale New Town. It was part of a rushed 'consultation process' set up by the recently elected New Labour government to discuss the contents of the proposed Crime and Disorder Bill. I went with Paul Prescott, an outreach youth worker whom I had known for years. The meeting was chaired by a former academic colleague, the then MP for West Lancashire. No children or young people had been invited. The evening very quickly turned into an unrelenting attack on 'kids', 'yobs' and 'thugs'. Paul and I raised the problems and issues faced by children and young people in the community, including the easy availability of drugs and alcohol and police harassment. We were shouted down and roundly condemned as 'do-gooders'. My attempt to discuss the media-infused public outcry around children and young people was mocked. A month later I addressed the annual meeting of North-West Emergency Social Workers on 'current developments in youth justice'. Only one person in the room knew of the Crime and Disorder Bill. I discussed its content, particularly focusing on the punitive potential of curfews, parenting orders and antisocial behaviour orders. There was disbelief among participants and a refusal by some to accept that what appeared to be welfare-oriented, diversionary measures could be interpreted as net-widening and criminalising.

As the 1998 Crime and Disorder Act was introduced I initiated research focusing particularly on the introduction of antisocial behaviour orders. Working together, Julie Read and I witnessed the pressures experienced by local authority officers to issue ASBOs, the lack of protection afforded by the courts and the 'naming and shaming' of children by the media. Subsequent qualitative research into early intervention programmes in a north-western town demonstrated clearly how a criminal justice ethos remained at the heart of preventive and supposedly restorative interventions. Yet the 'antisocial behaviour' bandwagon rolled on, gaining momentum and eventually fusing into the Labour government's 'respect agenda'.

Law 'n' order: the Blair project

In June 2006 the UK Prime Minister spoke on the 'future' of the nation and criminal justice as 'the culmination of a personal journey' (Blair 2006: 85). Representing the interests of 'ordinary, decent law-abiding folk' (ibid.: 86), who 'play by the rules' (ibid.: 92), he bemoaned the 'absence of a proper, considered intellectual and political debate' on liberty and the urgent need for a 'rational' return to 'first principles' (ibid.: 87). Critical analyses from left-leaning academics amounted to 'intellectual convulsions' proposing recidivism as 'entirely structural'. The 'political right' considered crime 'entirely a matter of individual wickedness'. Between these extremes 'rational' analysis had emerged, the 'conventional position' of 'New Labour' (ibid.: 89). To achieve its mission a 'complete change of mindset' was required, an 'avowed, articulated determination to make protection of the law-abiding public the priority' measured 'not by the theory of the textbook but by the reality of the street and community in which real people live real lives' (ibid.: 93). Despite calling for an informed, intellectual debate, Blair caricatured those researching and working in communities as theorists detached from reality.

Blair noted the dissolution of society's 'moral underpinning' (ibid.: 88) and the abandonment of the 'fixed order community' (ibid.: 89) through 'loosened ... ties of home', changes in 'family structure', increased divorce rates, single-person households and a reduction in the 'disciplines of informal control'. New Labour's 'tough on crime' agenda has been driven consistently by a moral imperative embodying dubious assumptions that, traditionally, personal hardship was matched by collective benevolence. Men 'worked in settled occupations', women 'were usually at home' and social classes 'were fixed and defining of identity' (ibid.). They constituted the bedrock on which community spirit and civic responsibility were built, reproducing social discipline through 'informal codes of conduct and order' (ibid.: 88). This portrayal of law-abiding, compliant and responsible communities socialising children into the values of decency, obedience and respect does not bear scrutiny.

The tone and content of Blair's carefully choreographed 'swansong' law and order speech to the September 2006 Labour Party Conference, delivered with a touch of arrogance, remained solidly consistent. Four years earlier he had described the 'Britain' inherited by New Labour: 'crime was rising, there was escalating family breakdown, and social inequalities had widened' (Blair 2002). Neighbourhoods were 'marked by vandalism, violent crime and the loss of civility'. The 'mutuality of duty' and the 'reciprocity of respect' had been lost; 'the moral fabric of community was unravelling'. The criminal justice system was outmoded, courts were slow and out of touch. Welfare considerations were prioritised over victims. An 'excuse culture' permeated youth justice. With police overburdened by peripheral duties, petty crime and antisocial behaviour had escalated.

Inter-agency initiatives were neither efficient nor effective and punishments no longer reflected the seriousness of offences.

Blair's persistent message affirmed the primary responsibility of parents and other individuals in achieving safe communities, reducing crime and protecting law-abiding citizens. Taking responsibility for challenging inti- midatory and abusive behaviour would secure a return to 'informal con- trols' and safer, integrated communities. For Blair, community required 'responsibilities as well as entitlements' (Gould 1998: 234). Rights, including access to state support and benefits, were the flip-side of civic responsibilities; social transactions between the 'self' and others where self- respect is attained.

Children of the ghetto

At the time of James Bulger's tragic killing, Blair deplored the 'moral vacuum' prevalent throughout British society. Instructing children and their disaffected communities in 'the value of what is right and what is wrong' offered the only salvation from the sure descent into 'moral chaos'. Recent events, he continued, were 'hammer blows against the sleeping conscience of the nation'. The metaphor, in the circumstances insensitive and dis- tasteful, resonated with New Labour's spin doctors. Blair's high moral tone fitted perfectly into the manufactured and manipulated 'crises' in 'child- hood', 'the family' and 'community'.

Reflecting on that period, Barry Goldson (1997: 129) notes the 'fer- menting body of opinion that juvenile justice in particular, and penal liberalism in general, had gone too far'. During the early 1990s a series of unrelated disturbances in towns throughout England and Wales raised the profile of youth offending. Media coverage focused on 'joyriding', 'ram-raiding', 'bail bandits' and 'persistent young offenders'. Senior police officers directed sustained pressure at government to address the 'issue' of repeat offending. As Goldson (ibid.: 130) states:

> A crude, reductionist assimilation of disparate behaviours was assem- bled and, in virtually no time, the consensus which had bound together over a decade of policy and practice developments began to crack. The conditions which would legitimise a complete repudiation of the prin- ciples of diversion, decriminalisation and decarceration and an explicit rejection of what had been the Government's position emerged at a furious pace.

In October 1993 the Secretary of State for Social Security Peter Lilley 'declared ... that while it had been considered politically incorrect to criticise the growth in unmarried motherhood, it was now time to break the taboo' (Durham 2001: 465). Home Secretary Michael Howard took Lilley's taboo breaking further, claiming that children 'without a male role model tended to be more aggressive and less likely to know the difference between right and wrong' (ibid.). Despite overwhelming evidence of the levels of harm inflicted within communities, particularly on women and children, by the violence of men, Conservative ministers maintained that children without contact with their fathers were ill disciplined, aggressive and irresponsible. Without any consideration of material circumstances, including lack of appropriate welfare support, 'single mothers' were characterised as incapable, amoral and nihilistic.

As the public debate rapidly degenerated and presumed a direct line of progression from low-level disruptive behaviour through to serious crime, a curious alliance between 'reactionary' and 'liberal' academics emerged. Charles Murray (1990), doyen of the New Right, argued that illegitimacy, violent crime and refusal to work provided structural foundations for the consolidation of an 'underclass'. In text reminiscent of turn-of-the-century commentaries on 'unemployables' and 'idlers', Murray's underclass was a rapidly expanding population 'stuck at the bottom of society because of its own self-destructive behaviour, lured on by well-intentioned reforms gone bad' (Murray 1994a: 10). In Murray's portrayal, 'illegitimacy' provided the 'best predictor of an underclass in the making' (Murray 1990: 4). All social problems were rooted in 'the continuing increase in births to single women' and families were destined 'to deteriorate among what the Victorians called the lower classes'. Using statistics compiled by British sociologist Patricia Morgan, he claimed a definitive link between 'illegitimacy' and a benefit system that 'rewards' unmarried parents and acts as a disincentive to paid work. In this scenario the underclass expands and its members choose neither marriage nor work. These social arrangements then become the learned behaviour of the next generation.

Children living in communities abandoned by fathers 'run wild' and become 'inordinately physical and aggressive in their relationship with other children' (Murray 1990: 12). Without fathers as 'role models', without nuclear families as social context, not only individuals, but entire communities are threatened with dislocation. Murray views young men as 'essentially barbarians' (1990: 23) who 'retaliate against anyone who shows the slightest disrespect ... sleep with and impregnate as many girls as possible' and promote 'violence as a sign of strength'. Their code is simple and frightening: 'To worry about tomorrow is a weakness. To die young is glorious ... inner-city boys articulate [these] as principles' (Murray 1994b: 12). They are reclaimed by the 'act of taking responsibility for a wife and children', the 'indispensable civilising force' at the heart of social order (ibid.: 23).

Murray (1994b: 12) questioned what might be expected of daily life in 'lower-class Britain'. His reply, based on 'observations and knowledge of the US underclass', was absolute:

> The New Rabble will be characterised by high levels of criminality, child neglect and abuse, and drug use. The New Rabble will exploit social benefit programmes imaginatively and comprehensively, and be impervious to social benefit programmes that seek to change their behaviour. They will not enter the legitimate labour force when economic times are good and will recruit more working-class young people to their way of life when economic times are bad. The children of the New Rabble will come to the school system undeveloped intellectually and unsocialised in the norms of considerate behaviour ... The New Rabble will provide a large and lucrative market for violent and pornographic film, television and music. Their housing blocks will be characterised by graffiti and vandalism, their parks will be venues for drugs and prostitution. They will not contribute their labour to local good works, and will not be good neighbours to each other ... the New Rabble will dominate, which will be enough to make life miserable for everyone else.

The end product, Murray predicted, would be a more segregated society in which 'sink estates' become no-go areas, welfare benefits 'sky-rocket', more girls become unmarried mothers, and the young male criminal population burgeons. He warned, 'British civility ... the original home of Western liberty ... is doomed' (ibid.: 13).

Going beyond Murray's underclass thesis, Halsey (1992) and Dennis and Erdos (1992) considered social breakdown more universal and far-reaching, although its components remained consistent: 'illegitimacy', 'dismembered families', rejection of the work ethic and spiralling crime. Starting from the premise that the traditional family established a 'coherent strategy for the ordering of social relations ... to equip children for their own eventual adult responsibilities', the 'breakdown' in family life had resulted in 'the emergence of a new type of young male ... weakly socialised and weakly socially controlled so far as the responsibilities of spousehood and fatherhood are concerned' (Halsey 1992: xiii). Thus the patriarchal pressure 'to be a responsible adult in a functioning community' had collapsed.

Dennis and Erdos (1992: 27) considered the demise of 'responsible fathers' to be crucial. Young men, they argued, 'no longer take it for granted that they will be responsible' for children. According to Dennis (1993: 69), 'cumulative evidence from common experience and statistical evidence' affirms 'beyond doubt the superiority, for the children and for the rest of society, of the family with two publicly and successfully committed natural parents'. Quoting directly Barbara Defoe Whitehead's words in *The Atlantic Monthly*, Dennis continued, 'family diversity in the form of single-parent and step-parent families does not strengthen the social fabric but ... dramatically weakens and undermines society' (ibid.: 70). For Dennis and Erdos (1992: 107) a 'new generation of feminists', in association with Marxist intellectuals, had embarked on 'a long march through the institutions', arriving at 'the family, altruistic anarchism, hedonistic nihilism'. This subversive process had 'weaken[ed] the link between sex, procreation, childcare, child-rearing and loyalty in the lifelong provision on a non-commercial basis of mutual care within a common place of residence'.

Pivotal to the polemics of Murray and the ethical socialists was the 'interlinking of "welfare dependency", single parenthood, undisciplined children and crime in an unbroken causal chain' (Carlen 1998: 71). They relied on, and promoted, a gendered imagery of 'disease and infection' providing a popular front to the underlying reactionary theories of moral degeneracy and social pathology. They reaffirmed a 'long tradition in which misogyny has combined with exploitative class relationships to ensure that "undeserving" poor women have been represented in both life and literature as being especially invidious bearers of moral and social contagion' (ibid.). As Pat Carlen records, the early 1990s folk devil of 'unattached youth' provoked 'penal fantasies – from hard labour for ten-year-olds, to bringing back corporal and capital punishments' (ibid.: 6). Alongside stood a second folk devil: 'single mothers – to be deterred from the single state by punitive changes in welfare and housing legislation'.

Bullen *et al.* (2000: 453) note that in a media context dominated by 'almost incessant, compulsive, prurient probing of those found guilty of any excess', the young single mother cut an 'abiding deviant figure' in the 'contemporary civic and political landscape'. She was represented as the 'sexual wanton' and 'welfare cheat' generating 'alarms and excursions over "teenage pregnancy"'. Violent and disruptive behaviour of boys, their persistent offending and lack of social responsibility, was laid at the door of 'fatherless families', the young, 'permissive' and 'never-married mothers' were held responsible (Carlen 1998:7). The 'old notion that all crime is explicable in terms of family structure and parenting' was re-established, 'together with the older calumny that women are the roots of all evil' (ibid.). In misrepresenting the 'harsh reality of single parenting' and 'further stigmatis[ing] an already stigmatised and alienated group' the 'moral agenda informing New Labour's social justice and education policy making' raised the 'possibility of illiberalism and neglect of the underprivileged' (Bullen *et al.* 2000: 453). Pat Carlen (1998: 7) is less equivocal. The renewed 'punitiveness' in family policy, she argues, was constructed around deep-rooted, institutional practices that already treated 'single mothers' harshly, thus consolidating a 'malign influence through the criminal justice and penal systems'.

The connection between Murray's under-researched yet assertive social commentary and the observations of the 'ethical socialists' is not a crude or forced representation formulated by critical reviewers. In his 1994 retrospective on the 'underclass' Murray lauded his new-found allies as 'courageous social scientists' prepared to speak their 'empirical' minds over 'illegitimacy'. He feigned disbelief that their critics could possibly dispute that 'the two-parent family is a superior environment for the nurturing of children' (Murray 1994b: 12). The right-wing Institute of Economic Affairs published Murray (1990), Dennis (1993), Dennis and Erdos (1992) and Halsey (1992). Its Director, David Green (1993: viii) called for the 'correction of fundamentals' through the restoration of 'the ideal two-parent family, supported by ... the extended family'. It was a version of the family as the primary 'civilising force', with 'dismembered' or 'dysfunctional' families classified through the affirmation of moral absolutes, regardless of material circumstance or structural inequality. This line of moral reductionism dominated the 'childhood debate' in the UK during the early 1990s. It was presented as a challenge to the post-1960s nihilists and hedonists, who were considered selfishly responsible for tolerating and excusing 'barbarism' and 'lawlessness' among children and young people.

'Who are you calling antisocial?'

> Property owners, residents, retailers, manufacturers, town planners, school authorities, transport managers, employers, parents and individual citizens – all of these must be made to recognize that they too have a responsibility [for preventing and controlling crime], and must be persuaded to change their practices in order to reduce criminal opportunities and increase informal controls.
>
> (Garland 1996: 445)

However clumsy the term, 'responsibilisation' carries a simple message. According to David Garland the state alone cannot, nor should it be expected to, deliver safe communities in which levels of crime and fear of crime are significantly reduced and potential victims are afforded protection. While private organisations, public services and property owners take measures to tackle opportunistic crime, thus turning private security provision into one of the most lucrative contemporary service industries, in addressing prevention the 'buck stops' with parents and individual citizens. Civil rights, including rights of access to state support, intervention and benefits, are presented as the flip-side of civic responsibilities. Being responsible for challenging intimidatory behaviour, small-scale disorder and criminal activity is part of a network of 'informal controls' contributing towards safer and more cohesive communities.

At the hub of this idealised notion of 'community' is the relationship between families and inter-agency partnerships working towards common, agreed social objectives. The live connection between a new form of communitarianism and the liberal tradition of shared responsibility underpinned the much-vaunted 'Third Way' politics of Clinton's Democrats and Blair's New Labour. It was a politics in which core values and principles were derived in mutually beneficial and benevolent social transactions between the 'self' and others; 'others' being the mirror in which self-respect is reflected, an image made tangible through 'communitarianism'.

Within this process of reclamation – itself a form of moral renewal – crime is a betrayal of the self and a betrayal of the immediate social relations of family and community. The corrective for crime – however petty – and for disruptive or disorderly behaviours, is two-dimensional. First, affirming culpability and responsibility through the due, presumed fair, process of criminal justice – from apprehension to punishment incorporating the expectations of retribution and remorse. Second, the reconstruction of and support for the proven values of positive families and strong communities.

Hard on the heels of the 1997 general election, the new Home Secretary, Jack Straw, commented: 'Today's young offenders can too easily become tomorrow's hardened criminals' supported by 'an excuse culture [which] has developed within the youth justice system' (*The Guardian*, 28 November 1997). It was an inefficient system that 'often excuses young offenders who come before it, allowing them to go on wasting their own and wrecking other people's lives'. Parents 'are not confronted with their responsibilities' and 'offenders are rarely asked to account for themselves'. Straw's message was unambiguous: victims are disregarded, the public is excluded. He reiterated four key elements held dear by his Conservative predecessors. First, when tolerated or indulged, children's disruptive and offensive behaviour leads inevitably to their graduation into serious and repetitive crimes. Second, within the community the primary responsibility for regulating and policing such behaviour, referred to by Garland as 'informal controls', rests with parents. Third, professionals entrusted with initiating purposeful, correctional interventions had betrayed that trust, excusing unacceptable levels of behaviour and their own lack of effectiveness. Fourth, existing processes and procedures over-represent the needs and rights of perpetrators while under-representing victims. Few political commentators were surprised that Straw shouldered the well-worn authoritarian mantle. A year earlier, while unfolding a vote-catching law and order strategy, Straw had promised an increase in secure accommodation for young offenders and 'curfews for 10-year-olds' (*Sunday Times*, 18 August 1996).

Straw's broadside against the youth justice system and its workers drew support from other sources. Just eight months before the 1997 election the Audit Commission (1996) criticised the youth justice system as expensive, inefficient, inconsistent and ineffective. Its controller, Andrew Foster, commented that the 'cycle of antisocial behaviour that has become a day-to-day activity' could be broken only through a 'systematic overhaul' of youth justice (*The Guardian*, 21 November 1996). Objectives for attention were clear: 'inadequate parenting; aggressive and hyperactive behaviour in early childhood; truancy and exclusion from school; peer group pressure; unstable living conditions; lack of training and employment; drug and alcohol abuse' (Audit Commission 1996: 3).

From within the prevailing political rhetoric, now endorsed by the independent Audit Commission, emerged the ubiquitous and conveniently elastic term, 'antisocial behaviour'. Its new-found status quickly consolidated as *the* key issue. As journalists, academics and practitioners sought a more precise definition, the fledgling government obliged with a less-than-precise definition via a rushed consultation document ahead of a Crime and Disorder Bill. Antisocial behaviour, stated the document, was that which 'causes harassment to a community; amounts to antisocial criminal conduct, or is otherwise antisocial; disrupts the peaceful and quiet enjoyment of a neighbourhood by others; intimidates a community or section of it' (Local Government Information Unit, 1997). It was a triumph of 'definition by committee'. The slide between 'criminal conduct' and 'antisocial behaviour' was embedded in the ambiguity of 'otherwise'. It was a definition open to broad interpretation and subject to conveniently wide discretion in its enforcement; a definition in the mind's eye of the beholder.

In response to the consultation, several established academics collectively attacked the conceptualisation of antisocial behaviour as 'neither sensible nor carefully targeted'. Ashworth *et al.* (1998: 7) condemned the proposed legislation for taking 'sweepingly defined conduct within its ambit', granting 'local agencies virtually unlimited discretion to seek highly restrictive orders', jettisoning 'fundamental legal protections for the granting of these orders', while authorising 'potentially draconian and wholly disproportionate penalties for violations'. Despite such opposition, the 1998 Crime and Disorder Act (CDA) became law within a year, obliging local authorities to present a crime strategy derived in a crime and disorder audit involving consultation with local communities, 'hard to reach' groups and all public sector agencies. It placed a responsibility on statutory agencies to participate in the operational planning, realisation and evaluation of local strategies.

It also established a framework for the much-trailed 'overhaul' of youth justice. With the principal aim of youth justice stated as the prevention of offending, including repeat offending, the CDA placed a duty on local authorities to ensure availability of 'appropriate' youth justice services, including provision of 'appropriate adults'; assessment and rehabilitation; bail support; remand placements; reports and community sentence; and post-custody supervisions. The CDA also introduced a national Youth Justice Board, obliging local authorities to establish multi-agency Youth Offending Teams (YOTs) working to annually reviewed Youth Justice Plans. In addition to the reconstruction of youth justice, the CDA abolished the presumption of *doli incapax*, allowing courts to draw inferences from the failure of an accused child to give evidence or refusal to answer questions at trial.

Parenting Orders would provide 'help and support ... in addressing a child's offending behaviour' through the restoration of 'a *proper relationship* between the child and its parent or guardian' (UK Government 1999: 181). In this process, counselling sessions instructed parents on 'how to set and enforce acceptable standards and behaviour' (ibid.). Child Safety Orders, directed at children under 10, were 'early intervention measure[s] designed to prevent children being drawn into crime' through offering 'an early opportunity to intervene positively in an appropriate and proportionate way to protect the welfare of the child' (ibid.). Child Curfews targeted 'unsupervised children gathered in public places at night' who were considered 'too young to be out alone' and who 'cause alarm or misery to local communities and encourage each other into antisocial and criminal habits' (ibid.: 182).

The most immediately contentious initiative, however, was the Anti-Social Behaviour Order (ASBO). A community-based civil injunction applied for by the police or the local authority, each in consultation with the other, could be taken against an individual or a group of individuals whose behaviour was considered 'antisocial'. Applications were made to the magistrates' court, acting in its adult jurisdiction and in its civil function. Professional witnesses could be called and hearsay evidence admitted. ASBOs were promoted as preventive measures targeting 'persistent and serious' antisocial behaviour. Antisocial behaviour was defined as 'acting in a manner that caused or is likely to cause distress to one or more persons not in the same household as himself [*sic*]'. Guidelines stated that 'prohibitions in the order must be such as are necessary to protect people from further antisocial acts by the defendant in the locality', targeting 'criminal or sub-criminal behaviour, or minor disputes' (*CDA Introductory Guide*, Section 1). Breach of the order without 'reasonable excuse' was a criminal offence. The guidelines stated that ASBOs would 'be used mainly against adults' (ibid.). This was affirmed by the UK Government's (1999) submission to the UN Committee on the Rights of the Child, in which it set out recent changes in legislation regarding children. While all other CDA orders were disclosed and their impact assessed, the ASBO was omitted.

Given that the CDA concentrated heavily on the criminal and disorderly behaviour of 10 to 18-year-olds, and was the vehicle through which youth justice was structurally reconfigured, it is unsurprising that it came to be viewed as legislation concerned primarily with the regulation and criminalisation of children and young people. The UK Government's 1999 submission to the UN Committee stated 'it is not unjust or unreasonable to assume that a child aged 10 or older can understand the difference between serious wrong and simple naughtiness'. But, it proposed, for children lacking 'this most basic moral understanding, it is all the more imperative that appropriate intervention and rehabilitation should begin as soon as possible' (ibid.: 180).

'Serious wrong' and 'simple naughtiness' were presented as opposite ends of a spectrum, yet no acknowledgement was made of the complexities of understanding, experience and interpretation that lie between. Also significant were issues of premeditation, intent and spontaneity. As Haydon and Scraton (2000: 429) state, '[r]educing these complexities, difficult to disentangle at any age, to simple opposites in the minds of young children amounts to incredible naivety or purposeful misrepresentation'. Further, the courts were proposed as 'the site most appropriate to intervene and rehabilitate'. Yet, the UK Government (1999: 180) stated that 'emphasis is firmly placed not on criminalizing children, but on helping them to recognise and accept responsibility for their actions and enabling them to receive help to change their offending behaviour'.

The combination of major institutional change in youth justice, new civil injunctions – particularly ASBOs – the removal of *doli incapax* and the right to silence and an expansion in secure units sealed the Labour government's intent to 'out-tough' its predecessors. As Johnston and Bottomley (1998: 177) state, while 'the Conservatives talked tough, it is Labour that introduced stringent measures such as child curfews, antisocial behaviour orders and parenting orders'. The result was a 'regulatory–disciplinary approach to crime prevention, combined with "welfarist" assistance to help people meet its standards'. What the CDA exemplified was the tangible outcome of New Labour's law and order rhetoric: 'an amalgam of "get tough" authoritarian measures with elements of paternalism, pragmatism, communitarianism, responsibilization and remoralization' (Muncie 1999a: 169). It was delivered, using the language and theory of 'risk', through a 'burgeoning new managerialism whose new depth and legal powers might best be described as "coercive corporatism"' (ibid.).

Allen (1999: 22) identified the net-widening potential of targeting antisocial behaviour alongside an increasingly 'coercive approach of zero-tolerance policing' interventions, leading to the promotion rather than eradication of 'social exclusion'. Thus, the 'promise of speedier trials, new teams and panels to monitor action plans, "restorative justice" and the inadequacies of the pre-1998 system' were the justification for the CDA, but academics and practitioners voiced concerns about 'its potential for net-widening, over control, lack of safeguards and what one can only call "joined-up labelling"' (Downes 2001: 9). Goldson (2000: 52) put it more strongly: 'Early intervention, the erosion of legal safeguards and concomitant criminalisation' had been 'packaged as a courtesy to the child'. Yet it was an intervention that 'promotes prosecution ... violates rights and, in the final analysis will serve only to criminalise the most structurally vulnerable children'.

Introduced without providing evidence of the 'graduation' of 'at risk' children and young people into crime, ASBOs received 'a degree of political backing out of all proportion to their potential to reduce crime and disorder', while the 'demonisation' of parents through Parenting Orders could only 'exacerbate a situation' that was 'already complex and strained' (Hester 2000: 166, 171). Hester accurately predicted ASBOs would be used primarily in 'poor communities' and 'by definition they will thus be disproportionately deployed' (ibid.: 172). Further, the regulation of children and parents within the most politically and economically marginal neighbourhoods placed an expectation on people to take responsibility in social and material contexts where they were least able to cope. As Pitts (2001: 140) reflects, the 'managerial annexation of youth justice social work ... effectively transformed [social workers] into agents of the legal system, preoccupied with questions of "risk", "evidence" and "proof", rather than "motivation", "need" and "suffering"'. In interpreting the Labour government's swift delivery of the CDA and its concentration on ASBOs, Gardner *et al.* (1998: 25) noted the contradiction in 'tackling social exclusion' while passing legislation 'destined to create a whole new breed of outcasts'.

Within a year, Jack Straw strongly criticised local authorities for failing to implement child curfews and ASBOs, thus intensifying pressure on local authorities to establish antisocial behaviour initiatives. Newly appointed or seconded staff, often under-trained and poorly managed, were impelled into using ASBOs without having the time or opportunity to plan appropriately for their administration or consequences. Local antisocial behaviour co-ordinators were reluctant to zealously seek ASBOs. Yet the political dynamics were considerable:

> There was massive pressure on us. We needed an ASBO. The [area] hadn't had one and the Chief Executive was on the case all the time. The police hadn't had one, the Council hadn't had one, so we had to get one.
>
> (Interview, 2002)

The investment in and success of the antisocial behaviour unit was tied to:

> how many evictions I get and how many antisocial behaviour orders, injunctions and how many notices seeking possessions I serve. It always gets in the paper and I know that's how my bosses think I'm doing my job well ... the more evictions and antisocial behaviour orders I get, the better I'm doing.
>
> (Interview, 2002)

ASBOs soon became a classic example of net-widening through which children and young people who previously would have been cautioned were elevated to the first rung of criminalisation's ladder. The vindictiveness of local media, alongside the triumphalism of local councillors and their officers, provide dramatic illustrations of the public humiliation associated with authoritarian policies conveyed through sensationalist reporting.

As had happened throughout the trial and incarceration of Jon Venables and Robert Thompson, the national media promoted the debate over children and antisocial behaviour, regularly running news stories and features that exploited the absence of reporting restrictions. Liverpool's first ASBO was served on a disruptive 13-year-old. On 5 June 2002 the *Liverpool Echo* dedicated its entire front page to the case. A large photograph of the child's face was placed alongside a banner headline: 'THUG AT 13'. Within a month he was sentenced to eight months for his third breach of the ASBO. Also in June 2002 the *Wigan Reporter* gave its front page to a 'mini menace' who was to be 'sent on a trip to a remote Scottish island' where 'there was nothing to break and nothing to steal'. The headline read 'COUNCIL FUND SCOTTISH TRIP FOR A TINY TERROR'. The caption under the colour photograph named the 13-year-old, stating: 'The youngster leaves court, pretending to play the flute with his screwed-up anti-social court order'.

In West Lancashire the local newspaper ran the front page headline: 'FIRST YOBBO TO BE BARRED: Tough new line to stop louts terrorising neighbourhoods'. It published two photographs alongside 10 conditions imposed to end the 'yob's reign of terror'. Within a year he was imprisoned for breaching conditions. The local authority's Chief Executive wrote an open letter 'on behalf of all law-abiding citizens', thanking the local newspaper 'for again giving front-page coverage to the crusade against crime'. The 'jailing' had 'remove[d] from the streets an individual who appears to be hell-bent on causing mayhem and who appears to show no remorse'. Also, 'particularly because of the high profile coverage and the fact that the [newspaper's] editorial line has not minced words on this issue – we have sent out a message loud and clear to '[Name] Wannabies' that the community will not stand idly by watching their thuggery go unchecked'. A further case in the area, banning a brother and sister from the neighbourhood, was headlined 'STAY OUT!' and 'Taming two tearaways' (*Skelmersdale Advertiser*, 30 May 2002). Such cases were not exceptions. Children, neither charged with nor convicted of any criminal offence, were named and shamed ruthlessly. In each case, communities were invited to note the conditions attached to ASBOs and report any breach.

On 20 March 2002, the *Mirror* devoted the full front page to the photographs of two boys, aged 15 and 17. Above their faces ran the headline: 'REVEALED: The lawless teenagers who are laughing at us all. Every town has them'. Beneath the photographs, occupying a quarter of the page was the word 'VILE'. Under each photograph were boxes arrowed to the boys' faces: 'Ben, age 17 Crimes: 97'; 'Robert, age 15 Crimes: 98'. The distinction between 'crime' and 'antisocial behaviour' was not made and the two-page coverage inside the newspaper would not have been permitted had they been convicted of crimes.

On 17 February 2004, the *Daily Express* devoted its front page to the headline: 'TERRORISED BY GIRL GANG BOSS AGED 13. She led 50 hooligans on violent rampage'. Alongside the story, particularly significant because of her age and gender, was her photograph and name. Under the page 9 headline, 'High on glue, the teen gang leader who spread alarm and fear to a city', were the 12 conditions of her five-year ASBO. She was barred from: mixing with 42 named young people, 'the Leeds Town Crew'; using the terms 'Leeds Town Crew, 'LTC', 'TWOC Crew', 'GPT', 'Cash Money Boyz', or 'CMB', in any correspondence, spoken or written; areas of central Leeds, unless accompanied by parent, guardian, social or youth worker; travelling on buses, unless accompanied by parent or guardian; wearing a hood or scarf that might obscure her identity. As she left the court she pulled up her hood to guard against the press photographers and instantly breached her ASBO.

The *News of the World* (10 October 2004) took 'naming and shaming' to new depths in exposing a young child and his family to serious risks of reprisals. Across two inside pages it ran its 'Exclusive': 'Stefan is first 11-year-old to have Anti-Social Behaviour Order served on him'. A full-page photograph showed the child behind a driving wheel, the headline took up half a page: 'YOUNGEST THUG IN BRITAIN!' Alongside a 'stamp' marked 'OFFICIAL', it listed the 'Tiny tearaway's rap sheet from hell'. The list included: 'Theft'; 'Drugs'; 'Booze'; 'Arson'; 'Joy-riding'; 'Truancy'. It concluded: 'TOTAL NIGHTS LOCKED UP IN JAIL: 50'. On the opposite page was a photograph of Stefan seated with his mother and father and seven brothers and sisters. Under the heading 'Crowded house', Stefan's face and those of his parents were visible. The faces of the other children were pixellated to 'protect their identities'. The headline was condemnatory: 'Yob's jobless parents rake in equivalent of more than £40k a year'. The story-line was unforgiving: 'He's 11 years old – and terrifying. A swaggering little shoplifting, fireraising, joyriding, fighting, drinking, drug-taking, nightmare doted on by his benefit-sponging parents.'

While child-protection issues in Stefan's case are self-evident, the *News of the World* was fortified by 'three yobs' earlier in the week failing 'in a High Court bid to prove that publicity about their ASBOs had infringed their human rights'. This was a reference to the 'right to privacy challenge' brought by three claimants supported by the civil liberties' group Liberty, against the Metropolitan Police Commissioner, the London Borough of Brent and the Home Secretary over naming and shaming in a leaflet delivered throughout the borough. The Court held that where 'publicity was intended to inform, reassure, assist in enforcing the orders and deter others, it would not be effective unless it included photographs, names and partial addresses'. Local residents had experienced 'significant criminal behaviour' over an extended period, the individuals concerned were well known in the area and the publicity was central to ending their antisocial activities. The publicity's 'colourful language' was necessary to draw residents' attention to the issue. The claimants had been 'stopped, searched arrested and brought before the courts', yet they had 'continued with antisocial behaviour and defiance of authority' (quoted in *The Guardian*, 8 October 2004). According to the Leader of Brent Council, the judgment had been awaited with interest by local authorities throughout England and Wales. A Home Office spokesperson considered it supported the principle that 'publicity is necessary to help with the enforcement of an order'.

Intensifying the pressure

As the academic debate regarding 'responsibilisation' and 'communitarianism' continued, the 'responsible community' was mobilised in the public domain as a blunt instrument to regulate, marginalise and punish children whose behaviour was labelled antisocial. While local authorities remained inconsistent in their implementation of the new legislation, new interventionist initiatives continued to develop. The Government's Social Exclusion Unit, through its National Strategy for Neighbourhood Renewal, set targets for measurable reductions in antisocial behaviour. Central to this process was the Youth Justice Board's adoption of a Risk Factors Screening Tool 'suggested by research' (YJB/CYPU, 2002: 15–16). Local authority, multi-agency specialist teams were expected to identify 'hard core' perpetrators and those 'at risk' to assess, track and monitor children and young people from birth to 16. Twenty-nine risk factors were specified, including: holding negative beliefs and attitude; involved in offending or antisocial behaviour at a young age; family members involved in offending; poor family relationships; friends involved in antisocial behaviour; hangs about with others involved in antisocial behaviour; underachievement at school; non-attendance at or lack of attachment to school; lack of participation in structured, supervised activities; 'lack of concentration'. Youth Justice Board approved schemes such as the unfortunately named GRIP (Group Intervention Panel) in Lancashire adopted, apparently without question, previously discredited forms of classification such as Criminogenic Risk Factors.

National policies for tackling antisocial behaviour were presented as thought-through, coherent and comprehensive, protecting those 'at risk', processing effectively a 'hard core' of repeat offenders and challenging 'deep-seated' problems within the most vulnerable and 'deprived' areas. Yet, as far as children and young people were concerned, antisocial behaviour units, and those recruited to them, were engaged in targeting by selectively employing subjective risk factors. These were new, broad, discretionary powers implemented by teams informed by an ideology of policing rather than welfare. For example, the opening sentence of Liverpool Anti-Social Behaviour Unit's draft strategy for 2003–6 stated that the Unit enjoyed 'notable success as a reactive punitive service' (Liverpool ASBU 2003: 1).

In November 2002 Home Office Minister John Denham renewed the call for a 'crackdown on antisocial behaviour' through maximising the use of ASBOs and extending powers through the 2002 Police Reform Act. These included: 'interim' ASBOs; widening of their geographical scope; extension of orders to people convicted of a criminal offence. In April 2003 voluntary agreements, Acceptable Behaviour Contracts (ABCs), were introduced, through which those 'involved in' antisocial behaviour contracted in to acceptable behaviour. Denham confirmed ASBOs and ABCs as 'key tools in tackling low level crime and disorder' while increasing 'the community's confidence in the ability of the local authority and the police to deal with the problem' (*Home Office Press Release*, 12 November 2002). Children and young people 'must be dealt with in a way that ensures they fully appreciate the consequences of their actions on the community'. He reinforced the demand for 'all areas of the community' to accept their professional and personal responsibilities in 'effectively tackl[ing] this problem that is such a blight on people's lives'.

Two days later the Home Secretary, David Blunkett, appointed the first Director of the Home Office Anti-Social Behaviour Unit, heralded as a 'centre of excellence on anti-social behaviour, with experts from across Government and local agencies' (*Home Office Press Release*, 14 November 2002). He stated the Unit's 'support' for 'local delivery' of policy and practice leading to the 'culture change' required 'to rebalance rights and responsibilities'. Simultaneously the Queen's Speech stated that the government would 'rebalance the criminal justice system to deliver justice for all' while 'safeguard[ing] the interests of victims, witnesses and communities' (*The Guardian*, 13 November 2002). A White Paper on antisocial behaviour was announced.

Introducing the White Paper, David Blunkett challenged parents, neighbours and local communities to take 'a stand against what is unacceptable ... vandalism, litter and yobbish behaviour' (Home Office, 2003: Foreword). He continued: 'We have seen the way communities spiral downwards once windows are broken and not fixed, streets get grimier and dirtier, youths hang around street corners intimidating the elderly ... crime goes up and people feel trapped.' Blunkett's agenda included: more police officers, the consolidation of community support officers, neighbourhood warden schemes, crime and disorder partnerships, increased use of ASBOs, fixed penalty notices for disorder offences and new street-crime initiatives. A central premise was that 'healthy communities are built on strong families' in which parents 'set limits' and 'ensure their children understand the difference between right and wrong' (ibid.: 21). Using the justification that children and young people were 'at risk', a 'new Identification, Referral and Tracking system (IRT)' was to be introduced. Information on antisocial behaviour given to the police would be 'shared with schools, social services, the youth service and other agencies'.

Families 'described as "dysfunctional"' or 'chaotic' would be targeted. Parenting classes were regarded as 'critical in supporting parents to feel confident in establishing and maintaining a sense of responsibility, decency and respect in their children, and in helping parents manage them' (ibid.: 23). Parenting Orders would be extended, giving schools and local education authorities powers to initiate parenting contracts. Refusal by parents to sign contracts would constitute a criminal offence, with intensive fostering imposed on families unwilling or unable to provide support. Youth Offending Teams were also given powers to initiate Parenting Orders 'related to anti-social or criminal type behaviour in the community where the parent is not taking active steps to prevent the child's behaviour ... ' (ibid.: 34). A concurrent Parenting Order would be issued to parents of children under 16 given an ASBO.

Based on 2001 figures (23,393 persistent young offenders in England and Wales) Intensive Supervision and Surveillance Programmes were initiated. These combined 'community based surveillance with a comprehensive and sustained focus on tackling the factors that contribute to a person's offending behaviour'. Individual Support Orders would be used to ensure that children aged 10 to 17 addressed their antisocial behaviour. Fixed Penalty Notices (FPNs) were to be administered by police officers, school and local education authority staff to parents who 'condone' or 'ignore' truancy. FPNs also could be issued to parents of children 'where the children's behaviour would have warranted action ... were they to be 16 or over' (ibid.: 9). The 'principle' remained 'consistent' – 'the protection of the local community must come first' (ibid.: 35). The White Paper was a clear demonstration that harsh measures and unprecedented discretionary powers had become central to authoritarian cross-agency interventions.

On 14 October 2003 the Prime Minister and the Home Secretary outlined the government's renewed and strengthened 'action plan' to confront antisocial behaviour. They quoted a Home Office survey which, on the basis of evidence from 1,500 organisations, recorded 66,000 antisocial behaviour incidents at an estimated daily cost of £13.4 million. Tony Blair stated that it was 'unacceptable' that the powers given to local authorities under the 1998 Crime and Disorder Act were not being used consistently. 'Loutish behaviour', he stated, 'is loutish behaviour wherever it is.' Powers should be used 'not occasionally, not as a last resort' but 'with real energy'. Should the extended powers of the imminent legislation prove insufficient 'we will go further and get you them' (*The Guardian*, 15 October 2003). The Home Secretary dismissed critics of ASBOs as 'garbage from the 1960s and 1970s', stating that it was inappropriate to be 'non-judgemental when you live next door to the neighbours from hell' (ibid.).

The potential for applying ASBOs with 'real energy' had not been lost on judges. In February 2003 a Manchester district judge lifted reporting restrictions on a 17-year-old and, in addition to serving an 18-months detention order, imposed an ASBO. Breach of the ASBO carried a further period in detention of up to five years. Eight months later, also in Manchester, another 17-year-old was served with a 10-year ASBO in addition to an 18-months' detention and training order. In this case, the ASBO was sought after sentencing and while the young person was detained in custody. The terms of the ASBO were not restricted to his home area but extended throughout England and Wales. A Manchester City Council representative was unequivocal regarding the purpose of the ASBO: 'It stands as a stark warning – behave or risk a long ban ... [he] must tread very carefully wherever he goes. One slip and he could find himself in custody again' (*Press Release*, Manchester City Council, 10 November 2003). In this context, ASBOs used alongside sentencing had become a form of 'release under licence'.

While Manchester City Council led the way in the use and expansion of the terms of ASBOs, the picture across the UK remained inconsistent. It is important to reflect on the limited statistical evidence. From April 1999 to March 2004, 2,497 ASBOs were applied for throughout England and Wales. Only 42 were refused by the courts, giving a 98.3 per cent success rate. In the 12 months to March 2004 more ASBOs were issued than in the preceding four years taken together and there was a 60 per cent drop in refusals. There were inconsistencies between local authorities with comparable demographics. For example, West Mercia used six times more ASBOs than did Gloucestershire. More ASBOs were issued in Greater Manchester than in any comparable area, but they were concentrated within two district authorities. Further, a quarter of all Greater Manchester ASBOs extended throughout England and Wales. Those local authorities that used ASBOs most regularly also had, proportionately, the lowest rate of refusals in the courts.

Throughout the five-year period 74 per cent of all ASBOs were issued against under-21s and of these 93 per cent were to boys or young men. Forty-nine per cent of all ASBOs were issued against children aged 10 to 17. Between June 2000 and December 2002, of those young people prosecuted and found guilty of breaching their ASBO 50 per cent were sentenced to a Young Offenders' Institution. The Home Office did not provide information on breach but, given the increase by a factor of five in the issuing of ASBOs between April 2003 and March 2004, it is fair to project the previous figures on breaches and custodial sentences by a similar factor. This suggested 300 to 400 custodial sentences each year for breach. Put another way, these children and young people received a custodial sentence without being charged with a crime other than a breach of a civil injunction.

The 2003 Anti-Social Behaviour Act was introduced 'to provide tools for practitioners and agencies to effectively tackle anti-social behaviour'. As expected, the new powers included: widening the use of Fixed Penalty Notices and applying them to 16–17-year-olds; interventions to close 'crack houses'; dispersal of groups in designated areas; aggravated trespass; unauthorised encampments; restrictions on replica guns; enforcing parental responsibility for children who behave 'in an anti-social way in school or in a community'; fly-tipping, graffiti and fly-posting; closure of establishments creating 'noise nuisance'; enabling landlords to act against antisocial tenants. Actions to 'improve the operation of ASBOs' were introduced in January 2004, followed by parenting contracts and orders, including their attachment to ASBOs, in February and increased powers to agencies to issue ASBOs in March. Fixed Penalty Notices were introduced for parents of truants (February), for graffiti and fly-posting (March) and for disorder (March). Curfew Orders and Supervision Orders were introduced in September.

Disrespecting children's rights

In June 2005 Alvaro Gil-Robles, European Human Rights Commissioner, reporting 'on the effective respect of human rights' in the United Kingdom entered into the controversy surrounding ASBOs and the regulation of children and young people (Gil-Robles 2005: 4). Expressing 'surprise' at the executive's 'enthusiasm' for the 'novel extension of civil orders', not least 'particularly problematic' ASBOs (ibid.: 34), he raised four principal concerns: 'ease of obtaining such orders, the broad range of prohibited behaviour, the publicity surrounding their imposition and the serious consequences of breach'. Given the limiting form of conditions in many cases, breach was 'inevitable'. ASBOs were 'personalised penal codes, where non-criminal behaviour becomes criminal for individuals who have incurred the wrath of the community'.

Gil-Robles questioned 'the appropriateness of empowering local residents to take such matters into their own hands', particularly as this was 'the main selling point of ASBOs in the eyes of the Executive' (ibid.: 35). More a public relations exercise 'than the actual prevention of anti-social behaviour itself', ASBOs had been 'touted as a miracle cure for urban nuisance'. The police, local authorities and others were placed 'under considerable pressure to apply for ASBOs' and magistrates, similarly pressured, 'to grant them'. He 'hoped' for some respite from the 'burst of ASBO-mania' with civil orders 'limited to appropriate and serious cases'.

While acknowledging the House of Lords judgment regarding the criminal standard of proof, Gil-Robles noted the continuing admissibility of hearsay evidence. Combining 'a criminal burden of proof with civil rules of evidence' was 'hard to square' as 'hearsay evidence and the testimony of police officers and professional witnesses' was not 'capable of proving the alleged behaviour beyond reasonable doubt' (ibid.: 36). Further, guidelines 'unduly encourage the use of professional witnesses and hearsay evidence' while failing to 'emphasise the seriousness of the nuisance targeted'.

Troubled that children between 10 and 14 could be considered 'criminally culpable', Gil-Robles concluded that ASBOs brought children to the 'portal of the criminal justice system'. He had heard evidence of 'excessive, victimising ASBOs' served on children. Their subsequent stigmatisation, imprisonment for breach and inevitable alienation risked entrenchment of 'their errant behaviour'. Widespread publicity of cases involving children, central to Home Office guidelines, was 'entirely disproportionate' in 'aggressively inform[ing] members of the community who have no knowledge of the offending behaviour' and had 'no need to know'. Naming and shaming constituted 'a violation of Article 8 of the ECHR' and potentially transformed 'the pesky into pariahs'.

Extended to the jurisdictions of Scotland and Northern Ireland, a version of ASBOs was introduced in Ireland in 2007. Despite a series of legal challenges, their continuing refinement and expansion of powers proceeded unabated. Yet they seriously breach the UN Convention on the Rights of the Child (CRC), undermining the 'best interests' principle, the presumption of innocence, due process, the right to a fair trial and access to legal representation. More specifically, conditions embedded in ASBOs regularly breach CRC Articles: separation from parents and the right to family life – Article 9; freedom of expression – Article 13; freedom of association – Article 15; protection of privacy – Article 16. Given the North of Ireland context, and the reality of paramilitary beatings as a consequence of ASBOs, Article 6 – the right to life, survival and development, and Article 19 – protection from abuse and neglect are, at best, compromised.

Imprisoning children for breaching ASBOs constitutes an egregious breach of Article 40. ASBOs fail to promote 'the child's sense of dignity and worth', have no consideration of age and inhibit 'reintegration' into the community (40.1). They conflate civil law and 'penal law' (40.2a), compromise the presumption of innocence (40.2bi), deny access to a 'fair hearing' (40.2biii), prevent cross-examination of evidence before the court (40.2biv) and fail to respect privacy throughout the proceedings (40.2bvii). Imprisonment for breaching a civil order rejects the principle of depriving a child of its liberty as a last resort, and fails to respond to children 'in a manner appropriate to their well-being and proportionate both to their circumstances and the offence'. Finally, significant child-protection issues are raised by naming and shaming children as young as 10. Taken together, these breaches and circumstances amount to the most serious attack on children's rights since the UK government ratified the UN Convention.

Ironically, while demonstrating lack of respect for the rights of children, the third term Labour government renewed its commitment to a 'respect agenda'. In May 2005 Tony Blair talked of 'respect' towards others as a 'modern yearning as much as a traditional one'. Street-corner and shopping-centre thuggery, binge drinking and yobbish behaviour, he railed, is derived in 'the way that parents regard their responsibility to their children, in the way their kids grow up generation to generation without proper parenting, without a proper sense of discipline within the family'. Lost streets would be reclaimed by parents and local communities joining 'law makers and law enforcers' to establish a 'proper sense of respect and responsibility'.

Yet the concept of 'strong community' remained rhetorical and aspirational, neglecting the context of conflict in communities riven and dislocated by deeper, structural inequalities evident in poverty, racism, sectarianism, misogyny and homophobia. As events in France in 2005 demonstrated, the full spectrum of disruptive behaviour is spawned and ignited by political–economic marginalisation and criminalisation. Most significantly, children and young people are well aware that for all the rhetoric of inclusion and stake-holding, they are peripheral, rarely consulted and regularly vilified. They endure disrespect as a daily reality. Blair, however, the end of his prime ministerial reign on the horizon, remained true to the New Labour project of moral renewal through a rule-of-law agenda. He regretted that new laws had 'not been tough enough', necessitating further legislation 'that properly reflect the reality'. Only by remedying imbalances, by addressing low-level crime and broadening the definitional scope of anti-social behaviour, could 'social cohesion' be restored to 'fragmented communities' (Blair 2006: 94).

Throughout this chapter the veneer of risk, protection and prevention coating a deepening, almost evangelical, commitment to discipline, regulation and punishment is starkly apparent. As the grip tightens on the behaviour of children and young people, minimal attention has been paid to the social, political and economic context. The reality is an authoritarian ideology, mobilised locally and nationally to criminalise through the back door of civil injunctions. In-depth, case-based research shows that the problems faced by children and families are exacerbated by the stigma, rumour and reprisals fed by the public process of naming and shaming. Yet the transactional perspective on rights and implementation remains a central theme of the Blair legacy. There is no evidence that it will be transformed. For, at the 2005 Labour Party Conference, his heir apparent, Gordon Brown, reminisced that his 'moral compass' was set by his parents; for 'every opportunity there was an obligation' and for 'every right there was a responsibility' (Conference address, 26 September 2005).

As concluded elsewhere:

> Children's offending and antisocial behaviour, like their other life experiences and personal opportunities, are located within powerful, structural determining contexts. Through unemployment, poverty and differential opportunities class impacts significantly on communities, families and children. The politics of reproduction, in the context of patriarchy, creates quite different possibilities – and probabilities – for girls and young women in both the private and the public spheres. Sexuality remains forbidden territory until puberty, when gendered ideologies reinforce femininity, hegemonic masculinity and heterosexism. Finally, racism – within the politics of neo-colonialism – remains a formidable barrier to equality of opportunity for any child defined as 'ethnic minority'.
>
> (Scraton and Haydon 2002: 326)

While not all situations for individual families and children are equally determined and resistance takes many forms, the arrogance and complacency at the heart of the Blair/Brown 'moral compass', 'moral renewal' rhetoric ignores the necessity of a 'fundamental shift in the structural relations and determining contexts of power which marginalize and exclude children and young people from effective participation in their destinies' (ibid.).

8 Children, young people and conflict in the North of Ireland

In October 2003 Northern Ireland's first Commissioner for Children and Young People (NICCY) began work by announcing the commissioning of a major study to research the state of children's rights, adequacy of provision for children and how rights and provision in Northern Ireland compared with other European jurisdictions. I was a member of a Queen's University-based research team that conducted the research and took primary responsibility for the work on youth justice and policing also having an input on mental health. With Clare Dwyer I carried out the qualitative research. The Northern Ireland Prison Service refused me access to the Hydebank Wood Young Offenders' Centre, although I gained access to young women in prison at the Mourne House Women's Unit, Maghaberry Prison. Ciara Davey and Siobhán McAlister took responsibility for much of the primary research in schools and with children experiencing particular vulnerability and disadvantage. The full report (Kilkelly et al. 2004) and a version for children (Haydon 2004) were published in 2004.

The legacy of conflict

While the impact on children and young people of political conflict in the North of Ireland is yet to be fully acknowledged, several generations have endured pervasive sectarianism, hard-line policing, military operations and paramilitary punishments. A combination of ceasefires, arms decommissioning and the 1998 Belfast (Good Friday) Agreement, reflected in the commonly used phrase 'peace process', suggested 'the conflict' had ended and a 'post-conflict' phase had emerged. Whatever the advances, transition is gradual and complex. Sporadic and opportunist violence occasionally flares between and within communities. An entrenched loyalist feud, triggering the displacement of numerous families and their children, has been one manifestation. Beyond these issues, however, is the legacy of 30 years of serious conflict and its impact on children who are now parents. In this context, the right to truth and to acknowledgement as part of the process of recovery are significant issues for children and the communities in which they live.

Smyth *et al.* (2004: 96) concentrated their research on areas 'relatively more exposed to the Troubles than average'. They note that relatively 'infrequent effects such as severe traumatisation tend to attract more attention from the media, researchers and organisations' concerned with the impact of the conflict on children's lives. These include: subjection to paramilitary punishment attacks; witnessing killings, shootings or punishments; rioting; being exiled; suffering school-related sectarian bullying. Less dramatic and often unaddressed are: 'chronic anger, lack of trust in adults, isolation and feelings of marginalisation, bitterness at other community or at the police; distrust of all authority; feelings of marginalisation; lack of contact with or knowledge of "other" community' (ibid.: 99). They found that vulnerability 'is not only experienced by individuals, but also by whole families and communities' and that 'adults to whom children could ordinarily turn for support or protection are more often than not exposed to the same traumatic events that the children are, and are themselves traumatised and sometimes incapacitated' (ibid.: 109).

Interviews with community-based workers raised unresolved problems faced by children and young people during the conflict: house arrests involving a heavy military presence; forced house entry during the night by the police; parents imprisoned, 'on the run' or killed; witnessing violent confrontations, including death, in communities. 'House raids are over to a point and the physical harm is over; but the emotional harm is there and it's not recognised' (Interview, community-based counsellor, August 2004). Those interviewed for the NICCY research felt that research studies had omitted to give sufficient priority to the impact on children and their attainment of house raids in particular. A typical response was: 'As far as we are concerned no allowances were made for them at school.'

Community workers in the most economically disadvantaged communities emphasised the significance of the 'emotional effects of the conflict'. They stressed the 'dire need' for appropriate medical intervention to support children and a reconsideration of how children in conflict with the law are defined and criminalised. A children's caseworker identified the issue graphically:

> When you're raising mental health care for this generation, post-conflict, we're dealing with a huge age range of people who've been the bereaved, the injured … And another generation who are the children of the children … the impact of the trauma, which they're calling trans-generational trauma … it's affecting children's education, their mental health and their ability to participate in society.
>
> (Interview, August 2004)

She stated that the cases dealt with by her organisation showed that

> the agencies that are dealing with people have no idea what the effects of trauma are, they don't put it into the equation when children are

displaying different symptoms, whether they are in education, the criminal justice system or whatever. The effects of trauma don't even factor there ... and the issue of the conflict doesn't even raise itself.

As Smyth *et al.* (2004: 43) note, those children deeply affected by the conflict had 'difficulties in concentration and the aggressive behaviour that followed their traumatisation was misinterpreted by others, being seen as deliberately disruptive behaviour' posing 'particular problems in school, where teachers did not always seem aware of the pupils' history or the difficulties faced by them, nor did they appear to be equipped to deal with such difficulties'. Despite the pressing need due to exceptional circumstances, the NICCY research identified a serious deficit in child and adolescent mental health services. No case research has been developed into the high number children and young people taking their own lives, particularly in North Belfast. The relationships between conflict-related trauma, persistent paramilitary threats, forced exiling, economic marginalisation and social exclusion are of particular concern. These are cumulative contexts in which hopelessness, helplessness and despair impact on the minds of children who self-harm. As one young woman stated when asked why she self-harmed, 'it's my only way of coping ... and I release the pain as well' (Interview, July 2004).

Research carried out in schools revealed 5 per cent of young children considered their movements restricted because of their religion and a further 4 per cent raised the issue of paramilitary activity when they drew images on being given the prompts 'police' and 'crime'. Paramilitary activity was of particular concern to young people aged 15–16 years (61 per cent). This is unsurprising, given that it is the target age for recruitment into paramilitary organisations. Yet young children from the age of 6 demonstrated a clear awareness of paramilitary activity in their areas. For example, a 6-year-old girl drew a vivid stick drawing of a punishment beating and a young boy drew a picture of a person being dragged from a car and assaulted by paramilitaries.

Eleven per cent of children and young people expressed a desire for peace that increased in significance as children grew older. The message from these children was direct:

I would like people to live where they would like to and for the Protestants and Fenians to live together. (Girl, aged 16)

Where I live there are people with a different religion who also live near and people give them a hard time. I wish there was no religion so that everyone could get on and there would be no fighting. (Boy, aged 13)

Among children and young people interviewed, the desire for 'peace' between and within communities was common. Yet the view from interface areas, where divided communities meet, is bleak and indicates resignation among children that differences have solidified. In her research Leonard (2004: 105) notes, 'while the situation was better [now] in some ways as there were less bombings and shootings', some children 'felt there was more hatred than in the past'. There was a pervasive 'sense of inevitability and permanence about the conflict' and all were 'pessimistic about the possibility for conflict resolution in Northern Ireland' (ibid.). In their lives and everyday experiences 'peace remained a distant vision' (ibid.: 107).

Parades are significant events in children's experiences of sectarianism, particularly in high-conflict working-class areas. In their study of the experiences and perspectives of 3 to 11-year-olds, Connolly and Healy (2004) note that 3 to 4-year-olds 'living under the shadow of sectarian violence' already tended to prefer events or symbols associated with their culture and a minority had begun to re-enact violent incidents through play. By 7 to 8 years they were aware of the distinction between Protestant and Catholic communities and some were routinely involved in interface violence, including stone throwing and verbal abuse. They exhibited strong negative attitudes towards the 'other' community and the majority were aware of local paramilitary groups, some already identifying with groups. Leonard (2004: 44) found that 14-year-olds often found rioting exciting and an escape from boredom. It also provided 'a mechanism for demonstrating religious/sectarian identity ... a way of emphasising the internal cohesiveness of the group'. In such situations, as Smyth *et al.* (2004: 104) note, children are recruited into paramilitary organisations.

Street violence is most common and most severe in interface areas. In her research with children in Loyalist and Nationalist areas of North Belfast, where 20 per cent of all deaths in the conflict occurred, Leonard (2004: 7) notes that the 'area has experienced the mass movement of people, open street rioting, clashes with security forces, shootings and intimidation'. The complexity of 'territory' is such that the area 'contains around 24 interfaces' and 'eight of the official Belfast peace lines'. Asked about the positive aspects of life in the area, the 14-year-olds specified 'strong ties, family, friends and neighbours'. But the 'amount of space devoted to highlighting positive aspects was insignificant' when contrasted to the negative: the area's appearance; lack of amenities; availability of alcohol and drugs; joyriding; paramilitaries; rioting.

Leonard (ibid.: 76) found the '[f]ear of verbal and physical intimidation and violence impacted on the movements of both groups' with places 'outside the children's immediate locality ... labelled as spaces of risk and fear'. Levels of violence experienced by children in and around their schools were extreme, including attacks on buses and vandalising or torching teachers' cars. Children attended school behind locked gates monitored by security guards. They could not use playgrounds for fear of being stoned. Verbal abuse and spitting were everyday occurrences as they made their way home. In-depth interviews with children showed that 'many young people curtailed their movements because of fear of physical and verbal intimidation by the other main religious community' and many 'recounted incidents where they had been direct victims of physical and verbal abuse' (ibid.: 133).

A most graphic and widely publicised example of sectarian violence and its impact on children occurred in 2001 over public access to the Roman Catholic Holy Cross Primary School, North Belfast. Following increased tensions within the area, exacerbated by the Loyalist feud and renewed violence towards the Nationalist community initiated by Loyalist paramilitaries, tensions were high. On 20 June a major disturbance took place as children from Holy Cross were leaving for home. There was further rioting throughout the following day. Shots were fired and 10 blast bombs and 60 petrol bombs were thrown. The police redirected children and parents from the road they used to walk to school, as their safety could not be guaranteed.

Following a troubled summer, the police reviewed their initial decision and made plans to allow children and their parents to take their normal route to Holy Cross. The intention was to protect access along the road by barriers and 'anti-spit' screens. While erecting the protection, the army and police were attacked by Loyalists. As the protest gathered momentum children, accompanied by their parents, walked through a corridor made by barriers. They were subjected to verbal abuse and violent threats. Between September and October the protests escalated. In statements taken from parents it is clear that the extreme levels of abuse and violence had a major impact. They record the severe distress and suffering endured by young children who feared for their lives, death threats received by parents and enforced displacement from the area. Children's rights organisations questioned the failure by the police to adequately protect children, safeguard their best interests and secure their right to education.

Intra-community violence has also impacted on children. Leonard (ibid.) found that within Loyalist communities the experience of being exiled had serious consequences for children. Some idea of the extent of displacement can be gained from what was identified as the 'largest forced movement of households since the 1970s' between August and October 2000 (Interagency Working Group on Displaced Families, 2000). Within the 263 families involved were 269 children, 178 of whom were aged 11 years or under. The Working Group noted that the 'figures [for those seeking relocation from the Housing Executive] do not present the whole picture' as 'many families are not living at home and are dispersed throughout the area because of death threats made on their lives. We estimate that approximately 1,000 individuals are directly affected by this situation.' Children's experiences of enforced moves included direct violence and assaults, houses ransacked or burnt and furniture damaged, destroyed or stolen. While agencies provided temporary accommodation, emergency payments and health care, including 'trauma counselling', this was on a short-term basis.

Baton rounds and the vulnerability of children

The use of baton rounds for crowd dispersal has been an issue of serious contention since rubber bullets were first introduced and used in the North of Ireland in 1970. Following deaths and injuries the 'more accurate' and 'less lethal' plastic bullet was introduced in 1974. In 1994 a 'more accurate' anti-riot launcher was introduced, followed in 2001 by a 'more accurate' and 'potentially less lethal' baton round, the L21A1. Throughout this period 17 people, eight of whom were children, were killed by rubber or plastic baton rounds. Many others, estimated in hundreds, were injured. Accurate statistics on baton-round injuries were not recorded by the police or hospitals. From interviews conducted with community-based support groups it is clear that physical and psychological trauma caused by serious injuries to survivors and to their families was, and remains, extensive. There is also evidence that lives have ended prematurely as a result of this trauma.

The use of baton rounds 'in situations of serious public disorder' is governed by the Association of Chief Police Officers' (ACPO) guidelines. While recognising that baton rounds can cause serious injury and have resulted in deaths, ACPO specifies that baton rounds and CS munitions constitute a 'less than lethal contingency in dealing with serious public disorder'. Once an operational decision has been taken to deploy baton rounds they 'should be fired at selected individuals and not indiscriminately at the crowd ... aimed to strike directly (i.e. without bouncing) at the lower part of the target's body (i.e. below the rib cage)'. The guidelines prohibit targeting the upper body because 'risk of serious and fatal injuries is significantly increased'. This instruction fails to recognise that a child's upper body and head might well be at a height consistent with an adult's rib cage.

Revised guidelines, issued in 2003, for the first time addressed risks to children. Referring to the *UN Code of Conduct for Law Enforcement Officers* they state:

> every effort should be made to exclude the use of firearms, especially against children ... Every effort should be made to ensure that children are not placed at risk by the firing of baton rounds in public order situations and children should not be directly targeted *unless their actions are presenting an immediate threat to life or serious injury*, which cannot otherwise be countered.
>
> (Para 1.9, emphasis added)

While appearing to establish a safeguard in principle, effectively the guidelines authorise the use of baton rounds against children and young people.

Between 2000 and 2002 over three hundred baton rounds were fired by the Police Service of Northern Ireland (PSNI) and just under a hundred by the Army (Omega Foundation 2003: 27). Of the 12 injuries caused in one year (2001–2), where the age of the person was known, eight were to children. During an incident in April 2002, when police officers and soldiers were deployed to contain disorder between nationalist and loyalist youths, baton rounds were fired by a police officer and soldiers. The Police Ombudsman investigated the case and consequently officers were given 'appropriate advice and guidance' on issuing weapons to officers who have no authorisation for their use. In this case the officer 'received appropriate advice and guidance'. The Ombudsman, however, supported the PSNI in the use of baton rounds on the basis that there was 'no viable and effective alternative' (Interview, August 2004). She agreed with the often-stated official position that baton rounds are preferable to live ammunition. A PSNI representative stated that 'in my opinion while some lives have been lost more lives have been saved by their use. They have been shown to be effective in riot and crowd control, more than any other method' (Interview, August 2004).

Research conducted by the Omega Foundation (2003: 27) on behalf of the Northern Ireland Human Rights Commission recommended the government to agree 'to a binding timescale for the completion of the search for an alternative and withdrawal of the baton round in Northern Ireland'. Sparse evidence was presented in defence of the introduction of the L21A1 and in supporting the UK government's reassurances that there was greater transparency in their use. In October 2002 the UN Committee on the Rights of the Child restated its concern 'at the continued use of plastic baton rounds as a means of riot control in Northern Ireland as it causes injuries to children and may jeopardise their life' (UNCRC 2002: 7). Consistent with the recommendations of the Committee against Torture, it urged the government 'to abolish the use of plastic baton rounds as a means of riot control'.

The Patten Commission (Patten 2000) also recommended alternatives to baton rounds. The PSNI introduced CS incapacitant spray as 'an additional less than lethal option as part of a graduated response to any situation where police or a member of the public may be subjected to attack or violence'. The phrase 'less than lethal' is of dubious merit, given that since its introduction in England and Wales CS spray has been involved in the deaths of several people. If administered at close quarters, particularly when a person is under physical restraint, it has lethal potential. The PSNI, however, states that CS spray 'is not an alternative to baton rounds, nor is it a tool for deployment in incidents of major public disorder'. Voluntarily, the PSNI is committed to referring all cases of its use to the Police Ombudsman to 'ensure that we learn all lessons possible for our use of CS Spray'.

The community-based groups interviewed rejected official reassurances regarding the comparative 'safety' of baton rounds, responding that if, like bullets, they have lethal capacity they constitute a form of 'live' ammunition and should be regarded accordingly. Citing both the Committee against

Torture and the Committee on the Rights of the Child, they maintained that the continuing use and sophistication of baton rounds placed children and young people at additional risk. A community group worker commented:

> The thing about the technology is this. No-one was being made to adhere to the rules – neither the police nor the army. The rules stated that they were never to be fired above waist level. And that they were never to be fired at less then 20 metres. And that they were never to be fired in non-riot situations. Yet the people who died including all the children, were hit in the head and upper body regions, some at point blank range ... All of the deaths, and let's not forget all of the injuries, including children with horrendous facial injuries, impacted on families.
>
> (Interview, August 2004)

This poignant observation leads to a further crucial issue – the failure of statutory services to provide long-term care and counselling for those bereaved or injured by baton rounds. An NGO representative stated a broader consideration:

> The whole impact of the plastic bullet on the injured has not been adequately assessed ... and many of the children injured have never been able to take their place in a normal society ... can't form relationships ... there's been no research at all into the long-lasting effects of plastic bullet injuries.
>
> (Interview, August 2004)

Finally, on the introduction of the L21A1, a community worker stated:

> They [the Northern Ireland Office] showed us the new bullet. There's very little difference between it and the one they use now. We asked them, 'Can you give us a guarantee that these are non-lethal?' They said 'No, we can't'. There's no guarantee they're non-lethal. Despite the Patten recommendations that they be phased out and a safer alternative found, that has not happened.
>
> (Interview, August 2004)

Children and differential policing

Deaths and injuries due to baton rounds fired by soldiers or by police officers represent the sharp end of a continuum of the state's discretionary use of force within the law. Strong opposition, particularly within Nationalist and Republican communities, reflects the controversial and bitterly contested history of policing in Northern Ireland since partition. Throughout three decades of conflict, and beyond the 1998 Belfast

Agreement, policing remained contentious. The Royal Ulster Constabulary (RUC) was perceived and experienced in Nationalist and Republican communities as a sectarian, paramilitary force incapable of making the transition to a community-oriented, human rights-compliant police service. Its legacy included shared cross-community concerns about the processing of serious complaints, particularly regarding the activities of the Special Branch and allegations of collusion between the RUC and Loyalist paramilitary groups. This connected to serious allegations of institutionalised corruption and abuses of power, particularly the use of informants afforded immunity against prosecution for grave crimes, including murder. Given the special powers and permissive discretion under which the police operated, their legal, organisational and political accountability was compromised, not least regarding the use of force and police technologies.

The 1998 Belfast Agreement established the basis for the Independent Commission on Policing in Northern Ireland (the Patten Commission). It recommended a police service

> professional, effective and efficient, fair and impartial, free from partisan political control; accountable, both under the law for its actions and to the community it serves; representative of the society it polices, and operat[ing] within a coherent and cooperative criminal justice system, which conforms with human rights norms.

Patten (2000) proposed that an effective, efficient and modern police service depended on the adoption of key principles: collective responsibility involving the active and democratic participation of local communities in building a partnership for community safety; the acknowledgement and protection of human rights for all through training and strategies; legal, political and financial accountability; transparency and openness, particularly with regard to covert operations.

In November 2001 the Police Service of Northern Ireland (PSNI) succeeded the RUC. New uniforms, badge and flag – issues of considerable dispute – were introduced in 2002 and a new programme of recruitment, training and agenda-setting, in line with Patten, was established under the broad direction of the PSNI Change Management Team. In this climate of critique and transition, and despite the inclusiveness central to the Patten Report and the work of the children's sector in achieving that end, minimal attention was given to the largest group in routine contact with the police: children and young people. Yet issues raised by children in recent studies are profound.

Hamilton, Radford and Jarman (2003) studied young people's views of police accountability. Although confined mainly to the 16 to 24 age range, 56 per cent of young men and 28 per cent of young women reported contact with the police in the previous 12 months. Being stopped and questioned by the police and being moved on were the most frequent reasons for contact and most young people regarded the circumstances as harassment. Their experiences of the police were 'predominantly negative' and 24 per cent were 'very dissatisfied' with the police. Ellison (2001: 133) refers to this as 'adversary contact'. 'Disrespectfulness and/or impoliteness' (58 per cent) was the main criticism and harassment 'included physical violence, a constant police presence and being watched, confiscation of goods and verbal abuse'. The research also found marked differences in young people's perceptions and experiences of the police, depending on their community.

Ellison noted that 14 to 17-year-old males were three times more likely to be stopped and searched by a police officer than were 18-year-olds. Children from 'socio-economically disadvantaged areas' were more than twice as likely to have been searched. His research also demonstrated a difference in perception and experience between Protestant and Catholic children: '92.6% of Catholic males who have been stopped and questioned by the RUC "too many times to remember" believed this to constitute harassment, compared to 60.3% of Protestant males' (ibid.: 133). Ellison's research was conducted post-Patten and he recorded considerable support among young Catholics for changes in the RUC, including name change. While a considerable minority (20.8 per cent) of Protestant young people agreed with slight reform, the majority remained resistant to change.

Quinn and Jackson (2003) researched the detention and questioning of children and young people. Their detailed study found that 55 per cent of those detained were released within three hours, 25 per cent between three and six hours, 13 per cent between six and 12 hours and 7 per cent between 12 and 24 hours. Most were held in a cell or juvenile detention room, sometimes overnight. Only 15 per cent of those detained were eventually charged. Seventy-eight per cent were searched, 52 per cent were photographed, 70 per cent were fingerprinted and 36 per cent had a sample taken for DNA testing. 'Some appropriate adults and solicitors complained that the taking of samples, fingerprints and photographs criminalised young persons' (ibid.: vi). According to custody staff, 'securing the prompt attendance of an appropriate adult' was 'a major problem' and 'often prolonged young persons' time in custody unnecessarily' (ibid.: vii).

There was inconsistency in the advice given to children and young people by custody officers. Solicitors 'complained that not enough was done to explain the importance of legal advice to young persons and their parents ... ' (ibid.: ix). Quinn and Jackson also found that solicitors 'generally agreed that there were difficulties in ensuring that young persons, particularly under 14 year olds, understood the advice which was given to them' (ibid.: x). Whether children understood the caution, and how it was explained, was a significant issue and 'it was suggested that 10–13 year olds would rarely understand the caution' (ibid.: xii). In terms of compliance with international standards and the UN Convention on the Rights of the Child regarding child protection it was unacceptable that 'interviewing officers had not received any special training on interviewing young persons' (ibid.: xii). Further, while 'the dominant approach ... was simply to put an allegation to the young person ... other interview styles' included 'an adversarial approach, a moralistic approach and an intelligence gathering approach' (ibid.: xii–xiii).

The NICCY research revealed children's routine, negative experiences of the police. Although all identified a 'need' for policing within their communities, most recounted experiences of unacceptable and unlawful policing. Focus groups in Belfast and Derry gave recent examples of aggressive and bullying policing, including assaults, occurring in non-confrontational situations. Typical comments were:

> The Peelers just push you around. You've got the attitude problem not them. If you come back at them they just give you a quick beating. It's not right but it goes on all the time. (Young male, aged 17)

> We were just standing by the fences there the other day and the police came and told us to move on. We said we're just havin' a smoke, we're here [in the building]. 'You're not allowed to stand there. Move on!' (Young female, aged 18)

> If you're on the street then you're up to no good, like. They just come and tell you to go and when you say 'Where?' they tell you to 'Fuck off, that's where'. (Young male, aged 17)

> They know you, your families an' all. They tell you 'You're next' and that you're up to no good an' they're watchin' for you. I got paranoid that I was scared to go out. (Young female, aged 17)

> One of the blokes [police officer] grabbed me by the scruff of the neck and threw me against the wall and had me up against the wall like this. I just said 'Nine one one, I've got your number.' (Young male, aged 17)

A youth worker recalled:

> I was parking the car and I just heard a screech and a car pulled over and a guy came out, about four or five inches taller than me, and grabbed a wee young fella up by the throat and threw him into the car. The wee fella was only about 14. He was wearing an Ireland football jersey and he was just grabbed by the throat and threw into the car and taken away.
>
> (Interview, June 2004)

In focus groups held in Derry with 80 child sector workers, 44 per cent recorded their dissatisfaction with the police and 13 per cent regarded the police as 'bullies'. Nineteen per cent considered there should be better coordination between the PSNI and community-based restorative justice projects. One worker commented, 'There needs to be an effective CRJ approach that tackles appropriately and effectively issues like under-age drinking and safety for young people and provides the opportunity for taking responsibility for misbehaviour and its consequences.'

The above accounts, across communities and from boys and girls, were consistent with the overall findings of the broader NICCY research conducted in schools. When asked to write, draw and discuss images that came to mind when they heard the words 'police' or 'crime', 143 out of 710 children (20 per cent) described the police as 'lazy' and/or 'not doing enough' to serve the community, said that they were slow to arrive at the scenes of crimes or accidents and that they should focus more on solving 'real' crime. Typical comments included:

> The police don't do anything about the people in [name of town], they just walk around the town at night and watch young people drink and take drugs. Over the past year our town has lost lots of things because of the teenagers and older people, for example, the circus and the fun fair festival. Some people suffer for the things they didn't do and they leave us with nothing. It's about time the police did something about it. (Girl, aged 12)

> The cops sometimes get it right by catching the robbers or killers but most of the time they are out to get the public who are not doing anyone any harm such as people who are slightly over the speed limit or people with no tax or even in some places they put a curfew on all kids even though it may just be a small percentage of the kids who are causing the trouble. (Boy, aged 14)

Thirteen per cent considered the police were only interested in harassing young people, a view echoed by older children in general and boys in particular. Seven per cent claimed that differential policing reflected sectarianism within the police and 6 per cent associated police with riots. Twenty-two per cent were concerned about the use of drugs, joyriding, drinking and noise in their community. Only 12 per cent of children interviewed held positive views of the police. Typical comments were:

> There should be more police about the area and the police should try to be a little more friendly. The police should try and let us play in our area because sometimes they would have a complaint saying we're not allowed to play in the streets but it's our street and we should be able

to. They should try and get the people causing the trouble off the street so we can have a safer time. They should try and get joyriders off the road because they are killing people and themselves. (Boy, aged 13)

The police are always up behind our house putting cameras in the field and watching our house. I found one about six months go in a field. I don't feel comfortable in my own house! My dog went over and started to bark at them in the field. The fucking bastards gave it a poisoned sausage and it died a few hours later. As they walk past our house they stick up their fingers at us and call us names like 'Catholic scum' and 'Fenian bastards'. They scare me with their guns. (Boy, aged 14)

The police are a bad thing to have driving about the streets and roads. They cause fights and riots on the roads. People's houses and cars are being damaged by people throwing things at the police. Just four days ago, our car tyres were busted by glass on the road. (Boy, aged 14)

Every time I see their cars I run an' all. I don't want them to see me. I'm not afraid I just don't want them to see me because each time they come they think I have done something bad. Sometimes I do. (Boy, aged 8, Traveller community)

Lesbian, gay, bisexual and transgendered (LGBT) young people claimed that when they reported abuse or assault to the police they were not taken seriously and suffered further alienation within communities for taking action. LGBT young people's distrust of the police was shared, regardless of religion or community. The group also emphasised the significance of 'multiple identities'. As one young person stated:

In Northern Ireland the focus is on whether you are a Catholic or Protestant and there is little attention given to other means of discrimination on the basis of class, gender or race. Yet these impressions can impinge on one another hence doubling or even tripling the oppression experienced by some young people.

(Focus group, May 2004)

Smyth *et al.*, (2004: 79) note that the 'lack of accountability of the police and the sense that young people had of police impunity was a significant source of anger and frustration, particularly amongst young Catholics'. It amounted to 'a strong sense of injustice and the powerlessness to challenge unfair treatment was a recurring theme in interviews'. An 11-year-old girl Traveller stated in a NICCY research focus group: 'They [the police] have guns and batons and they think they can do anything'.

A key issue raised by adult community groups across the sectarian divide was the use of children by the PSNI to gather low-level intelligence as informers, in exchange for immunity from prosecution. A community worker put it succinctly: 'They know that if they recruit a child as an informer they turn the child into a combatant and immediately put his life at risk' (Interview, August 2004). The suggestion that such practices reflected official police policy or practice was rejected by the PSNI and by the Police Ombudsman. Both referred to new legislation and strict operational guidelines governing the use of children as informers. Yet a PSNI representative commented that modern police forces are 'intelligence led' and young people would be considered appropriate for 'information gathering' on crime in an area (Interview, August 2004). In observing police interviews of children detained at police stations Quinn and Jackson (2003: 116) comment: 'it appeared indeed in some cases that the interview was being used, not so much to extract a confession from the young person or to provide an opportunity for exculpation, but rather to gather information about other matters or individuals'. The PSNI draws the distinction between the use of children as information gatherers primarily for political ends and as part of the routine policing of crime. It would be naive to assume, given recent history, that the issues are not connected, at least in those communities wary of police intervention.

Regulating 'antisocial behaviour'

In 2004 the Northern Ireland Office (NIO) published a consultation document, *Measures to Tackle Anti-social Behaviour in Northern Ireland*. It misrepresented the history of Anti-social Behaviour Orders (ASBOs) in England and Wales, stating: 'ASBOs were introduced to meet a gap in dealing with persistent unruly behaviour, *mainly by juveniles*, and can be used against any person aged 10 or over' (NIO 2004: 4 emphasis added). Considerable controversy surrounded the consultation, and the children's sector united in opposing the intended legislation. The Northern Ireland Commissioner for Children and Young People, with support from leading children's NGOs, challenged the introduction on several grounds, not least lack of consultation with children and young people. In rejecting the application Justice Girvan concluded:

> ... one wonders in practical and realistic terms what meaningful response could be obtained from children unless they were in a position to understand the legal and social issues to anti-social behaviour, the mechanisms for dealing with it. The shortcomings of existing criminal law and the effectiveness or otherwise of the English legislation and its suitability for transplant to the Northern Ireland context, and the interaction of Convention and international obligations [*sic*].

The Anti-Social Behaviour (Northern Ireland) Act was introduced in August 2004. Welcoming the legislation, the Home Office Minister for Criminal Justice, John Spellar, stated:

> Government is pleased to be introducing this important piece of legislation which provides another tool in dealing with behaviour of this kind which can ruin lives and local communities. It complements measures which already exist and lets those who act in an anti-social way know that they will face firm sanctions. We will be working with all the agencies to make sure this legislation is used early and effectively.
>
> (*NIO Press Release*, 25 August 2004)

At no point in the consultation document or in the statements made by the Minister or his associates was any reference made to the special circumstances prevalent within the North of Ireland. That antisocial behaviour among children had been identified previously by the NIO as an issue within communities was taken as sufficient justification to introduce legislation that was fast gaining notoriety in breaching children's rights in England and Wales. No serious consideration was given to the success of community-based restorative justice schemes or their potential disruption through a more directly punitive and criminal justice-oriented initiative. In its submission to the consultation, an umbrella young people's organisation observed that ASBOs had 'the potential to demonise and further exclude vulnerable children who already find themselves on the margins of society and the communities in which they live' (Include Youth 2004: 5).

Further, and carrying potentially serious consequences, was the relationship of ASBOs to paramilitary punishments of children. ASBOs and evictions were introduced in circumstances where naming, shaming, beatings, shootings and exiling already existed regardless of their effectiveness. As a children's NGO focus group concluded: 'It's seen and represented as justice. It's concrete and immediate ... a quick fix. It doesn't work. It's brutal, inhuman and ineffective and doesn't challenge antisocial behaviour' (Research Focus Group, Belfast, May 2004). Community negotiations regarding paramilitary and vigilante interventions in the lives of children and young people had been initiated and were making progress. Yet within this delicate climate, a process of political and social transition, the antisocial behaviour legislation was imposed. Additionally, as the Northern Ireland Human Rights Commission (2004: 8) noted: 'Information regarding the identity, residence and activities of those subject to an order [will] be in the public domain and could lead to the breach of a right to life were paramilitaries to act on that information.'

Within a month of the introduction of ASBOs a poster produced by Loyalist paramilitaries appeared throughout East Belfast:

DUE TO THE RECENT UPSURGE OF ANTI-SOCIAL BEHA-
VIOUR AND THE VERBAL AND MENTAL ABUSE ENDURED ON
A DAILY BASIS BY THE ELDERLY PEOPLE IN THE SURROUND-
ING AREA

YOU ARE FOREWARNED IF THIS DOES NOT STOP FORTH-
WITH IT WILL LEAVE US WITH NO ALTERNATIVE BUT TO
DEAL WITH THE SITUATION AS WE DEEM NECESSARY

NOTE: NO FURTHER WRITTEN OR VERBAL WARNING WILL
BE GIVEN

BE WARNED

A research focus group (May 2004) concluded: 'Supporting ASBOs and
supporting paramilitary beatings are derived in the same emotion: they're
about revenge.'

The debate about transition from conflict, particularly regarding the
control of the streets and public space within communities, returns the analysis to a material context. Regarding concentrations of poverty in the
North of Ireland, Hillyard *et al.* (2003: 29) state:

> ... the impact on the development and opportunities of these 150,000
> children and young people [living in poverty] should not be under-
> estimated. The wider consequences and costs for society as a whole must
> be a concern. These children and young people occupy ... 'spaces of dis-
> possession', growing up as excluded people in excluded families increas-
> ingly characterised by antisocial behaviour, insecurity and threat.

Antisocial behaviour among children in the North of Ireland cannot be
analysed in form or content alongside similar manifestations in Liverpool,
Glasgow, Birmingham, Dublin or Limerick. Their behaviours are rooted in
the recent history of the conflict. The following comments, from community-based or children's-sector NGO workers, are typical:

> These are children of those whose childhood was dominated by the
> Troubles. We're talking about the experiences of children: house
> arrests, military presence, parents imprisoned, parents on the run,
> parents shot and killed. These experiences and their lasting effects
> aren't recognised.

> Children and their parents are in dire need of medical support. The
> children are accused of misbehaving, of antisocial behaviour rather than
> their mental ill-health being recognised.
>
> (Interview, July 2004)

Whether it's antisocial behaviour or suicidal tendencies, you cannot disconnect that from the anger of death in the communities. Shoot-to-kill, plastic bullets, collusion ... these are the experiences. Children often took over running of the home. The physical and psychological impact means these children have never been able to take their place in society. Transgenerational trauma affects every part of their lives: education, mental health, social participation. And in schools, in criminal justice agencies, trauma is not even part of the equation.

(Interview, August 2004)

Without taking these dynamics into account and contextualising the perceived and experienced antisocial behaviour of children and young people in the North of Ireland's most economically marginalised communities, the authoritarianism of ASBOs as administered in England and Wales has the potential to feed into that which already exists. Further, they threaten to corrode significant advances in alternatives to 'criminal justice' by undermining, ideologically and politically, established parental support programmes and community-based restorative justice initiatives.

Resisting violence

Throughout the NICCY research young people in conflict with the law gave painful accounts of endurance and resilience. A young mother's reflections on the sense of helplessness in her short life were not unusual:

When you're desperate nowhere will take you because you'll get put out for fighting or smoking blow. When I was in [hostel] I ran away and they didn't even phone my mammy and let her know. I ended up on the streets, drinking heavily, doing drugs and sleeping in a subway. I felt worthless. Maybe this was what I was supposed to be. I was suicidal, so low. Soon after, I started to self-harm ... I had all this anger inside me so I did it to release it. I was getting used to the pain so I was getting deeper cuts. You don't think in the long run where you'll end up. You feel like you'll be like that for ever.

(Interview, July 2004)

A young man's account of the all-pervasive presence of violence in his personal history clearly illustrated the extent of isolation and danger that remains a reality for many children and young people:

I used to wait for my Da, like, and he'd take off on us for nothing ... belt, fists, anything he could use. I was bullied all through my childhood. There were always fights in the house, like. And then I got it at school. You were going through enough at home, you didn't expect it in school, like. Then it was on the street with the peelers. *You've* got the attitude problem. You feel like a hurt animal, just waiting to be released.

(Interview, July 2004)

Much of the violence negotiated by young people occurred within the family and at school, supposedly safe havens. They constantly feared assault when outside their community: "'You shouldn't be here, you Fenian bastard" ... then they started spitting on her [girl-friend] on the street. Then Social Services turn round and blamed her'. A young father stated: 'You've got to forget about your past, when you've got kids you don't want them to live what you've lived'.

It is often stated that the North of Ireland is a society 'emerging from conflict', going through a long process of 'transition'. The research reported here suggests that for many children the notions of 'post-conflict' or 'transition' remain distant possibilities, as sectarianism entrenches hatred for the 'other' physically, psychologically and culturally. This is a particularly harsh reality in interface locations. Communities are divided not only by sectarianism but also by class and poverty. The intersection of these two key determining contexts is crucial in the lives of children and young people. In the urban areas, people live in close geographical proximity but occupy entirely contrasting worlds. The focus in this chapter has been on those communities in which violence has become normalised, a feature of daily life. They are also communities rarely policed sensitively or effectively and where many community-based workers reported that the statutory services had given up on their responsibilities.

Serious issues to be addressed include: the persistent refusal to withdraw plastic bullets; differential policing and the targeting of children and young people, including rough justice by police on the streets; the lack of recognition afforded to community restorative justice projects; the inexplicable failure to respond effectively to the continuing impact of conflict and trauma on the lives of children and young parents; the institutional failure to provide basic child and adolescent mental health services; the over-representation of looked-after children in custody; the use of solitary confinement and restraint as responses to managing the most vulnerable and damaged children in custody. Perhaps the greatest challenge is to change a collective mindset, fuelled by irresponsible media coverage, portraying children in conflict with the law as products of individual pathology blended with social dysfunction. In a society where over 150,000 children live in poverty, where disadvantage is structurally located and where self-harm and suicide are the sharp end of a continuum of marginalisation and rejection, the rhetoric of exiling and punishment is reprehensible, whether scrawled on the gable-end wall or written in the statute-book.

9 Self harm and suicide in a women's prison

In late 2003 the Northern Ireland Prison Service (NIPS) agreed to a request by the Human Rights Commission (NIHRC) to allow independent research into the Mourne House Women's Unit at Maghaberry Prison, specifically to consider the regime's compliance with Article 2 (right to life) and Article 3 (right to be held in conditions that do not amount to inhuman and degrading treatment) of the European Convention on Human Rights (ECHR). The research followed a critical report by the Prisons Inspectorate on its 2002 inspection, the death of 19-year-old Annie Kelly, found hanging in a punishment cell in Mourne House in September 2002, and a subsequent visit to the Unit by NIHRC com-missioners. With Linda Moore, Senior Investigations Worker at NIHRC, I was commissioned to carry out in-depth qualitative research within Mourne House. The research took place at the prison and in the com-munity between February and April 2004, with subsequent visits in May. We uncovered a regime that had all but collapsed. Our findings and recommendations were published as The Hurt Inside: The Impris-onment of Women and Girls in Northern Ireland *(Scraton and Moore 2005).*

While we were conducting the research, Roseanne Irvine took her own life in highly controversial and disputed circumstances. Subse-quently we gave evidence at the inquests of Annie Kelly (November 2005) and Roseanne Irvine (February 2007). It was clear that our evidence had a significant impact on the jury's narrative verdicts and the decision of the Coroner to refer the cases and our report to the Secretary of State for Northern Ireland. In March 2007 the Northern Ireland Affairs Committee announced its intention to conduct an inquiry into Northern Ireland's prisons, with a particular emphasis on health. I also gave oral evidence to a judicial review concerning the holding of a child in isola-tion in punishment block strip conditions. As a direct consequence of that evidence, the judge ordered her immediate removal from the block. Views presented in this chapter are mine and are not attributable to the NIHRC.

An enduring legacy

In 1986 women prisoners in the North of Ireland were transferred from Armagh Jail to Mourne House, within the walls of the purpose-built high-security prison, Maghaberry. Women had always been incarcerated in Armagh. It was built between 1780 and 1819, and Corcoran (2006: 21) notes that in the 1970s Armagh's overcrowding was compounded by 'an overspill of internees and remands from Belfast Prison ... and a boys' Borstal'. Gender segregation, alongside the separation of 'different categories of women prisoners led to the *ad hoc* subdivision of the already congested wings'. In these difficult and demanding circumstances the 'needs of male prisoners prevailed over those of the women in the allocation of resources and facilities', with 'recreation facilities for all women [prisoners] ... restricted to one small room' (ibid.: 22). Outdoor exercise was confined to a 'small muddy patch of ground' and its use by women brought 'verbal abuse and obscenities' from the 'soldiers patrolling the perimeters'. Corcoran's research reveals the depth and seriousness for women of inadequate diet, poor medical provision, lack of training of medical orderlies and paternalistic educational provision. She also records the Northern Ireland Prison Service's assessment of these criticisms as 'ill-founded and vexatious' (ibid.: 24).

During the 1970s and 1980s, republican women prisoners protested for political status and refused to participate in prison work. In February 1980, they began a no-wash protest, continuing for over two years. Armagh women were also involved in the 1980 hunger strikes. The regime was brutalising. A woman prisoner described a confrontation during the 1981 protest for political status:

[The screws] herded us into the association room. Then they went up and wrecked our cells ... they took us one at a time to be searched ... all the screws were lining the walls ... I didn't have a chance to look at their faces before I was spread-eagled against the wall and searched. Then it was back to my cell. Four of the women had been up for adjudication for breaking some prison rule ... the screws went up to get them ... in full riot gear with shields and batons, and carried the women down the stairs. One of them was kneeling on Anne-Marie Quinn's stomach – a huge big man ... She was crying out with the pain ... As they were trailing [Eilish] down they were trying to pull the trousers and jumper off her.
(Fairweather, McDonough and McFadyean 1984: 219–20)

Strip-searching women prisoners in Armagh received international attention bringing, widespread condemnation. Another woman recalled:

All women prisoners in Northern Ireland are strip-searched every time they enter or leave their prison compound, like when they are going to meet a visitor, or taken to court on remand, or visiting the infirmary. You have to stand in a closed-off cubicle, take off all your clothes and hand them out to two screws. I knew one woman prisoner, and she was having a miscarriage. She was haemorrhaging on the way to the hospital, and they strip-searched her.

Sharon Pickering (2002: 179) notes the trauma of the strip search, 'Often making women's periods stop, anxiety attacks ... designed to humiliate, to degrade.' In her detailed accounts of strip-searching of women political prisoners she records women's resistance, 'which usually resulted in them being forcibly held and clothes torn from their bodies'. The physical assault and emotional trauma of the forcible strip search was exacerbated by women being charged with breaches of prison rules and/or assaulting staff. The use of force individually was matched by the use of punishment institutionally. Women prisoners, political or 'ordinary', were constantly reminded that they were powerless to resist the authority of the prison. Pickering concludes:

> Strip searching came to epitomise, for many, the resolve of the security services to have women submit to the process of criminalisation and surveillance by taking control of women's nakedness. The objective of 'breaking women' was understood by women in this study who had experienced strip searching as being particularly vicious.
>
> (Ibid.: 181)

Pickering (ibid.: 176) also notes in that in Armagh and Mourne House the 'objectification' of women prisoners not only relied on the imposition of femininity, of feminine appearance and motherhood, but also 'de-feminised' through abuse, calling women 'whores', 'sluts', 'bad mothers'. They were 'subject to limitations and expectations based on their sex and because the authorities were operating with firm assumptions about how women should behave' (ibid.). Fairweather, McDonough and McFadyean (1984: 210) were told by a woman prisoner that the authorities 'have the idea that good mothers, good wives and good girlfriends shouldn't be in jail ... you're destroying the ideals of what a woman should be like'. The dual construction and application of women's sexuality – simultaneously emphasising and negating femininity – represented a concerted effort to 'render women impotent in an already debilitating powerless situation'. As a woman prisoner stated, 'They are always attacking your sexuality in order to degrade you, to humiliate you and in order to beat you' (ibid.: 177).

Following the transfer of women to Mourne House in 1986, Armagh's harsh regime persisted. Strip searches as arbitrary punishment and assaults on prisoners by staff were endemic. The following account is from a Republican woman prisoner's experiences of 'a mass forcible strip search ... carried out by officers in riot gear against 21 Republican women prisoners' on 2 March 1992:

> They took the women down; they stripped them and battered them, then they charged ... I barricaded myself in my cell; after that I was charged with building a barricade and refusing to strip. I was protect-ing my body ... I did not have a say over my own body and that is why I refused to strip because it is my body ... because it [strip-searching] is another form of rape.
>
> (Pickering 2002: 179–80)

A woman imprisoned in Mourne House during the 1990s recalled:

> You always would have heard back to the days in Armagh Jail about the women being strip-searched. It wasn't until I was strip-searched that I realized what those women had been through because it was the most horrendous experience that anybody could go through. It takes away your whole dignity and there's nothing you can do.
>
> (Ibid.: 177)

Mourne House was Armagh's enduring legacy.

In the shadow of the conflict

In May 2002, the political prisoners released under the terms of the 1998 Belfast (Good Friday) Agreement, the Prisons Inspectorate conducted an inspection of Mourne House as part of Maghaberry Prison. It noted 'the potential dangers' inherent 'in situations where the needs of a small group of women ... can become marginalised' (Prisons Inspectorate 2002). The report continues: 'It is essential to avoid the identity of the units for women prisoners becoming confused with the larger prison site'. Given the distinct needs and contexts of women's imprisonment, 'safeguards' inclu-ded '*total* separation, *distinct* management and staffing teams and *separate* healthcare facilities' (emphases added). While highly critical of its regime, the Inspectorate considered 'Mourne House has the potential ... to operate as a high quality facility for women in custody' (ibid.: MH.01). Yet, as operated, it was managed as another house unit of the male jail, with 'no recognition of the different needs' of women prisoners. Staffing levels were inappropriately high and had not been reviewed since the unit held high-security politically affiliated prisoners. Eighty-seven officers were desig-nated to Mourne, which held an average of 25 female prisoners, and women were 'routinely escorted over short distances from house units to the healthcare centre' (ibid.: MH.24).

The regime was constructed around lengthy periods of lock-up and an inactive day. Some women had little to occupy them except cleaning duties, and activities were frequently cancelled due to 'operational difficulties'. Although the standard of educational provision was potentially good, classes were frequently cancelled due to 'operational considerations'. The Mourne House kitchen had been 'mothballed', preventing women from preparing their own food. The inspectors found an unhealthy balance of male staff to female prisoners, leaving many women prisoners feeling uncomfortable, especially if they were checked when using the toilet or washing. Violence and abuse in some women prisoners' histories contributed to their vulnerability. They were not transported separately, travelling in the same vehicles as male prisoners, and they were taunted on court visits. The inspectors found complacency over record keeping, even in relation to a young woman with a long history of self-harm. She was not identified as being at risk on her escort record.

Further criticisms included: strip-searching of women without specific reason; insufficient information and support for women during their first night in prison; no structured induction programme. The inspectors severely criticised the regime's treatment of suicidal and self-harming women, especially young women. In particular, they were disturbed by the use of the punishment block and the main male prison hospital to manage women enduring mental ill-health:

> It was not appropriate to accommodate distressed female prisoners in what were little more than strip cells in an environment which essentially centred on the care of male prisoners, many of whom who had mental health problems. This was more likely to increase feelings of vulnerability.
>
> (Ibid.: MH.36)

The inspectors were profoundly concerned to find a 15-year-old self-harming child held in strip clothing in the punishment block. They 'were told that staff were not good at recording all the work that had gone into trying alternative strategies with the young person before this action was decided upon'. No staff had child-centred or child protection training. The report presented detailed recommendations across the regime, including: using Mourne House as a discrete female facility; constructing a policy and strategic plan for the treatment of women in custody; gender-specific training for all staff and managers; initiating a low-security unit with significantly reduced staffing levels; reopening the women's healthcare unit. Between the inspection and the publication of the highly critical report in September 2002, one of the young women held in Mourne House, Annie Kelly, took her own life in a punishment block strip cell.

Annie's story

Annie Kelly, the tenth in a family of 12 children, was first in conflict with the law aged 13. Her family noted a significant change in her behaviour following the tragic death of her brother. A year later she received her first conviction. She was sent to Training School and then to a Juvenile Justice Centre, where she was served with a Certificate of Unruliness. In July 1996 she was imprisoned in Mourne House, her behaviour considered too difficult for a juvenile facility. Aged 15, she was held in a high security women's prison. Over a five-year period she received 28 custodial sentences. Her behaviour in prison was challenging, her convictions reflecting a range of offences, including assault on the police, riotous and disorderly behaviour, criminal damage, theft and common assault. A prison teacher who never felt threatened by Annie recalled her treatment:

> Nobody [prison staff] knew how to handle her. What happened was dreadful. She responded to the more aggressive staff by hitting out. She was held most of the time in solitary confinement. When I taught her our chairs were bolted to the ground.
>
> (Interview, March 2004)

Annie was regularly transferred to the male prison hospital. Agitated and disturbed, she 'heard voices' and self-harmed. She lacerated her arms, banged her head, inserted metal objects under her skin and strangled herself with ligatures, losing consciousness. Between 1997 and 2002 the records show numerous assaults on staff, cell wreckings and 40 incidents of self-harm. Her formal psychiatric assessment found no 'organic' impairment or mental illness. She was diagnosed as having attitudinal problems derived in a personality disorder. The diagnosis was offered as an explanation for her antagonistic behaviour towards staff, her self-harm and her 'suicidal ideation'. Outside, she drank heavily. Yet her medical assessments record a bright and intelligent young woman suffering from low self-esteem and self-denigration.

In April 2001 Annie was committed to prison over a weekend. Uncooperative and aggressive on reception, she was escorted to the punishment block where, according to official reports, she assaulted prison officers. She was put in isolation, unlocked only when three officers were present and a full-length shield formed a barrier between Annie and the officers. Following a self harm attempt she was strip-searched by officers. She resisted the search and a three-person control and restraint team, in riot gear, was deployed. She was restrained, handcuffed and medically examined. Officers alleged that, alone in the cell, she slipped the handcuffs and smashed the spy-hole glass.

Violence towards prison officers was the justification for her segregation. In June 2002 she wrecked a punishment-block cell. According to reports she wrenched the hand basin from the wall, removed the taps and used them to break through the cell wall. She was returned to the basic punishment regime in a 'dry cell'. Dressed in a 'protective' gown, she was given a 'non-destructible' blanket. There was no mattress, no bed and no pillow. She slept on a raised concrete plinth. According to officers, she considered the strip cell 'hers'.

Annie often lay on the plinth and banged her head on the floor. She tore ligatures from the supposedly indestructible clothing and blankets, but repeated acts of self-strangulation were not taken seriously by most officers, who believed she was faking or feigning suicide to irritate them. A clinical psychologist recorded concern that Annie might cause herself an accidental suicide. All staff were aware of this concern, as were other prisoners, one of whom stated:

> I talked to Annie. She was a very young girl. She needed a lot of attention and some of the girls upstairs [young prisoners] need the same. But we can't do anything. We know somebody's talking about it [suicide] and we tell staff but we don't know what they do with that. It's not really taken seriously ... some of them take it seriously but others will go, 'She's always at it'. That's not the attitude to have.
>
> (Interview, March 2004)

Annie was transferred to the male prison hospital. She wrote a harrowing account of the transfer to her sister (Personal letter, dated 13 August 2002, used with consent). It was her last letter home. 'You wouldn't believe the way I'm treated. You would need to see it with your own two eyes.' She described how the 'control and restraint team landed over and told me I had to take off my clothes and put a suicide dress on'. She complied when the all-male team told her they would hold her down and strip her.

> Then they all held me out in the corridor. I only had the suicide dress on and I was told I could keep my pants cause I'd a s.t. on. But when the men were holding me they got a woman screw to pull my pants off. That shouldn't have happened. Then they covered me in celatape to keep the dress closed and handcuffed me and dragged me off to the male hospital.

The male hospital was a 'dirty kip' and she 'stuck it out for 6 days cause they threatned [sic] to put me in the male p.s.u. [punishment and segregation unit] if I smashed it'. She 'wrecked' the hospital cell and was returned to the Mourne House punishment block. 'I'm just relieved to be back.' Still in a 'suicide dress', she had 'hung myself a pile of times. I just rip the dress and make a noose. But I am only doing that cause of the way their treating me. The cell floor is covered in phiss cause they took the phiss pot out the other night.' She complained of flies in the cell:

> They won't let me clean it. I haven't had a shower now in 4 days. I've had no mattress or blanket either the past few nights ... At the end of the day I know that if any thing happens me there'll be an investigation. I

never ripped the mattress or blanket nor did I block the spy. So if I take phenumia it'll all come out ... I think you can only last 10–12 days without drinking cause then you dehydrate and your kidneys go. I've no intention of eating or drinking again so their [sic] beat there. I know they'd all love me dead but I'd make sure everything is revealed first.

A management plan had been agreed. Annie was to be transferred from the hospital to a normal association landing alongside other women prisoners. She rejected the plan, demanding a return to the punishment block. When told she could not be transferred immediately she smashed the hospital cell. Annie was moved on 10 August. Between the 10 and 13 August, the day she wrote her letter home, she was held without basic sanitation or bedding. She refused food and water.

She moved from the strip cell to an intermediate cell in the punishment block. After six days she wrecked that cell and strangled herself, demanding a return to 'her' cell. She was moved into strip conditions, ripped her clothing and applied ligatures to her neck. On 30 August a member of the Board of Visitors found her refusing to eat. Food littered the cell floor. She had 'no ambition except to die'. The Board of Visitors considered a 'different approach concerning Annie should be made with some urgency – perhaps a medical approach, assessment and treatment elsewhere' (Internal Review, undated). Yet she was placed in solitary confinement in the punishment block for a further 28 days. On 5 September she made what was to be her final court appearance, was convicted of attempted robbery and burglary, and sentenced to 18 months.

The next day officers stated that Annie had tied ligatures around her neck. The doctor recorded faint marks. Her care plan was updated and she was classified 'at risk'. The doctor concluded: 'The whole area of what appears to be an increasing number of young disturbed females needs to be looked at with a view to having a regime in place including specialist help and training for staff in an environment which does not come under the standard application of the prison ethos' (ibid.).

Late on 5 September a confrontation took place between Annie and Night Guard duty officers. Following the incident, the senior officer headed a written statement: 'A. Kelly Fake Ligatures'. He was told by staff that she had blocked the spy hole. Minutes later Annie 'was lying on the cell floor with a ligature around her neck tied to the window'. The senior officer called for others 'to make up a control and restraint team' and for a hospital officer. As the team was about to be deployed the senior officer 'observed F929 A Kelly get off the floor laughing and get into bed'. He ordered officers to clear the cell 'of anything that could block the spies'. The team returned to the cell twice within five minutes to remove further ligatures from her neck. 'All the ligatures were made from her suicide blanket? [sic] one of them being 9ft long. Lack of female officers made it impossible to search or strip Kelly to prevent this' (ibid.).

That night a woman prisoner, in a cell directly above Annie, heard her screaming (Interview, May 2005). The following evening was significantly quieter. In the early hours of 7 September she heard noises from Annie's cell. A male voice, she assumed it to be a prison officer, was shouting, 'Come on, Annie, come on'. Then all was quiet. During the morning Annie was unlocked, taken to the shower and returned to her cell. No other prisoners were held in the punishment block. From prison officers' accounts the three officers on duty had minimal interaction with Annie.

Annie Kelly died in her cell during the early afternoon. A female officer checked the spy-hole. Annie was at the window, ligatures around her neck and her tongue out. The ends of the ligatures were attached to diamond metal mesh through a small gap between the inner window frame and its Perspex cover. Walking from the cell to the office, the officer told her colleagues that Annie was using ligatures again. Assuming Annie had staged 'another' incident the officer did not raise the alarm. The officers, in riot equipment, entered the cell. Not responding, the officers realised Annie was dead or dying.

Following Annie's death a case conference was held. It recorded 'the need for ... appropriate knowledge to deal with prisoners who suffer from acute personality disorders' and 'for a co-ordinated multi-disciplinary approach' (Internal Review, undated). These conclusions echo the concerns raised and transmitted by the Belfast Coroner to the Prison Service following the inquest into the death of Janet Holmes five years earlier. Of profound and continuing concern was how, given her history and recent behaviour, Annie had the means to end her life. She was in a strip cell modified specifically for her use. There were two observation windows in the cell door, a cell window protected by metal diamond mesh in a steel frame covered by Perspex. The ceiling was lined with sheet metal with no exposed seams. All conduits, ducting and pipes had been removed. There was no integral sanitation or electrical fittings. She was usually dressed in non-destructible, protective clothing, her blanket made from similar material. Yet officers and managers were aware that blankets and clothing could be torn. But modification to the cell windows enabled access to the metal mesh through a gap sufficiently wide to take ligatures and hold her weight.

The Prison Service internal inquiry recommended issuing electronic pagers or alternative means of contact to nursing staff for swift emergency response. It called for updating and replacing monitoring equipment and upgrading protective blankets and clothing. It also recommended an inspection of the cell to consider 'modifications that may be necessary as a consequence of this tragedy' (ibid.). More broadly, the inquiry team 'recognises and endorses the general concern ... that an adult institution is an inappropriate place to commit a juvenile female'. The Prison Service 'should consult with all relevant bodies to consider the provision of a secure community based facility for juveniles with personality based disorders within Northern Ireland'. The Prison Service Suicide Working

Group's terms of reference 'should be extended to include the management of juveniles with personality disorders' and staff training should be provided 'as a matter of urgency'.

Roseanne's story

Born in October 1969 in Belfast, Roseanne Irvine was the youngest in a family of seven children. According to a pre-sentence report, as a child she witnessed and was subjected to violence, although one of her sisters recalls a happy childhood. She enjoyed school, left at 16 to enrol at a youth training scheme and then worked in a local factory. In 1991 she became pregnant. Soon after the birth of her daughter she began to suffer depression, and alcohol dependency followed. From early 1994 until September 2001 she was treated on 38 separate occasions for anxiety, depression, alcohol intoxication, drug overdoses, self harm and attempted suicide. She was admitted to hospital, mental-health and psychiatric units on numerous occasions. In 2001 a consultant psychiatrist diagnosed 'chronic psychosocial maladjustment' exacerbated by alcohol abuse. This was interpreted as 'borderline personality disorder' (File notes).

She was considered a loving and caring mother, but because of 'repetitive episodes' of self-harm and alcoholism her daughter was placed on the Child Protection Register and cared for by her older brother and his family. In February 2002 another of Roseanne's brothers died, in a hostel fire. His sudden death had a deep impact on her mental health. She attempted suicide and was admitted to hospital. The day after her release she drank heavily and set fire to her home. With no previous record of offending behaviour, she was charged with arson. On the day she was remanded to prison, 22 March 2002, an IMR21 (prisoner at risk of suicide) was opened. She was located on the C2 committals landing, where a nurse officer carried out an initial check, but she was not seen by a doctor. A second IMR21 was opened six days later, confirming she was a 'potential suicide risk', but again the doctor did not visit her.

On 9 April 2002 a Prison Officers' Association (POA) representative wrote to the Governor informing him that Roseanne had attempted suicide during the previous night-guard period. She had strangled herself with a ligature and was 'lying face down'. She was examined by a doctor, who recommended her transfer to the male prison hospital for 'special care'. The transfer did not happen and Roseanne was taken to the Mourne House punishment block. She was dressed in an anti-suicide gown, without underwear and placed on 15-minute observation in a strip cell. Referring to criticisms of prison management following a previous death in custody, the POA letter asked:

> Why does the management of the Prison Hospital continue to ignore the contents of the Suicide Awareness Manual?

Why are the hospital management so reluctant to accept female prisoners and why are those prisoners who are admitted to the Prison Hospital returned to Mourne House after the briefest possible stay?

Why are IMR21's raised by Mourne Wing staff constantly brushed aside after a token examination by a Hospital Officer?

Why did it take approximately thirty-five minutes for the Night Guard Hospital Officer to reach C2 on the night of the incident in question?

Why was Irvine not admitted to the Prison Hospital immediately after attempting to take her own life?

Why was [she] placed in a Segregation cell in Mourne PSU [prison support unit]?

(Letter, dated 9 April 2002)

Subsequently, the POA reported another attempt by Roseanne on her own life: 'To our dismay once again the regulations laid down in the Suicide Awareness Manual were ignored' leaving her 'in her own cell and placed on fifteen minutes observation by the night guard' (Letter, undated). It had been agreed previously that prisoners on 'special watch' would not be accommodated on residential landings. Yet the Governor responsible for healthcare and the prison doctor were 'of the opinion that prisoners who are not in clinical need should be kept in a Residential House'. The POA considered that 'prisoners deemed to be at risk of self harm' should be 'placed in the Health Care Centre and treated by Nursing Officers'. Soon after, the POA registered a 'failure to agree' with the Governor stating:

Hospital management are continuing to ignore the regulations governing the treatment of prisoners who are attempting self-harm. This is placing an intolerable burden on discipline staff by placing these prisoners in residential units instead of the healthcare centre.

(Notification of Failure to Agree, 19 April 2002)

In May 2002 the POA Chairman advised a healthcare meeting that it was 'necessary to have a Health Care Officer in Mourne House during association and at night and requested the matter be looked into' (Meeting Minutes). This was a consequence of Roseanne's self-harming and attempted suicide. Subsequently he stated:

There are only two health care officers at night on the male side. If you have two medical emergencies you've had it. You must have a health care officer available for Mourne House at all times.

(Interview, March 2004)

Following another meeting, the POA noted that the Governor had accepted the 'manual' might not be used appropriately in responding to self-harming prisoners. He had stated that admission to the prison hospital was based on a medical assessment of clinical need and self harm was 'not necessarily a medical problem' but a 'multi-disciplinary problem'. Further, a working party on the implementation of new suicide-awareness arrangements was in process and a recent healthcare review had recommended handling 'at risk prisoners ... on normal location'. The POA requested 'a review into the possibility of re-opening Mourne [women's] healthcare centre' (Interview, March 2004).

In September 2002 Roseanne was involved in a further incident. Again the POA sent a memorandum headed: 'Treatment of Prisoners deemed to be at risk of Self Harm' (16 September 2002). It noted that Roseanne had 'committed an act of self harm on C2 landing' and 'As usual the regulations contained in the Inmate Suicide Awareness Manual ... were ignored by Prison Management'. The Duty Governor had 'left instructions that Irvine should be placed on fifteen minutes observation and remain in her cell on C2'. The POA commented, 'Once again Night Guard Staff untrained in medical procedures are being placed in an intolerable situation.' He was unequivocal that prisoners 'on special watch cannot remain on a residential unit'.

In October 2002 Roseanne was sentenced to two years on probation. She went to live at Bridge House, a therapeutic community for women with complex mental health needs. She settled in Bridge House but she was returned to prison in August 2003 for breaching her probation order. Again she was placed on an IMR21. By November she had served her time and was discharged from prison. She lived in a hostel, but with no therapeutic facility available her problems with alcohol, glue, gas and drugs worsened. She transferred to another hostel, where she was deeply disturbed because of intimidation by men living there. She moved to a flat, but her habit impelled her back to the hostel. According to a nun who visited her, Roseanne's 'mood became very low and she said she wanted psychiatric help' (Interview and correspondence, March 2004). She was expelled for one night from the hostel and left on the streets. The hostel social worker considered Roseanne required appropriate psychiatric care. She was given a psychiatric hospital appointment for early February 2004. On 21 January, while out with others from the hostel she was attacked by one of the group.

Within two weeks, following a further suicide attempt, Roseanne was admitted to hospital. The nun found her 'very withdrawn and depressed', but optimistic she would receive care and treatment following her hospital appointment. The next day the nun visited her again:

> When I arrived I could see Rosanne was very depressed and did not know what was happening to her. She had seen [the consultant] in a

room with many other people, which she found very distressing, and was unable to communicate. I went to see the ward sister who came with me to Roseanne's bedside and told her that she was being discharged under the care of the community health team. Roseanne was very distressed.

Roseanne was discharged from hospital without medication. The hospital had no information on her whereabouts. She was taken to the Homeless Advice Centre and allocated a place in a house occupied by men who suffered multiple problems, mainly alcohol and drugs related. She was 'very frightened' living at the house. The caretaker was on duty only from 7pm until 7am. Roseanne kept her February appointment with the consultant, who told her that she should be in hospital. An appointment was made for her to attend the day hospital for medication. The nun continued to visit Roseanne:

> I went to [the house]. I could not get in several times. Then on one occasion a drunk man answered the door and he told me Roseanne was out. I left a message for Roseanne to phone me. I eventually got to see Roseanne. I brought another sister with me as I was afraid to go into this house by myself. Roseanne was in a terrible state of depression, confusion. She said she was frightened 'out of her mind', had taken drugs, drink and glue and no medication.

Concerned that Roseanne had not been visited at the house to assess its suitability, the nun telephoned Roseanne's care manager and reported her 'depressed, suicidal and unable to stand, her eyes rolling'. The care manager arranged an outpatient hospital appointment. That evening Roseanne telephoned, 'drunk and suicidal'. Within a week she was in police custody and 'appeared in court in her pyjamas'. She had set fire to her room at the hostel and was charged with arson. On 20 February Roseanne was remanded in custody.

When Roseanne arrived at Mourne House she was 'health screened' by a Nursing Officer. She was assessed 'No risk indicated at present'. Yet a further entry recorded she had attempted hanging the previous week and she had self-harmed her face and arms three days earlier. No entry was made on information supplied by the police or other agencies regarding mental or physical health concerns. Yet the PACE form accompanying Roseanne to prison was explicit. It required the police to disclose any indication of potential exceptional risk. Under the heading 'May have suicidal tendencies' three ticks had been entered alongside two handwritten asterisks. Under 'Physical illness or mental disturbance' was one tick. In the section 'Supporting Notes' the words 'SELF HARM' were written in capitals, underlined, with two asterisks. There followed, also underlined, with accompanying asterisks, the handwritten comment, 'Informed C.P.N that she would cut herself if the opportunity arose'. The asterisks and under-lining were in red ink. On her arrival at prison the 'health screening' ignored the contents of the PACE form.

On 1 March Roseanne told a prison officer that she intended to hang herself. The officer opened an IMR21 and Roseanne was put in an anti-suicide gown, her underwear removed, supplied with an anti-suicide blanket, potty and a container of water and transferred to C1, variously labelled a 'close' or 'special' supervision unit. In reality it was the punishment block. Despite the Inspectorate's recommendations and Annie Kelly's death, women who self-harmed or threatened suicide continued to be 'managed' by solitary confinement in a strip cell, 23 hours a day. During the following morning two Governors and a Senior Officer discussed Roseanne's case but she was left on C1. A nursing officer also stated that Roseanne had threatened to set fire to herself. She was scheduled to attend 'sick parade' in line with the IMR21 requirements to be seen by a doctor. It was cancelled and the duty doctor was not informed of her condition. The healthcare section of the IMR21 remained blank. During the day an officer noted her distress in the strip cell and that she had torn hair from her scalp. Despite this, and without a doctor's medical assessment, she was returned to C2.

At risk, still on an IMR21 and without medical examination, Roseanne was returned to an ordinary cell. It had multiple ligature points and she had access to a range of ligatures. The next day sick parade was cancelled again and the doctor did not visit her. Officers reported her 'calm' and 'in good form'. In the afternoon she was visited by the prison probation officer. She informed Roseanne that her social worker had arranged a meeting to arrange a visit from her daughter. The probation officer stated she gave Roseanne a handwritten note to that effect. The note was never found. After the probation officer's visit Roseanne became upset. She told officers she might not be allowed to see her daughter again.

During a short evening unlock Roseanne stated that she had taken '5 Blues' supplied by another prisoner. Officers assumed the tablets to be diazepam. In fact they were Efexor. She was already on a range of medication including Efexor: omprazole; diazepam; chloral betaine; chlorpromazine, Inderal LA; Largactil. The Mourne House Governor, in another part of the male prison, was informed of the alleged overdose. He ordered an immediate cell search. This was not carried out and the women were locked in their cells for the night. The Night Guard with responsibility for C2 stated she did not know that Roseanne was on an IMR21, nor that she had taken a drugs overdose. At approximately 9.15pm Roseanne was sitting on her bed writing a note. She asked for the light to be switched off. Just over an hour later she was checked. She was hanging by the neck from the ornate bars of the window. The noose was a draw cord from her pyjama bottoms.

The aftermath

Its apparent inevitability made the death of Roseanne Irvine particularly shocking. As an officer put it: 'We have our own list, our own worries as to specific women who might have died ... she displayed the symptoms, the prior attempts. The warning bells were there' (Interview, March 2004). A professional worker stated, 'everyone realised that Roseanne had great needs but it [the provision] fell short because no-one put their hand up for overall responsibility' (Interview, March 2004). Given Roseanne's history of vulnerability, self-harm and attempted suicide, the lack of a personal care plan raised immediate concerns about the circumstances of her death. Deeply distressed, she was convinced that access to her daughter was under threat. Another prisoner recalled:

> She was always talking about her wee daughter. She loved her so much she talked about [her] every day. She hadn't seen her daughter for three weeks and she really missed her. She said to me that she did not think she would see her again because what her social worker told the prison officer to tell her. She told Roseanne that [her daughter] was happy and it would not be right to bring her up to the prison to see her. That really hurt Roseanne. You could see it in her face when she was telling me. It was Roseanne's child and she had every right to see her.
>
> (Interview, March 2004)

A prison officer stated that Roseanne 'was not getting to see her daughter' but did not know why. She continued:

> In a letter a week ago she told her daughter that she was not well, but that she really missed her and wanted to see her. She loved her daughter but she was ill and it [the illness] was no fault of her own.
>
> (Interview, March 2004)

From the accounts of other women prisoners Roseanne had suffered in the punishment block. One woman stated that 'she had had to lie on wood' and another commented that she 'was sore on her back after the punishment block' (Interviews, March 2004). In fact she had lain on a concrete plinth without a mattress or a pillow. Still considered at risk, her return to C2 gave her access to several ligatures in a cell with multiple ligature points, not least the patterned metalwork of the window bars. She received no counselling, had little meaningful contact with staff and was locked up, unobserved, for extended periods.

A woman prisoner stated that on the evening of her death 'Roseanne told me not long before we got locked up that the staff did not check on the women every hour and she said to me that one of these nights they will find someone hanging and they will be dead. That very night Roseanne was found dead' (Interview, March 2004). She continued:

> If the staff had checked on Roseanne more often that night she might be alive today. They knew she was down ... The girl needed help which she did not get. She was so down. This place is like hell on earth.

A woman in a C2 cell heard another woman 'squealing and shouting' to Roseanne but 'no buzzer went off'. She was convinced that the officers had turned off the emergency cell buzzers. Another woman stated:

> What happened to Roseanne was frightening. You think you're going to bed safe and you wake up and ask a warder where someone is and they say she hanged herself ... All she wanted was to see her child but they didn't listen to her. Roseanne's death could have been prevented.
>
> (Interview, March 2004)

The impact on the other women prisoners was immediate:

> The next day I just sat and cried. I then had panic attacks. They didn't get the nurse over. I pushed the [emergency] button and they came to the door. I asked to see the nurse and they just said 'No'. They said, 'You're not allowed to push the button. It's for emergencies only'. I said I was having a panic attack. They said, 'Take deep breaths'. It was early evening. I sat up on the bed with a pillow and cried and cried.
>
> (Interview, March 2004)

Roseanne's closest friend on the landing, Jane (pseudonym), was devastated and was transferred to the male prison hospital, where she was interviewed several days after Roseanne's death. The interview took place in an office and the level of constant noise outside was intense. It seemed out of place in a healthcare facility accommodating acutely disturbed and distressed patients:

> While we were talking the daily routine of the prison hospital was happening beyond the door ... loud male voices shouting and laughing; jokes and banter between staff; the constant rattling of keys; whistling; telephones ringing; people's names being shouted down corridors. All interpersonal communications seemed at full pitch.
>
> (Fieldnotes, March 2004).

Throughout the interview Jane was agitated and cried. She apologised constantly for her emotional and physical 'state':

The way that girl was treated the system let her down. There should be a hospital for women. It was disgusting, dirty in here ... I always told her not to do anything to herself. I tried to see her that night but we only got 20 minutes out [of the cells]. I started to write things down myself. I wrote there should be more support for women with mental health problems.

(Interview, March 2004)

Jane talked about her own mental health problems: 'You get no support, the staff ignore you'. She had twice received visits from a psychiatric nurse 'then it was stopped'; there was 'no support for women with depression'. In the prison hospital 'you're locked up 23 hours a day'. She continued:

If you're sitting there [in the cell] for hours there's stuff that goes through your mind. If I don't get out today I'll plan something. They think there's nothing I can do but I can. They think they know everything but they don't. I've got a plan, I know what I'll do. My first cousin hung himself.

She had not wanted to be transferred to the male prison hospital, 'it's filthy'. Jane was held in strip conditions. The bed was bolted to the floor and the metal toilet, with fixed wooden seat, was open to observation. It was described by a senior orderly as a 'basic suite' which the staff tried 'to keep as clean and tidy as possible given the circumstances'.

Jane wanted to go back to Mourne House, where she could have contact with other women. Initially she thought she would be in the prison hospital for 'one or two nights'.

The doctor doesn't want me to go back over there but I can talk better over there. Over here they don't even talk to you and it's supposed to be a hospital. Here, if you feel really down they don't care.

The isolation, particularly from other women, was the most difficult aspect of the 23 hour lock up: 'I've never been in prison before. I hate getting locked up ... it brings memories back to me'. She disclosed a history of sexual abuse, 'I'm lying trying to sleep, thinking about these things'. She continued:

In the hospital they [male prisoners] talk filthy and dirt with the other prisoners. A man exposed himself. Said, 'I'll give her one'. He thought 'I'll pull it out 'cos there's a woman there'. We were all outside together. One man is in for sexually abusing a child. We have to have association with them. They are crafty, some of them. I told them [staff] about what the man did but they never did anything about it. I did not feel safe around them.

Her account was deeply disturbing. The senior orderly on duty confirmed that Jane had been on association with male prisoners in the recreation room. He explained:

> There are difficulties housing women prisoners in a male ward. These are acutely disturbed prisoners ... Unlock depends if there's sufficient female staff. But they do have association with male prisoners.
>
> (Conversation, March 2004)

On hearing Jane's experiences in the recreation room the orderly stated they always ensured a female member of staff was present, but he did not contest Jane's account. The 'situation' in the prison hospital, he stated, was 'acute and volatile'. For Jane, grieving the loss of her friend while struggling with her past memories and current fears, the experience of incarceration was 'like a nightmare and you think it's never going to end'. She said that if 'they'd doubled me up [shared cell with Roseanne] then I could have saved her life. She was worried about whether she would ever see [her daughter] again'. Jane's concern was that 'there'll be more deaths in this prison because people don't get the help they need'. She wrote later:

> I have four kids and four grandkids and I miss them all so much. I keep thinking to myself I will never see mine again. I love them all so much too. But to me time is running out for me. I can't take much more. Every day is like a nightmare.
>
> (Letter, March 2004)

The inquests

The inquest into the death of Annie Kelly was held at Belfast Coroner's Court between 10 and 23 November, 2004; two years and two months after her death. Prison governors and officers portrayed Annie as a deeply disturbed, manipulative young woman beyond management or control; a danger to herself, to other prisoners and to staff. They considered her situation self-inflicted. She 'chose' the strip cell, 'her' cell; she 'faked' suicide to 'taunt' prison officers; she was capable of formidable violence; she could wreck cells and destroy anti-suicide blankets and clothing with her bare hands. As an officer stated previously, 'She wasn't mad but bad' (Interview, March 2004). Yet it was a representation not universally shared. A teacher who knew her well stated that after Annie died 'a lot of people had to look at their consciences. Some staff [officers] would respond positively to her, put a radio by her door, but other staff [Pause] ... Things did happen. Annie was goaded and she would hit out' (Interview, March 2004).

Annie's mother, Ann Kelly, recorded how prison visits to see Annie 'were difficult because of the strict supervision engaged in by Prison Staff who were both very hostile towards Annie and ourselves' (Written statement to the Inquest, with permission). Annie had complained 'on numerous occasions' to Ann 'about the rough treatment she was receiving from Prison Staff and being constantly under control and supervision of male staff'. This was particularly demeaning 'in situations where she was being searched'. She had also complained 'that she had been detained in exercise areas which were shared by male prisoners', a reference to her time in the male prison hospital. Ann accepted that it was Annie's intention 'to upset Prison Staff by engaging in mock suicide attempts to create panic and cause staff to feel upset about her and her detention'. Yet it was hostility from prison officers that had given 'rise to a lack of concern for Annie's safety and led her to be placed in a cell which increased the likelihood of Annie engaging in mock suicide attempts'.

Ann Kelly felt that 'strong hostility among Prison Staff and Governors towards Annie' resulted in complacency: 'I am not satisfied a proper regime was in place to supervise her given that there had been numerous instances of this nature which gave rise to her death prior to it happening'. Following a visit to the cell in which Annie died, to offer prayers, Ann concluded 'nothing had been done by Prison Authorities to ensure that she was placed in a safe environment which would have prevented these mock suicide attempts which were usually in the form of hanging'.

The jury was unimpressed by the proposition that Annie had brought death on herself. Detailed and thorough, its narrative verdict was unprecedented in indicting the Northern Ireland Prison Service for its endemic failures (Verdict, 23 November 2004). The jury found the 'main contributor' to her death 'lack of communication and training at all levels'. For prison managers, governors and officers the verdict offered no hiding place, no opportunity for buck-passing and no escape from responsibility. 'There was', concluded the narrative verdict, 'no understanding or clear view of any one person's role in the management and understanding of Annie.' They identified a 'major deficiency in communication between Managers, Doctors and the dedicated team' responsible for Annie's health, welfare and safe custody. There were 'no set policies to adhere to', specifically a lack of appropriate management and staff training. And there was 'no consistency in her treatment and regime from one Governor to the next'.

Having established that the Prison Service was institutionally deficient, the jury listed five 'reasonable precautions' to be acted on. The anti-suicide blankets were 'deficient' and an 'anti-ligature window should have been installed from the outset'. Given events immediately prior to her death, 'clearer guidelines on observation and monitoring' might have reduced the 'opportunity of making ligatures'. A cell search would have discovered ligatures and 'cell inspection should have been carried out frequently and thoroughly especially in regard to the window'.

The jury identified six further 'factors relevant to the circumstances of her death'. They criticised her 'very long periods of isolation' and the lack of appropriate 'female facilities'. They recommended better 'availability of resuscitation equipment within the Prison' and the availability of first-aid equipment 'on every landing'. Responding to evidence concerning the paucity of adolescent mental healthcare in the North of Ireland, the jury called for the provision of a 'therapeutic community'. Failing this, the 'Judicial system should strive to provide a like environment'. Finally, the 'Northern Ireland Mental Health Order needs to be updated to include personality disorders'. Given the failures in broader care provision, the deficiencies in communication and training 'at all levels' and the inadequate and inappropriate treatment of Annie, the jury decided she did not die 'by her own act'.

Just over two years later, on 13 February 2007 and following a week-long inquest into Roseanne's death, a different jury returned another damning narrative verdict. It stated: 'The prison system failed Roseanne'. She had taken her own life while the 'balance of her mind was disturbed'. Reflecting on prison officers' and managers' evidence that had demonstrated a fatal mix of complacency, incompetence and negligence, the jury noted the significance of 'the events leading up to her death, i.e. long history of mental health difficulties specifically the incidents that occurred from 1–3 March'.

The 'defects' in the system were: 'Severe lack of communication and inadequate recording'; 'The management of the IMR21 (failure to act)'; 'Lack of healthcare and resources for women prisoners'. These had contributed to Roseanne's death as follows: 'All staff were not aware of Roseanne's circumstances and could not act accordingly'; 'Priority should have been made to see a doctor'; the 'Hospital wing was inadequate for female prisoners'. The jury listed four 'reasonable precautions' that had been neglected: 'Could have been taken to an outside hospital/out of [hours] call doctor'; 'Full briefing during handovers'; 'Decisions to be moved from C1 to C2 should not have been made by a non-medically trained qualified staff member'; 'To be paired up with friend in cell – more checks'. 'Other factors' were: 'Prison is not a suitable environment for someone with a personality/mental health disorder. Under Northern Ireland's Mental Health legislation there is no other alternative'; 'more ongoing training on suicide awareness for prison staff'.

The Coroner announced his intention to write to the Director of the Prison Service and to the Secretary of State for Northern Ireland. Spontaneous applause from the three rows of family members erupted as the jury left the court. The verdict illustrated systemic failings in a prison that had been severely criticised by the Prisons Inspectorate following its inspection in May 2002. Four months later, Annie Kelly had taken her own life in a strip cell in the punishment block. At the time of the research, early in 2004, far from there being improvements in the regime to rectify its failings, it had deteriorated further. In particular, vulnerable women suffering mental ill-health endured the consequences (see Scraton and Moore 2005). In 2005 an inquest jury heavily criticised the Prison Service for its contribution to the death of Annie Kelly. The Human Rights Commission reiterated its call for a public inquiry into the circumstances surrounding both deaths, encompassing the broader issues of institutional failings, managerial incompetence and regime breakdown. It did so again following the jury's verdict at the Roseanne Irvine inquest. In March 2007 the Northern Ireland Affairs Committee announced an inquiry into healthcare in Northern Ireland's prisons.

Women in prison: towards abolition

This chapter opened with the 'Armagh legacy' and the shadow cast by the jail over Mourne House. To some commentators and researchers the imprisonment of those convicted of conflict-related offences and those convicted of 'ordinary' offences cannot be bracketed together. The 'special circumstances' of the war in the North of Ireland undoubtedly created and, to an extent, requires a distinct analysis. In the context of women's imprisonment at the time of the research, however, it was evident that many customs and practices associated with the imprisonment of politically motivated prisoners remained intact. Armagh was a prison in which the needs of women prisoners were secondary to those of men. Political imprisonment and sectarianism hardened the response to Republican prisoners, particularly the regular use of violent strip searches. Humiliation and degradation were the most common descriptions proffered by women prisoners, whose evidence demonstrates how prison officers used force to instil fear and terror. Nakedness became the most potent weapon against resilient women in the determination to break their mental resolve. 'Defeminisation' purposefully undermined women's femininity and sexuality, through persistent vilification. Alongside was the inevitable 'othering' of women prisoners, juxtaposing the 'good woman' as wife and mother to the 'bad woman', neglectful of her role, her family and herself.

These constructions are not confined to the imprisonment of politically motivated women prisoners. The research literature on the history and expansion of women's imprisonment in advanced democratic states is replete with examples of institutionalised sexism and misogyny. Pat Carlen's definitive study found women prisoners caught in a double bind. Institutionally they were defined as 'both within and without sociability, both within and without femininity; and, concomitantly, within and without adulthood' (Carlen 1983: 90). Being judged, assessed and, to some extent, classified on their capacity for social interaction; their femininity in terms of appearance, tidiness, motherhood; and on their maturity, by prison officers, governors and medical staff amounted to a triple bind.

Carlen's interviews revealed routine degradation as basic as denying toilet access. Women also 'received little sympathy regarding pre-menstrual tension and even less recognition of their need for increased access to washing facil-ities during menstruation' (ibid.: 104). Pat Carlen and Anne Worrall (2004: 61) note a general acceptance 'that women's healthcare needs in prison – both physical and mental are more various and complex than men's ... but the overwhelming experience of women in prison is that their health needs are not consistently dealt with in a respectful and appropriate way'. At best, they argue, 'women's unpredictable bodies' are considered 'a nuisance' and 'at worst, a threat to security'. Specific needs go beyond 'routine menstrua-tion' to include 'pregnancy, cervical cytology, and breast cancer screening, and miscellaneous hormonally-triggered "women's ailments" ... chronic mundane conditions such as constipation and other digestive problems'.

Blanche Hampton (1995: 143) found that for women sentenced to imprisonment the 'crime' was not only 'against society' but also 'against womanhood'; a proposition 'reinforced continually, you abandoned your children. So all this added guilt comes on top of your own problems.' Jude McCulloch (1995: 8) states that, once imprisoned, women 'generally endure worse conditions than men ... less access to education, recreation, employment, training and health services than their male counterparts'. Amanda George (1995: 15) notes that women's marginalisation in prison reflects their marginalisation in wider society: 'The institutional prison contains women who have suffered the worst excesses of a highly stratified sexist, racist and class-based society.'

The assumed 'exceptional' behaviour of women who offend is often interpreted as irrational, unpredictable and a denial of their servile gender. Heidensohn (1985: 75) identifies that the 'implicit assumption' is that women prisoners are 'less reclaimable, more vile, more "unnatural" than male'. The stereotypical woman prisoner, then, is predisposed to offending and antisocial behaviour through an inherent pathological condition com-bining psychological damage and personality disorder. Joe Sim (1990: 176) specifies the key themes within the 'disciplinary matrix' imposed exclu-sively in women's prisons:

> ... the individualization of women prisoners; the drive to normalize their behaviour; the close interconnection between different, usually male-dominated groups whose activities have been built on the perpe-tual surveillance of the women's physical and psychological response to imprisonment; the advent of intensive technological control ...; the resistance of women to that control and to medical and psychiatric categorization; and the continuing entrapment of women within catch-all psychiatric categories such as behavioural and personality disorder.

For the authorities and 'often for the women themselves, each return to prison' represents 'another failure', their recidivism taken as proof that they had no intention or motivation to reform (Carlen 1983: 194). Consequently the 'temporary classification "disorderly", gradually ossifies into the more permanent "disordered" ... untreatable ... beyond the remit of the treatment agencies, without hope and beyond recognition'. Over 80 per cent of admissions to prison had histories of mental illness, yet imprisonment amounted to a denial of those histories. They were 'clothed instead with the disciplinary needs of the "disordered"' (ibid.: 196). As the Mourne House research shows, it remains a process provoking a 'compression and dispersion of all those definitional conditions and effects which cluster around the related concepts of personality disorder and anti-social personality disorder'.

Carlen (1983: 209) concludes that in its 'simultaneous identification of 'personality disorder' and its refusal to recognise it as a category of 'mental illness', psychiatry succeeded in a 'masterly stroke of professional imperialism'. Neither mentally ill nor treatable, the 'personality disordered' woman becomes a 'residual deviant' beyond the scope of treatment. Worse still, once the classification has been made, the status ascribed, she has 'little chance of having the label removed'. Psychiatrically categorised women prisoners are 'neither wholly mad nor wholly bad' but 'treated to a disciplinary regime where they are actually infantilised at the same time as attempts are made to make them feel guilty about their double, triple, quadruple, or even quintuple refusal of family, work, gender, health and reason' (ibid.).

Hampton (1995: 107) notes that women 'who attempt suicide or self-mutilate ... can expect to be tranquillised and/or isolated ... They may or may not be counselled and are seen by custodial staff as attention-seeking'. George (1995: 23) found self-harming women 'put in isolation (solitary), deprived of sensory input and placed in a bare concrete cell with a canvas mattress and a canvas blanket in a canvas nightie'. A recent study by Tamara Walsh (2004: 16) in Queensland shows how 'special needs' of mentally ill women, particularly those self-harming, are met through segregation in observation cells: 'barren, rubber rooms where prisoners are subjected to 24 hours a day lighting, stripped down and dressed in a suicide gown, and often physically restrained'.

Cassandra Shaylor (1998: 386) notes the 'emerging use of the control unit, the prison within the prison, as the ultimate regulation of the female body'. While 'control units' did not exist in Mourne House, the incarceration of Annie Kelly and Roseanne Irvine shows how, for long periods, women are confined in isolation and held in the punishment block to 'manage' self-harming and parasuicidal behaviours. The punishment block amounted to a control unit. Shaylor (ibid.) proposes that solitary confinement is indicative of 'increasing brutality in women's prisons', including the persistent and often gratuitous use of strip searches.

The Mourne House research demonstrated that, while regimes and programmes were not gender specific in design or delivery, regulation, control and punishments were consistently gender specific. Fear, degradation and dehumanisation endured by women prisoners were institutionally genderised, most appropriately represented and analysed through their location on a continuum of violence and violation (see: Stanko, 1985; Kelly, 1988). This ranged from lack of access to telephones or baths, through lock-ups, to strip searches, personal abuse and punishment. The sharp end of the continuum, where the body is the site of self-harm and strip searches, is related directly to the sexual comments, innuendo and insults embedded in the prison's daily routine. The Mourne House testimonies provide bleak reminders of the destructive force of imprisonment. While not reduced to total passivity, nor completely incapacitated, women's voices were effectively silenced, their self-esteem consistently undermined and their physical and mental health deeply traumatised ... and two women died.

10 'Nasty things happen in war'

In the Preface I locate the events covered in this chapter in my deeply personal experiences of serious injury, illness and recovery. As a critical researcher, it demonstrates to me at least that you don't have to leave your room to use primary analysis to present alternative accounts. To many that is self-evident, but as an empirical researcher who listens and gathers I needed to be reminded of that ... perhaps not in such dramatic circumstances. As I digested the speeches and commentaries from the White House and Downing Street while watching war unfold from afar, the relationship between justificatory words and devastating destruction was clearly apparent. I set out to analyse texts and establish intent. In early 2002, when we published Beyond September 11: An Anthology of Dissent *(Scraton 2002c), three issues were apparent yet officially ignored or denied. First, that what had been unleashed against Afghanistan would strengthen rather than contain the 'terrorist threat' to which it was directed. Second, that Iraq was the main objective, whatever the legality of the war-in-the-making, and international standards would be rewritten or denied. Third, that the unlawful detention of those taken prisoner and forcibly removed to Guantanamo Bay was a visible manifestation of atrocities through torture and rendition committed by proxy in hidden holding centres. In 2005 I was preparing to give a public lecture at Berlin's Mud Club when news of Abu Ghraib broke. The talk was entitled 'Impunity of the Powerful'. As individual soldiers were denounced and charged for specific acts, those in power walked free from responsibility for the institutionalised excesses they had unleashed.*

War of words, acts of 'terror'

No country lightly commits forces to military action and the inevitable risks involved. The military action we are taking will be targeted against places we know to be involved in the al-Qaida network of terror, or against the military apparatus of the Taliban. The military plan has been put together mindful of our determination to do all we humanly can to avoid civilian casualties.

(Tony Blair, UK Prime Minister, 7 October 2001)

How political leaders respond in the aftermath of events of global significance, their language, rhetoric and posturing has a defining impact on the scope of debate and the potential for intervention. The profoundly shocking attacks against the United States on 11 September 2001 were the most dramatic and tragic manifestation of the possibilities open to those committed to terror as an international strategy. While people searched downtown Manhattan for lost loved ones and the enormity of the attacks, graphically symbolised by the collapse of the World Trade Center's twin towers, was realised, the US President, George W. Bush, remained silent and invisible. Nine days later he addressed Congress, setting an agenda that would come to change the face of international politics. Nationhood and patriotism were central themes in his defence of US freedom and democracy but, without subtlety, they laid the foundations for military intervention.

As a nation, Bush pronounced, the US had been 'awakened to danger and called to defend freedom' (Speech to Congress, 20 September 2001). Collective grief had 'turned to anger and anger to resolution'; 'our mission and our moment' had arrived. Justice would be delivered, whether 'we bring our enemies to justice or bring justice to our enemies'. This construction of 'calling', of 'mission' and of 'destiny' became the new hegemony replacing that which had underlain the rhetoric and politics of the Cold War. Al-Qaida, supported by Afghanistan's Taliban regime, was the 'new' enemy and would be eliminated along with its leader, Osama bin Laden. Under his leadership al-Qaida had recruited and trained 'thousands of ... terrorists in more than 60 countries'.

Bush placed three non-negotiable demands before the Taliban: surrender the al-Qaida leadership to US authorities; release all foreign nationals held in Afghanistan; provide access to all terrorist training camps. His message was unequivocal: 'hand over the terrorists' or 'share their fate'. In sustaining murderers, he argued, the Taliban government was complicit. Should the Taliban ignore or refuse the demands of the US administration, Afghanistan would bear the brunt of a full-scale military offensive. Justification for war against a sovereign state was predicated on the regime's harbouring and promotion of international terrorism. States sympathetic to and protective of al-Qaida posed a serious and imminent threat to international stability and democracy, thereby satisfying the criteria for a counter-offensive. They were safe havens for terrorists.

Against this threat, beginning with al-Qaida but extending to 'every terrorist group of global reach', Bush declared a 'war on terror'. All such groups would be 'found, stopped and defeated'. By their complicity those states supplying aid, resources or accommodation to 'terrorists' were legitimate targets. They faced an ultimatum: 'you are with us or you are with the terrorists'. There could be no compromise and no neutrality. On this basis the US administration positioned its own interests as representative of global interest, identifying states ambivalent to or tolerant of designated 'terrorists' as 'hostile'. Mobilisation was not simply 'America's fight', not only 'America's freedom', but a sustained 'fight' for the 'world', for 'civilisation', for 'pluralism, tolerance and freedom'. Considering NATO and its members' shared obligations, Bush proclaimed an 'attack on one is an attack on all'.

Bush was clear that the 'civilised world' was by 'America's side'. It became the defining comment in 'othering' civilisations. In setting the 'them' and 'us' agenda it denied any possibility that distinctive civilisations with different political ideologies and belief systems could co-exist. Effectively and purposefully, it portrayed the civilised 'self' threatened by the barbaric 'other'. The US would not be duped but would defend the 'advance of human freedom, the great achievement of our time'. Declaring the 'war on terror' was a mission for the world, a war against a ubiquitous, common enemy. Bush sought no international mandate. Military intervention against Afghanistan would occur regardless of allied support or limits set by international law or conventions. Over 60 nation-states were proscribed as hostile and those that did not align with the US administration would be regarded as part of its problem. As far as the administration was concerned, the 11 September attacks provided authority and legitimacy to define, name and eliminate 'terrorist' organisations, their members and their associates.

The UK Prime Minister, Tony Blair, attended Bush's Congress address, to which he gave unqualified endorsement. Bush was grateful, the US had 'no truer friend than Great Britain'. Both states had 'joined together in a great cause'. The following week Tony Blair addressed delegates at the Labour Party's annual conference. 11 September, he stated, was 'a turning point in history' (Speech to Labour Party Annual Conference, 28 September 2001). Emerging from 'tragedy' and 'evil' would be a force for 'lasting good' and the 'machinery of terrorism' would be destroyed 'wherever it is found'. A 'greater understanding between nations and between faiths' and 'above all, justice and prosperity for the poor and dispossessed' would be lasting outcomes. While long-term objectives were aspirational, Blair employed the Bush ultimatum in addressing the immediate issues of Osama bin Laden, al-Qaida and the Taliban: 'surrender the terrorists; or surrender your power. It's your choice.'

The terrorist attacks of 11 September, he argued, required a 'proportionate' and 'targeted' response. In a direct and emotionally charged reference to those passengers who resisted the hijackers on board United flight 93, the plane that failed to reach its target, Blair implored: 'Listen to the calls of those passengers on the planes. Think of the children on them, told they were going to die.' Civilian casualties would be inevitable but that was the price to be paid in responding to 'what we are dealing with'. Such losses had to be registered in the context of civilian deaths on 11 September. Blair's comparative loss account had the whiff of vengeance: the regrettable sacrifice of civilians as a response to terrorism but also as a brake on escalation.

Urgent UK law reform was imperative, 'not to deny basic liberties but to prevent their abuse and protect the most basic liberty of all: freedom from terror'. Internationally, governments would cooperate as an expression of the 'power of community asserting itself'. 'Confidence is global', and state interdependence would consolidate to define 'the new world we live in'. Mutual interests, 'woven together' would be secured by global politics 'driven by people'. The 'power of community' combined with 'justice', evolving and securing benefits for all nations. Returning to a central New Labour theme, Blair affirmed the 'governing idea of modern social democracy' as 'community' protecting and sustaining 'principles of social justice'. With missionary zeal he promised 'to deliver social justice in the modern world'.

Using sound-bites seemingly gathered during his Congress visit, Blair committed to the 'fight for freedom' and the 'fight for justice too'. His mission was as grand as it was arrogant: 'let us re-order the world around us'. Returning to his rhetorical stomping ground he invoked 'moral power', not locally or nationally derived but 'of the world acting as a community'. It is not difficult to appreciate just how conceited this vocabulary must have sounded to many of Blair's European counterparts. He was determined to cement the moral and political foundation for the 'war on terror', already endorsed and adopted regardless of electoral mandate. Self-righteously and in the soap-box rhetoric of 'community', 'justice', 'freedom' and 'equality' he mapped, then occupied, the moral high ground. Afghanistan, 'a country where millions [were] already on the verge of death from starvation' (Chomsky 2001: 76), without protection from air strikes, would be bombed into democracy and the greater good would be served.

Since its installation, repression, torture, summary executions and the universal subjugation of women and girls had been the characteristics of the Taliban regime. As their husbands condemned a regime that their respective states initially had supported, Barbara Bush and Cherie Blair publicly expressed solidarity with Afghan women. It had taken the 11 September attacks for the West to break its silence on an organisation supported by a regime that had wreaked terror at home and abroad. The hypocrisy was tangible. The 'war on terror' mobilised a climate high on moral indignation and aggressive retaliation, while utilising the rhetoric of universal justice and global peace keeping. Arundhati Roy commented that in his self-anointed determination to pursue the 'calling of the United States of America', Bush identified it as a 'free nation' founded 'on fundamental values that rejects hate, rejects violence, rejects murderers and rejects evil' (*The Guardian*, G2, 23 October 2001).

In contrast, Roy reflected on the litany of countries bombed by the US since 1945: China, Korea, Guatemala, Indonesia, Cuba, Belgian Congo, Peru, Laos, Vietnam, Cambodia, Grenada, Libya, El Salvador, Nicaragua, Panama, Iraq, Bosnia, Sudan, Yugoslavia and Afghanistan. A parallel list would demonstrate those interventions where the US actively promoted

and funded the overthrow of governments, most notably Chile on a previous 11 September, or destroyed political economies, reducing populations
to starvation through trade embargoes and crippling sanctions. Yet Bush
depicted a world not of poverty and desitution created through the protection and promotion of US economic self-interest, but one where the
'stars and stripes' symbolised freedom, justice and equality.

On 7 October 2001 the US and UK launched cruise missiles against
Afghanistan. As expected, the Taliban refused to recognise the demands
made by the US. 'War' had been the inevitable outcome, from the moment
Bush issued his Congress ultimatum. In going to war, despite UN proto-
cols, the US claimed the endorsement of a 40-nation coalition. According
to Bush, 'carefully targeted' military action had been 'designed to clear the
way for sustained, comprehensive and relentless operations to drive them
[terrorists] out and bring them to justice' (*The Guardian*, 8 October 2001).

From the outset the military attack on Afghanistan was portrayed as a
precursor to a more sustained, longer-term 'war on terror'. Bush was
unequivocal: 'To-day we focus on Afghanistan, but the battle is broader.'
He continued:

> Every nation has a choice to make. In this conflict there is no neutral
> ground. To-day's operation is called Enduring Freedom. We defend not
> only our precious freedoms, but also the freedom of people every-
> where.
>
> (Presidential Address to the Nation, 7 October 2001)

The 'goal' was 'just', therefore the war was just. Resources would be made
available to fulfil the 'duty' of fighting global terrorism. Blair also accepted
the 'cause' was 'just'. The eleventh of September had been an 'attack on
our freedom, our way of life and civilised values the world over ... our
determination in acting is total'.

From conception, the Bush/Blair 'war on terror' agenda was flawed. Like
so many social and societal reactions underpinned by moral indignation, it
had neither the intellectual grasp nor the political capacity to wage, let alone
win, such a war. In 'monstering' Osama bin Laden, the Taliban and al-
Qaida and their use of terror as strategy, the origins, definitions and manifestations of terrorism were reduced to simplistic assumptions and explanations. Internationally it has proved difficult to establish a shared and
operational definition of terrorism. This will always be so while states,
both internally and externally, depend on repression and oppression in
managing endemic structural inequalities. Civil rights and human rights
struggles have not been confined to totalitarian regimes. Western social
democracies, their political economies globalised around the inherent economic exploitation of advanced, and forever advancing, capitalism, are
compelled to manage the consequences of the extreme relations of wealth
and poverty. It remains, as it has been since democracy was grafted on to

capitalism, a form of political management underpinned ultimately by the authoritarian use of force and sanctioned state violence.

As Max Weber noted during capitalism's first period of international expansionism, the state held the monopoly on the use of legitimate violence. Those who resisted and fought totalitarian regimes, who sacrificed – for example – their relative peace to fight fascism in the Spanish Civil War, were celebrated for their heroism. Yet, those using force against the excesses of 'democratic states' or their economic allies have been castigated for their terrorism. This should not reduce the issue to the simplistic freedom fighter–terrorist equation. What it demands is that the complexity of definition, of relative motive, of historical and political context and of established objectives and 'just' targets, is considered. It is profound hypocrisy that social-democratic states have researched, developed and supplied weapons of mass destruction on 'free market' principles in order to further their political and economic interests, including bank-rolling bin Laden, only to object when that weaponry is pointed in their direction. In all contexts, justifications for the use of violence remain a matter of political judgement and moral relativism.

Having been empowered by the US when it suited, the longer-term consequences of that action – the abusive totalitarianism of the Taliban and the networking of al-Qaida – were the sanctioning and funding of the 11 September attacks. In utilising terror, Osama bin Laden had learnt well: no distinction between military and civilian targets, strike fear at the heart of all communities. But, if this construction is applied universally to all interventions where fear and insecurity are instilled throughout communities or populations, then what of those states, proclaiming freedom and democracy, that have used and supported terror? From the saturation fire-bombing of a defenceless Dresden and the wilful destruction visited on surrendering German cities and towns at the close of the 1939–45 war, to the catastrophic use of Agent Orange, napalm and carpet-bombing in Vietnam and Cambodia, the sacrifice of civilians by the UK and the US epitomised the legitimation of terror. These indefensible acts exacted revenge and, literally, burnt reprisal into the collective memory of populations. Calculated and purposeful, such ends exposed the cruelty of the means.

It is instructive that, as the 'frontiers' of expanding capital were pushed back, using soldiers and missionaries to commit acts of physical atrocity and cultural genocide against aboriginal populations, 'terror' was introduced as a tactic in clearing the way for economic settlement and exploitation. The 'infusion' of universal fear, to 'strike' or 'inspire' communities with terror, were essential strategies of domination at the heart of imperialist expansion. While today, in Western societies, much is made of the 'fear of crime' having consequences as debilitating as crime itself, the 'fear of atrocity' committed by the colonial powers was a purposeful and powerful weapon. There is no direct connection between contemporary state responses and those of earlier interventions, yet the legacy of political, economic and cultural domination – aided and abetted by the rule of law and its uncompromising enforcement – cannot be ignored. As the US and its allies congratulate themselves on freedom and justice as hallmarks of advanced democracies, they ignore the long-term and unresolved consequences of colonisation and appropriation.

Their convenient denial of the 'unfree' within their populations, the victims whose inheritance and daily life are dictated, if not determined, by endemic social injustice and inherent structural inequality, has long roots. What cannot be denied is that 'infusing', 'inspiring' and 'striking' indigenous and enslaved communities with terror was experienced as a deliberate strategy of domination that has not been forgotten. Indeed, it remains central to 'third world' definition and status and to persistent struggles over land rights, territory and reservations. Whatever the claims for an academic, post-modern interpretation of 'power' as relative and pervasive, contemporary definitions of 'terrorism' are derived in the 'absolute' and 'legitimate' power of political–economic interests central to the development, consolidation and sustenance of 'global' capitalism.

In discussing how 'terrorist acts' have become 'propagandist', meaning those acts 'committed by our enemies against us or our allies', Noam Chomsky (2001: 89–90) states:

> I understand the term 'terrorism' exactly in the sense defined in official US documents: 'the calculated use of violence or threat of violence to attain goals that are political, religious, or ideological in nature. This is done through intimidation, coercion, or instilling fear'.

Not restricted to colonialism and the pursuit of empire, this was the framework for military intervention, overt and covert, that came to define US foreign policy in the latter half of the twentieth century. In Arundhati Roy's litany of US offensives the violence was calculated, the goals were political and ideological. As will be seen, the 'war on terror', whatever the qualifications made regarding Islam, also carried a religious dimension.

The politics of atrocity

> It is our hope that they [Northern Alliance] will not engage in negotiations that would provide for the release of al-Qaida forces; that would provide for the release of foreign nationals leaving the country and destabilising neighbouring countries … So my hope is that they will either be killed or taken prisoner.
> (Donald Rumsfeld, US Defense Secretary, 19 November 2001)

The prosecution of the 'war on terror' against Afghanistan was conducted primarily from the air, using cruise missiles, carpet and cluster bombing.

Weak anti-aircraft defences and no effective Afghan air force enabled massive strikes virtually without risk. On the ground, the war was conducted by the notoriously fractured Northern Alliance, whose history of human rights violations, given the circumstances, made it an uneasy bedfellow for allied forces. Whatever the claims made regarding the use of special forces' intelligence to plan and orchestrate military action, as the war progressed it became increasingly clear that Northern Alliance commanders defined targets and established priorities.

The bombing was relentless and Taliban forces could not sustain effective resistance. Civilian casualties inflicted by air strikes were high and impossible to assess accurately. The Northern Alliance advance overwhelmed the Taliban defences and, given the recent history of Afghanistan, the US military command would have anticipated that the Alliance would show no mercy to Taliban forces, particularly the hated foreign recruits. In revealing his preference for the imprisonment or killing of foreign nationals, Rumsfeld and his advisers would have been aware that his words would be interpreted as tacit approval of torture, brutality and summary execution. Further, the US administration had placed al-Qaida forces outside the protection of the Geneva Conventions.

What ensued at the Qala-i-Jhangi fortress close to the northern town of Mazar-i-Sharif was as inevitable as it was appalling. Towards the end of November the Northern Alliance closed in on the northern city of Kunduz, a Taliban stronghold with 12,000 soldiers supported by 2,000 foreign nationals. A cessation in the fighting was negotiated, and safe passage for the Taliban command and elite guard was exchanged for unconditional surrender. The fate of foreign nationals, however, was unclear. Despite well-publicised rifts in its regional leadership, the Northern Alliance guaranteed prisoners of war fair treatment consistent with international law and conventions. Rumsfeld, however, issued a statement making it clear that the US was 'not inclined to negotiate surrender' (*The Guardian*, 24 November 2001). A 'British defence source' considered Rumsfeld's comment 'belligerent'. UK Foreign Secretary Jack Straw affirmed his government's commitment to avoiding 'a massacre'. Professor Adam Roberts (2001: 20) considered it 'shocking' that the Pentagon had been 'unclear on the basic and simple point that if the fighters in Kunduz surrender, they will not be massacred'.

Following surrender, several hundred Taliban fighters, of whom only a small number where Afghan, were imprisoned by the Northern Alliance, supported on the ground by a handful of US special forces personnel, at the Qala-i-Jhangi fortress near to the town of Mazar-i-Sharif. This allowed US forces to conduct intelligence-gathering interrogations. Within two days of the surrender, possibly as many as 400 lay dead. A group of prisoners, assuming they were about to be executed, as their hands were tied behind their backs, rebelled and seized weapons. In the ensuing panic, and following the shooting of a CIA interrogator, another US agent called in helicopters and troops. Within hours, 'American missiles plunged into the area ... killing hundreds of prisoners in an inferno'. The bombardment, to the displeasure of the Northern Alliance command, killed and injured many of its soldiers. A group of Taliban fighters, having taken weapons from the fort's armoury, resisted and British SAS soldiers assumed coordination of the operation. Eventually the insurrection was ended. There were few survivors and many died with their hands tied. Bodies were desecrated as Northern Alliance soldiers removed gold teeth.

Jonathan Freedland (2001: 21) reflected, 'many will baulk at calling this a massacre because the Taliban seemed to bring their fate upon themselves by rebelling, thereby forfeiting their right to Geneva Conventions protection as prisoners of war'. This was the position adopted by the British government. A source was quoted as stating that as Qala-i-Jhangi was a 'situation in which prisoners tried to break out with grenades and Kalashnikovs' it 'had to be dealt with and you cannot be too squeamish' (*The Guardian*, 29 November 2001). Yet significant questions required answers. Why, in an impromptu decision, were so many prisoners incarcerated in a compound known to house heavy weaponry? Why were so many killed when only a few rebelled? In what circumstances did prisoners die while remaining bound? What was the relationship on the ground between US personnel and the Northern Alliance? Was the force employed, particularly the aerial bombardment, proportionate?

As international criticism mounted, the US distanced itself, claiming the operation was the responsibility of the Northern Alliance. Amnesty International and the UN High Commissioner for Human Rights, Mary Robinson, called for a full inquiry. But UK Foreign Minister Peter Hain deemed an inquiry 'unnecessary':

> These things happen in war. Just remember that these people in the prison were al-Qaida fighters ... We do not see a need for an inquiry. Nasty things happen in war.
>
> (Peter Hain, *BBC Radio 5*, 29 November 2001)

Implicit in Hain's response was that rules and conventions of engagement and detention could be overridden because of the unlawful status of the prisoners (al-Qaida) and the 'nastiness' of war. Yet Jack Straw's initial assessment indicated that a massacre was possible. The massacre was not without precedent.

Two weeks earlier, at a school in Mazar-i-Sharif, independent eye-witnesses reported that many of 520 Pakistani recruits to the Taliban cause had been killed while trying to surrender (*The Guardian*, 24 November 2001). Attacked by US planes, survivors were taken prisoner by the Northern Alliance. The Red Cross estimated 250 had been killed either by the bombardment or by execution. As Kunduz was taken, confirmed reports emerged of wounded prisoners shot and left to die on the streets.

This followed similar summary executions and fatal beatings administered after the fall of Kabul.

According to a Northern Alliance commander, in the aftermath of a battle at Takteh Pol in southern Afghanistan, and in the presence of US military personnel, his soldiers lined up and machine-gunned 160 Taliban prisoners. On 23 December the inauguration of the interim administration took place in Kabul. The previous day, based on unattributed 'intelligence', US air strikes destroyed a convoy claimed by the Afghan Islamic Press to comprise delegates to the inauguration. Over 60 people were killed while offering no defence against the attacks. US military sources justified the use of force, claiming that those killed were Taliban or al-Qaida leaders.

As was clear at the onset of the military offensive, the overthrow of the Taliban was the beginning of the 'war on terror'. Rumsfeld reaffirmed the US commitment:

> Despite the progress in Afghanistan, the global war against terror is still in its early stages. The terrorist networks that threaten us operate in dozens of different countries, and terrorist threats against both of our nations' citizens and interests continue. Meeting the challenges ahead will require sacrifice, determination and perseverance.
> (Donald Rumsfeld, 2 December 2001)

The Taliban's fall was proclaimed a great success by the US and its allies. Anti-war campaigners were derided, as the Bush administration portrayed itself as liberationist. Amid triumphalism, the more detailed and profound consequences of military action were neglected. Osama bin Laden remained alive and free and the al-Qaida network, although punctured, was intact and recruiting. While the pernicious Taliban regime had been defeated, the US/allied role in the forcible removal of a government remained a troubling intervention. As Rumsfeld inferred, on the basis of US intelligence, simply naming a state as sympathetic to proscribed terror-ist groups was sufficient justification for US-led military intervention to secure regime change. The US assumed the power to intervene with impu-nity in domestic affairs of regimes which, by US intelligence criteria, did not meet with approval.

That impunity extended to denying responsibility for contributing to or investigating atrocities, and to the inflicting of civilian casualties. The US media showed little interest in the deaths of Afghan civilians, occasionally noting 'regret' over 'collateral damage'. Such deaths were 'rare', 'acci-dental' casualties of war. US and allied audiences were reminded of the thousands killed in the World Trade Center and Pentagon attacks, of the inhumanity of the Taliban and of 'who started the war'. While estimated casualties were high they did not include those who died, and continue to die, from their injuries and those dying from cold, hunger or home-lessness. Neither did they include military victims nor prisoners killed at

Mazar-i-Sharif, Qala-i-Jhangi, Takteh Pol, Kandahar and in other atrocities. Seumas Milne, questioning the morality of civilian deaths in the context of a 'just war' concluded that they were not 'an accidental by-product of the decision to overthrow the Taliban regime, but because of the low value put on Afghan civilian lives by US military planners' (*The Guardian*, 20 December 2001). Milne's argument was well illustrated by a chilling account of 93 villagers killed at Chowkar-Karez, randomly strafed by US gunships. He quoted a Pentagon official: 'the people there are dead because we wanted them dead'.

Prisoners of the States

These were the issues that drew sustained political opposition to the 'war on terror' throughout Western democracies. The backlash against the anti-war campaigns soon took hold. US law professor Patricia Williams (2001) noted, 'student demonstrators, global justice workers, civil libertarians, animal rights and peace activists' throughout the US were 'characterized as terrorist sympathizers'. By late November over 1,000 people in the US had been 'arrested and held, approximately 800 with no disclosure of identities or location or charges against them'. Widespread public support was polled for the use of torture to extract information relating to terrorism and the US Patriot Act, enabling law enforcers to 'gather information with few checks and balances from the judiciary', was introduced.

Williams argued that state-legitimated 'righteous lawlessness', previously institutionalised and 'practised in oppressed communities', had a substantial constituency in contemporary America. Given the rise and consolidation of excessive imprisonment over the previous decades, the denial of 'natural justice' embodied in draconian legislation and the promotion of capital punishment, the post-11 September attack on rights and liberties was unsurprising. The enthusiasm to 'embrace profiling based on looks and ethnicity; detention without charges; searches without warrants; and even torture and assassination', however shocking, was the inevitable consequence of what Christian Parenti (1999) had perceptively named 'Lock-down America'.

On 14 December 2001, just three months after the September 11 attacks, the UK's Anti-Terrorism, Crime and Security Act became law. The Act enabled unlimited detention of people suspected of terrorism who could not be removed from the country. Grounds for suspicion depended on information provided by the security and intelligence services, with no right of access to that information. Telecommunications providers were required to hold all data (internet, e-mails, telephone calls) for 12 months, with access granted for 'safeguarding national security' and 'for the purposes of prevention or detection of crime' or the 'prosecution of offenders' relating 'directly or indirectly to national security'. It would protect national security through policing 'terrorism' and 'subversion'. Police, customs and immigration services were given further powers, including the exchange of personal data and the retention for 10 years of fingerprints taken from asylum seekers and refugees.

Mary Robinson, the UN High Commissioner for Human Rights, requested 'all governments to refrain from excessive steps which would violate fundamental freedoms and undermine legitimate rights' (*The Guardian*, 30 November 2001). Anti-terrorism measures should 'protect human rights and democracy' and not 'undermine these fundamental values of our societies'. Support for tough measures, however, reflected a moral climate founded on righteous indignation and a calculus of retribution inviting more authoritarian powers and punitive sanctions. If the 'war on terror' was to succeed abroad, elimination of terror would begin at home.

Elliott Currie (1998: 186) notes how, in the US, harsher laws, zero-tolerance policing and uncompromising punishment regimes resulted in 'bursting prisons, devastated cities and a violent crime rate still unmatched in the developed world'. Nils Christie (1994) records his shock at discovering the 'new techniques' and instruments of containment, including the consolidation of super-maximum security prisons. Chains, manacles, isolation, natural light deprivation, 'non-lethal' weapons and ritual humiliation had become elements of acceptable confinement in the supposed 'free-world'. Christian Parenti's (1999: 174) detailed exposé of institutionalised violence endemic in California's maximum-security prisons identifies it as 'an extreme expression of the nation-wide campaign to degrade and abuse convicts'. To establish hard-line credentials, politicians perfected a 'rhetoric' built on the premise that 'going to prison is no longer punishment enough'. The volatile context of public clamour and political opportunism delivered 'a wave of political fads: from chain gangs and striped uniforms, to the stunning evisceration of prisoners' legal rights'. Within prisons, it led to terrifying outcomes of deprivation, rape, torture and even death. Over four decades, prisons functioned 'to terrorize the poor, warehouse social dynamite and social wreckage'. Pathologising the poor, the marginalised, the 'underclass', justified and legitimated 'state repression and the militarization of public space' (ibid.: 169).

Within the UK, with the exception of Irish political prisoners, the excesses of US incarceration had not developed throughout the system. Yet the social and political climate produced and sustained a popular commitment to longer sentences, harsher conditions and reduced prisoner rights. Certainly no effective challenge to the slogan 'Prison Works' emerged, and the escalation in imprisonment since 1997 brought no discernible concern. Despite evidence to the contrary, including the incarceration of children as young as 10 and the catastrophic failure of prisons 'on their own terms', the public perception remains that prisons are 'holiday camps' where prisoners enjoy rehabilitation and education programmes at the taxpayers' expense. The Prison Inspectorate has condemned conditions and regimes repeatedly, particularly those endured by women and children, and has criticised the squalor of Victorian prisons. It is of no significance to a media locked into a 'soft-on-crime' mindset. With virtually no public concern forthcoming regarding the appalling conditions inflicted on those sentenced for minor criminal offences, apathy was exchanged for outright hostility towards those convicted of 'terrorist' offences.

For three decades intimidation, abuse and degradation characterised the incarceration of Irish Nationalist and Republican prisoners, men and women, held in British jails. Yet it was early in 1997, following two aborted trials of high-security prisoners who had escaped from Whitemoor prison, that a judge abandoned proceedings because he deemed the accused mentally unfit to stand trial. The conditions of sensory deprivation in which they had been held since recapture had made them ill. The UK government's chief medical officer found that secure regimes within the special units were so 'cramped' and 'claustrophobic', lacking in 'meaningful work ... social contact and incentives', that 'it was likely over a course of years that a proportion of them [prisoners] would develop significant adverse effects to mental health'. This was, he concluded, unacceptable. All prisoners, regardless of offence, were entitled to the 'same rights as regards health and healthcare as any other person in the country'. The court ruling and the chief medical officer's findings amounted to a damning indictment of regimes which, however politically expedient and popular with sections of the media, had weakened the resolve and broken the spirit of individuals through inhumane and degrading treatments.

Against this backcloth, both in the US and the UK, the punishing regime inflicted on alleged al-Qaida or pro-Taliban soldiers taken prisoner in Afghanistan and incarcerated 8,000 miles away in Camp X-Ray at the US naval base, Guantanamo Bay, was established. The dramatic arrival of the first 20 prisoners immediately raised serious questions about the application of 'justice' pursued by the US administration. Denied prisoner-of-war status, they were held and transported without the protection of international law or the Geneva Conventions. Incarcerated outside US sovereign territory, they were unprotected by the US constitution and, in the event of prosecution, had no right to jury trial. With a Military Order issued on 13 November 2001 and entitled 'Detention, Treatment and Trial of Certain Non-citizens in the War Against Terrorism', a new form of stateless detention of the 'enemy' was born.

Donald Rumsfeld publicly rejected the 'prisoner of war' classification, naming captives 'unlawful combatants'. This enabled long-term detention without trial, unprotected interrogations, prosecution through military commissions under more permissive rules of evidence, and a lesser burden of proof to secure conviction than obtains in regular criminal courts. Within the terms of the Geneva Conventions, Rumsfeld did not have the authority to reclassify. The legal status of those captured in armed conflict should have been determined by an appropriate, recognised court or tribunal. Rumsfeld's 'doublespeak' denied the 'war on terror' was a war. He suggested that in the military conflict the only legitimate 'military' personnel belonged to the US and its allies. Having first defined the boundaries and theatre of war, the US ascribed status to combatants and appropriate forums for prosecution.

As the first consignment of 'unlawful combatants' arrived at Camp X-Ray the consequences of Rumsfeld's reclassification became fully apparent. Dressed in bright orange boiler suits, wearing caps, taped-over goggles and surgical masks, the prisoners were bound, shackled and, in some cases, sedated. Other than masks and enforced blindness, however, their appearance was consistent with that of regular prisoners in transit throughout the US penal system. Sensory deprivation and sedation were justified by the senior officer in charge of the security operation: 'We asked for the bad guys first'. These prisoners were the 'worst of the worst' and, according to Rumsfeld, would be 'perfectly willing to kill themselves and kill other people'. They were 'among the most dangerous, best trained, vicious killers on the face of the earth' (quoted in Rose 2004: 8). Vice-President Dick Cheney agreed: 'These are the worst ... devoted to killing millions of Americans, innocent Americans ... ' (ibid.). According to the US Joint Chief of Staff they 'would gnaw through hydraulic lines in a C-17 [troop carrying aircraft] to bring it down'. Bound, manacled, blindfolded and shackled, they were locked in 8ft by 8ft (2.4m by 2.4 m) outdoor chain-link cages. They slept on mats, sheets for bedding, under halogen floodlights. Affronting their cultural and religious beliefs, the military shaved their beards.

Within days of the international outcry over the classification and treatment of the prisoners the Pentagon embarked on a public-relations exercise that rebounded spectacularly. It issued full-colour photographs of the detainees, manacled and masked, kneeling before their armed captors. Their humiliation was palpable and the US soldiers' physical domination clearly more than symbolic. Presumably published to demonstrate the uncompromising response of the US administration to terrorism, the photographs not only caused grave concern throughout Western democracies but, within Muslim nations and communities, fuelled deep resentment of US double standards. As Richard Norton-Taylor commented, the photographs showed a 'complete disregard, not to say contempt, [within] the Bush administration ... for international opinion'. The prevalent view of the US administration was that it did 'not need to be bound by international law, any more than it does by international arms control treaties, and that military might is enough' (The Guardian, 22 January 2002).

The International Red Cross stated that all prisoners taken in Afghanistan should be held under the terms of the Geneva Conventions, with particular regard to international standards prohibiting 'cruel, degrading and inhumane treatment'. While Red Cross inspection teams do not disclose findings, it was clear that the organisation was at odds with the US administration over status, conditions and practices at Camp X-Ray.

Others voiced their criticisms. Kenneth Roth, Executive Director of Human Rights Watch, raised the paradox inherent within US procedures:

> Terrorists believe that anything goes in the name of their cause. The fight against terror must not buy into that logic. Human rights principles must not be compromised in the name of any cause.
>
> (*The Guardian*, 17 January 2002)

Rumsfeld dismissed the allegations of inhumane treatment at Camp X-Ray as 'utter nonsense'. 'America', he said, 'is not what's wrong with the world'. He continued: 'Let there be no doubt, the treatment of detainees is proper ... humane ... appropriate ... and fully consistent with international conventions'. The 'truth ultimately wins out' and 'the truth of the matter is they're being treated humanely' (*The Guardian*, 23 January 2002). Within days of Rumsfeld's uncompromising statement, and following an inspection by the International Red Cross and rumours of Colin Powell's concern over the classification and treatment of the prisoners, the US authorities announced a review of the conditions of containment.

Concerns were also expressed within the UK government. While the Foreign Office initially accepted the US administration's legitimacy in classifying prisoners, Defence Secretary Geoff Hoon commented that prisoners should be detained 'with proper respect for international law'. It emerged that British citizens were held within Camp X-Ray. This led to pressure to have them returned, if appropriate, to stand trial. In Britain, however, a debate unfolded about the incarceration of 'terrorist' suspects detained under the new legislation. At Belmarsh high-security prison detainees alleged inappropriate conditions. Locked in isolation, without natural light for 22 hours each day, initially they had been denied access to solicitors or families. Their lawyer, Gareth Peirce stated, 'These men have been buried alive in concrete coffins and have been told the legislation provides for their detention for life without trial' (*The Guardian*, 20 January 2002). Complaints included intimidation, abuse, strip searches and refusal of requests for medication. Not charged with any offence, they were a new generation of internees, technically innocent and held on suspicion of unspecified involvement in terrorist activities.

Two years later the European Committee for the Prevention of Torture visited the UK to consider the treatment of those held as suspects under anti-terrorist legislation. They found: psychiatric illness (depression, stress disorders, suicidal ideation); ill-treatment, including prisoners held naked, solitary confinement, lack of heating, abuse/ridicule/racism; inappropriate use of Broadmoor Special Hospital; internment without trial or prosecution for an indefinite period amounting to inhuman and degrading treatment; lack of understanding or management by the authorities; lack of access to appropriate legal representation and to appropriate medical care. These concerns came to a head with a House of Lords judgment that found the measures disproportionate and discriminating unfairly against foreign nationals.

Further, the European Commissioner for Human Rights, Alvaro Gil-Robles, expressed his concerns about the implementation of the 2005 Prevention of Terrorism Act. He stated that new powers introduced to administer control orders failed to meet procedural protections of the criminal courts, constituting a potential unlawful detention breach of Article 5 of the European Convention of Human Rights (ECHR). Further, he considered that control orders related to 'criminal' activities, thereby compromising Article 6 and the right to a fair trial. Gil-Robles was concerned that the 'ordinary criminal justice system' was being substituted by a 'parallel system run by the executive'.

Given the circumstances, and the protection afforded by international law and conventions, the treatment meted out to prisoners held at Camp X-Ray and within the US and the UK could not be defended. Lawyers able to visit their clients were certain that conditions amounted to degrading and inhumane imprisonment. The US administration's reluctance to determine prisoner status through an appropriate court or tribunal provided unequivocal evidence of political, and military, interference in the judicial process. Shifting definitions of 'war' made a mockery of the legitimacy of this first and frightful stage of the 'war on terror'. Yet public opinion in the US and the UK appeared to accept that the status, conditions and treatment afforded to prisoners held without charge were reasonable. So powerful was the 'moral panic' surrounding 'terrorism' that the 'civilised' values Bush and Blair proclaimed were lost in practice. It encompassed a significant shift in the application of international law, rationalised by the demands of new and exceptional circumstances, the rules of which were justified through constant reference to the attacks on the US and its vengeful, hateful 'war on terror'. The US administration used those held captive as the tangible manifestation of the terrorism responsible for the deaths at the World Trade Center and the Pentagon. By its labelling of those 'innocent until proven guilty' as the 'worst of the worst', the moral high ground was finally vacated.

Defending the 'civilised world'

On 29 January 2002 George W. Bush presented his State of the Union address. A President whose popularity bordered on the unelectable a year earlier, whose credibility at home and abroad appeared tarnished beyond repair, now enjoyed an 82 per cent rating within the US. The origin of this remarkable reversal was contained in his first words: 'As we gather tonight, our nation is at war ... ' (State of the Union Address, 29 January 2002). The biting economic recession at home, the international criticisms of US global domination and the consolidating alienation of populations throughout the Middle East and Asia were ignored for, 'the State of our

Union has never been stronger'. On 77 occasions waves of enthusiastic applause interrupted the address. It was triumphalism unrestrained; 'our nation has comforted the victims ... rallied a great coalition, captured, arrested, and rid the world of thousands of terrorists, destroyed Afghanistan's terrorist training camps, saved a people from starvation, and freed a country from brutal oppression'.

A speedy, efficient and total war had delivered victory in Afghanistan, the first in 'winning the war on terror'. The message was 'now clear to every enemy of the United States. Even 7,000 miles away, across mountains and continents, on mountaintops and in caves – you will not escape the justice of this nation'. This phrase captured the post-11 September consciousness – aerial, indiscriminate bombardment as the means to administer 'justice' as determined by the US administration on behalf of its 'nation'. Bush quickly moved to establish Afghanistan not as an end-point but as a point of departure. The 'war on terror' was in its infancy and 'tens of thousands of trained terrorists ... schooled in the methods of murder, often supported by outlaw regimes' remained at large. Eliminating terrorist training camps and bringing terrorists to justice, together with enforcing change on regimes 'who seek chemical, biological or nuclear weapons from threatening the United States and the world' was the longer-term agenda. While 'training camps operate' and 'nations harbor terrorists, freedom is at risk'. For the 'civilised world' the common 'war against terror is only beginning'.

The enemies of the 'civilised' were those states and their 'terrorist allies', collectively 'consitut[ing] an axis of evil'; regimes that 'pose[d] a grave and growing danger'. US intelligence understood 'the true nature' of North Korea, Iran, Iraq and Somalia. Iraq was 'a regime that has something to hide from the civilized world'. Operations continued in Bosnia, the Philippines and off the coast of Africa to 'eliminate the terrorist parasites'. Whatever 'necessary to ensure our nation's security' would be identified and carried through without hesitation or further provocation, for 'the price of indifference would be catastrophic'. Bush transformed collective responsibility for waging war into one of destiny and honour: 'History has called America and our allies to action, and it is both our responsibility and our privilege to fight freedom's fight.'

The speech noted the 'billion dollars a month' cost of the 'war on terror'. It would be increased through pay rises for the 'men and women in uniform'. The 'largest increase in defense spending' was 'the price of freedom and security ... is never too high. Whatever it costs to defend our country, we will pay.' The 'war' would be fully supported alongside the expansion of 'a sustained strategy of homeland security' prioritising 'bio-terrorism, emergency response, airport and border security, and improved intelligence'. The 'war on terror' and 'homeland security' would lay the ground for the 'final great priority ... economic security for the American people'. Bush's three objectives were: winning the war, protecting the homeland and revitalising the economy. Priorities were 'clear' and the 'purpose and resolve we have shown overseas' would succeed 'at home': 'We'll prevail in the war, and we will defeat this recession.' Bush's one-liners on jobs, energy, trade, tax cuts, welfare reform, teaching and health security amounted to a cynical exercise in mobilising the ideology of patriotism and the rhetoric of freedom to demand public tolerance of unemployment, low pay, long-term poverty and social exclusion. Criticism of any aspect of foreign or home policy was unpatriotic, giving sustenance to terrorism.

His speech was carefully choreographed and interminably rehearsed. It sought and received endorsement from the 'newly liberated', from those who had lost loved ones in action and from the heroes of war. Bush welcomed to Congress Hamid Karzai, the Afghanistan interim leader and Dr Sima Samar, the new Minister of Women's Affairs. In remembering those who died on 11 September he introduced Shannon Spann, the wife of the CIA officer killed at Mazar-i-Sharif. Profoundly emotional, the choreography of bereavement was transactional. While affirming commitment to homeland security, Bush acknowledged the bravery and intuition of two flight attendants who had apprehended the British 'shoe-bomber', Richard Reid, in flight. Reflecting on the 'courage and compassion, strength and resolve' of the American people, he presented 'our First Lady, Laura Bush'; she had provided 'strength and calm and comfort' to 'our nation in crisis'.

Bush committed to the expansion of the US Freedom Corps (homeland security) and the Peace Corps. The latter would expand 'development and education and opportunity in the Islamic world', central to 'a new culture of responsibility'. The US led the world in 'defending liberty and justice because they are right and true and unchanging for people everywhere'. There was 'no intention' to impose 'our culture' but the 'demands of human dignity: the rule of law; limits on the power of the state; respect for women; private property; free speech; equal justice; and religious toler-ance' were 'non-negotiable'. He concluded:

> ... steadfast in our purpose, we now press on. We have known free-dom's price. We have shown freedom's power. And in this great con-flict, my fellow Americans, we will see freedom's victory.

This was not merely a victory address, the valedictory for a reactive and reactionary operation that had deposed a brutal and brutalising regime. It was an inaugural. Bush was marking the initial success of an enduring military offensive that 'may not be finished on our watch'. As a super-power with lone-ranger status, the US would police 'rogue states', engaging selectively according to its criteria for naming terrorism, its definitions of lawful combat and its acceptance of international conventions regarding war. The shame and guilt of Vietnam had been laid to rest in the rubble of

Afghanistan. A 'just' war was a war so labelled; 'justice' was justice according to US values as established by Bush and his neo-conservative regime. The primary enemies, a 'terrorist underworld', were offered to the American nation: Hamas, Hezbollah, Islamic Jihad, Jaish-i-Mohammed.

With opposition understandably somewhat muted in the US, internationally Bush was criticised for unbridled escalation, particularly for endorsing populist assumptions about 'civilisation', 'evil' and 'terrorism'. He responded fiercely in condemning 'nations that developed weapons of mass destruction' that might 'team up with' or give shelter to terrorist groups (*The Guardian*, 1 February 2002). These were nations inscribed on the US 'watch list':

> People say, well, what does that mean? It means they had better get their house in order is what it means. It means they better respect the rule of law. It means they better not try to terrorise America and our friends and allies or the justice of the nation will be served on them as well.
>
> (Ibid.)

Carpet-bombing, cluster bombs, strafing civilian convoys, collateral damage, indiscriminate atrocities, civilian deaths, unlawful detention and Guantanamo Bay were the collective outcome of a nation's justice. In depicting the 'war' against 'tens of thousands of trained terrorists' as a vocation, Bush fed the potential of the existing real and present danger of terrorism. Throughout Asia and the Middle East the deep distrust of the US, the hate directed against its military–industrial complex, its cultural imperialism and its open disdain for human rights while mouthing rhetoric of the 'civilised' against the 'uncivilised', emphasised a profoundly riven world. For 'third world' nations already knew to their cost that politically, economically or culturally the US had never promoted globalisation to facilitate equal participation, distribution or opportunities.

The invasion of Iraq

> I could not ignore that it provided explicit authority, under the War Powers Resolution and the Constitution, to go to war. It was a blank cheque to the President to attack anyone involved in the September 11 events – anywhere, in any country, without regard to nations' long term foreign policy, economic and national security interests and without time limit.
>
> (Lee 2002: 38)

Barbara Lee was the lone Congress Democrat to vote against the military offensive in Afghanistan. She exposed the dangerous potential masked by the President's rhetoric of freedom and liberation. Her fears were soon

realised. In September 2002 the White House published the US administration's new National Security Strategy (White House 2002). Penned by
Condoleezza Rice, it reflected the confidence of an administration committed to strengthening the power and authority of its military–industrial
complex at the expense of the declining influence of an ineffectual United
Nations. In the Preface, Bush affirmed that the 'great struggles of the 20th
Century between liberty and totalitarianism' had ended, the 'victory for the
forces of freedom' had been 'decisive'. The resolution of the Cold War had
left 'a single, sustainable model for national success: freedom, democracy
and free enterprise' (White House 2002: Preface unpaginated). There had
been no compromise. Advanced capitalism, serviced by social democratic
governments committed to the management of inherent structural
inequalities, had defeated communist alternatives. Now, however, new,
grave danger had emerged at the 'crossroads of radicalism and technology'.
'Radicalism' was barely disguised code for 'Islamic fundamentalism',
'technology' for 'weapons of mass destruction'.

The Strategy stated that 'freedom and fear are at war' (ibid.: 7), that US
foreign policy would prioritise 'defending the peace, preserving the peace
and extending the peace' in the 'battle against rogue states': states that
'brutalize their own people'; 'reject international law'; 'are determined to
acquire weapons of mass destruction'; 'sponsor global terrorism'; 'reject
basic human values'. Most significantly, they 'hate the United States and
everything for which it stands' (ibid.: 14). They would be reminded that
the 'United States possesses unprecedented – and unequalled – strength and
influence in the world'. This would be reflected in the US National Security
Strategy 'based on a distinctly American internationalism that reflects *our*
values and our national interests' (ibid.: 1, emphasis added). For the 'war
on terror is a global war', with the United States 'fighting for *our* democratic values and *our* way of life' (ibid.: 7, emphasis added).

With 'justification' established, the conditions for further military action
against rogue states were revealed. The use of pre-emptive offensives was
an imperative, but remained unacceptable within the terms of the UN
Charter. The 'United States can no longer rely on a reactive posture as we
have done in the past' (ibid.: 15). While previously in international law the
legitimacy of pre-emption was predicated on evidence of an identifiable
threat of offensive mobilisation, 'we must *adapt* the concept of imminent
threat to the capabilities and objectives of today's adversaries' (ibid.:
emphasis added). What was proposed, however, was not adaptation but
change, definitional change, including other states' capacity to threaten:

> The greater the threat, the greater the risk of inaction – and the more
> compelling the case for taking *anticipatory action* to defend ourselves,
> even if uncertainty remains as to the time and place of the enemy's
> attack ... the United States cannot remain idle while dangers gather.
>
> (Ibid., emphasis added)

Even Henry Kissinger appeared concerned: 'It is not in the American national interest to establish pre-emption as a universal principle available to every nation' (*New York Times*, 16 August 2002).

The US Security Strategy established four key elements to its 'broad portfolio of military capabilities': defending the US homeland; conducting information operations; ensuring US access to 'distant theatres'; protecting 'critical US infrastructure and assets in outer space' (White House 2002: 30). In providing a framework for action beyond the globe, its reach had become literally universal. According to Bush, the 'moment of opportunity' had arrived (ibid.: Preface, unpaginated). What was this opportunity? To secure the 'battle for the future of the Muslim world'. To succeed in 'a struggle of ideas ... where America must excel' (ibid.: 31). In so doing, US objectives to 'meet global security commitments' and to 'protect Americans' would not be 'impaired by the potential for investigations, inquiry or prosecution by the International Criminal Court, *whose jurisdiction does not extend to Americans and which we do not accept*' (ibid., emphasis added).

Having reconstituted internationally agreed conditions for pre-emptive military action against nation-states, the US administration formally placed itself and its citizens beyond the reach of international criminal justice. There was one further dimension to be inscribed in the new Security Strategy: the US administration's respond to dissident former allies within the Western democratic power base. Bush responded by demanding loyalty to its project: 'all nations have important responsibilities: Nations that enjoy freedom must actively fight terror' (ibid.: Preface, unpaginated). If they refused to give the US a mandate for military action, the consequences would be direct: 'we will respect the values, judgement and interests of our friends and partners [but] will be prepared to act apart when our interests and unique responsibilities require' (ibid.: 31).

There could not have been a more unequivocal rejection of the United Nations and of US allies' independent political judgement. By rewriting the defence of pre-emption, the 2002 National Security Strategy revoked the conditional basis of a 'just war'. As with other internationally agreed conventions and legal restraints, it rejected outright the International Criminal Court. Finally, it delivered an uncompromising declaration of unilateralism. If its military might was to be mobilised, it would be on its own, unconditional terms – regardless of legal restriction or the political judgement of its allies and the United Nations. While weapons inspectors travelled the length and breadth of Iraq and debate raged over the interpretation and legitimacy of UN resolutions regarding Saddam Hussein's regime, the US administration prepared to invade. As far as the US hawks were concerned, the military offensive was not about establishing Iraq's capacity to mount a serious and imminent threat.

From the outset, whatever the games played with Hans Blix as head of the weapons inspectorate and the UN Security Council, the invasion was a fait accompli. Cornered in the Security Council, France and Germany failed the 'loyalty test'. In building its case for military invasion of a sovereign state, the US administration liberated itself from the unambig- uous boundaries of self-defence laid down in the UN Charter. Pre-emption was now recast as 'anticipatory action'. In its mission to 'secure the future of the Muslim world', regime change – informed and supported by Iraqi exiles whose political credentials and judgement were at best dubious – was the sole objective.

On the eve of the invasion Bush attempted to justify the offensive by alluding to Iraq's weaponry and the imminent threat it posed. Addressing the nation, he delivered the well-rehearsed script. He stated that, 90 days after the UN Security Council passed Resolution 1441 requiring Saddam Hussein to make a full declaration of Iraq's weapons programme, he had not done so, thereby failing to cooperate in the disarmament of his regime. He had not accounted for a 'vast arsenal of deadly, biological and chemical weapons' and had embarked on an 'elaborate campaign of concealment and intimidation' (Presidential Address to the Nation, 8 February 2003). The Iraqi regime not only possessed the 'means to deliver weapons of mass destruction' but harboured a 'terrorist network' headed by an al-Qaida leader. Connecting the regime to al-Qaida was central to the US adminis- tration's position. It provided a direct link to the events of 11 September. Bush concluded:

> Resolutions mean little without resolve. And the United States, along with a growing coalition of nations, will take whatever action is necessary to defend ourselves and disarm the Iraq regime.

The UK government was compromised. It had no conveniently recon- structed security strategy through which pre-emptive military action could be mobilised. It had to abide by the UN Charter while supporting the US administration's determination to affect regime change in Iraq. The only possible justification for a military offensive was self-defence, and for that it needed evidence of unambiguous, imminent danger posed by Iraq. It re- interpreted UN resolutions going back as far as 1991 and sought an emphatic statement derived in independent sources. The United Nations Inspectorate had not produced significant evidence. On the contrary, Hans Blix requested more time. The government relied on its intelligence and security sources to produce necessary evidence and a dossier duly arrived. In its Foreword Prime Minister Blair wrote:

> ... the assessed intelligence has established beyond doubt ... that Saddam has continued to produce chemical and biological weapons, that he continues to develop nuclear programmes, and that he has been able to extend the range of his ballistic missile programme. I am in no doubt that the threat is serious and current ... [Saddam] has made

progress on WMD [Weapons of Mass Destruction] ... the document discloses that his military planning allows for some of the WMD to be ready within 45 minutes of an order to use them.

(UK Government 2003: 3–4)

Disregarding mass protest against the 'war' in Iraq, Tony Blair used seriously flawed intelligence to legitimate his determination to support the US administration. He later revealed that the dossier had been drafted by the Joint Intelligence Committee chairman and his staff. They were also the source of the 45 minutes estimation and had drafted the Foreword, signed off by the Prime Minister (*Hansard*, 11 July 2003).

Reflecting two years later on the deployment of UK forces, Tony Blair stated, 'we went to war to enforce UN Resolutions' (*The Guardian*, 6 March 2005). It was a judgement based on the UK Attorney General's association of UN Resolution 678 (1990) and UN Resolution 1441 (2002). UN Resolution 678 authorised the use of 'all necessary means' to remove Iraq's forces from Kuwait. It included the 'restoration of international peace and security' throughout the region and the elimination of weapons of mass destruction throughout Iraq. It was directed towards the 1990 allied coalition to achieve these ends. What followed was a series of UN resolutions, culminating in 1441. In itself, 1441 sought the Iraq regime's compliance with the weapons inspectorate but its wording could not be interpreted as providing authorisation for invasion or war. As Lord Archer, former UK Solicitor General, stated: '1441 manifestly does not authorise military action' (*The Guardian*, 5 March 2004).

Despite this opinion, shared by numerous legal academics and practitioners, the US and UK governments continued to overstate Iraq's military capacity, capability and threat while persistently undermining the credibility of Hans Blix and the weapons inspectorate (see Blix 2004). On the eve of the invasion, the most recent intelligence doubted the veracity of the 2003 dossier's claims. Concerns were voiced that no hard evidence existed to verify Iraq as a serious or imminent threat. Lord Boyce, UK Chief of Defence Staff, was so troubled he demanded 'unequivocal' legal opinion in support of military action. What he received instead was the Attorney General's assertion that 'on the balance of probabilities' Iraq possessed weapons of mass destruction and posed a real and serious threat. On reflection, Blair stated: 'in fact everyone thought he [Saddam] had them [weapons of mass destruction]'. In remarkable doublespeak, recasting previous certainty as inference, he commented:

The characterisation of the threat is where the difference lies ... we are in mortal danger of mistaking the nature of the new world ... the threat we face is not conventional. It was defined not by Iraq but by September 11 ... September 11 for me was a revelation ... The global threat to our security was clear. So was our duty: to act to eliminate it ... If it is a global threat, it needs a global response, based on global rules.

(The Guardian, 6 March 2005)

The argument presented throughout the US Security Strategy document is embedded in Blair's few sentences. Because the world beyond 11 September changed, military invasion of sovereign nation-states became acceptable, whether or not evidence existed of a demonstrable 'threat'. His conceptualisation of 'global' was instructive. He provided no indication as to who were the definers of 'global'. These were sweeping assertions from a Prime Minister without the capacity alone to deliver global security. Given its determination to operate unilaterally if necessary, there is no question that the US administration regarded itself, and expected to be accepted, as the principal definer.

This was evident in the decision to persist with holding prisoners at Guantanamo Bay. Despite continuing criticism from other states, NGOs and human rights organisations, the US administration continued to deny the checks and balances of international conventions. As stated earlier, because soldiers captured in Afghanistan did not wear the uniforms of a recognised army, they were considered 'undistinguishable from the general population'. Article 4 of the 1949 Geneva Convention was not applied to them, redesignated 'unlawful combatants' rather than 'soldiers in action'. Yet Article 5 of the Third Geneva Convention states that, should there be ambiguity regarding a detainee's status, they should be classified 'prisoner of war' until a competent tribunal determines their status.

Once again, the White House Press Secretary demonstrated how 'global rules' were rewritten to suit US priorities. In a strident response to mounting criticism over the unlawful detention – without legal protection or due process of the law – of more than 600 men and boys, he stated: 'The war on terrorism is a war not envisaged when the Geneva Convention was signed in 1949. In this war global terrorists transcend national boundaries' (Press Secretary Statement, White House, 28 May 2003). Already Donald Rumsfeld had established the guilty status of the captives: 'These people are committed terrorists. We are keeping them off the streets and out of airlines and out of nuclear power plants' (22 January 2002).

As the UK brokered a 'special favours' deal to release several UK citizens, it became clear that many Guantanamo Bay prisoners were held in appalling conditions, enduring abuse and intimidation in the interrogation they received. David Rose (2004: 71) also notes the use of 'Extreme Reaction Force' in the case of Tarek Degoul. Following a cell and body search he refused a second search. Five soldiers from the punishment squad, in riot gear, ran into his cell:

> They pepper-sprayed me in the face, and I started vomiting ... They pinned me down and attacked me, poking their fingers in my eyes, and

forced my head into the toilet pan and flushed. They tied me up like a beast and then they were kneeling on me, kicking and punching. Finally they dragged me out of the cell in chains, into the rec yard, and shaved my beard, my hair, my eyebrows.

Such stories preceded the release of photographs of US soldiers, men and women, humiliating and degrading prisoners in Iraq. As in Vietnam 30 years earlier, the much-proclaimed 'most efficient' and 'best disciplined' army in the world, was exposed as brutal and sadistic. US soldiers, the recipients of relentless post-11 September propaganda before leaving for Iraq, considered those in captivity beneath contempt. When the enemy is dehumanised, stripped of human identity, it is a small step to strip their clothes, to force them to simulate sexual acts and to coerce them into masturbating for the camera. The degradation inflicted on the body reflects denigration assumed in the mind. Photographs become a visible manifestation and record of subjugation. For all time, they represent the institutional power of personal abuse. In the photographs, pleasure enjoyed by the captors increases in proportion to the pain endured by their captives. Pornography is explicit in the representation; the overt expression of absolute power without responsibility and with assumed impunity.

The torture, degradation and human rights violations at Abu Ghraib prison could not be dismissed as the shameful acts of a small clique of cowboy soldiers. Techniques used by military intelligence officers were institutionalised. The International Red Cross was excluded from visiting the interrogation block and announced that torture, inhuman and degrading treatment were endemic throughout the holding centres for prisoners. Assaults included cold water treatment, phosphorous liquid from broken lights poured on naked bodies, beatings with broom handles, constant threats of rape and actual rape with instruments. Abuse was not confined to the actions of vengeful soldiers. It extended to private contractors not governed by military rules. With Iraqi law in disarray and US civilians in Iraq outside US jurisdiction, private companies operated beyond the rule of law. Even had there been operational local law, their contracts guaranteed exemption.

In this highly volatile context, torture became institutionalised as an essential ingredient in the 'war on terror'. The allegations made by British citizen Benyam Mohammed reveal the full consequences of franchising torture to states that reject international rights standards. For 30 months he was ghosted from prison to prison throughout Afghanistan, Morocco and Pakistan. In Morocco:

They cut off my clothes with some kind of doctor's scalpel. I was naked. They took the scalpel to my right chest. It was only a small cut. Maybe an inch. At first I just screamed ... I was shocked. Then they cut my left chest ... One of them took my penis in his hand and began to make cuts ... I was in agony. They must have done this 20 or 30 times in two hours. There was blood all over ... One of them said it would have been better to just have cut it off as I would only breed terrorists ... they did it to me about once a month.

Mohammed was subjected to the process of rendition under which the US transferred prisoners to torturing states, thereby abdicating responsibility. The use of torture on terrorist suspects was derived in Rumsfeld's approval for 'special interrogation techniques'. An internal reappraisal was conducted to establish the 'lowest boundary' of what constituted torture. Employing legal defences of 'necessity and self-defense' the US administration argued that non-lethal but painful interrogation methods could be used if a direct or imminent threat to the United States and its citizens might be prevented. The classic example was the insertion of needles under fingernails.

Alberto Gonzalez, elevated in 2005 to US Attorney General, issued a memorandum in which he argued that torture occurred only when there was an intention to cause physical pain. Thus inhuman and degrading treatment would be permissible in meeting a higher moral purpose. Stan Cohen (2005) lists the techniques of what came to be defined as 'moderate physical pressure': hooding; withdrawal of painkillers; beating and shaking; sleep deprivation; harsh lights; loud noise; sensory deprivation; 'position abuse'. A former US Navy intelligence officer called these techniques 'torture-lite' (ibid.: 26).

Arguing that torture should be licensed through judicial warrants, liberal Harvard law professor Alan Dershowitz stated: 'I'm not in favour of torture, but if you're going to have torture, it should damn well have court approval ... if we have torture it should be authorised by law' (ibid.: 27). This raised the spectre of judges regulating torture by ruling on the duration and severity of infliction. The US Attorney General was in no doubt as to the criteria to be used in making such a judgment: 'physical pain amounting to torture must be equivalent in intensity to the pain accompanying serious physical injury, such as organ failure, impairment of bodily function or even death'. Put another way, torture constitutes torture when there is risk of death or permanent disability.

While arguing against the use of torture, Michael Ignatieff (2004) makes the distinction between that which constitutes a deliberate infliction of cruelty and the 'lesser evil' of coercive pain. The latter is 'nothing worse than sleep deprivation, permanent light or permanent darkness, disorienting noise and isolation'. It appears that lessons learnt from the miscarriages of justice that were the Birmingham Six, the Guildford Four, Castlereagh and the long litany of anti-Irish degradations, have been forgotten. Whether classified as torture or coercion, cruel interrogations that terrorise prisoners result in false confessions and unreliable information. They also diminish the interrogators and the regime under which they operate. It is not only the agency and its techniques that lose credibility, but the state and its rule of law.

'Puritanical zeal'

> Burning in the collective US unconscious is a puritanical zeal decreeing the sternest possible attitude towards anyone deemed to be an unregenerate sinner. This clearly guided US policy towards the native American Indians, who were first demonised, then portrayed as wasteful savages, then exterminated, their tiny remnant confined to reservations and concentration camps. This almost religious anger fuels a judgmental attitude that has no place at all in international politics, but for the US is a central tenet of its worldwide behaviour. Punishment is conceived in apocalyptic terms ... Sinners are condemned terminally, with the utmost cruelty regardless of whether or not they suffer the cruellest agonies.
>
> (Said 2000: 51)

For over a decade the West's demonisation and destruction of Iraq's people and its infrastructure were relentless. At the close of the 1991 Gulf War the US engineered an appalling massacre of retreating Iraqi troops, mainly young conscripts, on the Basra road. It was a vengeful bombardment of extermination. Between then and the 2003 invasion, over 70,000 tonnes of bombs were dropped on Iraq. Over half a million civilians died as a result of disease, malnutrition and poor medical care. Many were children. Sanctions on essential foods and medicine were maintained alongside indiscriminate and persistent bombing. The 2003 invasion of Iraq was retribution. It was the final act, the final solution to unfinished business. As with the Taliban in Afghanistan, there could be no defence for Saddam Hussein's regime, its brutalisation of the Iraqi people and attempted mass extermination of Kurds and other opponents. Yet prior to the 1991 Gulf War, these acts had been condoned through silence, supported financially and politically by Western states.

The 2003 self-styled coalition of liberation was a coalition of oppression. Effectively, preconditions on inspection; the language of pre-emptive military strikes; the demand for immediate regime change; the deceit over weapons of mass destruction; the propaganda of nuclear capability; the commitment to unilateral action; the vilification of France and Germany amounted to a catastrophic end-game. All credibility, any hope of reason and resolution in the context of growing terrorist cells, was sacrificed in the rubble of Afghanistan and Iraq. As civilian casualties and deaths mounted, redefined as unfortunate mistakes, as 'collateral damage' or as necessary sacrifices towards the 'longer-term', a new generation of armed activists and suicide bombers was recruited. In the UK, the USA and Australia, Islam became grounds for suspicion, and the ideology of 'otherness' underpinning and promoting punitive military offensives abroad supported and infected punitive policing and rights abuses at home.

Such marginalisation is formidable in its capacity to deny legitimacy, neutralise opposition and disqualify knowledge – ruling alternative accounts out of court. It pathologises victims, survivors and campaigners, using patriotism, loyalty and ostracism as means of silencing. Demonisation and vilification, first directed towards the 'terrorists', is redirected towards 'sympathisers', 'appeasers' and 'traitors'. Within this distorted world of 'with us or against us' the casualties of war, regardless of their status – military or civilian – are held responsible, their losses, their injuries, their suffering reconstructed as self-inflicted. With so much reporting and commentary derived in the manufacture and selection of news through spin and manipulation, it is not difficult for states and their administrations to deny responsibility for their part in atrocities, their part in the long-term consequences of war.

The US-led global 'war on terror' mobilised public outrage in seeking legitimacy for unlawful military offensives in Afghanistan and Iraq and for the atrocities and breaches of international standards regarding detention and torture that followed. In the climate of fear generated by bombings in Bali, Madrid and London, civil liberties and human rights were threatened by anti-terrorist legislation. Faith in the rule of law and the judges to provide necessary checks and balances to 'bad' law or unlawful detention remains overly optimistic. While the 2004 House of Lords judgment was a swingeing indictment of the rushed 2001 legislation and its interpretation, the judicial corrective does not compensate for the unlawful detention of 'terrorist suspects'. It does not deliver accountability for degrading treatment in maximum security conditions and the long-term damage to detainees' mental health and material welfare. The rationalisation of human rights abuses by means of appeals to exceptional circumstances resonates with those who understand the British state's response to the conflict in the North of Ireland. At all levels, the normalisation of special powers and their extension beyond the North of Ireland into UK legislation undoubtedly undermined the rule of law and the administration of justice, leading to egregious breaches of international standards and miscarriages of justice.

11 'Speaking truth to power': critical analysis as resistance

There's thirty people on the Bridge, they're standing in the rain
They caught my eye as I passed by, they tried to explain
Why they were standing there I did not want to hear
When trouble gets too close to home my anger turns to fear
With my eyes turned to the ground I moved along
I covered up my ears and I held my tongue
The rain poured down relentlessly upon the picket line
And the empty words fell from my lips, your 'troubles are not mine'
Though the rain made the colours run the message it was plain
Women are being strip-searched in Armagh jail

(Christy Moore 'On the Bridge', in Moore 2003: 136)

'Outsiders', 'Others' and Objectifying

This book opened with reflections on researching and campaigning with Irish Travellers in the mid 1970s. Witnessing their political and economic marginalisation and the brutal circumstances of eviction and exiling, I commented that Howard Becker's portrayal of 'outsider' was literal. One of the most-quoted passages in criminology texts includes the assertion that 'social groups create deviance by making the rules whose infraction constitutes deviance, and by applying those rules to particular people and labelling them as outsiders' (Becker 1963: 9). It continues, 'deviance is *not* a quality of the act a person commits, but rather a consequence of the application by others of rules and sanctions to an "offender" ... deviant behavior is behavior that people so label'. Note the quotation marks around 'offender'. They depicted and conveyed Becker's disdain for social science analyses that accepted 'crime' and 'criminal', 'deviance' and 'deviant', 'delinquency' and delinquent' as unproblematic categories. The process of labelling, the 'transaction' between a determining group and another to whom the label had been successfully ascribed, created 'outsiders' as an externally inflicted yet broadly shared identity. Becker was not alone in identifying the definitions, negotiations and reactions to such categories and the implications for those labelled.

In advancing his 'preoccupation with socio-psychological problems logically subservient to cross-cultural explanation and study', Edwin Lemert (1967: v) applied his background in sociology and anthropology to 'social control and its consequence for deviance'. In what became a classic quotation, he saw this project as 'a large turn away from older sociology which tended to rest heavily on the idea that deviance leads to social control'. The 'reverse' was 'equally tenable', offering a 'potentially richer premise for studying deviance in modern society': 'social control leads to deviance'. In a nutshell, as labels constituting 'crime' or 'deviance' were defined, popularised and applied to regulate, discipline and control individuals or groups they formed new contexts for subsequent responses and reactions, with deviance 'perpetuated by the very forces directed to its elimination and control' (ibid.).

Lemert's argument was consistent with Becker (1963: 11), who considered that the determination of an act as deviant depended 'on how other people react to it', carrying considerable 'variation' over time. Also significant was 'who commits the act and who feels ... harmed by it'. Out of context, Becker's analysis could be interpreted as relativist social analysis devoid of structural considerations, not least power relations. Yet he discussed differential responses in noting that 'rules' were applied 'more to some persons than others'. Class, corporate interests, race, gender and age were each and together key factors in the 'interaction between the person who commits the act and those who respond to it' (ibid.: 14). Recognising the broad range of differentiation within 'modern societies' – social class, ethnicity, occupation, culture – Becker also considered the contexts in which a particular group, through privileged status, could 'impose its rules on other groups in the society' (ibid.: 17). It was self-evident that this was 'a question of political and economic power'. He concluded:

> Differences in the ability to make rules and apply them to other people are essentially power differentials (either legal or extralegal). Those groups whose social position gives them weapons and power are best able to enforce their rules. Distinctions of age, sex, ethnicity, and class are all related to differences in power, which accounts for differences in the degree to which groups so distinguished can make rules for others.
>
> (Ibid.: 17–18)

Becker was clear that the imposition of rules and their validation in law was not an uncontested process but generated sites of 'conflict and disagreement, part of the political process of society'. In discussing the relationship between 'political marginality' and 'social deviance' Horowitz (1968: 113) noted that while, within limits, the 'right to dissent politically' was 'guaranteed', the 'right to dissent socially' was 'almost totally denied those without high social status'.

Responding some time later to the critique of interactionist theories of deviance (labelling) Becker (1974: 60) argued that, while being concerned with 'how social actors define each other and their environments', his focus was also on 'differentials in the power to define':

> Elites, ruling classes, bosses, adults, men, Caucasians – superordinate groups generally – maintain their power as much by controlling how people define the world, its components and possibilities as by the use of more primitive forms of control ... History has moved us increasingly in the direction of disguised modes of control of the definitions and labels applied to people.

For Horowitz (1968: 113–14), within the USA the 'line between the social deviant and the political marginal' had become 'an obsolete distinction', with political dissent increasingly subjected 'to the types of repression that have been the traditional response to social deviance'.

Nanette Davis (1975: 205) considered that the inter-related processes of 'institutionalization, defining, labelling and categorizing', at the core of Becker's work, provided 'commonsense reality' underpinning the mechanics and operation of social control. The context, she argued, was 'an unequal society divided by class, ethnicity, sex and political and economic differences' dominated by 'politically powerful groups' which drafted 'and enforce[d] rules ... detrimental to the interests and needs of powerless groups'. Given structural inequality, Hall and Scraton (1981: 465) interpreted Becker's appeal to 'take sides' as a 'clarion call to a more overt radical political commitment, with sociologists and criminologists taking up a clear, "partisan" stance'. It was a commitment 'directed against the hidden agenda of "control" behind the liberal front of welfare policies'. More recently, John Muncie (1999b: 128) notes that Becker exposed how academic social science underwrote the 'spurious legitimacy' enjoyed by oppressive state institutions.

In recognising the significance of social transaction and labelling as central elements within 'new deviancy theory', there has been a tendency to depict social interactionism as divorced from structural relations of power. Working with Irish Travellers and closely observing the differential policing to which white working-class Knowsley and black working-class Toxteth were subjected during the late 1970s, my experiences connected directly to the full, violent potential of the application of the 'outsider' label. Control and regulation imposed on communities by the state, ideologically or coercively, responded directly to assumed and real statuses of 'deviant' and 'criminal'. Yet, as communities organised politically and fought back through campaigns and protest, harsh institutional responses were unambiguous manifestations of the logic and rationale embedded within their structural role, as well as their institutional function. While the 'criminal' or 'deviant' label might in many situations receive popular, but not always informed, support, the threat posed to the established order by political dissent brought uncompromising policing and criminalisation as logical outcomes. 'Criminalisation', argue Hall and Scraton (1981: 488–9), provides the state with 'a particularly powerful weapon' as it 'mobilises considerable popular approval and legitimacy' in policing a 'criminal' act rather than repressing a 'political cause'.

In pursuing a more fully developed understanding of the structural context of 'outsider' status and its determination, a chance reading of Simone de Beauvoir's *The Second Sex*, first published in 1949, provided a defining link. In her extensive and incisive analysis of gender relations she foregrounded the social, cultural, political and economic construction of the 'Other'.

> ... humanity is male and man defines woman not in herself but as relative to him; she is not regarded as an autonomous being ... she is defined and differentiated with reference to man and not he with reference to her; she is the incidental, the inessential as opposed to the essential. He is the Subject, he is the Absolute – she is the Other.
>
> (De Beauvoir 1972: 16)

No group, she argued, conceives itself as the One, the essential, the absolute, without conceiving and defining the 'Other'. The 'Other' is the stranger, the outsider, the alien, the suspect community. Otherness begets fear, begets hostility, begets denial. De Beauvoir listed the 'Others' of her time: blacks in the USA; aboriginals in the colonies; proletarians within capitalist economies; women and girls throughout patriarchies. Acknowledging Hegel, she concluded: 'we find in consciousness itself a fundamental hostility towards every other consciousness; the subject can be posed only in being opposed ... the essential as opposed to the other, the inessential, the object' (ibid.).

In considering the relationship between structural relations and social action, Frantz Fanon's *The Wretched of the Earth* opened a profound yet seemingly obvious connection to de Beauvoir. In discussing physical subjugation by military occupation and police rule central to colonisation he identified the coloniser's dehumanisation of native populations:

> As if to show the totalitarian character of colonial exploitation the settler paints the native as a sort of quintessence of evil. Native society is not simply described as a society lacking in values, but also the negation of values ... the enemy of values ... the absolute evil ... corrosive ... destroying ... disfiguring ...
>
> (Fanon, 1967: 31–2)

The native as amoral, the quintessential 'other', 'disfiguring all that has to do with beauty or morality'; this not only provided the foundation for understanding colonial relations of power and their implications for racism throughout a failing 'Empire', but it was relevant to understanding marginalisation, subjugation and exclusion in all structural contexts. It also raised the central issue of state authority and the institutionalised processes of 'othering'.

Interpreting authoritarianism

The violent response of US authorities to the early civil rights protests revealed the lie at the heart of its politics. As noted earlier, far from being a democratic, pluralist society, the US not only held Native Americans on under-resourced reservations but also condoned apartheid as the most visible legacy of slavery. Those states that used the rule of law and social policy to 'protect' their white communities from the 'negro threat' also failed to protect the lives of their black, non-voting constituents from the hatred, brutality and terror that had become the assumed birthright of white Americans and the operational prerogative of local state institutions. Across Southern states, violence against people of colour was a common feature of daily life. For campaigners and activists enduring the full brunt of state force, the dilemma was to seek change through peaceful, non-violent means or to take the route of direct action.

The dilemma was not confined to the USA, and the debate about the substance of state power within democracies, particularly the relationship between coercion and consent, became a defining focus for critical analysis. Within Western criminology oppositional, alternative discourses, in part influenced by social and political conflict but also, as discussed above, derived in questioning social sciences' close association with the management rather than eradication of structural and institutionalised inequalities, emerged and quickly consolidated. 'New' or 'radical' criminology was grounded in the 'diverse and unique world of everyday life, the claimed location of the interactionists, yet it adapted and contextualized new deviancy theory within the structural dynamics of power and social control' (Scraton and Chadwick 1991: 165).

This radical break, derived in neo-Marxist analyses, emphasised the structural processes of economic marginalisation and criminalisation and their manifestation in class divisions and conflict, inherent within advanced capitalism. Taylor, Walton and Young (1973: 270) developed a critical agenda towards achieving 'a state of freedom from material necessity – a release from the constraints of forced production, an abolition of the forced division of labour, and a set of social arrangements, therefore, in which there would be no politically, economically, and socially induced *need* to criminalize deviance'. Dismissed as economic determinists or reductionists by mainstream theorists and pragmatists locked into administrative criminology, the 'new criminologists' and their challenge to academic orthodoxies 'returned to prominence the significance of structural relations, the question of power and the processes which underpinned its legitimacy' (Scraton and Chadwick 1991: 165). Their emphasis was derived in 'the *contexts* of social action and reaction' and 'the often less visible structural arrangements – the political, economic and ideological management of social worlds' (ibid.). Muncie (1999b: 128) considers the eventual success of critical analysis was its 'radical reconstitution of criminology as part of a more comprehensive sociology of the state and political economy, in which questions of political and social control took precedence over behavioural and correctional issues'.

Central to that achievement was understanding and analysing authoritarianism as a response to threats posed by the 'other', the 'outsider', and the language and vocabulary of dangerousness central to the assessment of 'risk'. As Barbara Hudson (2003: 35–6) notes:

> Since the inception of modern penal systems there have been special penal laws to protect society from dangerous and habitual (persistent) offenders ... A common worry is that the risk posed by people classified as dangerous is future and speculative, but the deprivation they face is real and immediate. The criteria of 'clear and present danger' are often proposed in liberal democracies, but operation of the criteria is difficult and the assessment can never be certain ... Similar worries affect measures to protect liberal societies from threats posed by people who are thought dangerous because of political as well as criminal potential behaviour ... Like 'dangerous offender' legislation, internment and other forms of protection against suspected 'enemies' are at the margins of law, often on a murky border between criminal law and national security regulations where they lack transparency and accountability and barely respect the liberal ideals of due process protections, and separation of governing powers.

Responding to the inexorable rise and consolidation of 'risk politics', Hudson goes to the heart of the debate, seemingly regarded as passé by many contemporary theorists, about the politics and practices of authoritarianism within advanced democratic states. She discusses the historical 'preoccupation' of liberal governance in regulating those considered threats to political stability, industrial expansionism and 'respectable' working-class compliance. 'Dangerousness' has been ever present in this political and ideological construction of disciplined and responsible citizenship: 'a label that attached to individuals as well as to classes and sub-groups' (ibid.: 35). The ubiquitous label has been invoked to cover a multitude of 'sinners', from 'deviant sexualities' (Mort 1987) and 'moral degenerates' (Stedman Jones 1977) to the criminal, the violent, the lawless and the militant. Taken together, a much-favoured pastime of the New Right, the 'dangerous' represented a collective 'enemy within'. Meanwhile, massing at the border, a metaphor only in part, was the 'enemy without': the 'illegal immigrant', the 'bogus asylum seeker', the 'international terrorist'.

Hudson (2003: 36) neatly summarises the 'principle of equal liberty' shared by most 'versions of liberalism': 'the maximum possible amount of freedom compatible with equal freedom of all'. Yet 'inherent tensions' persist 'which cannot be resolved without the surrender of important values and insights' (ibid.: 37). They include the relationship between utility and rights, between universality and particularity. Other 'challenges ... arise from the depth of difference in contemporary societies, with population movements making for cultural and religious differences of a degree unimagined by earlier writers on tolerance and diversity'. She also records a 'new consciousness of differences, for example, between the standpoints of males and females'. What this amounts to is a 'radical fissured pluralism'. This begs the question as to whether 'pluralism' has ever been anything other than fissured, consensus ever anything other than illusory.

The advanced democratic state is predicated on the recognition and political management of personal and social diversity. Its regulatory mechanisms include the rule of law, enforced and applied equally and impartially to settle competing differences. As a primary objective, the resolution of interpersonal and social conflicts reflects moral purpose while securing political stability, the assumption being that all disputes are resolved through the informal or formal administration of justice for the 'common good'. Underpinning the weight of argument generated by traditional and neo-liberal theorists is the expectation that in seeking the 'common good' as the means to universal societal freedom individuals, through reason, will adopt conciliatory and unselfish resolutions to conflict. The bottom line, however, is that the mutual accommodation of different 'wills', the fair resolution of 'competing interests' and the establishment of 'universal justice' cannot be achieved while structural inequalities persist. Liberal-democratic state institutions, whatever the claims made for them or the good intentions of their employees, function to manage rather than eliminate structural inequalities.

Structural inequality is not simply a political expression or ideological representation derived in theoretical relativism. The cruelties of early capitalism, slavery and patriarchy were material realities. They destroyed personal lives, communities and cultures. There was no transitionary period through which their legacies were transformed, their excesses fully acknowledged and reparations realised. Capitalism, in its global capacity, has advanced, in keeping with its uncompromising objective of capital accumulation, while slavery and colonialism provided the material and cultural foundations for neo-colonialism. It is not possible to analyse the material forces of globalisation without considering the economic, political and ideological dynamics of neo-colonialism. Further, all societies remain steadfastly patriarchal, whether assessment is made on political and economic opportunity, the politics of reproduction and child-rearing, or endemic violence against women and girl children. While there have been social, cultural and political shifts bringing, within limitations, significant changes in the lives of individuals, the structural, alienating inequalities of class, 'race', gender, sexuality and age remain the primary defining contexts of all people's lives in advanced democratic states, whatever their claims to liberal governance.

Within the UK, the post-war commitment of successive governments to welfarism, public education and affordable housing projected an image of benevolence and, consequently, one of potentially achievable equality. The 'age of consensus', alongside the much-heralded 'end of ideology', was illusory, as structural inequalities were maintained. Being materially better off and less discriminated against gave the appearance of fundamental change in structural relations, but the redistribution of earned income through taxation presented capitalism with the scope to reconstruct, consolidate and move outwards to globalisation. The relations of production, reproduction and neo-colonialism became more complex and interwoven but were, and remain, no less relevant in impact and no less potent in consequence. The chapter in this text on policing Merseyside demonstrates clearly the relationship between 'race' and class in regulating and containing marginalised communities. Within the UK and the USA the inexorable advance and expansion of the military–industrial complex, however, were inhibited by restrictions on the 'free market'. During the late 1960s and early 1970s Western states also experienced the heat of civil disobedience, political resistance, organised industrial action, cultural movements and international opposition.

The emergence and consolidation of New Right politics in support of free-market economics culminated in the much-vaunted 'special relationship' between Reaganism and Thatcherism. In the USA and throughout Western Europe it brought the authoritarianism inherent within liberal democracies to the fore. Poulantzas (1978: 77) argued that in 'issuing rules and passing laws, the State establishes an initial field of injunctions, prohibitions and censorship', thereby establishing the 'practical terrain and object of violence'. The rule of law became 'the code of organized public violence'. He considered that within advanced capitalist states physical repression had not been replaced by 'ideological-symbolic manipulation, the organisation of consent, and the internalisation of repression (the "inner cop")' (ibid.: 78). Power was not reducible 'to prohibition and symbolic or internalized oppression', as the state retained 'a monopoly of legitimate physical violence … a rational-legal legitimacy based on law' (ibid.: 80). The deployment of physical violence by state institutions, operating a rational calculus based on the principles of 'reasonable force' and 'humane containment', was central to the maintenance and promotion of public order, social discipline and civil obedience.

According to Poulantzas (ibid.: 81), 'state-monopolized physical violence permanently underlies the techniques of power and mechanisms of consent:

it is inscribed in the web of disciplinary and ideological devices; and even when not directly exercised, it shapes the materiality of the social body upon which domination is brought to bear'. Repression, however, 'is never pure negativity, and is not exhausted either in the actual exercise of physical violence or in its internalization' (ibid.: 83). A central dynamic was 'something about which people seldom talk: namely, the mechanisms of fear'. Poulantzas characterised the 'new form of state' generic to advanced capitalist democracies as 'authoritarian statism'. In this process, state control intensifies 'over every sphere of socio-economic life combin[ing] with a radical decline of the institutions of political democracy and with draconian and multi-form curtailment of so-called "formal" liberties, whose reality is being discovered now they are going overboard' (ibid.: 203–4). Taking the late 1960s and early 1970s as his point of reference, Poulantzas noted the expansion of 'an entire institutional structure serving to prevent a rise in popular struggles' (ibid.: 210). As Hall *et al.* (1978: 303) demonstrated, the 'deep structural shifts' in political–economic conditions 'involved the progressive intervention of the state' in the 'whole sphere of ideological relations and social reproduction'.

In this context the law, its selective enforcement and uneven application, did not correspond instrumentally to the needs or demands of material conditions, but through the intervention of its institutions it 'managed' consent and 'secured' hegemony. Hall (1985: 118) criticised Poulantzas for neglecting the purposeful construction and manipulation of popular consent that delivered legitimacy for authoritarian state interventions: 'harness[ing] support [of] some popular discontents, neutraliz[ing] the opposing forces, disaggregat[ing] the opposition and incorporat[ing] some strategic elements of popular opinion into its own hegemonic project'. According to Hall, the conjuncture identified by Poulantzas as authoritarian statism was more accurately portrayed as authoritarian populism.

As stated above, civil unrest during the early 1970s brought students, workers, political activists and campaigners into direct confrontation with repressive state institutions. Tougher policing and harsher penalties were directed towards trade unionists, student protestors, anti-Vietnam and anti-apartheid campaigners, welfare claimants, unions, black communities and women's rights activists. The deployment of the British Army on the streets of the North of Ireland following Nationalist and Republican civil rights marches came to a head on 30 January 1972 with the deliberate shooting dead in broad daylight of 13 unarmed Derry civilians by soldiers of the 1st Battalion, Parachute Regiment. The exceptional military presence that followed, spanning four decades, supported civil policing representative almost exclusively of loyalist and unionist communities. It also operated within a context of special powers, emergency legislation, covert security operations and politicised courts. It constituted authoritarian statism, visible and hidden, in its most refined and engaged form.

Hall *et al.* (1978: 317) explored the 'crisis of and for British capitalism' and its policing in British towns and cities as a struggling economy attempted 'to stabilise itself in rapidly changing global and national conditions, on an extremely weak, post-imperial base'. The 'crisis' was not confined to cyclical booms and slumps of world trade and its volatile markets. It also prevailed in the 'relations of social forces' as a consequence of economic instability. It was a 'crisis in the political class struggle and in the political apparatuses'. The 'state' faced the challenge to secure 'conditions for the continued expansion of capital' through which its growth could be managed effectively (ibid.: 318–19). In this analysis, the role and function of the state was to encourage and secure consent and legitimacy for its political–economic strategies within civil society. Yet a 'crisis in political legitimacy, in social authority, in hegemony and in the forms of class struggle and resistance' prevailed (ibid.: 319).

These critiques argued that the liberal-democratic notion of consensus was illusory. Consent had to be manufactured through a coalition of social forces. The rule of law and its promotion as the core of social discipline was vital to forging consent, 'in winning over the silent majority to a definition of the crisis ... making it more legitimate for "public opinion" to be recruited ... in favour of a strong state'. It was the perceived constant in the 'ebb and flow of authoritarian populism', defining and reproducing 'social discipline' for the common good (ibid.: 304–5). The 'authoritarian' or 'strong' state, managing dissent and regulating conflict, could not progress without winning the hearts and minds of a broadly aligned constituency. As Poulantzas had proposed, sustaining social stability through a period of economic austerity and hardening political–legal intervention necessitated shrewd ideological management, including orchestrating mechanisms of fear, of threat, of danger.

This is not to underestimate the consciousness, potential and mobilisation of resistance within civil society. People are active agents in their own destinies and are not reducible to mere 'dupes'. Yet the spin of politics follows closely the spin of advertising, and the success of shrewd political and ideological management rests on the mobilisation of traditions, nostalgia, prejudices and fears within diverse communities. Hall *et al.* (ibid.: 278) identified a 'pincer movement' connecting the 'popular moral pressure from below' to the 'thrust of restraint and control from above'. They noted the state's mobilisation of repressive forces against the 'enemy in any of [its] manifold disguises'. The gradual 'shift to control' involved 'the law, the police, administrative regulation, public censure ... [a] qualitative *shift* in the balance and relations of force' amounting to 'a deep change' (ibid.: 278). As noted in the earlier chapters, within a few years Margaret Thatcher effectively deployed the phrase 'the

enemy within' against those who opposed her second, draconian administration.

In building the New Right agenda, Thatcherism popularly mobilised
against a moribund, out-of-touch Labour government. 'Folk devils' were
easily identified and targeted:

> ... the issue of the 'power of the unions' slotted in neatly alongside
> other essentialist strands: the dependency-creating welfare state and
> the pervasiveness of 'scrounging'; the 'decline' of education standards
> and performance due to comprehensive education; the escalation of
> street crime, crimes of violence and 'political terrorism'; the growth of
> 'permissiveness', the 'decline' of morality and the undermining of the
> family unit. (Scraton, 1987: 156).

Stuart Hall identified 'a deep and decisive movement towards a more disciplinary, authoritarian kind of society' in which 'the drive for "more Law
and Order" is no short-term affair'. In their doomsday pronouncements,
politicians and media commentators reflected a 'regression to a stone-age
morality' (Hall, 1980: 3). The populist appeal triggered a 'blind spasm of
control', as the only remedy for an 'ungovernable' society endorsing the
'imposition of order through a disciplinary use of the law by the state'
(ibid.: 3). The 'language of law and order', was 'sustained by moralisms' –
'where the great syntax of "good versus evil", of civilised and uncivilised
standards, of the choice between anarchy and order' divided and classified
social action (Hall, 1979: 19). Populism, argued Hall, was not a 'rhetorical
device or trick' but was derived in and responded to 'genuine contradictions' with a 'rational and material core' (ibid.: 20).

The appeal to 'tradition', to 'Britishness', to 'moral discipline' created
the illusion of a Golden Age of greatness and fairness at home and
abroad undermined by permissiveness, protest and selfishness. It provided the 'law and order crusade' with its 'grasp on popular morality and
common-sense conscience'. Laws became increasingly prohibitive and
repressive, the police operated outside the checks and balances of political accountability, sentencing hardened and prison conditions worsened.
It is no coincidence that this was a period of heightened civil disobedience,
industrial conflict and prisoner protest. These were manifestations of the
iron grip of New Right law-and-order ideology. A strong expression of
deep-seated ideologies and opportunistic political strategies consolidated,
securing and reproducing a lasting constituency within popular discourse.

Critics of Hall and his co-authors rejected the influence of authoritarian
populism, maintaining that they overemphasised ideological determinants
while underestimating political–economic conditions and their impact.
Jessop *et al.* (1988) concluded that there was no evidence to support the
thesis that Thatcherism had delivered hegemony or legitimacy through

securing coherent popular consensus. Hall denied that authoritarian populism had been conceived as a comprehensive analysis of Thatcherism and there had been no assumption that hegemony had been secured by the New Right. Acknowledging Gramsci, Hall (1985: 120) argued that hegemony could be neither conceptualised nor achieved without positioning the economy as the 'decisive nucleus' around which civil society operated. Authoritarianism, as an inherent feature of liberal-democratic states, resolved the economic crisis politically, through expanding and centralising powers within the 'permanent agencies of the state', particularly 'in relation to the maintenance of public order, the handling of emergencies and the gathering of intelligence' (Gamble, 1988: 183).

Thatcherism created a discourse that harmonised two apparently contradictory propositions. First was the well-established right-wing claim that the state, especially its welfare components, had become too influential, too over-indulgent and too interventionist in people's lives. It had created dependency, encouraged idleness and diminished potential. Second was the harnessing of state power to manage consent, systematise regulation, secure hegemony and crush opposition. In 1981 the deaths of 10 Republican hunger strikers in the North of Ireland were proclaimed as a marker for uncompromising government against the enemy within. The following year the Falkland/Malvinas war was celebrated as an uncompromising victory over the enemy without. Turning to the power of trade unions, the second Thatcher administration took on the powerful and popular National Union of Mineworkers, defeating it through a combination of free-market economics and overtly hostile and aggressive policing and prosecutions. Hard-line state responses to uprisings in black communities in 1980, 1981 and 1985, well documented in this text, were directed towards mining communities and others who engaged in industrial action or public protest to challenge the New Right project.

Reflecting on this period, Paddy Hillyard and Janie Percy-Smith (1988: 14) argued that while 'most people in Britain ... see the activities of the state as legitimate and its structures as democratic', democracy in the sense of participation, information access, accountability and 'respect for individual and collective liberties' had been 'debased':

> It is our contention that the contemporary British state falls a long way short of democracy in this sense. Rather it is better characterised as 'coercive' ... decision-making and administration are exclusive ... workings of the state are shrouded in secrecy ... scrutiny of the work of those with power is inadequate ... accountability is weak. While those with power or influence can operate relatively free from external constraints, the powerless, and in particular, certain especially vulnerable groups, are subjected to intrusive investigation and surveillance of their lives through a multiplicity of different state

agencies ... provid[ing] numerous opportunities for imposing punitive or coercive sanctions ranging from the withdrawal of social security benefits to eviction from council housing; from the removal of children into local authority care to arrest, detention and imprisonment.

(Ibid.: 15)

Simply to state, as many critics have, that 'the state' is multi-layered, its institutions complex and sometimes contradictory, provides no comfort to those who continue to endure the harsh realities of authoritarian policies and practices. Of course state power is not unidimensional, nor is it monolithic. However restricted, there has always been room to manoeuvre. State institutions are slightly and selectively open to negotiation, occasionally offering space for critical ideas. In the 1970s this realisation gave rise to the 'in and against the state' debates within the Conference of Socialist Economists and the National Deviancy Conference. Yet state institutions, and the police, prisons, mercenaries they subcontract, also operate as blunt instruments of force, punishment and collusion. Discourses and mechanisms based on regulation by 'consent' have always offered a socially oriented pathway to the effective maintenance of structural inequalities within democratic societies, yet it remains a route underpinned by the forces of coercion.

Throughout the research, from that unforgettable and humbling moment in Walsall, the mobilisation of fear, the appeal to the 'authoritarian within', has formed a consistent prelude to the deployment of exceptional force, restraint and incarceration. State institutions have politically managed and contracted out that deployment. A recurring theme is how, in the USA and in the UK, the 'tough on crime', 'zero-tolerance policing' mantras became embedded within the political manifestos of all parties. As the previous discussion illustrates, the populist appeal of authoritarian rhetoric is its promotion and provocation of material policy outcomes. Hudson concludes that 'deserved retribution', 'protection from dangerous or persistent offenders' and 'strong action against kinds of offending that become suddenly prevalent' (Hudson, 1996: 55) became firmly established as priorities within Western criminal justice processes. Consequently a 're-active framework' unleashed a 'new situation' in which 'an unlimited reservoir of acts' was 'defined as crimes', bringing 'unlimited possibilities for warfare against all sorts of crimes' (Christie, 1994: 24).

The contemporary 'war on terror' abroad was preceded politically and ideologically by the 'war on drugs', the 'war on crime' at home. Analysing the seemingly exponential 'growth in the instruments of coercion and punishment' in 1970s America, Paul Takagi (1981: 218) noted the rapid move 'towards a garrison state' under the cloak of democracy. Following the post-11 September US administration's clampdown, Henry Giroux

(2002b: 143) states that what 'emerged is not an impotent state but a garrison state that increasingly protects corporate interests while stepping up the level of oppression and militarization on the home front'. In this context, 'repression replaces compassion' and 'social problems are now criminalized' (ibid.: 144). For Mike Davis (2001: 45) this represents the escalation of the 'fear economy', the exploitation of a 'national nervous breakdown' where security becomes a 'fully-fledged urban utility like water and power'. While, as the previous chapter demonstrates, on foreign terrains the self-fulfilling prophesy of the globalisation of fear unfolds: 'Terror', states Davis, 'has become the steroid of Empire' (ibid.: 50).

Whose 'knowledge'? What 'truth'?

Nils Christie's (1998: 121) blunt comment that crime 'does not exist' but is 'created' through a complex process in which certain acts are ascribed criminal status at first appears absurd. Yet the observation is as profound as it is simple. 'Crime' and 'criminals', 'deviance' and 'deviants', as has been stated above, appear self-evident classifications, the application of which is consequent on breaches of law or convention. In contrast, 'new deviancy theory' proposed the centrality of social reaction in ascribing negative status to the breach of established conventions and social rules. Becker's point was that outsiders are socially created, marginalised and excluded. Nils Christie locates the ascription of crime within the institutional and classificatory processes of the state. 'Crime' and 'deviance' are invested with meaning in the socio-cultural and political–economic contexts of definition, enforcement and application of the rule of law. As the previous sections demonstrate, these are dynamic processes resulting in the historically specific and materially relevant construction of criminalisation.

In contextualising the 'social phenomenon' of 'mugging', Stuart Hall and his co-authors advanced critical analysis by stressing the centrality of ideology in representing and reconstructing material reality. Criminalisation is not a process restricted to 'the application of the criminal label to a particular social category'; it extends to 'political containment', mobilising 'considerable popular approval and legitimacy behind the state' (Hall and Scraton, 1981: 488–9). Thus, it became a defining aspect of the political management of 'dissent' and 'opposition' discussed earlier. Given the 'meaning' ascribed to certain acts and groups, it also became essential to the political management and differential policing of perceived identity. As discussed above, this theme was prominent in Hall *et al.*'s *Policing the Crisis*, particularly their empirical analysis of the relationship between street crime, black youth and policing. It was an analysis derived in previous work on negative identity (folk devils) and social reaction (moral panics).

In the early 1970s two studies were published in the UK presenting qualitative research on much-publicised issues of the time. These were Jock

Young's research with 'drug takers' and Stan Cohen's research into 'mods and rockers'. Their work explored how identifiable individuals or groups were represented publicly, through actions defined 'criminal' or 'deviant', as posing demonstrable and serious threats to the established social and political order. Occurring 'in times of rapid social change when traditional values are shaken up and disturbed, the ensuing public disquiet is resolved by the media by identifying certain social groups as scapegoats or folk devils' (Muncie and Fitzgerald 1981: 422). Folk devils were 'visible symbols of what is wrong with society' and the publicity they received amplified their ascribed 'deviance' and promoted moral panics. As Cohen (1972: 9) stated:

> A condition, episode, person or group of persons emerges as a threat to societal values and interests; its nature is presented in a stylised and stereotypical fashion by the mass media; the moral barricades are manned by editors, bishops, politicians and other right-thinking people; socially accredited experts pronounce their diagnoses and solutions; ways of coping are evolved or resorted to ... [sometimes] it has serious and long-lasting repercussions that might produce such changes as those in legal and social policy or even in the way society conceives itself.

Within a relatively short period 'folk devils' and 'moral panics' entered popular vernacular. Critiques noted their relativism and ubiquity, arguing that conceptually they were ideological constructions without roots in material conditions. Yet in their creation, and in the social and societal reactions they induce, folk devils are tangible. Returning to Horowitz (1968: 120), the moment at which perceived deviant activities and behaviours gain political impetus is when the 'breakdown in the distinction between crime and marginal politics' creates conditions for significant change through conflict. Using 'race riots' as an example, he argued that in seeking 'structural change' marginalised groups adopt 'political means that are both accessible and effective' but 'illegitimate rather than legitimate', thus further reducing the 'distinction between social deviance and political insurgency' (ibid.: 121).

Far from being the outcome of arbitrary social reaction, a moral panic is an orchestrated, hostile and disproportionate response emanating from state institutions that mobilise surveillance, containment and regulation. Tangible and material, they are reactive, involving concrete strategies, techniques and resources with social, political and economic consequences. Strident interventionism gains legitimacy from 'heightened emotion, fear, dread, anxiety, hostility and a strong sense of righteousness' (Goode and Ben-Yehuda, 1994: 31).

> During the moral panic the behaviour of some of the members of a society is thought to be so problematic to others, the evil they do, or

are thought to do, is felt to be so wounding to the body social, that serious steps must be taken to control the behaviour, punish the perpetrators, and repair the damage ... typically [it] entails strengthening the social control apparatus of society – tougher or renewed rules, more intense public hostility and condemnation, more laws, longer sentences, more police, more arrests and more prison cells ... a crackdown on offenders.

(Ibid.)

Far from being ideologically reductionist, political and material consequences are directly related to structural inequalities: 'the more power a group or social category has, the greater the likelihood it will be successful in influencing legislation ... consistent with the views, sentiments and interests of its members ... ' (Goode and Ben-Yehuda, 1994: 31). The moral outrage around a particular act or sequence of events is accompanied by a widely and immediately disseminated rush to judgement, invariably feeding highly publicised calls for increasingly regulatory interventions. More broadly, moral panics 'form part of a sensitizing and legitimizing process for solidifying moral boundaries, identifying "enemies within", strengthening the powers of state control and enabling law and order to be promoted without cognisance of the social divisions and conflicts which produce deviance and political dissent' (Muncie, 1996: 55). The 'public anxiety and uncertainty' triggered and sustained by moral panics stigmatises, criminalises, ostracises and exiles the 'other', the 'outsider', the 'outlaw'.

For identifiable groups or communities the consequences can be severe. In his exhaustive analysis of the 'construction' of the Irish in Britain as a 'suspect community' Paddy Hillyard (1992: 260) concludes that the Prevention of Terrorism Act '*criminalised* Irish people living in Britain' through a process of 'detecting and investigating alleged law breaking and subsequently arresting, charging and prosecuting those under suspicion'. In this process criminalisation 'cover[ed] not only the processes by which certain *types of behaviour*' were 'designated prohibited acts by either statute or case law, but also the way certain *categories of people*' were ' drawn into the criminal justice system simply because of their status and irrespective of their behaviour'. More broadly, Hillyard argues, 'free and open debate' on Ireland was 'restricted' and individuals were 'forced to give up their political activity for fear of being arrested, detained and possibly excluded', resulting in 'an insidious and long-term impact on the democratic process itself' (ibid.: 264). Thus 'suspect communities' become silenced communities.

More recently Stan Cohen (2000: 41–2) discusses the 'ease with which the moral discourse of evil, sin, monstrosity and perversion is coupled with the medical model of sickness, pathology and untreatability':

The term 'folk devils' that I used 30 years ago to describe the media construction of the mods and rockers is more benign. It remains adequate for the cultural updates of skinheads, punks, hippies and social drug users. The moral panic line is crossed when the problem is seen as too horrible and its risk too threatening for mere cultural boundary-setting. For this we need *true victims*: their suffering is obvious and they are unambiguously victims ... We also need *essentialist offenders*: their actions not the product of fashion, situation, setting, opportunity or chance, but express the essence of the type of person they are and always will be.

(Ibid.: 40)

In this text the imagery of evil essentialism was evident in the portrayal of Thomas Hamilton in the killing of primary school children and their teacher in Dunblane. It was there in the media coverage, politicians' comments and the trial judge's concluding comments following the killing of James Bulger. It was mobilised by the police and authorities in the headlines that depicted Liverpool fans as callous killers at Hillsborough. That a false story claiming prisoners had executed and butchered 'sex offenders' could be sustained in the media throughout the Strangeways rooftop protests demonstrated the powerful imagery associated with monstering prisoners. Not dissimilar images were presented by the US administration and its allies in attempting to rationalise atrocities in Afghanistan and Iraq and to justify the use of unlawful detention and torture in holding centres and at Guantanamo Bay. In quite different circumstances the core issues remained consistent: the creation of the 'folk devil' or 'monster', the orchestration of the 'moral panic' and the shaping of 'truth'.

The proposition is not that official discourse as 'truth' is monolithic or universal, the exclusive domain of powerful definers, but that institutional processes and professional interventions within advanced democratic states are expressions of power constructing and legitimating self-serving versions of truth. The relationship between power and knowledge, manifested in the construction of official discourse as truth, is 'dispersed through the body of society' and central to the processes of 'discipline, surveillance, individualization and normalization' (Sim 1990: 9). Within these dynamics the marginalised, the excluded, the 'appeasers', the 'enemy within' or at the frontier, are denied the structural, material worlds they occupy. State institutions cast aside critics through denials and rationalisations and the ensuing moral panic is promoted and regulated, formally and informally, through targeting easily recognised folk devils.

The research presented here into deaths of children and women in custody, at Hillsborough and at Dunblane Primary School shows how the 'factual' and 'public' truth of controversial deaths was reconstructed through criminal investigations, coroners' inquests and government inquiries. It reveals how, in quite different contexts, limits were placed on evidence through the rules of disclosure and manipulation of testimonies. Together, the case studies demonstrate how, in the public domain information, was managed via public relations and media organisations more concerned with news manufacture than with conveying fact. A key issue arising from the range of cases is the abuse of institutional, discretionary powers with impunity, followed by inadequate, partial investigation. As the bereaved, survivors and campaigners were silenced through their pathologisation, and alternative accounts were disqualified through vilification, state institutions and their employees profoundly refused to acknowledge responsibility. Such persistent denial of a broader, moral culpability undermines legitimacy and weakens authority. It prevents the bereaved and survivors from coming to terms with the pain of their loss, exacerbates the suffering of 'not knowing'.

Establishing 'what actually happened' and 'who was responsible' – individually and institutionally – is central to any process of reconciliation. While 'truth' might be effective in 'releasing the dead from silence', it would be as unacceptable as it is difficult to convince victims that 'justice' should be sacrificed for 'truth' by granting amnesty to perpetrators who become 'truth-givers'. The bereaved and survivors, the wrongly accused and the abused continually reiterate their desire for truth, their demands for accountability, and their need for acknowledgement. This should not be perceived as vengeful or punitive. Nor should it be interpreted as an abandonment of due process or just deserts. Reconciliation can be attempted only if ethical responsibility is established through recognisable due process. A human rights and social justice framework, supported by an effective inquisitorial process recognising and responding to those bereaved by or surviving state violence, institutionalised brutality, gross negligence or neglect, would provide an alternative to flawed inquiries and inadequate inquests (Rolston and Scraton, 2004). It would challenge the context and consequences of state-sanctioned regimes of truth, recording and registering the 'view from below'. While accepting that all acts are ascribed meaning at the micro-level at which they occur, they can only be interpreted fully through analysis of their historical and material contexts. As Messerschmidt (1997: 6) states, 'structural action' is 'what people do under specific structural constraints'.

Critical research and analysis emphasise the significance of 'structural constraints' or determining contexts. These are: relations of production and distribution and the consequent uneven distribution of wealth, income and welfare; relations of reproduction, gender and sexuality and the subordination of women within diverse patriarchies; relations of neo-colonialism and the subjection of 'ethnic groups', asylum seekers, first nations people and aboriginals to racism; relations of age and the marginalisation and exploitation of children and young people. Each determining context is evident at the cutting edge of subjugation, exploitation and violence. Poverty, wherever the breadline is drawn, blights the daily lives, health and welfare of the low paid and unemployed. Women, despite 'equal opportunities' legislation, remain unequally paid and endure physical and sexual violence regardless of class, 'race', religion or age. Black, Asian and Traveller families are routinely subjected to racist abuse and violence across a spectrum to fire-bombings and murder. Sectarianism persists as a lasting consequence of British rule in Ireland. Children and young people, whether in 'families' or in 'care', are routinely physically chastised, degraded and abused. Each instance of impoverishment, sexism, homophobia, racism, sectarianism or child hate as an expression of agency has its particular circumstances and lived history. Yet they cannot be researched, analysed and fully comprehended without location in the determining contexts of structure.

As the relativism of 'post-structuralist' analyses, particularly in the interpretation and representation of power relations, replaced the assumed reductionism of 'grand theory', attention was deflected from the determining contexts of advanced political economies whose privileged, global reach required protection and security. As discussed in the previous chapter, the 2002 US Security Strategy unashamedly used the libertarian rhetoric of freedom, opportunity and justice to proclaim the defeat of communism and eliminate the threat of Islamic fundamentalism. Behind Bush's ranch barbecue discourse of 'good guys' and 'bad guys' lay the fear that Western economic interests and their pre-eminence were under threat. What would be the longer-term destiny of these interests in a new era of Pacific-Rim economic growth? How might the unrivalled benefits of wealth be sustained as natural resources run dry and supply routes are destabilised? Selective interventionism by the US and its allies might proclaim moral legitimacy as its motivation, but its global policing and regulation is driven by political economic self-interest.

In analysing power and authority within advanced capitalism it is remarkable how the intersections of state interventionism, economic determinants and ideological representation have been consigned to history. In the UK, as Thatcherism deregulated, privatised and opened the 'free market' for unfettered trading, the consequences of public underinvestment in marginalised communities, minimal welfare provision, 'sink' estates, 'special measures' schools, unsafe transport systems, polluted environments and unhygienic hospitals soon became tragically apparent. Recurrent crises within the food industry and its farming methods provided further evidence of a cavalier disregard for people's long-term well-being in pursuit of short-term profit. It is a cynicism evident from a cursory glance at the adaptability of predatory corporate interests. At its most simple, the rich rewards from the production of alcohol and tobacco are matched by those from the production of drugs and healthcare in response to the catastrophic effects of dependency and addiction. Returns on investment in manufacturing weapons of mass destruction are matched by contracts to rebuild infrastructures decimated by those weapons; to train and equip law-enforcement agencies, having induced lawlessness; and to construct prisons to hold new enemies of the state. Free-market adventurers, like mercury, retain their consistency while flowing to the fissures opened by conflict.

Critical analysis and the politics of resistance

Writing a quarter of a century after C. Wright Mills, Nils Christie (1994: 58) illustrates how pervasive and pernicious has been the 'invasion' of 'management ideology' and vocational 'correspondence' within universities. The demand for 'useful knowledge' is passed from 'managers within the state and business' to students and, given the pressure to attract increased numbers of students, to academics. Consequently 'university standards of critical thinking' are compromised and 'the moral power of the question-makers' is diminished. Just as social sciences in general served the post-war military–industrial complex, so administrative criminology today serves the punishment–industrial complex. Never has there been a more potentially lucrative period, as Christie famously put it, for 'crime control as industry'. In the aftermath of 11 September, Edward Said castigated 'prominent intellectuals and commentators' who employed 'self-righteous sophistry ... uncritical self-flattery ... [and] specious argument' to tolerate and justify the 'Bush programme' (*Al-Ahram Weekly*, 2 March 2002). As discussed earlier, academic inquiry does not proceed unfettered by sponsors and gate-keepers. It feeds off and into what John Berger (1977) refers to as prevailing 'ways of seeing', reflecting and reinforcing centres of power.

Consequently 'mainstream' or administrative criminology, with its ties to police and penal institutions, has become a lucrative business for university departments, private institutes and management consultants. The primary focus of this work, from cognitive behaviour therapy programmes, to anger management modules, to training in risk management, is locked into individual and social pathology rather than challenging institutional and structural contexts. Critical criminology has amassed an impressive research-based literature, yet it remains under-represented in established academic and professional journals and curiously absent from criminological 'handbooks' and 'textbooks'. Within mainstream criminology and criminal justice institutions, critical analysis has been marginalised. Significant for the research within this text, government departments and state institutions regularly refuse or restrict access to academic researchers whose 'independence' they cannot monitor or regulate. Those who commission independent research are equally liable to tie researchers into restrictive contracts inhibiting academic freedom and intellectual property rights.

Academic knowledge is incorporated into the state's general politics of truth within which hierarchies of credibility are constructed and maintained. Within academic and state institutions the process relies on self-defining 'scientific discourses' producing and exchanging formally sanctioned knowledge. As Henry Giroux (2002a) notes: 'The impoverishment of many intellectuals, with their growing refusal to speak about addressing, if not ending, human suffering is now matched by the poverty of a social order that recognises no alternative to itself'. In contrast, critical analysis foregrounds power, its relations to authority and its processes of legitimacy. It contextualises the determination of and resistance to the containment of personal action and social interaction. It turns individual cases and personal troubles into public issues. Edward Said considered 'the intellectual' as a 'voice in opposition to and critical of great power' with the capacity to challenge and restrain, 'so that the victim will not, as is often the case, be blamed and real power encouraged to do its will' (*Al-Ahram Weekly*, 2 March 2002). In challenging the social and political constructions of crime, disorder, terror, evil, and the consequent differential administration of criminal justice and military power, critical analysis responds to Noam Chomsky's appeal for intellectual responsibility.

While academic entrepreneurship produces 'pessimism of the intellect', critical research retains an 'optimism of the will' (apologies to Gramsci and Rolland). As Hudson states in her critical analysis of penal policy and punishment, 'legal theory and criminology' are unable to provide adequate explanations of crime, social problems, criminal law and the administration of criminal justice. Rather, it is necessary to construct a 'critical theory of the contemporary state' as the 'structural context in which criminal justice is enacted', where the 'rhetoric of law and order, crime and punishment has prevailed over treatment' (Hudson, 1993: 6–7). Hudson's analysis identifies the 'defining tradition' of 'critical social science' as intellectual engagement 'on behalf of those on the downside of power relations'. In his critique of prisons Thomas Mathiesen (1990: 138) argues that society's bifurcation 'between the productive and the unproductive ... places prisoners in a [structurally] powerless position'. As the earlier discussions of violence show, prisoners endure powerlessness and are stigmatised within brutalising institutions that are marketed as 'healthy', rational and rights compliant, thus 'appear[ing] meaningful and legitimate' (ibid.).

Simultaneously, 'by relying on the prison, by building prisons, by building more prisons, by passing longer prison sentences' politicians and civil servants 'obtain a method of showing they act on crime ... that they are doing something about it, that something is presumably being done about law and order' (Mathiesen, 1990: 139). As previously mentioned, prisons become places where the moral panic dynamic ultimately is played out. It remains a remarkable 'achievement' of authoritarian populism that despite nearly doubling the prison population and increasing sentencing in England and Wales in one decade, despite sending children to prison earlier and in greater numbers than any other Western European state, despite locking up hundreds of children who have not committed a crime other than breaching a civil injunction, despite holding prisoners in infested, overcrowded Victorian jails condemned for demolition a quarter of a century ago – all in the context of a marked reduction in 'crime' – public opinion overwhelmingly and persistently berates the government for being 'soft on crime'.

Reviewing 30 years of empirical research while remembering discussions with many activists, community groups, undergraduates, postgraduates and professionals *en route*, my initial proposition remains strong: critical analysis has a significant role in resisting the political and ideological imperatives of official discourse, state-sponsored evaluations of official policy initiatives and the correspondence of vocational training to the requirements of the crime-control industry. Returning to Wright Mills, it is an agenda contextualising the experiential realities of personal troubles as public issues, analysing and exposing prevailing regimes of truth within official discourse. Further, it locates state interventionism within structural relations. In seeking out, representing and valuing the 'view from below', critical criminologists promote structural change within social democracies, undermining the 'complex discourse of denial' and procedural arrangements that provide a sophisticated 'legal defense' (Cohen, 1996: 517).

Reece Walters (2003: 166) argues for 'criminology of resistance' that 'promotes critique, that challenges concepts of power and social order, that wrestles with notions of truth and adheres to intellectual autonomy and independence'. It is a resistance to the 'commodification' of approved knowledge, to the 'corporate management' goals of entrepreneurial universities and to the tightly defined and controlled demands of external funders. As this text shows, knowledge *as* resistance requires the researcher to oppose such regulation. Politically, the significance of critical research is marked by close association with people's movements and community campaigns. For the harm, suffering and exclusion endured by those struggling for social justice, formal acknowledgement and 'truth' provide the least deniable evidence of the incursion of authoritarianism into everyday life. It is at this level of inquiry and contextualisation that cases are transformed into issues, experiential moments of agency challenge the often-disguised processes of structure and the doublespeak of manufactured official discourse becomes enmeshed in its own rhetoric and spin.

Whatever the complexities and interweaving of power, however dispersed within the multi-layered state, government quangos and contracted private corporations, the case studies collectively demonstrate the self-serving degradation of truth and denial of justice. The previous chapters consistently reveal to a greater or lesser extent a combination of the following: abuses of institutional, discretionary powers with confidence and impunity; initiation of official inquiries as mechanisms of neutralisation, incorporation and legitimacy; the management and manipulation of information; inadequate and partial investigation and lack of disclosure of privileged evidence; the marginalisation, condemnation and silencing of victims and campaigners. These related processes of reconstruction and representation are central to the state's denial of responsibility and diminution of accountability. Through public condemnation of 'their' personal identity and reputation, the punitive consequences of authoritarianism are presented as self-inflicted. 'They brought it on themselves ... '; 'It was their own fault ... ' and so on. 'They' being the 'quintessential others', openly demonised and dehumanised, their histories decontextualised, their present marginalised, their futures diminished.

Henry Giroux (2002a) states, in the context of 'increasingly oppressive corporate globalism ... educators need to resurrect a language of resistance and possibility'. For, 'Hope is the precondition for an individual and social struggle ... the mark of courage on the part of intellectuals in and out of the academy who use the resources of theory to address pressing social problems.' Critical work is more than this: bearing witness, gathering testimonies, sharing experiences, garnering the view from below and exposing the politics and discourses of authoritarianism. It moves beyond the resources of theory into praxis, recognising the self-as-academic as the self-as-participant. It takes political responsibility. It is also unforgiving. As Stan Cohen (2001: 286) concludes: 'Intellectuals who keep silent about what they know, who ignore the crimes that matter by moral standards, are even more morally culpable when society is free and open. They can speak freely, but choose not to.'

Bibliography

Ahmed, K., Hicklin, A., Murray, G. and Smith, G. (1996) 'The Dunblane Tragedy: Why?' *Scotland on Sunday*, 17 March.

Allen, R. (1999) 'Is What Works What Counts? The Role of Evidence-based Crime Reduction in Policy and Practice', *Safer Society* 2, 22–3.

Ashford, M. (1996) 'The Trial Process in England and Wales', in P. Cavadino (ed), *Children Who Kill*, Winchester: Waterside Press, 67–72.

Ashworth, A., Gardner, J., Morgan, R., Smith. A. T. H., von Hirsch, A. and Wasik, M. (1998) 'Neighbouring on the oppressive: the Government's "Antisocial behaviour order"', *Criminal Justice* 16, 7–14.

Audit Commission (1996) *Misspent Youth: Young People and Crime*, London: Audit Commission.

Baldwin, J. (1964) *The Fire Next Time*, London: Penguin.

Becker, H. S. (1963) *Outsiders: Studies in the Sociology of Deviance*, New York: Free Press.

—— (1967) 'Whose Side Are We On?' *Social Problems* 14, 3: 239–47.

—— (1974) 'Labelling Theory Reconsidered', in P. Rock and M. McIntosh, eds. *Deviance and Social Control*, London: Tavistock.

Berger, J. (1977) *Ways of Seeing*, Harmondsworth: Penguin.

Blair, T. (2000) 'My vision for Britain', *The Observer*, 10 November.

—— (2006) 'Our nation's future: The criminal justice system', in R. Garside and W. McMahon (eds), *Does criminal justice work? The 'Right for the wrong reasons' debate*, London: Crime and Society Foundation, 85–97.

Blix, H. (2004) *Disarming Iraq*, New York: Pantheon Books.

Boyle, J. (1991) 'Foreword' in P. Scraton, J. Sim and P. Skidmore (eds), *Prisons Under Protest*, Milton Keynes: Open University Press.

Bourne, J. (2001) 'The life and times of institutional racism', *Race and Class* 43, 2: 7–22.

Bridges, L. (1999) 'The Lawrence Inquiry – incompetence, corruption, and institutional racism', *Journal of Law and Society* 26, 3: 298–247.

Bullen, E., Kenway, J. and Hay, V. (2000) 'New Labour, social exclusion and educational risk management: the case of "gymslip mums"', *British Educational Research Journal* 26, 4: 441–56.

Carlen, P. (1983) *Women's Imprisonment: A Study in Social Control*, London: Routledge & Kegan Paul.

—— (1998) *Sledgehammer: Women's Imprisonment at the Millennium*, Basingstoke: Macmillan

Carlen, P. and Worrall, A. (2004) *Analysing Women's Imprisonment*, Cullompton: Willan Publishing.

Chadwick, K. and Scraton, P. (2001) 'Criminalization' in E. McLaughlin and J. Muncie (eds), *The Sage Dictionary of Criminology*, London: Sage, 68–70.

Chippendale, D. and Horrie, C. (1992) *Stick It Up Your Punter: The Rise and Fall of The Sun*, London: Mandarin.

Chiswick Report, The (1985) *Report of the Review of Suicide Precautions at HM Detention Centre and HM Young Offenders' Institution, Glenochil*, Edinburgh: Scottish Home and Health Department, HMSO.

Chomsky, N. (2001) *9-11*, New York: Seven Stories Press.

—— (2005) *Imperial Ambitions: Interviews with David Barsamian*, London: Hamish Hamilton.

Christie, N. (1994) *Crime Control as Industry*, London: Routledge, 2nd edn.

—— (1998) 'Between Civility and the State', in V. Ruggiero, N. South and I. Taylor (eds), *The New European Criminology: Crime and Social Order in Europe*, London: Routledge.

Clendinnen, I. (1998) *Reading the Holocaust*, Melbourne: Text Publishing.

Clough, B. (1995) *Clough: The Autobiography*, London: Corgi.

Cohen, D. (1991) *Aftershock: The Psychological and Political Consequences of Disasters*, London: Paladin.

Cohen, N. (1999) *Cruel Britannia: Reports on the Sinister and the Preposterous*, London: Verso.

Cohen, S. (1972) *Folk Devils and Moral Panics*, London: MacGibbon and Kee.

—— (1981) 'Footprints in the Sand: a further report on criminology and the study of deviance in Britain', in M. Fitzgerald, G. McLennan and J. Pawson (eds), *Crime and Society: Readings in History and Theory*, London: Routledge & Kegan Paul.

—— (1985) *Visions of Social Control*, Cambridge: Polity Press.

—— (1993) 'Human rights and crimes of the state: the culture of denial', *Australia and New Zealand Journal of Criminology* 26, 2: 97–115.

—— (1996) 'Government responses to human rights reports: claims, denials and counter claims', *Human Rights Quarterly* 18, 517–43.

—— (2000) 'Some thoroughly modern monsters', *Index on Censorship* 29, 5: 36–43.

—— (2001) *States of Denial: Knowing about Atrocities and Suffering*, Cambridge: Polity Press.

—— (2005) 'Post-moral torture: From Guantanamo to Abu Ghraib' *Index on Censorship* 31, 1: 24–30.

Coleman, S., Jemphrey, A., Scraton, P. and Skidmore, P. (1990) *Hillsborough and After: The Liverpool Experience*, Liverpool: Liverpool City Council.

Connolly, P. and Healy, J. (2004) *Children and the Conflict in Northern Ireland: The Experiences and Perspectives of 3–11 Year Olds*, Belfast: Office of the First Minister and Deputy First Minister.

Connors, J. (1973) 'Seven weeks of childhood: An autobiography', in J. Sandford (ed.), *Gypsies*, London: Secker and Warburg.

Corcoran, M. (2006) *Out of Order: The political imprisonment of women in Northern Ireland 1972–1998*, Cullompton: Willan Publishing.

CRC (2002) *Concluding Observations of the Committee on the Rights of the Child: United Kingdom of Great Britain and Northern Ireland*, Committee on the Rights of the Child 31st Session, 4 October.

Cullen, The Hon. Lord, (1996) *The Public Inquiry into the Shootings at Dunblane Primary School on 13 March 1996*, Cm. 3386, Edinburgh: The Stationery Office.

Currie, E. (1998) *Crime and Punishment in America*, New York: Holt.

Davis, H. and Scraton, P. (1997) *Beyond Disaster: Identifying and Resolving Inter-Agency Conflict in the Aftermath of Disasters*, London: Home Office Emergency Planning/CSCSJ.

—— (1999) 'Institutionalised conflict and the subordination of "loss" in the immediate aftermath of UK mass fatality disasters', *Journal of Contingencies and Crisis Management* 7, 2: 86–97.

Davis, M. (2001) 'The Flames of New York', *New Left Review* 12, November–December.

Davis, N. J. (1975) *Social Constructions of Deviance: Perspectives and Issues in the Field*, Dubuque, IA: W. C. Brown Co.

De Beauvoir, S. (1972) *The Second Sex*, Harmondsworth: Penguin.

Dennis, N. (1993) *Rising Crime and the Dismembered Family*, London: Institute of Economic Affairs.

Dennis, N. and Erdos, G. (1992) *Families without Fatherhood*, London: Institute of Economic Affairs.

Downes, D. (2001) 'Four Years Hard: New Labour and crime control', *Criminal Justice Matters* 46: 8–9.

Durham, M. (2001) 'The Conservative Party, New Labour and the Politics of the Family', *Parliamentary Affairs* 54: 459–74.

Ellison, G. (2001) *Young People, Crime, Policing and Victimisation in Northern Ireland*, Belfast: Institute of Criminology and Criminal Justice, Queen's University.

Emergency Planning Society (1999) *People's Rights – Organisational Wrongs: Transcript of Proceedings, 14 April 1999*, London: Emergency Planning Society.

Fairweather, E., McDonough, R. and McFadyean, M. (1984) *Only the Rivers Run Free: Northern Ireland the Women's War*, London: Pluto Press.

Fanon, F. (1967) *The Wretched of the Earth*, Harmondsworth: Penguin.

Foucault, M. (1980) *Power/Knowledge: Selected Interviews and Other Writings 1972–1977*, C. Gordon (ed), Brighton: Harvester Wheatsheaf.

Franklin, B. and Petley, J. (1996) 'Killing the Age of Innocence: Newspaper Reporting of the Death of James Bulger', in J. Pilcher and S. Wagg (eds), *Thatcher's Children? Politics, Childhood and Society in the 1980s and 1990s*, London: Falmer Press.

Freedland, J. (2001) 'Playing the Great Game', *The Guardian Comment* 21.

Gamble, A. (1988) *The Free Market Economy and the Strong State*, London: Macmillan.

Gardner, J., von Hirsch, A., Smith, A. T. H., Morgan, R., Ashworth, A. and Wasik, M. (1998) 'Clause 1 – The Hybrid Law from Hell', *Criminal Justice Matters* 31.

Garland, D. (1996) 'The limits of the sovereign state', *British Journal of Criminology* 36, 4: 445–71.

Gateway Exchange (1987) *The Roof Comes Off: The Report of the Independent Committee of Inquiry into the Protest at Peterhead Prison*, Edinburgh: Gateway Exchange.

George, A. (1995)'The Big Prison', in Women in Prison Group (ed.) *Women and Imprisonment*, Melbourne: Fitzroy Legal Service.

Giddens, A. (1998) *The Third Way*, Cambridge: Polity Press.

Gil-Robles, A. (2005) *Report by Mr Alvaro Gil-Robles, European Commissioner for Human Rights on his visit to the United Kingdom, 4th–12th November 2004*, Strasbourg: Office of the Commissioner for Human Rights.

Giroux, H. A. (2002a) 'Global Capitalism and the Return of the Garrison State: Rethinking Hope in the Age of Uncertainty', *ARENA Journal* 19: 141–60.

—— (2002b) 'Democracy and the Politics of Terrorism: Community, Fear, and the Suppression of Dissent', *Cultural Studies, Critical Methodologies* 2, 3: 334–42.

Goldson, B. (1997) 'Children in Trouble: State Responses to Juvenile Crime', in P. Scraton (ed.), *'Childhood' in 'Crisis'?* London: UCL Press: 124–45.

—— (2000) 'Whither Diversion? Interventionism and the New Youth Justice' in B. Goldson (ed.), *The New Youth Justice*, Dorset: Russell House.

Goode, E. and Ben-Yehuda, N. (1994) *Moral Panics: The Social Construction of Deviance*, Cambridge, MA: Blackwell.

Gould, P. (1998) *The Unfinished Revolution: How the Modernizers Saved the Labour Party*, London: Little Brown.

Gouldner, A. W. (1971) *The Coming Crisis in Western Sociology*, London: Heinemann.

—— (1973) 'Foreword' in I. Taylor, P. Walton and J. Young (eds), *The New Criminology*, London: Routledge and Kegan Paul.

Gramsci, A. (1971) *Selections from the Prison Notebooks*, London: Lawrence and Wishart.

Green, D. (1993) 'Foreword', in N. Dennis *Rising Crime and the Dismembered Family*, London: Institute of Economic Affairs.

Hall, S. (1979) 'The Great Moving Right Show', *Marxism Today*, January.

—— (1980) *Drifting Into a Law and Order Society*, London: The Cobden Trust.

—— (1985) 'Authoritarian populism: a reply to Jessop *et al.*', *New Left Review* 151: 115–24.

Hall, S. Critcher, C. Jefferson, T. Clarke, J. and Roberts, B. (1978) *Policing the Crisis*, London: Macmillan.

Hall, S. and Scraton, P. (1981) 'Law, class and control' in M. Fitzgerald, G. McLennan and J. Pawson (eds), *Crime and Society: Readings in History and Theory*, London: Routledge & Kegan Paul/The Open University Press.

Halsey, A. H. (1992) 'Foreword', in N. Dennis and G. Erdos, *Families Without Fatherhood*, London: Institute of Economic Affairs.

Hamilton, J., Radford, K. and Jarman, N. (2003) *Policing, Accountability and Young People*, Belfast: Institute for Conflict Research.

Hampton, B. (1995) *Prisons and Women*, Kensington, NSW: UNSW Press.

Harvey, L. (1990) *Critical Social Research*, London: Sage.

Haydon, D. (2004) *Children's Rights in Northern Ireland: What children and adults who work with them had to say about children's lives*, Belfast: Northern Ireland Commissioner for Children and Young People.

Haydon, D. and Scraton, P. (2000) '"Condemn a Little More, Understand a little less": The political context and rights implications of the domestic and European rulings in the Venables-Thompson case', *Journal of Law and Society* 27, 3: 416–48.

Heidensohn, F. (1985) *Women and Crime*, London: Macmillan.

Herman, E. S. and Chomsky, N. (1988) *Manufacturing Consent: The Political Economy of Mass Media*, New York: Pantheon Books.

Hester, R. (2000) 'Community Safety and the new youth justice' in B. Goldson, (ed.) *The New Youth Justice*, Lyme Regis: Russell House.

Hillyard, P. (1992) *Suspect Community: People's Experience of the Prevention of Terrrorism Acts in Britain*, London: Pluto Press/Liberty.

Hillyard, P. and Percy-Smith, J. (1988) *The Coercive State: The Decline of Democracy in Britain*, London: Fontana/Collins.

Hillyard, P., Kelly, G., McLaughlin, E., Patsios, D. and Tomlinson, M. (2003) *Bare Necessities: poverty and social exclusion in Northern Ireland – key findings*, Belfast: Democratic Dialogue, 16.

Home Office (1998) *Crime and Disorder Act 1998: Introductory Guide*, London: Home Office Communication Directorate.

Home Office (2003) *Respect and Responsibility – Taking a Stand Against Anti-Social Behaviour*, White Paper, London: Home Office.

Horowitz, I. L. (1968) *Professing Sociology: Studies in the Life Cycle of Social Science*, Chicago, IL: Aldine Publishing Co.

Hudson, B. A. (1993) *Penal Policy and Social Justice*, London: Macmillan.

—— (1996) *Understanding Justice*, Milton Keynes: Open University Press.

—— (2000) 'Critical reflection as research methodology', in V. Jupp, P. Davies and P. Francis (eds), *Doing Criminological Research*, London: Sage.

Hudson, B. (2003) *Justice in the Risk Society*, London: Sage.

Human Rights Commission (2004) '*Measures to Tackle Anti-Social Behaviour in Northern Ireland*': *The Response of the Northern Ireland Human Rights Commission*, Belfast: NIHRC.

Ignatieff, M. (2004) 'Evil under Interrogation: Is Torture ever Permissible?', *Financial Times*, 15 May.

Include Youth (2004) *Response to Measures to Tackle Anti-Social Behaviour in Northern Ireland Consultation Document*, Belfast: Include Youth.

Interagency Working Group on Displaced Families (2000) 'Briefing Paper', unpublished, 22 October.

Jessop, B., Bennett, K., Bromley, S. and Ling, T. (1988) *Thatcherism*, Cambridge: Polity Press.

Johnston, G. and Bottomley, A. K. (1998) 'Introduction: Labour's Crime Policy in Context', *Policy Studies* 19, nos 3–4.

Jupp, V. R. (1989) *Methods of Criminological Research*, London: Allen & Unwin.

Kelly, L. (1988) *Surviving Sexual Violence*, Cambridge: Polity Press.

Kerr, J. H. (1994) *Understanding Soccer Hooliganism*, Milton Keynes: Open University Press.

Kilkelly, U., Kilpatrick, R., Lundy, L., Moore, L., Scraton, P., Davey, C., Dwyer, C. and McAlister, S. (2004) *Children's Rights in Northern Ireland*, Belfast: Northern Ireland Commissioner for Children and Young People.

Krisberg, B. (1975) *Crime and Privilege: Toward a New Criminology*, Englewood Cliffs, NJ: Spectrum Prentice-Hall.

Lee, B. (2002) 'Why I Voted Against the War' in S. Hawthorne and B. Winter (eds), *September 11, 2001: Feminist Perspectives*, Melbourne: Spinifex Press.

Leigh, D. (1980) *The Frontiers of Secrecy*, London: Junction Books.

Lemert, E. M. (1967) *Human Deviance, Social Problems, and Social Control*, Englewood Cliffs, NJ: Prentice-Hall.

Leonard, M. (2004) *Children in Interface Areas: Reflections from North Belfast*, Belfast: Save the Children.

Lewis, J. M. and Scarisbrick-Hauser, A.-M. (1994) 'An analysis of football crowd safety reports using the McPhail categories', in R. Giulianotti, N. Bonney and M. Hepworth (eds), *Football, Violence and Social Identity*, London: Routledge.

Liverpool ASBU (2003) *Liverpool Anti-Social Behaviour Unit: Draft Strategy*, Liverpool: ASBU, March.

Local Government Information Unit (1997) *Community Safety: Consultation in Advance of the Crime and Disorder Bill*, London: Home Office.

McCullin, D. (2002) *Unreasonable Behaviour: An Autobiography*, London: Vintage.

McCulloch, J. (1995) 'Women, prison, law and order', in B. Hampton (ed.), *Women and Imprisonment*, Melbourne: Fitzroy Legal Service.

McLure, J. (1980) *Spike Island: Portrait of a Police Division*, London: Macmillan.

McMillan, J. (1971) 'Some Notes and Observations on the Prison Subculture', unpublished.

Macpherson, Sir W. (1999) *The Stephen Lawrence Inquiry: Report*, Cm. 4262-I, London: The Stationery Office.

Mathiesen, T. (1990) *Prison on Trial*, London: Sage.

Messerschmidt, J. (1997) *Crime as Structured Action*, Thousand Oaks, CA: Sage.

Moore, C. (2003) *One Voice: My Life in Song*, London: Hodder and Stoughton.

Mort, F. (1987) *Dangerous Sexualities: Medico-Moral Politics in England since 1830*, London: Routledge & Kegan Paul.

Muncie, J. (1996) 'The Construction and Reconstruction of Crime', in J. Muncie and E. McLaughlin (eds), *The Problem of Crime*, London: Sage.

—— (1999a) 'Institutionalised intolerance: youth justice and the 1998 Crime and Disorder Act', *Critical Social Policy* 19: 147–75.

—— (1999b) *Youth and Crime: A Critical Introduction*, London: Sage.

Muncie, J. and Fitzgerald, M. (1981) 'Humanizing the deviant: affinity and affiliation theories', in M. Fitzgerald, G. McLennan and J. Pawson (eds), *Crime and Society: Readings in History and Theory*, London: Routledge & Kegan Paul/The Open University Press.

Murray, C. (1990) *The Emerging British Underclass*, London: Institute of Economic Affairs.

—— (1994a) 'Underclass: The Crisis Deepens', *The Sunday Times*, 22 May.

—— (1994b) 'The New Victorians ... and the New Rabble', *The Sunday Times*, 29 May.

Neuman, W. (1994) *Social Research Methods: Qualitative and Quantitative Approaches*, Boston, MA: Allyn and Bacon.

NIO (2004) *Measures to Tackle Anti-Social Behaviour in Northern Ireland: A Consultation Document*, Belfast: Criminal Justice Policy Branch, Northern Ireland Office.

North, M. (1999) 'Storm clouds the issues', *Analysis, Scotland on Sunday*, 21 March: 17.

—— (2000) *Dunblane: Never Forget*, Edinburgh: Mainstream Publishing.

Omega Foundation (2003) *Baton Rounds: A review of the human rights implications of the introduction and use of the L21A1 baton round in Northern Ireland and proposed alternatives*, Belfast: Northern Ireland Human Rights Commission.

Oxford, K. (1981) *Evidence to the Scarman Inquiry*, Liverpool: Merseyside Police.

Parenti, C. (1999) *Lockdown America: Police and Prisons in the Age of Crisis*, New York: Verso.

Partington, M. (1995) 'Salvaging the Sacred', *Guardian Weekend*, 18 May.

Patten, C. (2000) *A New Beginning: Policing in Northern Ireland*, The Report of the Independent Commission on Policing Northern Ireland.

Penal Affairs Consortium (1995) *The Doctrine of 'Doli Incapax'*, London: Penal Affairs Consortium.

Pickering, S. (2002) *Women, Policing and Resistance in Northern Ireland*, Belfast: Beyond the Pale Publications.

Pitts, J. (2001) *The New Politics of Youth Crime: Discipline or Solidarity?* Basingstoke: Palgrave.

Platt, T. and Takagi, P. (1981) 'Intellectuals for Law and Order: A Critique of the New "Realists"', in T. Platt and P. Takagi (eds), *Crime and Social Justice*, London: Macmillan, 30–58.

Polsky, N. (1971) *Hustlers, Beats and Others*, Harmondsworth: Penguin.

Popplewell, Mr. J. (1985) *Committee of Inquiry into Crowd Safety and Control at Sports Grounds: Interim Report*, Cmnd. 9585, London: HMSO.

Poulantzas, N. (1978) *State, Power, Socialism*, London: Verso.

Preston, P. (1996) *Dunblane: Reflecting Tragedy*, London: British Executive International Press Institute, September.

Prisons Inspectorate (2002) *Mourne House Women's Unit*, London: Her Majesty's Inspector of Prisons.

Quinn, K. and Jackson, J. (2003) *The detention and questioning of young persons by the police in Northern Ireland*, Belfast: Northern Ireland Office.

Reynolds, H. (1999) *Why Weren't We Told? A Personal Search for the Truth about our History*, Melbourne: Viking.

Roberts, A. (2001) 'Crisis at Kunduz', *The Guardian Comment*, 24 November, 20.

Rolston, B. (2000) *Unfinished Business: State Killings and the Quest for Truth*, Belfast: Beyond the Pale Publications.

Rolston, B. and Scraton, P. (2004) 'In the Full Glare of English Politics: Ireland, Inquiries and the British State' *British Journal of Criminology* 45, 4: 547–64.

Rose, D. (2004) *Guantánamo: America's War on Human Rights*, London: Faber & Faber.

Roy, A. (2001) 'Brutality smeared in peanut butter', *G2*, 23 October.

Said, E. (2000) 'Apocalypse Now', *Index on Censorship* 29, 5: 49–53.

—— (2002) 'Thoughts about America', *Al-Ahram Weekly*, 2 March.

Samson, P. and Crow, A. (1997) *Dunblane: Our Year of Tears*, Edinburgh: Mainstream.

Scarman, The Rt. Hon. Lord, (1981) *The Brixton Disorders 10–12 April 1981*, Cmnd 8427, London: HMSO.

Scraton, P. (1981) 'Policing and Institutionalised Racism on Mersyside', in D. Cowell, T. Jones and J. Young (eds), *Policing the Riots*, London: Junction Books: 21–38.

—— (1987) 'Unreasonable Force: Policing, Punishment and Marginalisation', in P. Scraton (ed.), *Law, Order and the Authoritarian State: Readings in Critical Criminology*, Milton Keynes: Open University Press.

—— (1997) 'Whose "Childhood"? What "Crisis"?' in P. Scraton (ed.), *'Childhood' in 'Crisis'?* London: UCL Press/Routledge.

—— (2000) *Hillsborough: The Truth*, Edinburgh: Mainstream Publishing, rev. edn.

—— (2002a) 'Defining "power"and challenging "knowledge": critical knowledge as resistance in the UK', in K. Carrington and R. Hogg (eds), *Critical Criminology: Issues, debates, challenges*, Cullompton: Willan Publishing.

—— (2002b) 'Lost lives, hidden voices: "truth" and controversial deaths', *Race and Class* 44, 1: 107–18.

—— (ed) (2002c) *Beyond September 11: An Anthology of Dissent*, London: Pluto.

—— (2004) 'Streets of Terror: Marginalisation, Criminalisation and Moral Renewal', *Social Justice* 31, 1–2: 130–58.

Scraton, P. and Chadwick, K. (1987a) *In the Arms of the Law: Coroners' Inquests and Deaths in Custody*, London: Pluto.

—— (1987b) 'Speaking Ill of the Dead: Institutionalised Responses to Deaths in Custody', in P. Scraton (ed.) *Law, Order and the Authoritarian State: Readings in Critical Criminology*, Milton Keynes, Open University Press.

—— (1991) 'Challenging the New Orthodoxies: The Theoretical and Political Priorities of Critical Criminology', in K. Stenson and D. Cowell (eds), *The Politics of Crime Control*, London: Sage.

—— (2001) 'Critical Research', in E. McLaughlin and J. Muncie (eds), *The Sage Dictionary of* Criminology, London: Sage.

Scraton, P. and Haydon, D. (2002) 'Challenging the criminalization of children and young people: securing a rights-based agenda', in J. Muncie, G. Hughes and E. McLaughlin (eds.), *Youth Justice: Critical Readings*, London: Sage/The Open University.

Scraton, P. and Moore, L. (2005) *The Hurt Inside: The Imprisonment of Women and Girls in Northern Ireland*, Belfast: Northern Ireland Human Rights Commission (revd edn).

Scraton, P., Jemphrey, A. and Coleman, S. (1995) *No Last Rights: The Denial of Justice and the Promotion of Myth in the Aftermath of the Hillsborough Disaster*, Liverpool: Liverpool City Council/Alden Press.

Scraton, P., Sim, J. and Skidmore, P. (1991) *Prisons Under Protest*, Milton Keynes: Open University Press.

Sereny, G. (1974) *The Case of Mary Bell*, London: Arrow.

—— (1997) *Cries Unheard*, London: Macmillan.

Shaylor, C. (1998) '"It's like living in a black hole": Women of Color and Solitary Confinement in the Prison Industrial Complex', *New England Journal on Criminal and Civil Confinement* 24, 2: 385–416.

Sim, J. (1990) *Medical Power in Prisons: The Prison Medical Service in England 1774–1989*, Milton Keynes: Open University Press.

—— (2003) 'Whose Side Are We Not On? Researching Medical Power in Prisons', in S. Tombs and D. White (eds), *Unmasking the Crimes of the Powerful: Scrutinizing States and Corporations*, New York: Peter Lang, 239–60.

Sivanandan, A. (1990) *Communities of Resistance: Writings on Black Struggles for Socialism*, London: Verso.

Smyth, M., with Fay, M. T., Brough, E. and Hamilton, J. (2004) *The Impact of Political Conflict on Children in Northern Ireland*, Belfast: ICR.

Stanley, L. (1990) *Feminist Praxis*, London: Routledge.

Stanko, E. A. (1985) *Intimate Intrusions: Women's Experience of Male Violence*, London: Routledge & Kegan Paul.

Stedman Jones, G. (1977) *Outcast London*, Harmondsworth: Penguin.

Straw, J. and Michael, A. (1996) *Tackling Youth Crime, Reforming Youth Justice: A consultation paper on an agenda for change*, London: Labour Party.

Stuart-Smith, Rt. Hon. L. J. (1998) *Scrutiny of Evidence Relating to the Hillsborough Football Stadium Disaster*, Cm. 3878m, London: The Stationery Office.

Takagi, P. (1981) 'A Garrison State in a "Democratic" Society', in T. Platt and P. Takagi (eds), *Crime and Social Justice*, London: Macmillan, 205–19.

Taylor, I., Walton, P. and Young, J. (1973) *The New Criminology*, London: Routledge & Kegan Paul.

Taylor, L. J. (1989) *The Hillsborough Stadium Disaster: 15 April 1989, Interim Report*, Cm. 765, London: HMSO.

UK Government (1999) *Convention on the Rights of the Child: Second Report to the UN Committee on the Rights of the Child*, London: Department of Health.

—— (2003) *Iraq's Weapons of Mass Destruction: The Assessment of the British Government*, London: The Stationery Office.

UNCRC (2002) *Concluding Observations of the Committee on the Rights of the Child: United Kingdom of Great Britain and Northern Ireland*, Geneva: UNCRC.

Van Heil, K. P. and Hoo, R. (1998) 'The Dunblane Incident', http://www.nas.net/~ccep/ccepnews

Walsh, T. (2004) *Incorrections: Investigating prison release practice and policy in Queensland and its impact on community safety*, Queensland: QUT.

Walters, M. (2001) *Acid Row*, Sydney: Allen and Unwin.

Walters, R. (2003) *Deviant Knowledge: Criminology, politics and policy*, Cullompton: Willan Publishing.

White House, The (2002) *The National Security Strategy of the United States of America*, Washington: The White House, September.

Williams, P. (2001) 'By Any Means Necessary', *The Nation*, 26 November.

Wright Mills, C. (1959) *The Sociological Imagination*, New York: Oxford University Press.

YJB/CYPU (2002) *Establishing Youth Inclusion and Support Panels (YISPS): Draft Guidance Note for Children's Fund Partnerships and Youth Offending Teams*, London: Youth Justice Board.

Young, K. (1991) 'Sport and Collective Violence', *Exercise and Sports Sciences Reviews* 19, 539–86.

Index